GOVERNMENT BEYOND THE CENTRE

SERIES EDITOR: GERRY STOKER

The world of sub-central government and administration – including local authorities, quasi-governmental bodies and the agencies of public–private partnerships – has seen massive changes in recent years and is at the heart of the current restructuring of government in the United Kingdom and other Western democracies.

The intention of the *Government Beyond the Centre* series is to bring the study of this often-neglected world into the mainstream of social science research, applying the spotlight of critical analysis to what has traditionally been the preserve of institutional public administration approaches.

Its focus is on the agenda of change currently being faced by sub-central government, the economic, political and ideological forces that underlie it, and the structures of power and influence that are emerging. Its objective is to provide up-to-date and informative accounts of the new forms of government, management and administration that are emerging.

The series will be of interest to students and practitioners of politics, public and social administration, and all those interested in the reshaping of the governmental institutions which have a daily and major impact on our lives.

GOVERNMENT BEYOND THE CENTRE

SERIES EDITOR: GERRY STOKER

Published
Richard Batley and Gerry Stoker (eds)
Local Government in Europe

Clive Gray
Government Beyond the Centre

John Gyford
Citizens, Consumers and Councils

Richard Kerley
Managing in Local Government

Desmond King and Gerry Stoker (eds)
Rethinking Local Democracy

Steve Leach, John Stewart and Kieron Walsh
The Changing Organisation and Management of Local Government

Arthur Midwinter
Local Government in Scotland

Lawrence Pratchett and David Wilson (eds)
Local Democracy and Local Government

Yvonne Rydin
The British Planning System

John Stewart and Gerry Stoker (eds)
Local Government in the 1990s

David Wilson and Chris Game
Local Government in the United Kingdom (second edition)

Forthcoming
John Stewart
The Nature of British Local Government

Government Beyond the Centre
Series Standing Order ISBN 0–333–69337–X
(*outside North America only*)

You can receive future titles in this series as they are published by placing a standing order. Please contact your bookseller or, in the case of difficulty, write to us at the address below with your name and address, the title of the series and the ISBN quoted above.

Customer Services Department, Macmillan Distribution Ltd
Houndmills, Basingstoke, Hampshire RG21 6XS, England

LOCAL GOVERNMENT IN THE UNITED KINGDOM

Second Edition

David Wilson and
Chris Game

MACMILLAN

First edition 1994
Second edition 1998

Published by
MACMILLAN PRESS LTD
Houndmills, Basingstoke, Hampshire RG21 6XS
and London
Companies and representatives
throughout the world

ISBN 0–333–69471–6
ISBN 0–333–69472–4

A catalogue record for this book is available
from the British Library.

This book is printed on paper suitable for recycling and
made from fully managed and sustained forest sources.

10   9   8   7   6   5   4   3   2   1
07   06   05   04   03   02   01   00   99   98

Copy-edited and typeset by Povey–Edmondson
Tavistock and Rochdale, England

Printed and bound in Great Britain by Creative Print and Design (Wales), Ebbw Vale

Contents

List of Figures and Exhibits

■ Figures

■ Exhibits

Preface to the Second Edition

There is a scene in the well-known screen musical, *Gigi*, in which an
elderly Maurice Chevalier vainly endeavours to infuse his younger but
worldweary companion, Louis Jourdan, with his own *joie de vivre* by
pointing out some of the attractions of Paris:

> Don't you marvel at the power
> of the mighty Eiffel Tower,
> knowing there it will remain ever more –
> climbing up to the sky
> over ninety storeys high. . .

> How many storeys?   Ninety
> And yesterday?   Ninety
> And tomorrow?   Ninety
> It's a bore!

French local government, in that purely arithmetical sense, can also seem
a bit unexciting. Much of its remarkable structure, including its more
than 36,000 communes – the equivalent of our district or borough
councils – has remained essentially unchanged since the Napoleonic
era in the early 19th century. Local government in the UK could hardly
be more different. During the last two decades in particular it has
changed constantly, in almost every respect – its external structure and
internal management, its politics and political complexion, its finances
and financial discretion, its service responsibilities, its relations with
central government and with its various publics.

In the first edition of this book, which we wrote mainly in 1992/93, we
tried to convey something of both the character and detail of this almost
perpetual change that practitioners in the world of local government –
the elected councillors, professional officers and all the other thousands
of council employees – had to come to terms with. We dealt with some of
the major legislation – but only some, since there had already been nearly
150 Acts affecting local government passed since 1979. We described the
dramatic poll tax saga, in which the nearly 400-year-old local rates system
was abolished and replaced by the hugely unpopular poll tax, which was
itself soon replaced by the council tax, taking its Prime Ministerial
advocate, Mrs Thatcher, with it. We were also able to give an early
state-of-play report of a nationwide restructuring of local government
that was under way – the second on that scale in just twenty years.

That new structure is now in place, if not fully in operation. We have
been able to include maps of all the new local authority boundaries in

England, Scotland and Wales, as well as in Northern Ireland, the one part of the UK untouched by this latest reorganisation. We have been able to update tables summarising the party or non-party political control of all these authorities, including the results of those new unitary and county council elections held on the same day as the 1997 General Election.

In coming years, these 'synchro-elections' may prove to have been the turning point in the Conservative Party's local government fortunes. Four years of unprecedentedly disastrous local elections had left them with no councils under their control at all in Scotland and Wales – just as they had no MPs after May 1997 – and with only a handful of mostly small English councils to their name. On General Election day, though, the Party at least had the consolation of winning back several county councils, as well as gaining control of two of the new unitary councils. The Conservatives are still left with significantly smaller numbers of councils and councillors than the Liberal Democrats, while Labour dominates the local government landscape just as massively as it does the House of Commons. But while the Parliamentary picture will still be much the same for a time, the local government map could well be extensively transformed.

For, to bring us to potentially the biggest change of all, we have of course a Labour Government. There are few relationships in the social sciences that approach the status and certainty of scientific laws, but one of the stronger candidates is that governments in power nationally lose votes locally, and indeed can start to do so very quickly. The Blair Government will need no reminding that its grotesquely inflated almost 2 to 1 Parliamentary majority rests on an actual vote of under a third of the potential electorate: a modest level of popularity that could easily turn to voter discontent in the local elections which take place every year somewhere in the country.

To its democratic credit, the Labour Government indicated in its manifesto that it wants all councils to have a proportion of their members elected annually in the future. This particular legislation did not feature in the Government's first Queen's Speech, but several other important, and in some cases constitutionally innovative, measures did. There are the Scottish and Welsh devolution Bills, and a further referendum-based proposal for the re-establishment of an elected Greater London Authority with – perhaps the most exciting bit of all – a directly elected executive Mayor for the first time in its history. Other cities and towns too are likely to get the chance to pilot their own democratic experiments, as well as being required, with all other councils, to involve their citizens and service users in the production and monitoring of annual performance plans. More early legislation affecting local government and its services includes two Education Bills, a Bill aimed at increasing council house building and thereby reducing homelessness, and a first step in the process of bringing directly elected regional government to England, as well as to Scotland and Wales. In short, further change on top of – and in some cases actually reversing – that of recent years.

Embarking on this second edition, we faced two fundamental decisions. How much do we need to change, and when should we stop writing? The first decision, we felt, was largely made for us. If this edition, like the first, was to be as up-to-date as possible, several chapters, particularly in Parts 1 and 3, would simply have to be rewritten, rather than just amended. In the event, not a single chapter survived completely intact – not even the History one.

The question of timing, we have to say, was not helped by former Prime Minister John Major's determination to delay calling the General Election until almost the last constitutionally permissible moment. Our decision was to allow ourselves enough time to take full account of the 1997 General Election and of the new Labour Government's legislative programme and early decisions in individual chapters rather than in the form of an 'update' chapter.

Other things too have changed since the first edition, and more debts of gratitude are incurred. This revised edition has been entirely written by the two named authors. Some of the material provided for the first edition by our colleagues, Steve Leach and Gerry Stoker, has survived our revisionary axe, and we accordingly express our appreciation while absolving them from any collective responsibility for the book as a whole.

Particular thanks must go to Sharon Moore at INLOGOV – for the excellence of her secretarial skills, her diligence and unfailing good humour, and for even being prepared, in the interests of 'the book', to conspire with the first-named author against the second. At De Montfort University Caroline Hime provided secretarial support of the highest standard throughout the enterprise. We wish her well as she switches career to go into teaching. Carole Shaw's skill at desk-top publishing has also been greatly appreciated. Steven Kennedy, our publisher, has once again had his forbearance sorely tested, but he has continued to be a source of constant support and encouragement.

Readers will note that, along with the maps and other figures and exhibits, we have increased the number of cartoons in this edition. We and the publishers are therefore pleased to thank Patrick Blower and the *Local Government Chronicle* for permission to reproduce the cartoons in Figures 9.2, 10.1 and 17.2, and John Clark and the Local Government Information Unit for those in Figures 9.1 and 17.1.

We trust that such illustrations contribute to this book's merit. For any defects, errors and for the views expressed we, of course, accept full responsibility.

DAVID WILSON
CHRIS GAME

Preface to the First Edition

This book is an attempt to present contemporary local government in a way that will strike both the academic reader and the practitioner as being of relevance to their world and experience.

David Wilson and Chris Game wrote the bulk of the book, with Steve Leach and Gerry Stoker providing some material on specific topics. All four of us work in universities. But we also spend much of our time working *outside* our respective institutions – directly with local government officers and councillors. We lead what can sometimes feel like a hybrid existence. – divided between our student teaching and our management training, research and consultancy work for local government. This book is a product of that hybrid existence.

While we are responsible for the conception and content of the book, we have necessarily incurred a number of debts. We should therefore like to thank especially: Professor George Jones at the LSE, whose detailed comments (both the substantive and the idiosyncratic) on the penultimate draft were challenging, encouraging and immensely helpful; his frequent collaborator, Professor John Stewart of INLOGOV, whose ideas have shaped the thinking of all those of us concerned with and for local government; Clive Gray from De Montfort University, Dr David King from Stirling University, and insights from numerous other colleagues and local government practitioners have also helped to shape the finished product.

Many other people have contributed to the production of the book. Our publisher Steven Kennedy has provided constant help and encouragement and sorely tested tolerance. Caroline Hime bore the brunt of the typing with great fortitude and good humour. Carole Shaw and her colleagues also proved to be a tremendous resource.

Our respective families have put up with a good deal while we both wrote and liaised in the production of the book – thanks to you all. Also to the generations of students who will recognise several of these chapters as transmogrified lecture notes.

Finally, we accept full responsibility for any errors and for the views expressed in these pages.

DAVID WILSON
CHRIS GAME

PART 1

LOCAL GOVERNMENT: THE BASICS

■ *Chapter 1* ■

Introduction – Our Aims and Approach

■ The excited Professor

In July 1996 an important report about UK local government was published by an all-party House of Lords Select Committee, chaired by Lord Hunt of Tanworth. We refer to its recommendations in Chapter 7. As such committees do, it received a lot of written evidence from concerned individuals and relevant organisations and then questioned in person a variety of expert witnesses. One of these witnesses was Professor John Stewart, to whom we pay tribute in our Preface. He introduced himself to the Committee with the following remarks:

> 'Reading some reports of your evidence, I get the impression that some people have been saying that local government is a dull world. I can quite understand that, if you are looking at the *national* world of local government – because, once you reduce local government to a uniform view, it is rather a dull world.
> 'I have had the good fortune to visit 300 local authorities over the last few years, interviewing leaders and chief executives, and what impresses me is *the excitement of local government*. It is the excitement of how one authority differs from another, because of the nature of the area, and because of the quality of the leadership. I am impressed too by the extent of innovation that has been taking place, sometimes in response to government legislation, but sometimes by the local authorities themselves. It is very exciting . . . to see city or town leaders wrestling with tremendous urban problems. I do not want you to get the impression that the world of local authorities is dull.'
> (House of Lords, 1996, Vol. II, pp. 461–62 – our emphasis)

Hear! Hear!, Professor. We could not have put it better ourselves.

■ A dull world? Not any more!

One of our chief aims in this book is precisely the same as the task Professor Stewart set himself in talking to the Lords Committee – to dispel any idea you, our readers, may have that the world of local government is narrow, uniform or dull. It is, in fact, quite the reverse.

3

Narrow is something local government has never been. That local authorities 'look after you from the cradle to the grave' is both a cliché and an unfashionably paternalistic view of councils' wide-ranging responsibilities. But it is also literally true, in that they will register your birth, death and, if necessary, any intervening marriage, and then finally dispose of you, in cemetery or crematorium according to taste. Much more to the point, our local councils and the services that they provide have a far more immediate, continuous and comprehensive impact on all our daily lives than many of the so-called 'bigger' issues that make the parliamentary headlines.

Nor have these local councils ever been uniform – except in the sense that the whole land mass of our planet would look uniform if viewed from far enough away. Local government is the government of localities, and an institutionalised recognition of their widely varying characteristics – geographic, demographic, social, economic and, by no means least, political. We cannot take you physically on Professor Stewart's tour of local authorities, but we try to do the next best thing – by illustrating, wherever possible, the differences that exist even between councils of the same type and a similar size, and also by encouraging you to discover for yourselves the uniquenesses of your own local councils, or what you might call the microcosmos of local government.

As for being dull, the very suggestion would be likely to raise a pitying, and self-pitying, smile from most of those working in or with local government over the past few years. 'If only!' would be the more likely response from a workforce that has had to come to terms with change and upheaval on every front: privatisation and the contracting out of services; opt-out ballots of tenants and school parents; the introduction and almost instant abandonment of a 'poll tax', followed by a council tax, and tax capping; neighbourhood offices, customer contracts, complaints hot-lines, one-stop shops, service guarantees, environmental audits, enabling councils . . . all against a backdrop of continuous financial constraint and the actual or threatened rearrangement of the country's whole local government structure.

Few of these ideas and developments would or could have found their way into a book on local government published even a dozen or so years ago. Their origins are mixed. Some came from within the world of local government itself. But many, as Professor Stewart noted, stem from central government and from the unprecedented quantity of legislation directed at local councils in recent years. It has been this interventionist and legislative attention of central government that has raised the profile of local government, made it regular front-page news, and thereby:

> succeeded in doing the unthinkable [and] rescued students from the terminal boredom of lectures on local government by making the subject interesting, even humorous for those with a taste for black comedy.   (Rhodes, 1991, p. 86)

But whose responsibility was it that there was an image of 'terminal boredom' to dispel? Partly, presumably, local councils themselves, who have all too often failed to project themselves in such a way as to stimulate the interest – let alone the sympathy and support – of those they claim to represent and serve. To be fair, this criticism is one that many of them would now acknowledge and claim to be doing their best to rectify. We shall be drawing attention to some of their more enterprising efforts throughout this book.

Authors too, however, have their responsibilities. Part of our job must be to stimulate the interest of *our* public in the activities of local government: to convey, as directly as possible, a sense of its 'feel' and atmosphere. So who are our public?

■ You and us

We assume that most of our readers will not themselves have worked in local government, or at least not for any great length of time. We assume that, for most of you, your principal experience of local government will have been as customers, consumers, clients and citizens; perhaps also, to add a fifth C, as complainants. You will probably have had various more or less memorable contacts over the years with council officials and employees, and perhaps also with your locally elected councillors. You will certainly be at least one and probably several of the following: council tax payers, education grant recipients, state school or college students, council house tenants, social services clients, library borrowers, sports and leisure centre users, pedestrians, bus travellers, car drivers, taxi riders, planning applicants or protesters, domestic refuse producers, and so on. You will probably be registered local electors, and possibly actual voters. Yet perhaps oddly, given this degree of personal involvement, you are likely to consider yourselves to be 'outsiders' in relation to the world of local government.

If so, then in this sense we too are outsiders. We are not employed *in* local government either; but we do work very closely *with* local government. In various ways – through teaching and lecturing, research and consultancy – we are in virtually daily contact with local councils, their members and staff. A key part of our jobs involves trying to link together, or at least narrow the gap between, the 'academic' and 'practitioner' worlds of local government, and that is the task we have set ourselves in this book.

Our aim is to present a picture of local government comprising both facts and 'feel'. The balance, we believe, is vital. Certainly, we would reject what might be labelled the 'Gradgrind' approach, after Charles Dickens's schoolmaster in *Hard Times*: 'Now, what I want is Facts. Teach these boys and girls nothing but Facts. Facts alone are wanted in life.' But if facts alone are insufficient, *some* facts are indispensable – and not just for those of you required to sit exams. We are concerned, therefore, that our readers acquire a factually accurate knowledge of what local government is about and how it works. We are even more concerned, though, that you acquire something of what we describe as the 'feel' of local government: an appreciation of the interests, viewpoints, motivations, satisfactions and frustrations of those involved, and an awareness of the range, the nature and the complexities of the issues they face.

■ Get to know your own council

With this latter objective in mind, we now put forward a few important suggestions or recommendations. First, you should try to make whatever use you can of the fact that you yourselves will, depending on exactly where you live, be residents of at least one local council, and possibly two or three. These councils produce a mass of information in different forms about the services they provide and the activities with which they are involved. They may produce and circulate their own council newspaper, or insert a couple of pages regularly into one of the local daily or weekly papers. They will certainly deliver to you personally a statement of their annual budget to accompany your local council tax demand.

They will also produce all sorts of other leaflets, brochures, cards and pamphlets about particular services which should be available from your local town or county hall. So go along and ask! You may be surprised by what you get, even if you may not be able to match the collection of publications (and other material) set out in Exhibit 1.1 that one of us received from a particularly helpful London borough council – in which he wasn't even a resident!

If you're of a lazier, 'nerdlike' disposition, you can try surfing. By mid-1997 there were already more than 150 local authority World Wide Web sites, from Western Isles in Scotland (http://www.open.gov.uk/west-isle/wiichome.htm), publishing in both English and Gaelic, to Weymouth and Portland in Dorset (http://www.weymouth.gov.uk), trying to persuade you to take a seaside holiday in the area. Like everything else produced by local authorities, the early Web sites varied greatly in quality, from the enterprising and sophisticated to the embarrassing. But both their existence and their content will serve to tell you something about the kind of council yours is.

■ An early definition

Examining the material outlined in Exhibit 1.1 we were struck by how, even if we had had no previous knowledge at all about local government, we would have been able to piece together a reasonable impression of the kind of institution a *local council* is.

Exhibit 1.1 *Information available from one council's reception area*

* The council's Annual Report and Accounts
* An application for a 'Res Card' – a card, available only to residents of the borough, entitling them to various concessions when using council and other facilities in the area
* The latest copy of the council's 12-page newsletter, 'Around the Houses', delivered door-to-door about four times per year
* A separate Leisure Services Newsletter, 'Leisure Times', partly translated into Spanish as well.
* A map and leaflet about the council's leisure services: libraries, sports and leisure centres, gardens, parks, etc.
* An application form for a Security Grant – available to the elderly and disabled, to make their homes more secure
* A leaflet reporting various environmental improvements made by the council – more public seating, tree and shrub planting, play equipment for children, refurbishment of statues and fountains
* A leaflet announcing a series of consultation meetings with residents in a particular area of the borough
* A City Watch form, with an attached reply-paid card on which a complaint could be sent to the council about defective street lights, uneven paving stones, abandoned vehicles, vandalism, graffiti, etc.
* A residents' guide to how to object to the granting of entertainments licences
* Individual leaflets advertising:
  – the Home Library Service; the Business Reference Library
  – the Video Loan Service; the sale of pooper scoopers
  – the hire of rubbish compactor skips from the council
  – a 'Want to be a Writer?' festival sponsored by the council
  – a Family Link project, providing short breaks for children with special needs
  – a Taxicard scheme, providing subsidised trips for the disabled
  – waste paper and glass recycling schemes
* Leaflets about some of the campaigns in which the council was engaged, either on its own or working with other organisations:
  – against litter
  – against drug abuse (plus a badge!)
  – against unauthorised estate agents' boards
  – against the local health authority's planned closure of two local hospitals
  – for the sponsorship of floral hanging baskets by local traders for home ownership
* And finally, a plastic bag with the council's 'Leisure for Life' slogan, in which to carry away all these trophies.

Your Local Council

* a large, geographically-defined, multi-functional organisation,
* pursuing a variety of social, political and economic objectives,
* either through the direct provision,
* or through the sponsorship, indirect funding, regulation, or monitoring of
* a very extensive range of services to its local community.

This is by no means a fully comprehensive definition of what a local council is and how it operates, but it is a useful starting point.

■ Your council's Annual Report

Even if an initial visit to your own local council were to prove less productive than ours, you should at least be able to obtain a copy of the council's Annual Report. This document is something which, together with a set of audited Annual Accounts, all councils are required by law to produce. Indeed, nowadays the Report and Accounts are often combined in the same publication.

You will quickly discover, though, that there is no standard format or style for the production of these Annual Reports. Like councils' use of the Internet, they vary enormously, from the 100-page, glossily illustrated and expensive-looking brochure-cum-book to the more downbeat, down-market tabloid newspaper format, designed for comprehensive circulation among the council's residents. But, whatever its style, a council's Annual Report – just like a university prospectus – can tell you a great deal about itself: both about the kind of organisation it is, and also about the kind it wishes to be seen as being. Like a prospectus, it is the council's best single opportunity to make a public statement and presentation of its activities and achievements, its internal management and external relations, its future plans and its past performance.

In particular, a good Annual Report is likely to contain two useful features that we shall refer to explicitly in later chapters. First there will be a presentation of the council's *budget* and overall *financial profile*: how much was spent, on what services, and where the money came from. Since you yourselves will have provided at least some of that money – in the form of local and national taxation, local fees, charges and rents – and since you will also be users of some of the council's services, we feel that one of the best ways of introducing the sometimes rather threatening topic of local government finance is through your own council's budget and accounts. Understand how your own money is spent, and the services it helps to provide, and you are well on the way to under-standing the system.

A second feature of many Annual Reports is the *comparative* one. All councils are required to compare the scale, costs and efficiency of their services – their so-called Performance Indicators – with those of other authorities of the same general type. Some councils will provide this comparative information in their Annual Reports, but all are required to make it available somehow through the local press. So ask for your council's most recent publication of its performance indicators and check for yourself how, say, its pupil-teacher ratios, provision of nursery school places, per capita library loans, housing rent arrears, household waste recycling record, or council tax collection rates compare with those of other authorities – and, more importantly, see what explanations may be offered for any apparently unfavourable figures.

■ Organisation of the book

The book is divided into three parts. Part 1 is concerned with the *basics* of local government. The aim is to provide you with a good basic knowledge of the purposes and origins of local government, its structures, functions and finances, and the context in which it operates. At the end of Part 1 you should, we hope, feel reasonably confident about the fundamentals of local government.

Part 2 looks at the *dynamics* that drive the system. What makes local government 'tick'? The focus moves on to the people and institutions that make decisions, provide services and seek to influence the activities of their locality. We become more directly concerned with politics since our aim is to understand how various interests involved in local government perceive their situation and try to realise their objectives.

Part 3 turns to the agenda of *change*. As already indicated, a defining characteristic of local government in the current era is that it is experiencing a profound challenge to its traditional roles, structures and activities. The book therefore concludes with an attempt to grapple with 'the shape of things to come'.

Guide to further reading

An additional way of developing your 'feel' for local government and politics is through what might be called the 'trade press' of local government: the regular weekly publications that are read mainly by local government personnel themselves, not least for the job advertisements. Most widely available are probably the *Local Government Chronicle* and *Municipal Journal*, the former also responsible for LGCNet, local government's most comprehensive news and information service, should you be fortunate enough to have access to it (http://www. emap.com/lgc). If you have the opportunity to read these 'practitioner' publications, and in particular their 'front-end' news sections, we would strongly recommend it; and don't ignore completely those job adverts – they (and their salaries) can be quite revealing. It is even more important that you scan as frequently as possible the local government news items in both the national and your local press. Hardly a day passes without there appearing at least one or two news articles about the activities of local councils, which will illustrate, expand upon, or update the contents of this book.

■ *Chapter 2* ■

Themes and Issues in Local Government

■ Introduction

This chapter introduces some of the main current issues and themes in UK local government and the key defining characteristics of the local government system. We start by trying to demonstrate the value of our own advice about the benefits of following local government in the national and local press. If, for example, you had been scanning the press in the summer of 1996, the headlines that might have caught your eye would almost certainly have included some of those in Exhibit 2.1.

■ Change and uncertainty

Our dozen news headlines collectively illustrate several of the most prominent themes of 1990s' local government, starting with its state of apparently perpetual motion. In almost every aspect it continued – as throughout the 1980s – to be subject to change, much of it of the most fundamental, structural kind (News Items 1–3).

As Exhibit 2.2 demonstrates, for much of the decade even the total number of councils was changing – or, to be specific, *falling* – from year to year. There are fewer councils as we write than there were at the start of the year, and there will be fewer still when you read these words. If as a reader you find it confusing, just try imagining yourself as a council worker, not knowing whether your employing authority will still be in existence in a couple of years' time, let alone what powers and service responsibilities it might have (News Items 5 and 6), or how it might be managed and financed (News Item 4).

In England in 1992 a team of Commissioners embarked upon a county by county review of the structure of non-metropolitan local government. Its final proposals were approved by government Ministers in the summer of 1996 and the last of 46 new 'unitary' councils were elected in 1997 to become operational in April 1998. In Scotland and Wales similar restructuring reviews were undertaken by the respective Secretaries of State and, as recorded in News Item 1, local government in these

---

Exhibit 2.1   *Selected local government news headlines, 1996*

1. 64 NEW UNITARY COUNCILS SPRING TO LIFE
   The Government's restructuring programme proceeds, with 29 new Scottish and 22 Welsh unitary councils taking over all local government responsibilities from the previous two-tier system of regions/counties and districts. Likewise 13 of a planned 46 new unitaries in England. Over 10 million residents affected, and nearly 500,000 staff.

2. LONDONERS TO VOTE ON NEW STRATEGIC COUNCIL
   Labour Party leaders confirm that a future Labour Government will set up a new Greater London Authority, but only after the electorate's approval in a referendum.

3. EDUCATION AUTHORITIES VANISH IN ULSTER SHAKE-UP
   Restructuring too in Northern Ireland, as five area education boards are reduced to three.

4. GOVERNMENT STAMPS ON RELOCALISED BUSINESS RATES
   A group of top company directors on the Conservative Government's advisory Deregulation Task Force recommends that responsibility for the setting of business rates be handed back to local councils. The advice is swiftly rejected.

5. MINISTER PLANS TO SPEED UP CCT
   Environment Minister, Sir Paul Beresford, announces plans to increase the proportions of 'white collar services' – financial and legal services, personnel, computing, housing management – that councils must expose to Compulsory Competitive Tendering by private sector firms.

6. COUNCILS TO LOSE STUDENT GRANTS?
   Ministers are reportedly preparing to move control of the student grant system from local authorities to a single grants agency because of the 'unacceptable variations in service' received by students.

7. LORDS' REPORT BACKS NEW LOCAL POWERS
   House of Lords inquiry warns of the danger of central government eating away at local government's power 'until nothing meaningful is left', and calls for councils to be given a 'power of general competence'.

8. THREE QUANGOCRATS FOR EVERY COUNCILLOR
   A Democratic Audit report reveals that there are over 70,000 people appointed to various 'Quasi-Autonomous Non-Governmental Organisations', responsible for billions of pounds of public money, compared to some 25,000 elected councillors.

9. WESTMINSTER'S WAR ON ILLEGAL SEX
   Westminster City Council has its own City of Westminster Act 1996, giving it powers to close unlicensed sex shops and sex cinemas, as well to refuse licences and prosecute owners.

10. EAST AYRSHIRE SCHOOLGIRL ON AREA COMMITTEE
    School student Emma McKay is elected as one of the community members and the first pupil representative on East Ayrshire's new structure of nine area committees.

11. BIRMINGHAM TESTS ITS 5-YEAR-OLDS
    Birmingham City Council has started voluntary testing of 5-year-olds, so that when national curriculum testing starts at 7, 11 and 14, there is a baseline measure from which to calculate 'value added' by the school.

12. GLASGOW'S BAN ON BEVVYING
    Glasgow Council's licensing board makes Clydeside the country's biggest area to ban all drinking in public, with arrests and fines of up to £500.

areas of the UK became wholly unitary in 1996, following elections in April–May 1995.

Structural reform, however, goes on. The Labour Government's first Queen's Speech in May 1997 (see Exhibit 20.2) included several Bills with important structural – indeed, constitutional – implications: the referendums paving the way for a Scottish Parliament, Welsh Assembly, and later an elected authority for London; also proposals for Development Agencies in the remaining English regions.

The management of many individual services too is set to change, or to continue to change, significantly. Under Conservative governments local education authorities were scaled down repeatedly as they lost responsibility for polytechnics, further education and sixth-form colleges, school budgets, and opted-out schools. At one point it was mooted, presciently, that student grants would be next to go (News Item 6). Council housing was sold off or transferred to new managements. Social services departments have taken over community care provision but have little extra funding to meet their additional obligations. Technical services – refuse collection, cleaning, catering, repairs and maintenance – and more recently 'white collar' professional services (News Item 5) were increasingly contracted out to the private sector. For a country used to long-term stability in its governmental institutions, this breadth, scale and speed of change are at least remarkable and to many constitutionally and democratically threatening (News Item 7). Inevitably, it is one of this book's key themes.

■ Non-elected local government

There is a trend detectable in much of this recent and potential change: the spread of non-elected local government (News Item 8). It is not in itself a new phenomenon. The National Health Service structure of District Health Authorities and self-governing Trusts is non-elected; so too were the New Town Development Corporations, and the Scottish and Welsh development agencies, on which the planned English regional development agencies are modelled.

What is new is the rapid growth of additional non-elected or indirectly elected bodies *at the expense of* directly elected local councils. Throughout the 1980s and early 1990s service responsibilities were removed from local authorities and given to mainly single-purpose Government-appointed agencies: Urban Development Corporations (UDCs) for inner city development, Training and Enterprise Councils (TECs), Housing Action Trusts (HATs) and governing bodies of further education colleges, for example. It amounted, in the judgement of Jones and Stewart (1992, p. 15), to a 'fundamental change' in our system of local government:

Exhibit 2.2 How many councils this year?

YEAR	ENGLAND					SCOTLAND	WALES	NORTHERN IRELAND	TOTAL
	Non-metropolitan			Metropolitan					
	Counties	Districts	New unitaries	London	Metropolitan boroughs				
1994	39	296	0	33	36	65	45	26	540
1995	38	294	1	33	36	65	45	26	538
1996	35	274	14	33	36	32	22	26	472
1997	35	260	27	33	36	32	22	26	471
1998	34	238	46	33	36	32	22	26	467
1994–8	–5	–58	+46	–	–	–33	–23	–	–77

Government is being handed back to the 'new magistracy' from whom it was removed in the counties more than 100 years ago. Elected representatives are being replaced by a burgeoning army of the selected ... the unknown governors of our society.

It is a change that was intended as a challenge to elected local government – all too often itself 'unknown' to its citizens – and is one that is being positively taken up, in the form of more collaborative and partnership working. While continuing to argue the case for quangos operating more openly, democratically and accountably, councils nowadays are increasingly working *with* and *through* these external organisations – to deliver services, monitor other organisations' service provision, and apply for government grant funding.

■ Diminished discretion

As some powers have been taken away from local government, those remaining have been increasingly constrained: subject to greater national direction and control. Switchback changes in local government finance have been accompanied by the imposition of steadily tighter conditions: Government ministers and civil servants becoming more directly involved in declaring what *they* calculate each local council ought to be spending on different services, as we see in more detail in Chapters 9 and 10. The outcome, as suggested in Figure 2.1, has been a perceptible reduction in local discretion, in the ability of local councils either to decide for themselves or to finance effectively services that they would wish to provide for their local communities.

We shall be encountering later many of the specific governmental initiatives itemised in Figure 2.1. We shall note too the contrast between this centralising trend in the UK and the generally decentralising policies that were being pursued by most other European central governments, but which here have been more the exception than the rule. For the present we merely draw attention to the general shape of what we label the funnel of local authority discretion.

Like a funnel, there is a definite tapering from one end to the other. But there is no suggestion that all local discretion has been eliminated. Councils still have some opportunity, Figure 2.1 implies, to determine their own political priorities and to embark on their own policy initiatives in response to the needs and wishes of the residents in their particular local communities. They may feel increasingly hemmed in by central government dictates and directives, they may protest their unfairness, but they have by no means been robbed of all initiative and individuality.

16

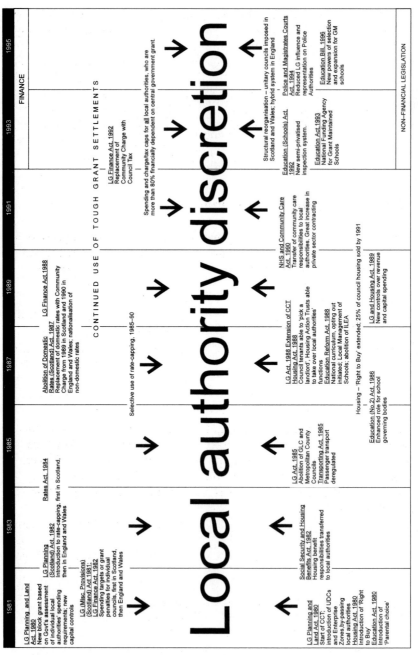

Figure 2.1 *The funnel of local authority discretion*

Source: Adapted from Hollis *et al.* (1990, p. 22)

■ Diversity and innovation

Proof of that last assertion may be found among our own news headlines in Exhibit 2.1, and will surely be in any similar selection you may assemble for yourselves. Examples will range from the momentous and contentious to the barely newsworthy. But Birmingham's school tests, the crack-downs on drinking and sexploitation by Glasgow and Westminister, and East Ayrshire's community democracy initiative all share one thing in common: they are all examples of local councils freely deciding to do something differently from how it was being done before, differently from what other councils were doing, and *not* merely in response to any central government demand or requirement.

■ Contracting, competing, enabling

The picture of contemporary local government that is emerging is one of inevitable subordination to central government, but hardly craven sub-servience; councils with perhaps less freedom of action than previously, but far from emasculated.

As for the future, the goal that the last Conservative Government appeared to have in mind at one time was expressible as a pun. The combination of that Government's removal of some functions from the control of local authorities and its encouragement of the contracting-out of others to the private sector led to the coining of the term: 'the *Contracting Authority*'. Both in size and in the nature of its work, the local authority of the future, it was suggested, would be a contracting one!

The end of the 1980s brought a slight change in terminology. Contraction was still the objective, and contracting out still one of the key means to that end. But there were other means too, spelt out in the Government's 1987/88 legislative programme, in which a whole clutch of measures signalled a fundamental change in the role and operation of local authorities.

There was the community charge legislation for England and Wales, of which more in Chapter 10. Potentially even more far-reaching were the plans for housing, education and many of the technical services provided by local councils. Council tenants would be able to choose their own landlords and vote themselves out of local authority control. Similarly, the parents of children in state schools could vote to 'opt out' of their Local Education Authority and become grant maintained directly by the then Department for Education. Services such as refuse collection, street cleaning and school catering, which most councils had been used to providing themselves with their own workforces, would now have to be open to competitive tenders or bids from the private sector.

One depiction of the future, therefore, was that of 'the *Competitive Council*' (Audit Commission, 1988): required to compete with private companies, with the voluntary sector, and even with central government itself, if it wished to continue to provide some of its most long-standing services.

The phrase, though, which achieved wider currency than either the Contracting or the Competitive Council was that of the *Enabling Council* (Clarke and Stewart, 1988; Brooke, 1989; Ennals and O'Brien, 1990; Wistow *et al.*, 1992; Leach *et al.*, 1996). Local authorities' traditional role as large-scale and mainly self-sufficient service *providers* would – in almost any conceivable political future, it was argued – be reduced, and they would instead become 'enablers'. They might in many instances retain the ultimate responsibility for service provision. But, rather than do everything themselves, with their own directly employed workforces, they would stimulate, facilitate, support, regulate, influence and thereby *enable* other agencies and organisations to act on their behalf. The Enabling Authority thus became the new vogue term – and sometimes, it seemed, the new vague term, given the widely varying interpretations put upon it (see Chapter 20).

■ The quest for quality

By no means all recent change in local government has been externally prompted. Increasingly over the past decade or so local councils have begun of their own volition to examine more self-critically their performance record and to look for ways of improving it and thereby enhancing their public image. They have sought to develop – to quote two buzz phrases – a Public Service Orientation or customer service culture.

Too often in the past, councils will now concede, they were inclined to act as what in many ways they were: unchallenged monopolistic service providers *to* – rather than *for* or *with* – a largely captive public. The last distinction is a crucial one. Rarely, until fairly recently, were service recipients actually asked about the type or quantity or quality of service they required or were prepared, through their own local taxes, to finance. Rarely, in short, were they treated as *customers*: people able to make choices, with the right to the information on which to base those choices, the right of redress if dissatisfied with the service received, and the right to go to other providers.

Local council services were, for the most part, professionally managed, competently delivered, and tolerably efficient. But the emphasis tended to be on quantity rather than quality, with relatively little consideration paid to issues of flexibility, variety and consumer relevance. This emphasis was already changing – in advance of, as well as in response to, John Major's Citizen's Charter initiatives under the last Conservative Government.

Local authorities have been developing a wide range of their own initiatives to improve the quality of their services and get 'closer to their customers': neighbourhood offices, 'one-stop' shops, community meetings, public attitude surveys, 'focus group' discussions on specific issues with selected groups of residents, council newspapers, complaints hotlines, public question times at council meetings, and even video boxes, in which you can make your own video telling the council what you think of it. Once again, keep a look out for anything noteworthy your own council may be doing.

■ The present system: defining characteristics

Having identified some of the principal themes and concerns of local government in the 1990s, we now pause for some stocktaking. If the world of local government is changing as momentously as we suggest, what is it changing *from*? What, in broad introductory terms, does the present system look like? What are its main features and its overall rationale? In the remainder of this chapter we introduce some of the key defining characteristics of our local government system.

□ *Local government, not local administration*

We should start with a fundamental distinction, and explain why we have so far been using, unquestioningly, the term 'local government', rather than 'local administration'. It will serve too as a further introduction: to why the university department for which one of us works is called the Institute of Local *Government* Studies (INLOGOV), and not Local *Administrative* Studies.

All countries of any significant size find it necessary to decentralise or disperse some of the basic tasks of governance. Some do so much more extensively and more enthusiastically than others. Switzerland, for example – albeit a somewhat exceptional one – has never had a national Ministry of Education or a Ministry of Health (Allen, 1990, p. 1). The Swiss decentralise these services entirely to the control of local authorities, and mostly very much smaller authorities than those in Britain.

When central governments decentralise, they may choose to do so in different ways and to different degrees:

* *Administrative decentralisation, or delegation*
    They may choose to delegate purely administrative decision-making to dependent field offices of a central ministry. All major policy decisions will continue to be taken centrally, but the service will be delivered and routine administrative decisions taken by locally based but centrally employed civil servants. The most obvious

example in Britain is the Department of Social Security's Benefits Agency, whose *cash payments* to the sick, disabled and unemployed are made from local offices of the DSS or in Northern Ireland the Social Security Agency. They are thus quite separate – unlike the practice in many countries – from the local authority social *services* provided to many of the same people.

* *Functional decentralisation*
  Secondly, central government can create semi-independent agencies to run specific services. Here the most obvious example is the National Health Service, with its structure of District Health Authorities and Trusts, overseen by boards of appointed and nominated members. It may look a little like the structure of local councils, and in many countries the health service is a fully integrated part of the local government system. But Britain's health authorities and trusts are quite separate: funded by and ultimately accountable to central government via the NHS Executive, and thus part of the growing 'quangocracy' referred to above.

* *Political decentralisation, or devolution*
  Thirdly, central government can devolve policy-making responsibilities in a wide range of service areas to relatively autonomous and directly elected regional, provincial or local governments. This political decentralisation, in which a constitutionally superior body chooses to hand over certain powers to constitutionally dependent ones, is clearly distinguishable from *federalism*, in which *both* the national (or federal) and the local bodies are assigned their powers equally and separately by the constitution. But it is just as clearly distinguishable from local administration.

Local authorities are far more than simply outposts or agents of central government, delivering services in ways and to standards laid down in detail at national ministerial level. Their role, as representative bodies elected by their fellow citizens, is to take such decisions themselves, in accordance with their own policy priorities: to govern their locality. If this were not so, there would not be the often dramatic variations in the service costs and performance measures revealed in councils' annual reports, and in the increasingly popular league tables of local council statistics. Nor would we have seen in several of our News Items examples of ways in which councils can, to a certain extent at least, determine and pursue their own initiatives.

☐ *Local self-government?*

So, does the system of local government – councils of elected politicians making policy decisions on behalf of their local communities – amount to local *self-government*? Do localities and communities have the rights and resources genuinely to manage their own public affairs in what they see as their own best interests? Some writers appear to think so, and use the terms 'local government' and 'local self-government' almost interchangeably. Thus one recent textbook suggests that today 'local government means the self-government of Britain's counties, cities and towns' (Kingdom, 1991, p. 3).

Others, however, are more hesitant. Local government *ought* to mean local or community self-government, they seem to suggest; it ought to be about democratically elected representatives collectively deciding how best to respond to all the differing needs and wishes of the residents of their area. In practice, though, that is not how it works in the UK. Let us look at a particularly forceful quote from the Bains Committee, responsible in the early 1970s for one of the most influential reports on post-war local government:

> Local government, in our view, is not limited to the narrow provision of a series of services to the community . . . *It has within its purview the overall economic, cultural and physical well-being of the community.* (Bains, 1972, para.2.10, our emphasis)

It sounds like the first half of an exam question, followed perhaps by: 'Discuss, with reference to UK local government over the past twenty years.' If it were an essay question, you would certainly want to focus on that slightly quaint word 'purview'. For it has at least two shades of meaning. One is that which the Bains Committee apparently had in mind: scope of outlook or concern. Local councils, they were saying, *should* properly be concerned with and involved in *all* aspects of community life, not just those areas of responsibility allocated to them by Parliament.

That is the situation in many countries, especially those formed historically by the coming together of several small communities for mutual help and support – e.g. Switzerland, the Netherlands, Italy, the Scandinavian countries. Local councils or municipalities in such countries have, on average, much smaller populations than UK local authorities. Yet they have something that, as we saw in News Item 7, British councils have not had: *a power of general competence.* They have a general right to undertake any activities which they feel to be in the interests of their citizens, unless such activities are actually forbidden or assigned to other bodies. Like private citizens, they can do anything they are not expressly forbidden from doing. As Allen (1990, p. 23) puts it:

> Local government is not looked upon as just a mechanism. Rather, it is seen as the organic self-expression of the people themselves, whose powers are not yielded to the centre, but retained by the citizens of each community in the country to provide necessary local services for themselves.

In the UK, with its long monarchical history, the formal constitutional position is almost precisely the reverse: local councils can do *only* what they are statutorily permitted to do. Their rights and competences are not general, but specific. To quote Allen again (1990, p. 22):

> Local government is looked upon essentially as a subordinate mechanism created by the state for its own convenience. It is no more than one of several alternative agencies through which the paternalist central government can arrange the provision of services for the state's citizen-subjects.

Underlying their subordinate status, the common law doctrine under which councils operate is known as *ultra vires*, a Latin term which translates as 'beyond the powers'. If a local council does something or spends money that it is not statutorily authorised to, it will be deemed to have acted *ultra vires*: beyond its powers, and therefore illegally. Moreover, the elected councillors who collectively agreed to the action become individually punishable and personally liable to refund any money illegally spent – a potential punishment often out of all proportion to the 'crime', in the view of the Nolan Committee on Standards in Public Life (1997) and which the Labour Government may therefore agree to abolish.

This reference to the legal framework of UK local government brings us back to the Bains Committee. For 'purview' has an alternative narrower and particularly legal meaning: the body of a statute, containing the enacting clauses. This meaning was probably not that intended by the Bains Committee, but it serves as a cautionary reminder that, legally and constitutionally, local government in the UK can .concern itself with the 'overall economic, cultural and physical well-being of the community' *only* in as far as the national Parliament gives it the statutory authority to do so. It cannot do so entirely on its own initiative.

☐ *Creatures of statute*

The doctrine of parliamentary supremacy derives from the fact that the UK, like over 80 per cent of the world's nations, is a *unitary* state, not a federal one. There is a single source of constitutional power and authority: the Westminster Parliament, in which usually nowadays one party has an overall majority of members and thus forms the Government of the day. Parliament, processing legislation introduced by the Government, can make or unmake law on any subject whatever – including local government.

In federal systems – the US, Canada, Australia, India, Germany and Switzerland, for example – legislative power is divided, between the federal government at the centre and the governments of decentralised states or regions. No such division exists in Britain. Scotland and Wales, as nationalists in those countries are acutely aware, have no parliaments of their own at the present time, although change is likely (see Exhibit 20.2). Northern Ireland, which for 50 years had its own Stormont Parliament, saw that body's constitutionally subordinate status emphatically underlined in 1972, when Mr Heath's Conservative Government suspended it and imposed direct rule over the province.

Local authorities are in essentially the same constitutionally subordinate position as was Stormont. They are literally the creatures, the creations, of parliamentary statute. Their boundaries, duties, powers, memberships and modes of operation are laid down by Acts of Parliament. Naturally, therefore, they can be abolished by Parliament – as were the Greater London Council (GLC) and the six English metropolitan county councils in 1985/86, and as others are being even as we write.

☐ *Partial autonomy*

To summarise: the UK has a constitutionally subordinate system of local government, without the wide-ranging competence of many European continental systems, yet which is far more than a network of field agencies of central government. It could be described as semi-autonomous.

There are semantic purists who will insist that there can be no such phenomenon as partial autonomy – but we find it useful to be able to describe one governmental institution as having relatively less autonomy than another, or less than it possessed itself at some time in the past. Indeed, such imprecise terminology fits appropriately our uncodified and convention-based constitution. Most European countries have formal, written constitutions, which usually include some provision for, and protection of, the principle of local self-government.

In the UK, with no comparable single constitutional document, there is in theory no limit to the sovereignty of Parliament. There is correspondingly no constitutional protection for local government: neither for the rights of individual councils nor for the system as a whole.

In practice, however, as we shall see in Chapter 4, much of the history of UK local government, particularly during the early decades of the 20th century, has been about governments determining and Parliaments legislating to devolve powers and responsibilities to local authorities. Local councils have been seen, in Allen's phrase, as a usefully democratic and effective 'subordinate mechanism' for the delivery of all kinds of services which central government has decided should be publicly provided.

Statutory powers can assume various forms. At one extreme they may be *detailed* and *compulsory*, requiring local councils to undertake certain

activities to tightly defined and rigorously enforced standards. Alternatively, they may be *permissive* or *discretionary*, leaving councils to decide
for themselves whether or not to provide a particular service, and to
what standard. Traditionally, much of the legislation affecting local
government has had what might be termed a high 'discretion factor'.
Local councils have had considerable say in how they deliver their
services and, in some cases, whether or not they do so. But discretion
has no guarantee. It can be curtailed and ultimately withdrawn: hence
the aptness of the label 'partial autonomy'.

☐ *Directly elected*

The characteristic responsible above all others for whatever degree of
autonomy local authorities do possess is that of their direct election. They
are not composed of locally based civil servants or central government
appointees. They consist of local people, chosen at regular and regulated
elections to represent the interests of the communities in which they
themselves also live and work.

These representatives – known as *councillors* or *elected members* –
collectively constitute the local council and are the embodiment of its
legal authority. On the basis of that authority, they recruit and employ a
wide range of staff – professionally qualified 'officers', other administrative, technical and clerical 'white collar' staff, and various categories of
manual or 'blue collar' workers – to carry out the policies and deliver the
services that they, as democratically elected representatives, determine.

Direct election does not, in the UKs unitary system of government,
make councillors the constitutional equals or rivals of Members of
Parliament. Councillors may have to face their electorates more frequently than MPs, and there are far more of them: nearly 40 times as
many. But elections can always be suspended, just as councils can be
abolished, at any time that the Government, through Parliament, decrees.
Until that happens, though, councillors' elected status accords them a
legitimacy quite different from that of, say, the appointed members of
health authorities or urban development corporations.

Councillors have had to present themselves and their policy proposals
for consideration and approval by the electorate. That local democratic
approval represents a uniquely potent bargaining counter in any subsequent negotiations, whether with ministers, Whitehall civil servants, or
their own local officers. Their critics may, perhaps with some cause,
question voters' genuine understanding of the complex issues involved
and their relatively low turnout rates in local elections. But the very fact
of electoral backing in any even aspiring democratic society has a force of
its own – as the unelected Soviet President Gorbachev found in 1991
when confronted by the recently elected Russian President Yeltsin.

□ *Multi-service organisations*

If electoral accountability is the primary distinguishing feature of local authorities, the second is their range of responsibilities. They are involved in some way or other, it can sometimes seem, with an almost infinite variety of different services.

We referred earlier to councils looking after people from the cradle to the grave. Another way of illustrating the same point is through the A to Z service directories produced nowadays by many councils. The directories are designed for the councils' own sometimes understandably confused residents: to publicise the services that may be available to them and, even more importantly, where to go for them and who to contact. The listings in Exhibit 2.3 assume a unitary authority, like a metropolitan district council, responsible for all local government services. But, to emphasise how extensive can be the range of services provided by even a *single council department,* the services listed on the right of most entries are from a similar A to Z guide produced by Lewisham London Borough Council's Environmental Services Department.

□ *Multi-functional organisations*

All the services listed in Exhibit 2.3 have some degree of council involvement. But by no means are they all directly provided by the council itself. Historically it is true that councils' principal function has been that of *direct service provider.* They themselves have purchased the land, provided the buildings and equipment, and employed all the staff necessary to deliver their services.

Councils have always, though, had other functions and roles as well, and it is these roles that are likely to become relatively more important in the future. In many cases the local authority is the *regulator* or *monitor* of the activities of other agencies and organisations. They issue licences for public entertainments, theatres, cinemas, sex establishments, street trading, taxi drivers, animal boarding establishments, hairdressers, late night cafes, performing animals, pet shops, and caravan sites. Similar responsibilities include the *registration* of private residential homes, and the *certification* of sports ground safety, as the public became acutely aware following the Bradford and Hillsborough football disasters.

A further role is as *facilitator,* providing advice, assistance and possibly finance to individuals or organisations undertaking activities consistent with the policy of the council. Thus a Local Action Team of council officers will provide help in setting up credit unions as part of the council's work in alleviating poverty and debt. Start-up grants and loans are available for the establishment of new businesses and workers' co-operatives, and grants are given also to an extensive range of arts,

Exhibit 2.3 *An A to Z of council services*

	A METROPOLITAN CITY COUNCIL	LB LEWISHAM ENVIRONMENTAL SERVICES ONLY
A	Adult education; adoption and fostering; allotments; architecture	Abandoned vehicles
B	Births, marriages, deaths; bus passes; bottle banks; BMX tracks	Bridges and footbridges
C	Careers advice; cemeteries and crematoria; child care; cinema licensing	Cycle routes
D	Day centres; debt counselling; disabled people's facilities; dustbins	Dog fouling
G	Gay centre; golf courses; gritting; garden cultivation	Gully cleansing
H	Home helps; homeless families; historic buildings; housing benefit	Health education
I	Inner city development; insulation grants; insect control	Infectious diseases
J	Job creation; Jewish Library	Job vacancies
K	Keep fit classes, Kurzweil Reading Machines; Kabbadi facilities	
L	Land use planning; leisure passes; luncheon clubs; libraries	Listed buildings
M	Meals on wheels; museums and art galleries; markets	Meat inspection
N	Nature conservation; neighbourhood offices; nature reserves	Noise nuisance
O	Office development; oil spillage removal; on-street parking	Orange badge scheme
P	Planning applications; public lavatories; pre-school playgroups	Parking meters
R	Recreation services; recycling; residential homes; refuse disposal	Road safety
S	Sheltered housing; schools; street cleansing; sports centres	Street trading
T	Trading standards; traffic signals; truancy; talking books	Tree preservation
U	Unitary development plan; urban wildlife conservation	Urban design
V	Vocational education; voluntary organisation grants	Video jukebox licensing
W	Welfare rights advice; women's unit; weights and measures	Water pollution
Y	Youth clubs; youth training	
Z	Zebra crossings	Zoo licensing

recreation, social and community groups. Finally, moving a further step away from direct service provision, there is that most rapidly developing of council roles to which we have already alluded: that of *service contractor.*

☐ *Power of taxation*

Vital though we argued that it is, electoral authority is essentially a moral force. To be effective, it needs something more tangible: the right to tax. A further crucial characteristic of local authorities, therefore, is that they have the power to tax local residents. Other local agencies are funded by government grants and from their own trading income. Local authorities too receive much – indeed most – of their income from these sources. But for almost 400 years they have also been able to set the levels of and collect their own taxes.

In the past few years the local tax system has undergone an unprecedented series of reforms. Part of the outcome has been that local authorities' taxation power is no longer, as lawyers might say, an unfettered one. As we noted earlier, Conservative Government Ministers capped or limited councils' levels of spending and their right to tax their own residents, thereby effectively controlling their budgets. So, while the power to tax still distinguishes local councils from other agencies of public administration, it is a power exercised nowadays with central government constantly looking over their shoulders. Change under the current Labour Government is unlikely to be dramatic. The 1997 Manifesto stated: 'Although crude and universal council tax capping should go, we will retain reserve powers to control excessive council tax rises.' Central control is not set to disappear although its intensity could change.

■ Conclusion

We have identified in this chapter a set of characteristics that, individually and collectively, serve as a definition of UK local government.

UK local government defined

* a form of geographical and political decentralisation, in which
* directly elected councils,
* created by and subordinate to Parliament,
* have partial autonomy
* to provide a wide variety of services
* through various direct and indirect means,
* funded in part by local taxation.

This is a slightly more elaborate definition than that we worked out in Chapter 1, and it will serve as a reference point for several of the remaining chapters in Part 1 of the book.

Guide to further reading

Our first recommendations for further reading are those we made in Chapter 1. Find out about the practical workings of local government from your own local councils. Go along to the reception and ask: the response you get will be an interesting test of their customer consciousness! Couple this with a regular – if possible daily – scanning of the Home News pages of a 'quality' or 'broadsheet' national newspaper – *Guardian, Independent, Telegraph* or *The Times;* and don't forget your local press, especially around the January/February budgeting and April/May election times. For a more cynical view there is *Private Eye's* fortnightly 'Rotten Boroughs' column. Among the best textbook introductions to local government are those by Byrne (1994) and Elcock (1994). Fuller accounts and interpretations of the recent developments we identify are available in Cochrane (1993a) and in the compilations edited by Stewart and Stoker (1989 and 1995) and Leach *et al.* (1996). To follow up our references in this and succeeding chapters to other countries' local government systems, the most accessible source is Chandler (1993).

■ *Chapter 3* ■

Why Elected Local Government?

■ Introduction

In this chapter we address that deceptively simple question: why elected local government? In Chapter 2 we identified the defining characteristics of the UK local government system and some of the challenges it faced in the 1990s. We look now at the principles underpinning that system, at its rationale and *raison d'être*, its value and values. Most of this chapter will emphasise the benefits and positive attributes of elected local government as we defined it in Chapter 2. The emphasis reflects a bias to which we readily admit: a predisposition in favour of decentralisation of power and against its undue concentration.

■ The problems of local government

To central government, it often seems, the commonest 'problem' of local government is when it refuses to do what central government wishes: when local councils pursue demonstrably different goals from those of the party in power nationally. An alternative interpretation of such a battle of wills is that it demonstrates the health and robustness of a governmental system. Far from constituting a problem, it ought to be seen as an affirmation of precisely what local government should be about: locally elected and accountable representatives developing policies embodying *their* judgement of the best interests of *their* local community, not the judgement of the centre.

Our own reference to 'the problems of local government' is intended to suggest something rather more subtle and complex. We mean the potential costs and considerations involved in any decision to devolve administrative responsibility, let alone political power. In several cases these potential costs are merely the obverse of possible benefits. But it is still useful to enumerate some of what Allen (1990, ch. 1) terms the disadvantages of decentralisation.

The first argument deployed against decentralisation is that of *financial cost*. Decentralisation duplicates scarce financial resources and staff.

Things could be run more cheaply from the centre, critics suggest, whether the centre in question is London or, when considering the case for area or neighbourhood offices, a council's own headquarters.

Closely linked to finance is *efficiency*. It may be difficult to attract experienced staff and enterprising management, especially if the decentralised units are relatively small and poorly resourced. These staffing problems can in turn lead to *inertia* and a reluctance or inability to change.

A different kind of argument is that of *inequality*. The more genuinely decentralised a service, the greater are likely to be the resulting disparities among geographical areas and social groups. Then, depending on the response of the centre to such disparities, the demand for further devolution and even *separatism* may grow.

Finally, there is the charge of potential *corruption*, levelled probably more frequently at local than at national government, and as much in the news in the 1990s as it was in the 1970s, at the time of the notorious 'Poulson Affair'. In 1974 several leading politicians and senior public sector employees were found guilty of having improperly and corruptly secured contracts for the Yorkshire private architect, John Poulson. The case led to the important formulation of a National Code of Conduct for the guidance of both councillors and officers, and it is remembered primarily as a case of *local* government corruption, despite the fact that 'Poulson's cadre' (Doig, 1984, p. 142) embraced a cabinet minister, MPs of both parties, civil servants, health service and nationalised industry employees, as well as councillors and officers.

The equally high profile case of the 1980s and 1990s was the 'homes for votes' affair involving Dame Shirley Porter, former Leader of Westminster City Council. In a case much more to do with political power than personal financial gain, Dame Shirley and five councillor and officer associates were found guilty by a local government district auditor of operating a housing sales policy specifically for the electoral benefit of the Conservative Party and thereby of costing their council many millions of pounds. It is true that aspects of this case were considered in 1996/97 by the Government's Committee on Standards in Public Life, chaired by Lord Nolan. But it should also be remembered that that Committee was set up in the first place to investigate allegations of misconduct and 'sleaze' in the *Palace*, not the City, of Westminster, and on the part of MPs and ministers, who significantly had no equivalent of councillors' Code of Conduct to guide their behaviour.

Our point is not that any set of politicians – local or national, male or female, Party A or Party B – is intrinsically more virtuous or more corruptible than any other; merely that we should retain a sense of perspective and keep in mind Allen's warning (1990, p. 12) that, despite all the national and international evidence that central agencies are often at least as incompetent, inefficient or corrupt as local bodies, local authorities are perennially in the news for alleged corruption and graft . . . one or two notorious cases can suffice to keep the whole concept of local government in disrepute.

■ The values of local government

These alleged 'problems' of local government are not to be dismissed lightly. But they can be more than balanced by the advantages of decentralisation or, as various authors have phrased it, the justifications of local government (Clarke and Stewart, 1991, ch. 3; Smith, 1985, ch. 2; Young, 1986b). In the remainder of this chapter we group our justifications under the seven headings itemised in Exhibit 3.1. It is a grouping derived from a long-standing and at times complex theoretical debate, further details of which may be followed up by use of our references in the Bibliography.

Exhibit 3.1 *The values or justifications of elected local government*

Elected local government is likely to be better than a combination of central government and local administration at:

1. Building and articulating community identity
2. Emphasising diversity
3. Fostering innovation and learning
4. Responding swiftly, appropriately, corporately
5. Promoting citizenship and participation
6. Providing political education and training
7. Dispersing power.

☐ *Building and articulating community identity*

In Chapter 2 we concentrated particularly on local *government* and its contrast with local administration. We now focus on *local* government: the government of a particular geographical area and, if the relevant boundaries have been appropriately drawn, the government of a community. The institutions of local government *ought* both to reflect and reinforce people's sense of place and of community:

> A local authority has the capacity to shape an area, to preserve it, to develop it, to change it, and in doing so to give it a new identity. (Clarke and Stewart, 1991, p. 29)

Goldsmith goes further, adding a local council's capacity

> to act as the *advocate* of a locality, a function clearly recognised in such
> countries as France, where the local mayor is frequently also the local MP, and
> Italy, where party links between the locality and the centre are particularly
> strong. In present-day highly centralised Britain, with its adversarial partisan
> form of national politics, the voice of the locality far too often goes
> unheard.   (Goldsmith, 1986a, p. 2)

But necessarily these things take time and need encouragement, both
of which have been at a premium in recent years. We contrasted in
Chapter 2 the kind of 'bottom-up' local self-government found in some
European countries, which grew out of local communities coming
together for mutual help and support, and the UK's more 'top-down'
version, deriving from parliamentary statute and the drawing of boundary lines on maps. The inevitable danger of over-frequent 'top-down'
restructuring is the severing of any link between a local authority and
community identity, the most visible sign of which must be the imposition of alien council names that at best bewilder and at worst infuriate.

The reorganisation of the early 1970s produced countless examples of
these 'artificial' names, initially as unfamiliar to their own residents as
they still are to many outsiders. Some have already disappeared in the
latest reorganisation: the non-metropolitan counties of Avon, Cleveland
and Humberside, together with the equally short-lived and much-mis-
pronounced Welsh counties of Clwyd and Dyfed. But plenty of others
remain: the metropolitan districts of Calderdale and Kirklees (respectively the areas around Halifax and Huddersfield), Knowsley (east of
Liverpool) and Sandwell (West Midlands); and, among the many non-
metropolitan district candidates, Adur (West Sussex), Craven (North
Yorkshire), Gravesham (Kent), Three Rivers (Herts), and the doubly
confusing Wyre (coastal Lancashire) and Wyre Forest (Worcestershire).
They and their like can be seen as testaments to a national political
culture that is inclined to build and restructure its local government
system 'more on bureaucratic and professional principles than upon
local needs and community identities' (Lowndes, 1996, p. 71).

☐ *Emphasising diversity*

A sense of place and past implies *distinctiveness*: of an area's distinctive
geography, history, economy, social and political culture, and of its
consequently distinctive preferences and priorities. It is the recognition
that even local authorities of the same type, with the same statutory
powers and responsibilities, can be utterly different from each other and
have completely different governmental needs.

In a federal system like the US, where the states can pass as well as promote their own legislation, the diversity of local demands and circumstances can appear extreme and even bizarre. In Indiana it is illegal to ride on a bus within four hours of eating garlic, in South Carolina to drink water in a bar, and in Kentucky to carry an ice cream cone in one's pocket. But UK local authorities too can differ so greatly in character that it is possible to imagine their enacting almost equally singular legislation, given the chance.

Bristol, Berwick-upon-Tweed and Blackpool were all, until the recent reorganisation, English non-metropolitan districts. Yet, apart from their initials, they shared little in common. Bristol is one of the country's oldest cities and was the largest of 296 non-metropolitan districts with a population of over 375,000. It was a county in its own right for several centuries, then an all-purpose county borough from 1889 until 1974, whereupon it had some difficulty coming to terms with its diminished status as a district council within the county of Avon. The City (now Unitary) Council is invariably Labour-dominated and its politics fiercely partisan. It leases to the British Port Company a major commercial dock undertaking, has its own international airport, licenses one of the largest entertainment complexes in Europe and, even after recent sales, has a stock of over 35,000 council houses and flats.

Berwick-upon-Tweed Borough Council covers nearly nine times the area of Bristol but has about one-fourteenth of its population. By this latter criterion it is almost the smallest council in England. Notwithstanding its team's membership of the Scottish Football League, the medieval walled town itself lies two miles south of the Scottish border. But most of the borough is rural, its economy based on agriculture, fishing and light industry, plus summer tourism attracted by its picturesque coastline and the Northumberland National Park. The politics of the 28-member council are predominantly Liberal Democrat, with Independents in a strong second place.

Blackpool's tourism is on an altogether different scale, bringing into the town over £500 million a year. Its 146,000 residents are massively outnumbered by the 18 million tourist visitors, and all the council's biggest recent investments – mostly undertaken in conjunction with private enterprise – are in leisure and recreation: the showpiece flat green bowling centre and all-weather sports stadium, the Zoo Park and the Sandcastle water entertainments centre – with its new 'World of Coronation Street' – the refurbishment of the Promenade, not to mention its nearly £2 million spent each year on the famous illuminations.

Any other random selection of B-initialled districts would produce just as great a diversity. Yet central government's instinct is to focus on the relatively few similarities of such authorities and to play down their obvious contrasts. Ministers and civil servants struggle to devise formulae that will enable all such councils to be dealt with as a single group.

A thriving local government does the reverse. It emphasises and gives voice and expression to the distinctiveness of local communities. It is the *government of difference* or of diversity – or, more accurately still, of multiversity.

☐ *Fostering innovation and learning*

By responding to diverse local circumstances and acting as the government of difference, local authorities are almost bound to enhance the learning capacity of government. They will develop their own solutions and initiatives, some of which may prove unsuccessful or applicable only to their specific locality, but some of which may be adaptable – either by other local authorities or even by central government.

Local authorities are constantly learning from each other – through official bodies like the Audit Commission and the Local Government Management Board, publicising examples of 'best practice'; through the dozens of local government professional magazines and journals, conferences and seminars; and by simple word of mouth. Refer back to our own selection of News Items in Exhibit 2.1. You can be sure that Glasgow councillors and officers will have looked very carefully at other authorities' attempts to reduce public drinking and drunkenness before finally deciding to introduce their own ban. Similarly, with a Labour-controlled council like Birmingham seeking to go beyond the last Conservative Government's national curriculum by testing pupils at the age of five, the rest of the education world, including the Department for Education and Employment, will study with great interest what constitutes for them a free experiment. For, as a former Director of Education, Donald Naismith, has argued:

> When government brings in legislation, most of what they want to do has arisen because of local education authorities doing it first . . . Look at teacher appraisal. Suffolk pioneered it. Local management of schools? That was Cambridgeshire. Assessment of children at 7, 11 and 14, you could say Croydon. (Crequer, 1991)

Almost every local authority in the country has played its part in developing or piloting some new service which has subsequently been adopted or adapted for use elsewhere. Tower Hamlets provides all its profoundly deaf residents with an interactive portable keyboard and accompanying telephone handset, enabling them to communicate by phone. Brighton was the first town to scrap all its parking meters in favour of a more environmentally friendly, completely hardware-free parking system. Oxford has a licensed rickshaw taxi service to help reduce city centre congestion and pollution. Leicestershire provides an annual grant to the Post Office to run a rural 'post bus' service through villages cut off from public transport. North Yorkshire has what it believes to be the world's first 'green graveyard' – a combined cemetery and nature reserve for people wanting an alternative to an ecologically unsound burial in a regimented cemetery. Milton Keynes was the first council to introduce a door-to-door recycling scheme. Camden Council requires all its licensed night clubs to provide free water, in an attempt to reduce deaths from the drug Ecstasy.

The list is huge. Yet it would be longer still, were central government to recognise more frequently than it does the experimental and piloting potential of local government. Local councils are regularly invited by government departments to test policy and service ideas, but more often, it would seem, small ideas rather than large ones. Model 'poop scoop' by-laws, giving councils powers to ban dogs from beaches and other designated areas, were carefully piloted in Gosport, Rochester and, yes, Barking and Dagenham. But studying the impact of, say, a temporary relaxation of the financial controls over economic development, or of the restrictions on cross-boundary competitive tendering, is likely to be deemed either dangerous or irrelevant – unless, as with the testing in 1995/96 of nursery school vouchers, it has an immediate national political objective.

☐ *Responding swiftly, appropriately, corporately*

Distance delays. It can also distort perception. Being the multi-service, multi-functional organisations that they are, local councils on the spot ought to be able to identify better and faster than can central government the most appropriate response to any local situation. They should also be able to organise that response themselves, quickly, co-ordinatedly and, possibly, more economically. Sharpe (1970, pp. 155, 165) terms this ability the 'knowledge value' of local government:

> central government is not equipped to grasp the inimitable conditions of each locality. Local government is preferable precisely because locally elected institutions employing their own specialist staff are better placed to understand and interpret both the conditions and the needs of local communities . . . out-stationed field agencies could not . . . co-ordinate their activities with each other.

An exceptional but vital example of such co-ordination was provided by Kent County Council's emergency support operation following the bomb explosion at the Royal Marines' barracks at Deal in September 1989 which killed 11 bandsmen. The operation involved almost the whole range of council departments:

* the Fire Service
* the Police, who initially notified . . .
* the Emergency Planning Unit, who co-ordinated the ensuing support work, calling in, where necessary, organisations like the British Red Cross, the ambulance service, and Dover District Council
* Social Services, providing temporary shelter for those evacuated from their homes, meals-on-wheels, care and counselling support
* Education, as schools were requisitioned as rest centres
* the Schools Meals Service, providing food and hot drinks for both the rescued and rescuers
* Building Design and Highways, whose structural engineers were needed to advise on partially collapsed buildings
* Supplies, called upon to provide waterproofs and other protective equipment.

The relevant management jargon here is 'horizontal integration', as explained in the Widdicombe Committee Report:

> Local authorities can respond corporately to multi-dimensional local issues, such as inner city problems, in a way which national services are less able to do. This is an advantage of multi-purpose units of government which is not easily replicated in a system of local administration. Thus, while the health service might maximise efficiency in its vertical integration of a single service between district health authority and Whitehall, local government will tend to have the advantage in horizontal integration of a range of services at local level.   (Widdicombe, 1986a, p. 52)

□ *Promoting citizenship and participation*

Local *administration* is about acceptance: local officials' acceptance of nationally determined policy, and service recipients' acceptance of those officials' implementation of that policy. Local *government* is about choice and challenge. It actively encourages citizen involvement and participation. It has what Sharpe (1970, p. 160) calls 'democratic primacy' over central government, 'because it does enable more people to participate in their own government'.

Most obviously, elected local government involves citizens as voters and elected representatives. The regularity of local elections means that we have the chance to vote for our councillors far more frequently than for our MPs. Compared to many countries, the UK has an exceptionally large number of MPs and an exceptionally small number of councils. Even so, for every MP or parliamentary candidate there are roughly 40 county, district, borough and unitary councillors and candidates.

These figures, moreover, completely exclude the country's 90,000 or so parish and town councillors. There are 8,000 parish and town councils in England, and some 2,000 community councils in Wales and Scotland, with an average of nine elected members each, albeit some of them doubling as district councillors or borough councillors as well. Some of these councils are larger than our smaller district councils, representing communities of over 30,000 people. Most, however, are much more localised, nearly two-thirds comprising populations of under 1,000 and 40 per cent under 500 (Ellwood *et al.*, 1992). These latter councils in particular are likely to be run on a voluntary basis with no paid staff and little expenditure. Yet in some countries even these smaller councils would constitute prominent, influential and major service-providing institutions of local government.

It is not primarily their size, therefore, that reduces the governmental significance of parish and town councils and accounts for the limited attention they will receive in this book. The chief reasons are that, unlike county and district councils, and unlike similarly sized local councils in other countries, they are *not universal* and they have no *specific duties* to provide services or facilities. They greatly extend local government participation, but their service-providing role is very limited and entirely discretionary.

In England and Wales, parish, town and community councils are confined to predominantly rural areas. They represent a total of just under one-third of the population, the remaining two-thirds living in 'unparished' areas. The councils may, and many do, provide a wide range of services, either on their own initiative or acting as agents for their county or district councils: village halls, allotments, playing fields, gymnasia and baths, open spaces and camping sites, shelters, war memorials, public clocks, street lighting, car parks, burial grounds, footpaths and churchyards. But all these services are *discretionary*: there is no requirement that they be provided. Where they are provided, they are financed partly by fees and charges and partly by means of a precept added to the local tax collected by their district council from the area's taxpayers. In addition to this limited access to tax revenues, these local councils have the right to be notified and consulted by their respective district and county councils about local planning applications, footpath surveys, and certain bylaws.

Scottish community councils are rather different. They are entirely optional, have no automatic right of access to public funds, and cannot therefore be properly regarded as an additional tier of the local government system in the way that the English and Welsh councils can. Their principal functions are not the provision of services, but consultation and representation: ascertaining and articulating the views of their local communities.

Parish and community councils have a variety of consultative processes available to them. There are the regular meetings of the council itself, nowadays increasingly open to direct participation by members of the public. There is the traditional annual meeting of the whole parish – able, if it so determines, to instruct the council to carry out a parish poll on a particular issue. It is said that 'the incidence of parish/town polls is minimal – only 2 per cent of councils . . . reporting holding such a poll in 1989/90' (Ellwood *et al.*, 1992, p. 34). Yet, extrapolating across the country, that 'minimal' figure would have resulted in some 160 polls, all paid for by the electors themselves, which seems a phenomenon of at least passing interest in a country generally so sceptical of the methods of direct democracy.

Far more widespread is the use made by local councils of their own surveys of local needs and views, over a quarter of councils reporting such activity in 1989/90. Most frequent were housing needs surveys and village appraisals, the results of which would in turn be communicated to the appropriate district and county council departments and other agencies.

There is, in short, immensely more, and more varied, participation in local government than is often supposed by those who simply study local election contests. Elections are only the tip of the participation iceberg.

□ *Providing political education and training*

Participation is itself a form of political education. In the UK, political education is a largely neglected field of study in our schools and colleges. In such a society, governmental institutions and processes – particularly at the local level – have a key role to play as stimuli of political learning.

Local elections are especially important. Even non-voters are likely to have their political awareness and governmental knowledge increased through the heightened media attention given to local issues and candidates during the campaign period. All UK local elections take place in April or May, shortly after councils have made their budgets for the new financial year and sent out their local tax demands. Councillors and candidates, through their election addresses and manifestos, have to defend their actions or propose alternative policies. Statistics are produced, challenged and debated. Surveys may show that many people still remain unaware of who our councillors are and what our councils do, but without elections that ignorance would be almost total.

For its most active and involved participants local government provides not just education, but a training and apprenticeship for a professional political career. There is, however, much less career overlap between national and local politics in Britain than in many countries. It is not so much that fewer UK parliamentarians come from local government backgrounds, but that those who do mostly choose to resign as councillors at the earliest opportunity – regrettably, it may be felt, given the quantity of legislation directed at local government in recent years. In recent General Elections, though, there has been no single more important recruiting ground than local government – for all political parties. Of the record 1997 intake of 259 new MPs, 161 (62 per cent) had some local government experience, bringing the Commons total as a whole to 368 (56 per cent). This latter figure includes two-thirds of the 418 Labour MPs – now almost a parliamentary party of municipal politicians – over 60 per cent of Liberal Democrats, and 30 per cent of Conservatives.

Striking though these figures are, Young (1986a, p. 15) would argue that they only represent part of the political training potential of local government. He emphasises its value as a training ground not just for national politicians, but for democracy itself: for the learning of the crucial political skills of argument, persuasion and winning consent by 'that inevitably small proportion of the population who will hold office at any one time. The quality of democracy is in their hands'.

☐ *Dispersing power*

These references to democracy bring us to arguably the most fundamental value or justification of local government: that of *pluralism*. As the Widdicombe Report put it:

> the case for pluralism is that power should not be concentrated in one organisation of state, but should be dispersed, thereby providing political checks and balances, and a restraint on arbitrary government and absolutism. (Widdicombe, 1986a, p. 48)

Ten years earlier another Government report, this time by the Layfield Committee of Inquiry into Local Government Finance, had seen local government's role in almost identical terms:

> By providing a large number of points where decisions are taken by people of different political persuasion. . . it acts as a counterweight to the uniformity inherent in government decisions. It spreads political power   (Layfield, 1976, p. 53).

It is the same idea that is to be found on the opening page of any dictionary of quotations: Lord Acton's famous aphorism that 'power tends to corrupt, and absolute power corrupts absolutely'. Like many supposedly well-known quotations, it is frequently misquoted, but for our purposes the placement of the emphasis is insightful. The dispersal of power *may* lead to corruption, but Acton's certainty is reserved for its concentration.

■ Conclusion

Let us be clear. We are *not* in this chapter making allegations about corruption in the governmental system. Nor are we challenging the ideas we dealt with in Chapter 2 about a unitary state, parliamentary sovereignty and the constitutional subordination of local government in such a state. We are, however, suggesting that a significant dispersal of power away from the centre, by extending choice, encouraging initiative and innovation, and enhancing active participation, is likely to do more for the quality of government and the health of democracy than will its centralisation and concentration. The problems associated with democratic decentralisation are minimal compared with the problems associated with the excessive centralisation of power. The historical development of democratic decentralisation (i.e. elected local government) is the focus of our next chapter.

Guide to further reading

We have already quoted from what is still one of the best introductions to the values of local government: the article (1970) by L. J. Sharpe, an Oxford academic who was Director of Intelligence for the Redcliffe-Maud Royal Commission on Local Government. Hill (1974) is a book-length treatment of the subject from about the same time. More recently, Professors George Jones (LSE) and John Stewart (INLOGOV) have been the most prolific advocates of elected local government, starting with (1985) and continuing in their monthly 'Agenda' column in the *Local Government Chronicle*. Stewart is also joint author, with Michael Clarke (then Director of the Local Government Management Board), of a short but stimulating book (Clarke and Stewart, 1991). It is timely too to draw attention to the Commission for Local Democracy: an independent body that in 1995 produced a radical report designed to promote the cause of democratic local government and whose commissioned research is summarised in Pratchett and Wilson (1996).

■ *Chapter 4* ■

The Development of Local Government

■ Modern institutions, ancient origins

Why have we included an essentially historical chapter in a book on contemporary local government? Why not just concentrate on the present system and structure as we do in Chapter 5? The answer is disarmingly simple. It is just not possible properly to understand the present without at least some appreciation of how that present came about, of how it developed out of and differs from the past. That much would be true for any country. But it is especially true in Britain, where the system of local government, like most other institutions, has evolved gradually and piecemeal over the centuries, uninterrupted by an invasion or violent revolution that might have prompted a formal constitutional settlement.

In Britain there is no codified constitutional document setting out the rights and responsibilities of local authorities and their relationship with national government. Instead there is a set of institutions and practices, some centuries old, that were created and have been adapted in response to changing circumstances. Thus there are shires, and some shire county boundaries, dating back to Anglo-Saxon times – which, in the recent debates on reorganisation, many people made clear they did *not* want abolished and replaced by new unitary councils. There are historic cities – like Bristol, Oxford, Newcastle, Norwich, Aberdeen and Dundee – that were granted Royal Charters during the 12th century and were centres of genuine municipal self-government until they were forcefully incorporated into their respective counties and regions in the local government reorganisation of the early 1970s.

There are magistrates or Justices of the Peace, first appointed as local agents of the Crown in the 14th century, some 500 years before the emergence of political parties. It is understandable that they cling on fiercely to their independent representation on modern-day police authorities – but also that the 'new magistracy' was the phrase chosen by Jones and Stewart to describe the recent spread of non-elected local government agencies (see pp. 13–15 above). There used to be a local property tax – the rates – that originated with the Elizabethan Poor Law of 1601. Predictably enough, having been abolished by the Conservative

Government in 1988, it was recognised to have had significant merits lacking in the new community charge and, when the latter was almost instantly abandoned, was substantially reincarnated in the form of the council tax.

Some sense of history and of historical continuity, therefore, is important. But this *is* primarily a contemporary account of local government, and so we confine ourselves, and you, to a fairly breathless review of indisputably major trends and developments.

■ The 19th-century tangle

It is an irony in the history of British local government that the term 'local government' itself was coined only in the 19th century – at the very time when it was becoming larger and *less* local than ever before. Nonetheless, the early 19th century is our most appropriate starting point. Just across the English Channel, following its 1789 Revolution, France already had not only a clearly defined *system* of local government, but one that in its essentials still exists today:

* a municipality in each town, borough, parish or rural community, to be termed a *commune,* and all 36,000 and more, from the smallest hamlet to Paris itself, with the same constitutional status;
* each commune to have its own assembly, elected by universal suffrage, and a mayor responsible to central government as well as to the commune.

In Britain, by contrast, there was no such 'system'; nor would there be for most of the 19th century. Rather, there was what Patricia Hollis has graphically labelled 'a tangle' (Hollis, 1987, pp. 2–3), comprising principally the three traditional units of British local government: the parish, the county, and the borough.

Parishes, of which there were over 15,000 by the 1830s, appointed various unpaid officers – constables, highway surveyors, overseers of the poor, as well as churchwardens – to take responsibility respectively for law and order, road maintenance, and the provision of either work or financial relief for the poor. *Counties,* into which most of the country had been divided in the Middle Ages, were administered by Justices of the Peace. These Crown-appointed officials had both a judicial role, exercised through the county quarter sessions, and increasing administrative responsibilities, for highways and bridges, weights and measures, and general oversight of the parishes. The 200 or so *boroughs,* or corporate towns, were exempt from this jurisdiction of JPs and effectively governed themselves through Corporations established by Royal Charter. They had the right to determine their own systems of government – sometimes elected, sometimes self-appointed – to decide how to raise the money due to the King, and to run their own courts. This same principle of local self-rule was being developed and extended in Scotland through a considerably larger number of *burghs*, with their councils of burgesses.

There were in addition all kinds of *ad hoc authorities*, established by local Acts of Parliament, each providing a specific service within a particular area whose boundaries might not coincide with those of any other authorities. Thus there were Turnpike Trustees, who could levy tolls on road users to maintain and provide new roads; and Improvement Commissioners, who provided rate-funded services such as paving, lighting, street cleansing, and later fire engines and gas and water supplies.

It was the pressures brought about by the Industrial Revolution – urban poverty and unemployment, overcrowding and poor sanitation, disease and crime – that showed up this 'tangle' for what it was and demonstrated the urgent necessity of reform. The existing patchwork of institutions simply could not cope with the demands of a developing industrial society.

The response of government took two contrasting forms, each reflected in the two major reform Acts of the 1830s. On the one hand, the *Poor Law Amendment Act 1834* heralded the creation of *more single-purpose ad hoc authorities*. The Act replaced the parishes for the administration of poor relief with some 700 unions, or groupings of parishes, under *elected* Boards of Guardians. These Boards were subject to strong central direction from the national Poor Law Commissioners, but the very fact of their election and resulting electoral accountability distinguishes them from most of the single-purpose authorities created more recently. Plenty of other *ad hoc* bodies followed – local health boards, highways boards, elementary school boards – products in part of the delay in any more comprehensive reform of sub-national government.

The nearest the early 19th century came to such a reform was the second of the two 1830s statutes: the *Municipal Corporations Act 1835*. By creating some 78 *multi-purpose elected local authorities* which were not concerned with the administration of justice, this Act can be seen as the foundation of our present-day local government and it thus constitutes the first entry in our summary of structural legislation in Exhibit 4.1. The powers of these new councils were limited and their franchise even more so – restricted to male ratepayers of over three years' residence – but the principle of elected local self-government had been established.

■ A dual system emerges

Despite the reforms of the 1830s, there was nothing until almost the end of the 19th century that could even vaguely be called a *system* of local government. There still remained a tangle of appointed and elected

---

Exhibit 4.1   *The evolution of modern local government: keynote legislation*

1835   **Municipal Corporations Act** – birth of directly elected corporate boroughs in England and Wales to replace self-electing and frequently corrupt medieval corporations.

1888   **Local Government Act** – established 62 elected county councils and 61 all-purpose county borough councils in England and Wales. Paralleled by Local Government (Scotland) Act 1889.

1894   **Local Government Act** – established within the county council areas a network of 535 urban district councils (UDCs), 472 rural district councils (RDCs) and 270 non-county borough councils. The same Act revived parish councils. Equivalent Scottish structure established by Town Councils (Scotland) Act 1900.

1899   **London Government Act** – completion of the 'modern' structure of local government. Established in the London County Council (LCC) area a network of 28 metropolitan borough councils (plus the City of London Corporation) to replace the 38 vestries and district boards.

1929   **Local Government Act** – abolished Boards of Poor Law Guardians and transferred their responsibilities to local authorities. More extensive restructuring and transfer of powers in Scotland under Local Government (Scotland) Act 1929.

1963   **London Government Act** – established, from 1965, the Greater London Council (GLC), 32 London Boroughs, and in the former LCC area the Inner London Education Authority (ILEA). City of London Corporation survived the changes.

1972   **Local Government Act** – abolished county boroughs and reduced the number of counties in England and Wales to 47, incorporating 333 non-metropolitan district councils. In urban England established 6 metropolitan counties and 36 metropolitan districts. Came into force from April 1974.

1972   **Local Government (Northern Ireland) Act** – replaced 73 local authorities with 26 single-tier district councils in Northern Ireland elected by proportional representation.

1973   **Local Government (Scotland) Act** – introduced a rationalisation of Scottish local government and established 9 regional councils, 53 district councils and 3 island councils to replace the over 400 authorities which had existed from 1929. The new system came into operation from May 1975.

1985   **Local Government Act** – abolished the GLC and the 6 metropolitan county councils with effect from April 1986.

1988   **Education Reform Act** – abolished the Inner London Education Authority with effect from April 1990.

Exhibit 4.2   *Administrative tangle*

A selection of the bodies that constituted the local government of England and Wales towards the end of the 19th century:

302	municipal boroughs
31	Improvement Act districts
574	rural sanitary districts
58	port sanitary districts
2,302	school board districts
362	highway districts
6,477	highway parishes
1,052	burial board districts
618	poor law unions
13,755	ecclesiastical parishes
15,000	civil parishes

Source: quoted in P. Hollis, 1987, p. 3.

---

bodies, of both single- and multi-purpose authorities, as recited on one occasion to the House of Commons by the President of the Local Government Board, who apologised just in case there were any he had overlooked (see Exhibit 4.2).

Rationalisation was clearly overdue, and it came in the form of a group of Acts passed in the last dozen years of the century. The *Local Government Act 1888* created 62 county councils, including one for London (the LCC), and 61 county boroughs, all directly elected. *County councils* varied enormously in size, from nearly 3½ million in Lancashire to 20,000 in Rutland. Initially they had only a limited range of powers – responsibility for highways and bridges, asylums, weights and measures, and partial control of the police – but, as we shall see, these would grow steadily as the 20th century progressed.

County borough councils were all-purpose authorities, independent of the counties. The status was originally intended to be reserved only for large towns with populations of over 150,000, but this was reduced during the passage of the legislation through Parliament to just 50,000, to the considerable resentment of the counties, whose financial viability could be seriously threatened by the loss of even a single county borough. Parallel legislation in Scotland established 33 elected county councils, with the four largest burghs – Glasgow, Edinburgh, Dundee and Aberdeen – becoming all-purpose *counties of cities*: in effect 'independent islands' like the English county boroughs.

The *Local Government Act 1894* completed the reform of English and Welsh local government outside London by creating elected *urban district councils* (UDCs) and *rural district councils* (RDCs) based on the former sanitary districts. An attempt was also made to revive parishes in rural areas, even though they had by this time lost many of their powers to larger authorities. Every parish within a rural district with more than 300 residents was required to have a *parish council*, and those without councils were to hold *parish meetings*.

In Scotland equivalent legislation extended the elective principle to parish and town/burgh councils in 1894 and 1900 respectively, although for a time, as in England and Wales, there continued in existence a complex network of *ad hoc* bodies: school boards, police commissions, county road boards, district and joint standing committees.

The *London Government Act 1899* established 28 *metropolitan borough councils* to provide the capital with a second tier of local government under the LCC. The unique City of London Corporation, with its then 700 years of history, its Lord Mayor, Court of Aldermen and Common Council – a legislative assembly in its own right – remained untouched, as it was to in subsequent London government reforms.

Between them, these Acts at the close of the 19th century had brought about a small constitutional revolution: a *dual system* of elected local government throughout the country: all-purpose county boroughs/ burghs in the largest towns (outside London), and a two- or three-tier system elsewhere, with powers shared between the county, district/ burgh and parish councils. With each level or tier of council protective of its own responsibilities and self-sufficiency, it was not necessarily the most harmonious of systems, but it was one that in its essentials was to last for three-quarters of a century.

■ Structural tinkering, functional growth

The population of England and Wales was growing by an average of over 1 per cent per annum throughout the early years of the 20th century. More significantly, this growth was distinctly uneven: concentrated in the towns which consequently spread or sprawled into the surrounding countryside. Nineteenth-century boundaries began to look outdated and there was an inevitable conflict of interest between urban and rural authorities, as more and more towns qualified for and sought county borough status. Between 1889 and 1925 21 new county boroughs were created and over 100 county borough boundary extensions granted: changes which, as Byrne notes (1994, p. 38), 'cost the county councils an estimated 3 million loss of population and some £14.5 million loss of rateable value (revenue)'. To their relief, the Local Government (County Boroughs and Adjustments) Act of 1926 increased the minimum qualifying population for county borough status to 75,000 and made the procedure considerably more difficult, with the result that no new county boroughs were established between 1927 and 1964.

Other structural changes were ushered in by two pieces of legislation in 1929. The *Local Government (Scotland) Act* completed the process of reform and rationalisation described above. The bewildering variety of burghs was reduced to two types – 21 *large burghs*, responsible for most services apart from education which by now was county-based, and 176 *small burghs*, responsible for housing, public health and amenities – the dividing line being a population of 20,000. Parishes, district and standing joint committees were all abolished and replaced in rural areas by nearly 200 *district councils*, thus completing the creation of a two-tier system across the whole of Scotland outside its four big cities.

In England and Wales the *Local Government Act 1929* began to tackle the problem of the balance of urban and rural authorities, and particularly the number of very small authorities. The outcome of ensuing boundary reviews was that between 1929 and 1938 urban districts were reduced by 159, rural districts by 169, and some 1,300 boundaries were altered. Nevertheless, many small authorities still survived. Structural reform across all authorities needed tackling in a much more concerted manner, but this did not happen until the post-war years.

A second major consequence of the Local Government Act 1929 was the abolition of what was by then the only remaining *ad hoc* authority, the Guardians of the Poor, whose functions – poor law, civil registration, and the hospital service – were transferred to the county and county borough councils. In a similar measure, responding to the growing number of motor vehicles on frequently inadequate roads, the highways powers of rural districts were also taken over by the county councils.

These kinds of functional change, and the steady acquisition of additional service responsibilities by the county and county borough councils, were what characterised the history of local government in the first half of the 20th century far more than the comparatively minor structural reforms. The process can be visualised as the rising section of a symmetrical arch, the whole arch representing a kind of legislative and functional history of the first hundred years of county government, with its keystone or pinnacle in about the early 1930s, termed by some commentators the 'golden age of British government' (e.g. Byrne, 1994, p. 22).

Almost immediately following their establishment in 1889 the new elected county councils had begun to add to their initially modest portfolios of responsibilities, and the process continued through until at least the 1930s: further and technical education, road maintenance, elementary education, vehicle and driver registration, school meals, maternity and child welfare, careers advice, mental health services, secondary education, 'home help' schemes, libraries, unemployment relief, planning and development control, civil defence. At the same time the county boroughs were spearheading the 1920s council housing drive and acquiring control of the public utilities – water, gas, electricity, public transport – as well as, in some instances, docks, airports, telephone systems, theatres, crematoria and slaughterhouses.

The turning point, and the start of the falling section of the arch, was signalled by the responsibility for the payment of unemployment relief or the 'dole': fleetingly assumed in 1931 and lost three years later to central government in the guise of the Unemployment Assistance Board. But the real downturn came after the Second World War, with the Labour Government's massive programme of health, welfare and nationalisation legislation, all of which took services away from local councils.

■ Serious structural reform at last

In the post-war years the structural problems already evident in the 1920s and 1930s were becoming ever more acute. Structures were becoming increasingly irrational as the residential pattern of communities changed. There were major disparities of size between local authorities of the same type – in particular, many authorities were far too small to provide efficient services. The sheer number of authorities caused a good deal of confusion, as did the fragmentation of responsibility for service provision and the need for cumbersome co-ordinating machinery. Pressure for change was mounting, and it came first in London.

□ *London*

Following a three-year review by a Royal Commission, the *London Government Act 1963* created a new two-tier structure: a substantially larger *Greater London Council* (GLC) to replace the old LCC, pushing out into the Home Counties, and 32 *London boroughs* (see Figure 4.1). As in the 1890s, the City of London Corporation survived the reform process unscathed. The 32 boroughs – 12 in Inner London to replace the metropolitan boroughs, and 20 in Outer London – were allocated the bulk of services: housing, social services, non-metropolitan roads, libraries, leaving the GLC with the more 'strategic' functions of fire, ambulances, main roads and refuse disposal. There was one maverick: education. There was a concerted attempt to preserve the education system built up by the LCC, so it was determined that the inner London boroughs would have their education service administered by a special committee of the GLC, known as the Inner London Education Authority (ILEA), consisting of elected councillors from these boroughs.

Inevitably, reaction to the 1963 Act was mixed. Some argued that no reform was necessary; others maintained it did not go far enough, that the GLC boundaries had been too tightly drawn, and that it did nothing to alleviate the problems caused by the division of services between two

49

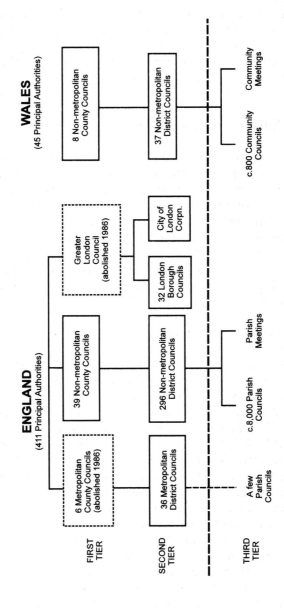

Figure 4.1 *Elected local government in England and Wales, 1974–95*

separate tiers of councils. But, whatever its merits or defects, the reform
of London government had at least demonstrated that wholesale change
was possible without services being totally dislocated. It also established
'the principle that an entire conurbation, in this case with a population of
eight million, should be governed as a single unit' (Elcock, 1991, p. 28).
Almost inevitably, reform of the rest of the system followed.

☐ *England and Wales*

In 1966, separate Royal Commissions were established, one for England
(led by Lord Redcliffe-Maud) and one for Scotland (chaired by Lord
Wheatley). Both reported in 1969. Wales, as in the 1990s reorganisation,
was treated differently from England. A Commission was not deemed
necessary; a White Paper from the Secretary of State for Wales would
suffice.

The English Royal Commission produced two reports; one by the
majority of the Commissioners favouring a structure based predominantly on all-purpose unitary authorities embracing both town and
country; the other a Memorandum of Dissent by Derek Senior advocating a multi-tier system of provincial councils, city regions, district and
local councils. The Labour Government substantially accepted the majority report and set out its legislative intentions in a White Paper
published in February 1970.

In June 1970, however, that Labour Government was voted out of
office, its plans for unitary local government disappearing with it. In its
place came a Conservative Government committed to the retention of a
two-tier system. As Alexander notes (1982a, p. 36), the 'philosophical
and partisan advantages of retaining the counties ensured that the Tories
would, in the end, propose a county-based two-tier system'. They did,
producing in early 1971 White Paper proposals for a two-tier system
across the whole of England and Wales based mainly on existing
counties.

The *Local Government Act 1972*, which became operative from April
1974 (see Figure 4.1), abolished all county boroughs and reduced the 58
county councils in England and Wales to 47 with populations ranging at
that time from 100,000 (Powys) to 1.5 million (Hampshire). Within these
counties 1,250 municipal boroughs, urban and rural districts were
replaced by 333 *district councils* also with hugely varying populations:
from 18,760 (Radnor) to 422,000 (Bristol). In the major conurbations six
metropolitan county councils were established – Greater Manchester,
Merseyside, West Midlands, Tyne and Wear, South Yorkshire and West
Yorkshire – and 36 *metropolitan districts* with populations ranging from
172,000 (South Tyneside) to almost 1.1 million (Birmingham).

Outside the metropolitan areas the old county boroughs, mostly
Labour strongholds, were absorbed as district councils into the new

counties. These old 'independent islands', often with several centuries of self-governing existence and a fierce civic pride, lost their positions of strength based on large-scale service provision. The loss of education and social services functions to the generally more Conservative counties was an especially bitter blow. Indeed, the maintenance of two principal tiers continued to make co-ordination of policy and administration difficult, and in those services where counties and districts had concurrent powers (e.g. planning, leisure services) the problems in some areas proved to be particularly acute.

At third tier in England outside the major cities the parish was retained. Of the more than 10,000 parishes, about 8,000 have elected councils, some of which are known as town councils. Small parishes, with under 200 electors, can instead hold parish meetings which all local electors can attend. In Wales, parishes were replaced in 1974 by *communities*, which have either elected councils or community meetings on a similar basis to English parishes. Additionally, in some urban areas neighbourhood councils have been formed which can provide a sounding board for local opinion.

☐ *Scotland*

The (Wheatley) Royal Commission on Local Government in Scotland saw its proposals for a two-tier system largely adopted by the Conservative Government in the *Local Government (Scotland) Act 1973* and implemented in May 1975. As in England, the Scottish Commission identified the large numbers of small authorities as constituting a fundamental weakness of the existing system. In the final legislation those numbers were reduced proportionately by even more than had happened in England and Wales: 431 county, city, burgh and district councils being amalgamated into 9 *regions*, ranging from 100,000 (Borders) to almost 2.5 million (Strathclyde); 53 *districts*, from 9,000 (Badenoch and Strathspey) to 850,000 (Glasgow); and 3 *'most purpose' island authorities* for Orkney, Shetland and the Western Isles (see Figure 4.2). Additionally, some 1,350 communities set up their own optional *community councils* as a kind of third tier, though these have no statutory powers and a lower status than even parish councils.

The network of regional and district councils which Wheatley had proposed fitted with the Conservative Government's preference for two-tier local government. Inevitably, the size and remoteness of the regional tier were heavily criticised; as in England, shared responsibilities between districts and regions for certain services would also pose difficulties. Some small tidying up of structures occurred in the early 1980s but essentially the post-1975 system remained intact until April 1996, with the huge Strathclyde Region comprising almost half of Scotland's total population.

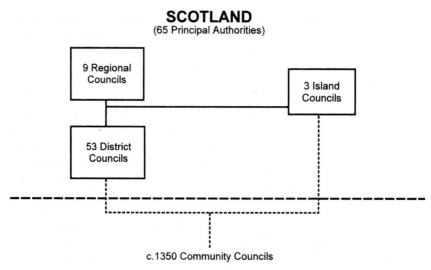

Figure 4.2   *Elected local government in Scotland, 1975–96*

□ *Northern Ireland*

It will be noted in Exhibit 4.1 that Northern Ireland's local government was reformed at the same time as that in the rest of the United Kingdom. That reform, though, and the significantly different structures it produced, need to be understood in the context of the political conflicts between the province's Unionist and Catholic communities which had intensified during the 1960s.

At that time – indeed, since the Local Government (Ireland) Act 1898 – Northern Ireland had a structure of local government very similar to that on the mainland. There were two all-purpose county boroughs – Belfast and Londonderry – and a two-tier system of six counties and 55 urban and rural district councils. The majority Unionist population had ensured that boundaries were drawn in such a way as to give them control of most councils and exclude the Catholic parties from any significant influence.

The resulting inequalities of service provision and particularly discriminatory housing allocations were among the principal grievances of civil rights protesters, and eventually in 1969 a Review Body was set up, chaired by Patrick Macrory. Influenced by the Wheatley Commission, the Macrory Report proposed a reformed two-tier model of elected local government. Most services – education and libraries, planning, roads, water and sewerage, fire, health and social services – would be provided by elected regional bodies, and there would be a greatly reduced number of district councils.

The *Local Government (Northern Ireland) Act 1972* implemented some of these recommendations, but, with the suspension of the Stormont government in the same year and the introduction of direct rule from Westminster, the proposed elected regional tier never materialised.

Local democracy in Northern Ireland, therefore, was and is limited to 26 *district councils*. These are elected, uniquely in the UK, by the Single Transferable Vote (STV) system of proportional representation, but have a very restricted range of responsibilities comprising mainly refuse collection and disposal, public conveniences, cemeteries and crematoria recreation and tourism – or, as the citizenry have been known to summarise it: bins, bogs and burials. All other services are provided by area boards and other quangos: 116 bodies in all, 'appointed by a Minister from a government which does not have a single MP anywhere in the six counties' (Vize, 1994, p. 16). District councils nominate up to 40 per cent of the members of some of these boards, but 'policy power remains with Westminster and its Stormont Castle outpost' (Vize, 1994, p. 17).

■ The Thatcher years: non-stop change

By the mid-1970s, then, the dual town/country structure of local government, set up at the end of the 19th century and fundamentally unchanged throughout most of the 20th, had been comprehensively reformed. A new tiered system was in place across almost the whole country. It had its inevitable tensions – competing mandates, resource jealousies, the blurring of lines of responsibility and accountability for service provision – but it would, surely, see us through to the next millennium? Hardly, as you will already have gathered from Exhibit 4.1 and Figure 4.1. Parts of this new structure were to be dismantled almost before they had had a chance to establish themselves.

As Newton and Karran remind us (1985, p.116), within weeks of Mrs Thatcher taking office in 1979, 'local government was strongly criticised by ministers who claimed that it was wasteful, profligate, irresponsible, unaccountable, luxurious and out of control'. The result was a barrage of legislation aimed at remodelling the pattern of local authorities, notably their pattern of finances.

Initially, changes in the structure of government did not seem to be a major priority for the Thatcher administration. Then in May 1983 the Government introduced into its General Election manifesto a pledge to abolish the six English metropolitan county councils and the GLC. As Elcock notes (1991, p.39), the

> official reason given for this hasty proposal was that these authorities had few functions and were therefore redundant: but in 1981 all seven had fallen under

Labour control and the GLC Leader, Ken Livingstone, had emerged as a colourful and effective antagonist with his headquarters just across the Thames from Mrs Thatcher's.

There was, in other words, a party political dimension to this structural reform in just the same way as there had been to the reforms of the 1970s, and as there is bound to be in any reorganisation of sub-central government in a unitary state. We should not be surprised when politicians behave politically.

In this case, the Government's arguments and the amplification of its manifesto proposals were set out in a White Paper, *Streamlining the Cities* (DoE, 1983b) published in October 1983. The title was significant, emphasising the Government's concern to reduce bureaucracy, duplication and waste and generally to 'roll back the frontiers of the state'. By abolishing the top-tier authorities in the metropolitan areas and transferring the bulk of their already limited range of functions to the borough and district councils, it would be bringing government closer to the people, making it more comprehensible and accessible, and thereby enhancing local democracy. In doing so, of course, it would also be removing the irritation of the attendant policy conflicts between the top-tier metropolitan authorities and central government whenever the two were controlled by different political parties. That was certainly the case after the local elections of May 1981, with the Labour-dominated councils pursuing – and, even more significantly, spending money on pursuing – policy priorities very different from those of the Conservative Government: public transport subsidies (eventually outlawed in the courts and in subsequent legislation), major economic development and employment provision programmes, greater police accountability, anti-nuclear sympathies and a scepticism towards civil defence.

Even with its recently elected 140-seat House of Commons majority, the Government did not find it at all easy to get this contentious legislation through even the lower House, let alone the House of Lords, where it met with fierce opposition from peers who saw their role as being to act as at least some kind of brake on radical constitutional change. The *Local Government Act 1985* was, however, eventually passed and from 31 March 1986 the GLC and the six metropolitan county councils ceased to exist.

Their responsibilities were taken over partly by the London boroughs and metropolitan district councils, but partly also by a range of joint boards, joint committees, *ad hoc* agencies and central government departments. The result is a degree of complexity that can seem not so much a 'streamlining' of our cities as a return to the administrative 'tangle' of the 19th century. Hebbert and Travers (1988, p.198) showed, for example, that almost 100 bodies with 21 different methods of revenue raising were engaged in the provision of services in Greater London. There are some two dozen *centrally appointed* bodies (e.g. Greater London Arts, London Docklands Development Corporation, London Regional Transport). There are 16 *London-wide nominated* bodies comprising councillors from the constituent boroughs (e.g. London Fire and Civil Defence Authority, London Waste Regulation Authority). Additionally, there are numerous *localised nominated* bodies for specific parts of London with a number of participating boroughs and a lead borough (e.g. North London Waste Authority – 7 boroughs with Camden as the lead; South London Waste Disposal Committee – 5 boroughs with Croydon as the lead).

In the metropolitan areas outside London the picture was a little less complex: fewer functions were taken over by quasi-government agencies, but those that were so transferred were among the biggest spending and highest profile services. So in each of the six metropolitan areas there were three *joint boards* for passenger transport, police, fire and civil defence. In both Greater Manchester and Merseyside there were joint boards responsible for waste disposal. In addition, *joint committees* were established dealing with matters such as recreation, arts and economic development. As Leach *et al.* (1987) point out, the precise patterns of working relationships vary a good deal from area to area, but one thing is common: none of these joint boards is *directly elected*. The bulk are controlled by councillors *nominated* from the constituent metropolitan districts. Directly elected local government is now weaker and more fragmented than before 1986; indirectly elected and appointed bodies have become increasingly numerous and important.

One of the problems with the structural reorganisation of local government – particularly when it has acquired strong political overtones – is that, once begun, it develops a momentum of its own. It becomes part of the national political agenda and each party produces its own ideas and blueprints of what the local government map should look like. Thus it was that at the 1992 General Election, to the amazement of most overseas observers, each of the three major parties had their own proposals for far-reaching structural reform which they would implement if elected (see Wilson and Game, 1994, pp. 262–3). Part of the 1986 London Government reforms, however, did not even make it through to that election.

The abolition of the GLC had the effect, as we have seen, of increasing the number of part-London local bodies. The *Inner London Education Authority* had been a sub-committee of the GLC, so when the latter was abolished a new arrangement was needed. What was created, very unusually for this country in the 20th century, was a *directly elected unifunctional council*, somewhat similar to the elected school boards in particularly the West and Midwestern United States. It could have provided an interesting study of an alternative form of local democracy. In the event, though, its almost inevitable Labour domination, allied to its high expenditure levels and perceived enthusiasm for 'progressive' education, led to its early abolition in the *Education Reform Act 1988*. Responsibility for education services passed to the individual Inner London boroughs with effect from 1 April 1990.

■ Summary: into the 1990s

Later that year, in November 1990, Mrs Thatcher was replaced as Conservative Party Leader and Prime Minister by John Major. Mr Major's biggest local government headache by far was the hugely unpopular poll tax or community charge and how to get rid of it. By comparison, the structure of the system might have seemed reasonably straightforward and unproblematic.

A similar structure of elected local government existed throughout the *non-metropolitan areas* of England and the whole of Wales and mainland Scotland (see Figures 4.1 and 4.2). Throughout these areas there were two principal tiers of local authorities with each tier providing a range of services, although the division of services between tiers in Scotland was slightly different from that in England and Wales. In England and Wales the upper tier authorities were known as *counties*; in Scotland they were designated *regions*. The lower tier authorities were known as *districts*, some of which are entitled, for historic reasons, to call themselves *cities* or *boroughs*. In much of non-metropolitan Britain there were also third-tier, or 'sub-principal', authorities known as parish councils in England and community councils in both Wales and Scotland.

In *metropolitan* England and London there was – and is – only one elected tier of local government – *metropolitan districts* and *London boroughs* – and these are *unitary* or *most-purpose* local authorities. Instead of sharing responsibility for service provision with other elected authorities, they operate alongside other indirectly elected or nominated bodies. The superficial simplicity of a single elected tier is far from a reality, given the mosaic of joint authorities and boards responsible for major services such as fire and civil defence and passenger transport: hence our preference for the term 'most-purpose', rather than 'all-purpose'.

In Northern Ireland there was – and again still is – a one-tier system of local government comprising 26 district councils with a very much more limited range of service responsibilities than even their non-metropolitan district counterparts on the mainland. The major functions of health, social services, education and libraries are organised through *area boards* made up of approximately one-third district councillors and two-thirds ministerial appointees. Responsibility for public sector housing is with an appointed Northern Ireland Housing Executive, administered through six regions.

Guide to further reading

Keith-Lucas and Richards (1978) provide the best general introductory history of English local government in the 20th century, covering all aspects of its development: functions, councillors and staff, party politics, as well as structure. Pearce (1980) focuses more specifically on structural change, and from the interesting perspective of a civil servant. There are several accounts of the structural reforms of the 1960s and early 1970s, including Alexander (1982a); Wood (1976); and, for London, Rhodes (1970). Dearlove (1979) offers a more political, and critical, commentary. On the abolition of the GLC and metropolitan county councils, see our 'further reading' suggestions in Chapter 5. There are several interesting commemorative publications: Loughlin, Gelfand and Young (1985), itself a commemoration of a 1935 celebration of 'A Century of Municipal Progress'; Young (1989) on 100 years of county government; and Game's (1991b) collective review of the centennial publications of 28 of the 39 English counties. Last, but very far from least, there is an outstanding history of the role of women in early English local government by Patricia (now Lady) Hollis (1987).

■ *Chapter 5* ■

Current Structures

■ Introduction: external and internal structures

This chapter divides into two main sections. The first section deals with so-called *external* structures and brings up to date the historical account of our system of local government begun in Chapter 4. We present literally a map of British local government at the very end of the 20th century. The second section looks at local authorities' *internal* management structures, at the machinery of committees and departments through which they conduct their business. Both topics are returned to later in the book. Chapter 17 examines in more depth the structural reorganisation saga, while Chapters 13, 17 and 18 pick up a range of issues related to internal management.

■ External structures: a reform too far?

□ *England – the arrival of hybridity*

We made the point in Chapter 4 that structural reform, once it becomes part of the agenda of national political debate, can acquire a momentum of its own. That is perhaps as good an explanation as any of why, following the reorganisations of local government in London in the 1960s, in the rest of the country in the 1970s, and in metropolitan England in the 1980s, we saw a further country-wide structural reform during the 1990s. Critical observers have contrasted the situation confronting the Redcliffe-Maud Commission with that thirty years on:

> In the 1960s there was a good deal of tangible evidence of the need for a reorganisation, including the palpable inability of large numbers of small authorities to deal effectively with the growth-associated problems of development and movement, especially in the more urbanised parts of the country. It is difficult to identify similar problems that underpin the present reorganisation, in which far too much has been made of the supposed 'problems' of conflict, overlap and duplication in the existing two-tier system. (Leach, 1995, p. 50)

Few people in local government felt any compelling need for further structural reorganisation, faced as they were already with the upheaval of the poll tax and other reforms of education, community care and CCT. 'The most convincing explanation' for its emergence, Leach goes on to suggest:

> centres on the political ambition of one individual. It was part of the vision . . . of a contender for the leadership of the Conservative Party, who became instead Secretary of State for the Environment.   (Leach, 1995, p. 50)

The minister's name was, of course, Michael Heseltine. As Environment Secretary, he gave impetus to reform proposals by producing a series of consultation papers in early 1991, thereby ensuring that local government reorganisation would feature as a prominent commitment in the 1992 Conservative Party manifesto: 'We will set up a commission to examine, area by area, the appropriate local government arrangements in England', the main objective of the examination being to decide 'whether in any area *a single tier* of local government could provide better accountability and greater efficiency' (our emphasis). Following the 1992 election there was a Cabinet reshuffle in which Heseltine was replaced as Environment Secretary first by Michael Howard and then, barely a year later, by John Gummer. Neither minister appeared fully to share Heseltine's reformist enthusiasm, but the reorganisation process lurched on, though with less far-reaching impact than had initially been envisaged.

The Government had wanted, as it made clear in its original *Policy Guidance*, 'a substantial increase in the number of unitary authorities as a result of the Commission's reviews'. At one time, following the Commission's draft recommendations of almost 100 new unitary councils embracing more than two-thirds of the population of the English non-metropolitan counties, that looked likely to be the outcome. But, confronted with a public opinion mostly sceptical about the likely benefits of such radical change, the Commission adapted many of its draft recommendations to 'hybrid' solutions: one or two mainly large town unitary authorities in otherwise unchanged two-tier counties. If it sounds familiar, it is: a return in effect to those 'independent islands' that featured in Chapter 4 as county boroughs.

The end result of the review is presented in Figures 5.1 and 5.2. By 1998 there will be a total of 46 new unitary authorities, covering just over a quarter of the population of non-metropolitan England. These new unitaries will have begun their lives variously from 1995 to 1998 (see Exhibit 5.1). Only four of the 39 former county councils will have disappeared entirely from the local government map – Avon, Cleveland, Humberside and Berkshire – the Isle of Wight having become a unitary county in 1995. In the remaining 34 counties the two-tier system has been wholly or largely retained.

Exhibit 5.1   Has your council changed recently? The new English unitaries and the districts they replace

	COUNTY	NEW UNITARY	FORMER DISTRICT COUNCIL(S)
1995	ISLE OF WIGHT	Isle of Wight	Medina BC; S. Wight BC
	Total	**1**	**2**
1996	AVON	Bristol	Bristol City C
		S Gloucestershire	Kingswood BC; Northavon DC
		North Somerset	Woodspring DC
		Bath and NE Somerset	Bath City C; Wansdyke DC
	CLEVELAND	Hartlepool	Hartlepool BC
		Middlesbrough	Middlesbrough BC
		Redcar and Cleveland	Langbaurgh-on-Tees BC
		Stockton-on-Tees	Stockton-on-Tees BC
	HUMBERSIDE	Kingston upon Hull	Kingston upon Hull City C
		E Riding of Yorkshire	E. Yorkshire BC; Holderness BC; Beverley BC; Boothferry BC (part)
		N Lincolnshire	Glanford BC; Scunthorpe BC; Boothferry BC (part)
		NE Lincolnshire	Great Grimsby BC; Cleethorpes BC
	NORTH YORKSHIRE	York	York City C (including parts of Ryedale DC, Selby DC, Harrogate BC)
	Total	**13**	**20**
1997	BEDFORDSHIRE	Luton	Luton BC
	BUCKINGHAMSHIRE	Milton Keynes	Milton Keynes BC
	DERBYSHIRE	Derby	Derby City BC
	DORSET	Bournemouth	Bournemouth BC
		Poole	Poole BC
	DURHAM	Darlington	Darlington BC
	EAST SUSSEX	Brighton and Hove	Brighton BC; Hove BC
	HAMPSHIRE	Portsmouth	Portsmouth City C
		Southampton	Southampton City C

LEICESTERSHIRE	Leicester	Leicester City C
	Rutland	Rutland DC
STAFFORDSHIRE	Stoke-on-Trent	Stoke-on-Trent City C
WILTSHIRE	Swindon	Thamesdown BC
Total	**13**	**14**
1998 BERKSHIRE	Bracknell Forest	Bracknell Forest BC
	Newbury	Newbury DC
	Reading	Reading DC
	Slough	Slough BC
	Windsor and Maidenhead	Windsor and Maidenhead RBC
	Wokingham	Wokingham DC
CAMBRIDGESHIRE	Peterborough	Peterborough Cit y C
CHESHIRE	Halton	Halton BC
	Warrington	Warrington BC
DEVON	Plymouth	Plymouth DC
	Torbay	Torbay BC
ESSEX	Southend-on-Sea	Southend-on-Sea BC
	Thurrock	Thurrock BC
HEREFORD and WORCESTER	Herefordshire	Hereford City C; S Herefordshire DC; Leominister DC (most); Malvern Hills DC (part)
KENT	Medway Towns	Rochester City C; Gillingham BC
LANCASHIRE	Blackburn with Darwen	Blackburn BC
	Blackpool	Blackpool BC
NOTTINGHAMSHIRE	Nottingham	Nottingham City C
SHROPSHIRE	Wrekin	The Wrekin DC
Total	**19**	**22**
GRAND TOTALS	**46**	**58**

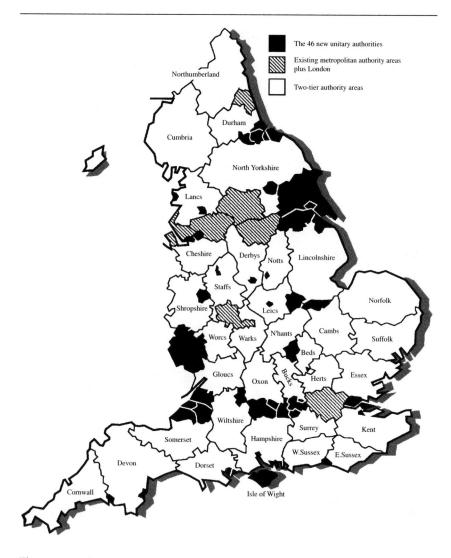

Figure 5.1 *The new local authority map of England*

As for the Local Government Commission, it will continue in existence, to undertake what are known as periodic *electoral reviews*. These
authority-by-authority reviews will examine the total number of councillors, the number in each electoral division or ward, the ward boundaries, their names, and the timing of elections. It will also consider the
idea of councils being allowed for the first time to have paid, full-time
executive councillors. It will not, though, re-review the boundaries
between councils or their functions.

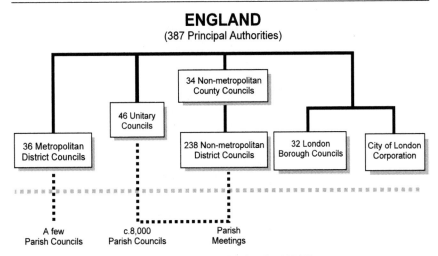

Figure 5.2 *Elected local government in England, 1997/98*

□ *Scotland – Minister halves number of councils*

In Scotland there was no 'rolling commission' to examine alternatives and make recommendations area by area. Instead the Secretary of State for Scotland was deputed to conduct the review. A preliminary consultation paper was published by the Scottish Office in 1991 advocating a single-tier system of smaller authorities which it was claimed would have greater local identity, would be more efficient and more accountable. A White Paper was produced in 1993 proposing 25 single-tier councils plus the retention of the three island councils. During the committee stage of the Bill's passage through Parliament, four councils were added, to give a total of 29 new unitary authorities and 32 in all. Following elections in 1995, these councils came into full operation in April 1996 – see Figure 5.3.

But, as we saw with the earlier abolition of the GLC and the English metropolitan county councils, 'single-tier' does not necessarily mean simplification. In the Strathclyde Region, for example, there are now more bodies responsible for fewer services than there were previously, but significantly fewer of them are directly elected – see Exhibit 5.2. The fewer elected councils inevitably cover larger areas than the former districts and also – though this was *not* inevitable – have far fewer councillors. It will be noted that, whereas the Local Government Commission review in England produced a reduction of less than 6 per cent in the number of elected councils, the ministerially-driven reorganisation process in Scotland resulted in a reduction of over a half. The number of councillors was cut from 1695 to 1245 or by more than a quarter, the implications of which are discussed in Chapter 17.

1 Clackmannanshire
2 Falkirk
3 East Dunbartonshire
4 West Dunbartonshire
5 Glasgow
6 Renfrewshire
7 Inverclyde
8 East Renfrewshire
9 City of Edinburgh

10 North Lanarkshire
11 West Lothian
12 Midlothian
13 East Lothian
14 North Ayrshire
15 South Ayrshire
16 East Ayrshire
17 South Lanarkshire

Figure 5.3 *Scotland's 32 new unitary authorities, operational from April 1996*

Exhibit 5.2 *Single-tier but hardly streamlined: the case of Strathclyde*

Until April 1996:
    Strathclyde Regional Council
    + 19 district councils

After April 1996:
    12 new single-tier or unitary councils, ranging from Glasgow (627,000) to E. Renfrewshire (88,000)
    7 joint boards for police, fire, passenger transport and valuation – made up of councillors nominated from the 12 councils
    3 strategic planning joint committees
    2 new quangos: the West of Scotland Water Authority, appointed by the Scottish Secretary to take over the water and sewerage services that, uniquely in Scotland, were previously the responsibility of the regional councils; also an appointed Water Customers Council
    1 new quango to run the Children's Panel Reporter service
    No responsibility for trunk roads, taken over by the Scottish Office

---

☐ *Wales – more ministerial unitaries*

In Wales too it was the Secretary of State who drove the reform process. In 1991 a 'consultation paper' was produced, suggesting various possible solutions of 13, 20 or 24 unitary authorities. The number that finally emerged, following a good deal of negotiation with the Welsh local authority associations, was 22: as in Scotland a reduction of the former 45 elected councils by more than a half. Again as in Scotland, these new unitaries came into operation in April 1996 – see Figure 5.4. Ten of the 22 new authorities are based on former district boundaries with, at most, minor modifications. The rest represent mergers of districts. Most previously county services, such as education, social services and transport, will now be provided at a more local level. Some, however, have moved to larger-scale provision: for example, there are now three fire authorities instead of eight.

☐ *Northern Ireland*

There has been no corresponding restructuring of local government in Northern Ireland. The position remains essentially as outlined in Chapter 4. Most services affecting people's daily lives – housing, education, libraries, health, community relations – are administered on behalf of the Northern Ireland Office by appointed quangos and other public

1 Swansea
2 Neath and Port Talbot
3 Bridgend
4 Rhondda, Cynon, Taff
5 Merthyr Tydfil
6 Caerphilly

7 Blaenau Gwent
8 Torfaen
9 Newport
10 Cardiff
11 Vale of Glamorgan

Figure 5.4 *The 22 new unitary authorities in Wales, operational from April 1996*

bodies. Elected local government is confined to 26 district councils, relatively small in British terms, and responsible for far fewer services than their counterparts elsewhere in the UK – see Figure 5.5.

Democratically, the most that can be said is that the more pro-active councils and the councillors themselves make a lot of their limited powers. In the absence of any provincial elected assembly, they act as an important debating forum for any key issue affecting Northern Ireland. They have developed an important advocacy role, both for their own local areas and for helping individual residents, who turn out to vote in local elections in far greater numbers than on the mainland. In 1994 they were given the important power to spend money on economic

1 Belfast
2 Newtownabbey
3 Carrickfergus
4 North Down
5 Castlereagh

Figure 5.5 *Northern Ireland's 26 district councils*

development in return for Unionist support of the Major Government in the parliamentary vote on the Maastricht Treaty. Some of them also, to an extent that frequently goes unrecognised, work closely with councils on the other side of the Irish border, and have proved highly effective in negotiating development funding from the European Commission. The fact remains, though, that the devolution of further significant powers to elected councils must surely depend on there being substantial and consolidated progress in the peace process. Until that time, local government in Northern Ireland will remain something of a pale imitation of that elsewhere in the UK.

□ *Joint arrangements*

Alongside the directly elected structures is a network of *nominated or indirectly elected joint bodies* and other joint arrangements between councils. As described in Chapter 4, following the 1986 abolition of the GLC and the metropolitan county councils, services such as police, fire and public transport were administered by such bodies in metropolitan England. One of the consequences of the abolition of the two-tier structure in Scotland, Wales and parts of non-metropolitan England, and the creation of many new unitary authorities with populations of under 100,000, is that an increasing range of council services will now be provided by councils co-operating through various kinds of joint arrangements. There are three main forms of joint arrangements:

* *Joint boards.* These are legally constituted bodies set up by two or more councils to provide statutorily required services. They are created by order of a minister and their membership and management are subject to ministerial approval. They do, however, have independent financial powers, which include the power to raise money by 'precept' from their constituent authorities. In the English metropolitan areas there are joint boards for, principally, fire and public transport. The Local Government etc. (Scotland) Act 1994 recognised that some of the new unitary authorities would not be able to provide police and fire services on their own and created joint boards for these services. It also gave the Scottish Secretary powers to create new Joint Valuation and Joint Planning Boards.
* *Joint committees.* Two or more local authorities can determine to establish joint committees of councillors to carry out specific council functions. Such committees, unlike joint boards, are not separate legal entities and cannot employ staff. Some of the new unitary authorities are too small to provide on their own the full range of specialist services previously delivered by county or regional councils; joint committees provide one possible form of alternative arrangement. For example, facilities such as specialist schools or residential homes might be situated in one council but used by a number of others.
* *Contracts.* Local authorities can make contracts with each other for the provision of services. These have been in existence for some time (e.g. highways agency agreements between county councils and district councils), but they are likely to increase as more councils develop and explore the possibilities of their role as 'enablers'.

As noted at the end of Chapter 4, it is the proliferation of these different kinds of joint arrangements that leads critics to question the labelling of this country's unitary councils as 'all-purpose' authorities. They may constitute the only directly elected local authorities in their area, but they are more accurately designated 'most-purpose' councils. Joint boards and joint committees may often offer efficient and effective services and some manage to involve their constituent authorities in their decision-making. But they do inevitably add to the *fragmentation* of local government, to the potential confusion and uncertainty of the public, and to the dilution of electoral accountability. Those concerned about such developments are quick to point out that in this, as in many other respects, Britain is unusual: Luxembourg and Finland are the only other Western European countries to have unitary local government systems!

☐ *Sub-principal authorities*

While this book focuses chiefly on the activities of the 'principal' local authorities in the United Kingdom, there is in non-metropolitan Britain a network of sub-principal authorities which should not be ignored. These sub-principal authorities – parish councils in England, community councils in Scotland and Wales – have survived the traumas of recent structural reorganisations and, indeed, have seen their role and powers enhanced (see Exhibit 5.3).

In England, there are approximately 10,200 parishes of which about 8,000 – predominantly in more rural areas – have parish or town councils, on which serve some 75,000 elected councillors. In urban areas experiments with neighbourhood and community councils 'have some-times been seen as a means of extending the parish tier of government into the towns and cities' (Elcock, 1991, p. 35). In Wales there are some 900 'communities', about 750 of which have established councils. Elect-ions to both English parish councils and Welsh community councils take place every four years.

As described in Chapter 3, these sub-principal authorities have a number of discretionary powers, notably providing local services such as allotments, playing fields and sports centres, community centres and public conveniences, and also acting as consultation points on issues such as planning applications. To pay for these services, the councils may raise money in the form of a 'precept' collected from their local residents by their district council. These precepts vary greatly across the country, from under £10 to £100 per council tax-band D property, reflecting the equally great variation in the councils' activities. As important as their service provision, however, is their advocacy function: the fact that they can 'act as pressure groups on behalf of local people in commenting on and resisting proposals that affect their electors made by local author-ities, nationalised industries, other statutory undertakings and govern-ment departments' (Elcock, 1991, p. 36).

Given their closeness to the people, there is a sense in which parish councils can be seen as the most democratic of all local authorities, and one of the final enactments of the last Conservative Government was an extension of their powers, and perhaps their role in rural community life through the Local Government and Rating Act, 1997 – see Exhibit 5.3.

Exhibit 5.3   *A boost for parishes?*

The Major Government's Local Government and Rating Act, 1997

* **More consultation** – on planning and other issues by district and county councils.
* **Reduced business rates** – for village shops, post offices and other vital local businesses.
* **Transport powers** – parish councils to be able to establish car-sharing schemes, make grants to voluntary bus services, arrange concessionary taxi fare schemes, and contract county councils to install traffic calming measures.
* **Crime prevention powers** – parish councils to be able to install CCTV cameras aimed at preventing crime, run community policing schemes, or make grants to their police authority in return for a village constable.

BUT no extra funding from central government for any additional expenditure, apart from the reduced business rates financed by the Treasury.

In Scotland, as noted in Chapter 4, the Local Government (Scotland) Act 1973 set up a rather different kind of community council system. Scottish community councils have no statutory basis and no access, as of right, to public funds. Rather, their role is to ascertain the views of their communities and to convey those views to the relevant elected council and other public authorities. They serve as one further reminder of how even bodies with the same name can sometimes differ in status and function in the different constituent parts of the multinational state that is the United Kingdom.

■ Internal structures

It is time now to address in a little more detail some of the terms we have so far referred to in passing, but without further explanation: local authorities, councils, councillors, elected members, committees, departments, officers. *Local authorities*, as we saw in Chapter 2, are semi-independent, politically decentralised, multi-functional bodies, created by and exercising responsibilities conferred by Parliament. The term is often used – and has already been used by us – interchangeably with *councils*. Strictly speaking, though, the council is the legal embodiment of the local authority: the body of *elected councillors* who collectively determine and are ultimately responsible for the policy and actions of the authority. In recognition of this legal responsibility, councillors are often referred to as the elected *members* of the authority, which distinguishes them from its paid employees, the *officers* and other staff.

As we have already seen, British local authorities are mostly very large organisations and, with the spread of unitary authorities, getting larger still: 467 from 1998 for the whole of the UK, or one council for every 125,000 of us. Several have more than 100 councillors and tens of thousands of full-time and part-time employees. In most authorities it would be impossible for councillors to take all necessary policy decisions in full council meetings, or for officers to manage and deliver the multitude of local government services, without some kind of internal structural divisions. The way in which local authorities in this country have traditionally organised themselves is through *committees* of councillors and professionally-based *departments*.

☐ *Councillors and committees*

It is the committee system that enables multifunctional authorities to work efficiently and effectively, and at the same time democratically – without elected councillors handing over all policy-making to paid officers. Committees can be seen as a council's workshops, where councillors' local knowledge and their political assessment of local needs are brought together with officers' professional and expert advice to produce, hopefully, democratically responsive and implementable policy.

Committees, therefore, are composed of and chaired by elected councillors and advised by officers. A few, such as education and social services, are *statutory* and must be set up by councils with these responsibilities. Most, though, are *permissive*, enabling councillors themselves to decide how they are going to arrange and divide up their council's work. Leicestershire County Council, for example, whose committee and sub-committee structure is set out in Figure 5.6, has nine main committees. Nottinghamshire, with exactly the same set of service responsibilities, has 10 – see Figure 5.7. In addition both councils appoint elected members to the newly created (1995) independent Police Authorities. Prior to 1995 each had its own Police Committee. The councillors in Nottinghamshire have chosen to have separate full committees for Finance and Resources; to emphasise the importance they attach to Equal Opportunities issues by having a full committee, rather than a sub-committee of Policy and Resources; and to incorporate Emergency Planning into Public Protection.

For a council that is not an education or social services authority there is in fact no law that says it has to delegate its work to committees at all. Indeed, before the recent reorganisation, a couple of small district councils in Scotland and Wales did choose to work entirely through full council meetings, albeit of only about a dozen councillors. Historically, the tendency has been the reverse: for councils to acquire over time a proliferation of committees and sub-committees with correspondingly

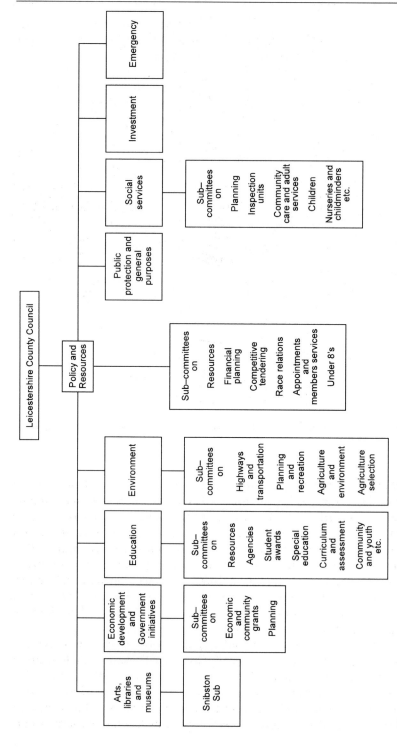

Figure 5.6 *Leicestershire County Council: main committees and sub-committees, 1996*

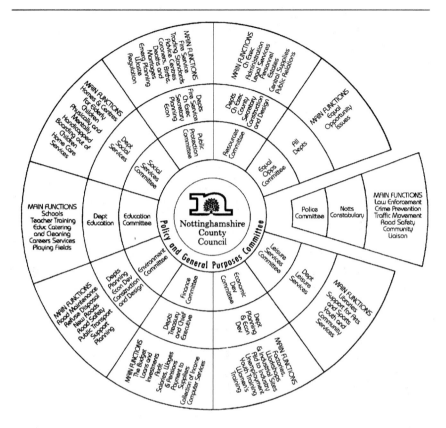

Figure 5.7   *Committees and departments, Nottinghamshire County Council 1994/95*

vast numbers of meetings. Despite some genuine pruning, Leicestershire County Council in 1993/94 had more than 90 committees, sub-committees, working parties, joint bodies and panels, holding a total of well over 700 meetings between them. Some councils, though, have drastically reduced the number of their principal committees to, say, four or five, each taking responsibility for a portfolio of strategically related services – as with Nottinghamshire's Environment, Public Protection, and Leisure Services committees. Other councils, as we shall see in Chapter 18, have investigated the feasibility of more radical options in their internal management systems.

One feature found in almost all councils nowadays is some kind of *central management committee*, usually known as Policy and Resources, sometimes as Finance and Management or some similar variant. The purpose of this committee, often chaired by the Leader of the Council and made up of some of its most experienced members, is to co-ordinate the work of specialist committees and to provide the council with overall policy leadership. During the 1980s some of these policy committees on councils heavily dominated by a single political party used to be composed only of members of that majority party – in the same way as the Prime Minister's Cabinet. But since the Local Government and Housing Act 1989 one-party committees and sub-committees have been effectively outlawed and they must instead have proportional numbers of all political groups represented on the council.

Committees – and perhaps more especially member-officer working groups – enable councillors to acquire specialist knowledge in specific policy areas, thereby hopefully producing more informed decision-making. In such forums there is also an element of informality which often encourages councillors to speak more freely. At the same time, however, the committee system has been criticised for lengthening the decision-making process, often by networks of sub-committees. Also, while members acquire expertise in specific areas, they can sometimes become blinkered and fail to appreciate the work of the council as a whole. Indeed, committee rivalries are by no means unknown. The deficiencies of the committee system, notably the compartmentalisation or fragmentation of decision-making inside an authority, have led to increased attention being devoted to strategic management, where the aim is to plan on an authority-wide basis rather than departmentally. Central to such thinking is the *senior management team*, usually headed by the Chief Executive, which brings us to the officer side of the local authority.

☐ *Officers and departments*

Notwithstanding the development of strategic management in recent years (see Chapter 18), many local authorities still carve up their work between *departments* with a *professional* focus. Each department is headed by a *chief officer* or *director*, a qualified specialist in the functional area concerned, and will employ relevant specialist and generalist staff at lower levels. *Service departments* – such as education, social services, leisure, public protection – provide services direct to the public, while central departments – such as the Chief Executive's, the Treasurer's, Personnel, Construction and Design – have more of a servicing role for other departments.

As with committees, local authorities have considerable discretion in the departmental structures they adopt and the officers they appoint. The Local Government Act 1972 enables them to appoint 'such officers as they think necessary for the proper discharge of their functions'. At the same time, however, this and other legislation *requires* relevant local authorities to appoint certain chief officers, for example: Chief Education Officer (Education Act 1944); Chief Fire Officer (Fire Services Act 1947); Director of Social Services (LA Social Services Act 1970).

As for departments, we saw in Figure 5.7 that Nottinghamshire County Council lists eight, plus the county constabulary. Leicestershire, on the other hand, had 12, including separate departments for trading standards, libraries and information, and for museums, arts and records: a slightly more fragmented structure but one that the council's members and officers felt worked for them.

Chief officers have overall responsibility for implementing council policies relating to their respective departments. Though highly trained, professionally qualified and, by most standards, extremely well paid, the chief officer is as much an employee and 'servant' of the council as the most recently recruited manual worker. Unlike councillors – often far less formally educated and trained and certainly much less handsomely remunerated – they have not been elected, and their role is to ensure that the policy laid down by the councillors is implemented and that all their reasonable and lawful instructions are carried out.

Most local authorities have a *Chief Executive* who is the chief officer in overall charge of the council and its departments – or 'head of the paid service', as it tends to be known. An additional requirement since the Local Government and Housing Act 1989 has been that all councils must have a 'monitoring officer', to check that the council is operating within the law. This role too is commonly taken by the Chief Executive. The Chief Executive is a kind of officers' team leader, and will generally chair, either weekly or fortnightly, a Chief Officers' Management Team, on which will sit most or all chief officers. Precise patterns vary from authority to authority, but almost all will have some such mechanism for ensuring effective liaison and policy co-ordination across departments.

The internal organisation of departments has traditionally been characterised by two elements: *professionalism* and *hierarchy*. Senior positions in departments have been held by the dominant profession in that department, with professional boundaries marking and reinforcing departmental territories. In parallel to this there has been a strong commitment to formal accountability and hierarchical control. In service departments staff have invariably been arranged in a hierarchy of accountability running from field-worker to chief officer and through the chief officer to the committee. In such a system the span of control of any one officer is inevitably limited, and in some traditionally structured authorities over a dozen tiers could separate the chief officer from the staff involved in providing services to the public.

This constitutes a problem both for the public and for junior officers; finding a route through the numerous lower tiers to deal with top-tier officers is often very difficult. The trend in recent years, therefore, has been towards 'flatter' departmental structures with fewer tiers, although some authorities have been reluctant to move away from the profess-ional/hierarchical model of organisation. The dynamics of relationships between the various elements of officer hierarchies are dealt with in some detail in Chapter 13. Meanwhile, Exhibit 5.4 summarises this section of Chapter 5 on internal structures.

■ Internal management – some key themes

While individual authorities have considerable freedom to determine their own internal organisational patterns in the light of local circumstances, some variation on a department/committee theme invariably emerges. This section examines four major reviews of internal management which took place in the period 1967–86: Maud, 1967; Bains, 1972; Paterson, 1973; Widdicombe, 1986a. More recent developments will be discussed in Chapter 18. Before examining these reports it must be emphasised that each authority has its own particular local history, traditions and culture – hence different authorities will respond very differently to recommendations from official reports. These four reports have, nevertheless, provided frameworks for much of the internal management change of the past thirty-odd years.

☐ *Maud 1967 – chief executives in, management boards out*

The Committee on the Management of Local Government, chaired by Sir John Maud, later Lord Redcliffe-Maud, sat at the same time as the Royal Commission on reorganisation referred to in Chapter 4. It was appointed to consider how local government 'might best continue to attract and retain people (both elected representatives and principal officers) of the calibre necessary to ensure its maximum effectiveness' (Maud, 1967, vol. 1, p. iii). The report was very critical of the existence 'of a nineteenth century tradition that council members must themselves be concerned with actual details of day-to-day administration' (Maud, 1967, vol. 1, p. ix). Detailed matters rather than strategic issues appeared to dominate the multiplicity of committees. In the light of what it found, the Maud Committee came up with some radical proposals.

All but the smallest local authorities should, it argued, have a *Management Board* of between five and nine senior councillors. It would have wide delegated powers and would be the sole channel through which business done in committees reached the full council. Maud also proposed a radical pruning of committees and departments – it thought about six would be sufficient. Third, the Committee argued that a chief executive officer should be appointed in each authority – not necessarily a lawyer, like the traditional Town Clerk – who would be the undisputed head of the authority's paid staff.

The instinctive universal response of most local authorities to the Maud Report was one of hostility. It was felt to have elitist connotations

Exhibit 5.4 *Internal management structures: a summary*

COMMITTEES	DEPARTMENTS
Local authorities are **governed** by **councillors** or **elected members**, who meet regularly and publicly in **full council** to take authoritative decisions for their local area.	Local authorities are **organised** into **departments**.
Most councils **delegate** much of their work to **committees** and **sub-committees** of councillors which concentrate on a particular area of the council's work and are responsible for determining the council's policy in that area.	These departments are staffed by **appointed officers** and **other employees** – administrative, professional, technical and clerical staff, manual workers – who legally are the **paid servants** of the elected council.
Each committee will have a **chairman**, who chairs its meetings, speaks and acts on its behalf, and liaises with relevant officers.	These officers and staff **implement council policy** as determined by its councillors, and run the authority on a day-to-day basis.
Council meetings are presided over by the **mayor** or **chairman** of the council, elected annually by and from all members of the council.	Departments can be divided into **service departments**, providing a service directly to the public, and **central** or **co-ordinating departments**, providing a service for the authority as a whole.
The **leader of the council**, its key political figure, is generally the elected leader of the majority or largest party group on the council.	Each department has a **chief officer**, usually a professional specialist in the work of the department and responsible for it to a committee and its chair.
Most authorities have a co-ordinating **policy (and resources) committee** of mainly senior councillors, usually chaired by the council leader.	Most authorities have a **chief executive**, the head of the council's paid service, responsible for co-ordinating the operation and policy of the council, usually through a **Chief Officers' Management Team**.

A council's POLICY is the outcome of the formal and informal interaction between elected councillors and their appointed officers. Councils have considerable discretion over their internal organisation; no two councils, therefore, will have precisely the same departmental and committee structures.

and many councillors were fearful of becoming second-class members of their councils, excluded from the Management Board, and with little or no policy influence. Likewise, the suggested drastic reduction in both departments and committees was widely thought to be unrealistic. Nevertheless, as Hampton (1991, p. 80) reminds us, Maud acted as something of a catalyst, although 'some of its less contentious proposals simply represented an encouragement to practices already being developed in larger local authorities'. Numbers of committees *were* rationalised in many authorities and some *did* appoint chief executives. So, despite the widespread hostility, Maud served as an important stimulus to change. This process was further encouraged by the publication in the early 1970s of the Bains Report (England and Wales) and the Paterson Report (Scotland): reports which were very similar in orientation.

□ *Bains 1972 and Paterson 1973 – corporate icing, traditional cake*

These two committees were set up in 1971 to provide advice on internal management structures for the new local authorities which were established under the Local Government Acts of 1972 in England and Wales and 1973 in Scotland. Their reports received far more favourable reaction than that previously accorded to Maud. Essentially they argued that the traditional departmental attitude which permeated much of local government needed to give way to a broader corporate, or authority-wide, outlook. Maud's controversial idea of an elite Management Board was not revived.

While the Bains/Paterson reports were wide-ranging, there were three major recommendations:

1. the appointment of a *chief executive* as leader of the officers of the authority and principal adviser to the council on general policy matters;
2. the creation of a *policy and resources committee* to provide co-ordinated advice to the council in the setting of its plans, objectives and priorities;
3. the establishment of a *senior management team* of principal officers responsible, under the chief executive's leadership, for the general co-ordination and implementation of these plans.

The vast majority of the newly established local authorities appointed chief executives; likewise, most appointed policy committees and management teams if they did not already exist. There was, therefore, in many authorities a good deal of internal *structural* change following Bains, although the effect on day-to-day working practices is far more

difficult to determine. New organisational structures do not automatically change style or working processes. Looking at the extent of real
change, Alexander (1982b, p. 76) argues that Bains's influence could well
have been more apparent than real.

Organisation charts changed but often political realities hardly moved.
New *forms* of management emerged, corporate in orientation, but values
often remained largely unaltered. The strong co-ordinating chief executive envisaged by Bains remained the exception rather than the rule. To
quote Alexander (1982b, pp. 77, 78), the evidence seems to suggest that
in many authorities, despite the hype, the influence of Bains was, 'at
worst, superficial in that it led to a widespread adoption of corporate
management forms. At best, it was catalytic in that it stimulated the new
authorities (as were the old authorities by the Maud Committee in 1967)
to examine their procedures and to create management structures and
processes best suited to local circumstances.' A similar conclusion
applies to the impact of the Paterson Report in Scotland: namely,
wholesale adoption of new administration *forms* but rather less certainty
about the reality of changed *processes* in line with the report's recommendations. The adoption of corporate structures did not easily sub-
merge the specifically professional approach of chief officers at
departmental level. Structural change is relatively easy to implement;
deeply rooted cultural change is another matter.

☐ *Widdicombe 1986 – overdue recognition of party politics*

The Widdicombe Committee was appointed in 1985 at a time when the
Thatcher Government was particularly concerned about the policies and
campaigning activities of a number of urban Labour authorities on what
came to be labelled the Municipal or New Urban Left, or 'loony left' as
such councils were known in the tabloid press. A mainly younger
generation of Labour councillors in London and certain other cities came
into office committed to using local councils as a testing ground for new
radical, interventionist policies in economic development, housing,
transport and planning, and to defending their communities against
central government spending cuts. Their search for a more assertive role
for their councils and for themselves as elected members was seen by the
government as a challenge to the traditional role of local government and
prompted the principal terms of reference given to the Widdicombe
Committee:

> To inquire into practices and procedures governing the conduct of local
> authority business in Great Britain, with particular reference to:
> (a) the rights and responsibilities of elected members;
> (b) the respective roles of elected members and officers.

The Maud, Bains and Paterson Committees had focused mainly on organisational structures, rather less on the role of councillors, and scarcely at all on their role as party politicians. Their managerial prescriptions consequently largely ignored the increasingly prominent party political dimension of the country's local government. Widdicombe, by contrast, addressed the issue head-on.

The Committee acknowledged the spread of party politics in local councils; also its increasing formalisation and intensity. Moreover, it welcomed many of its consequences: more contested elections, clearer democratic choice, greater policy consistency, more direct accountability. The key policy determining role played by the majority party group on many councils was seen as inevitable, legitimate, and one that should be properly recognised in a council's operational arrangements.

At the same time, the Committee was concerned to safeguard the position of minority parties and of individual and non-party members. Its recommendations led, as already noted, to an effective banning in the Local Government and Housing Act 1989 of one-party committees and sub-committees. Membership of decision-making committees should reflect the party composition of the full council and should consist only of elected councillors, with no voting co-optees. Senior officers were to be barred from all public political activity.

The impact of the Widdicombe Committee was, therefore, to introduce a number of 'checks and balances', without seriously challenging the right of a majority party to determine and see implemented its policy proposals. It injected a new air of realism into discussions about local authority management, providing a useful platform for future debate.

■ Conclusion

This chapter has outlined both external and internal structural basics. It has focused on institutional perspectives since these provide the framework within which the practice of local government takes place. Later chapters examine the ways in which both structural reorganisation and internal management are still very much at the forefront of change in local government. New organisational patterns are being shaped by new ideologies and values. New cultures are evolving which to some authorities represent a threat but which to others are seen as windows of opportunity.

Guide to further reading

As for Chapter 2, the first place to turn to for additional information is not the library catalogue, but your own town or county hall. It is both easier and more useful to learn about your own local authorities than about councils 'in general', and most nowadays produce leaflets or booklets describing 'how the council works' and listing their services. A council's Annual Report may also contain committee and departmental organisation charts. The 'external structure' of our local government system is going to continue to feature regularly in the news over the coming few years, as it did in our own crop of news items in Chapter 2. Accounts of how the existing structure came into being in the 1960s and 1970s are provided by Wood (1976), Alexander (1982a), and, much more summarily, by Chandler (1988). Chandler also covers the abolition of the GLC and the English metropolitan county councils, other accounts of which include Flynn *et al.* (1985) and ex-GLC Leader Ken Livingstone's entertaining autobiography (1987). Outlines of the complex post-abolition governmental structures are available in Leach *et al.* (1992) and Hebbert and Travers (1988). On internal management there are relevant sections in the various textbooks listed in Chapter 2, while the Widdicombe Committee Inquiry and subsequent legislation are comprehensively dealt with in Gyford *et al.* (1989).

■ *Chapter 6* ■

Changing Functions: From Government to Governance

■ Introduction – the continuing primacy of service provision

In the previous two chapters we have emphasised the elective, democratic history and character of the UK system of local government: that the councillors and councils we elect constitute 'the government' of our city, town, county or district in the same way that ministers and the Cabinet constitute the government of the country. There are, however, some fundamental differences between these two levels of government.

First, we do not directly elect our national government in the way we do our local councils. Rather, we elect the MPs from among whom the government is drawn and whose job collectively is to scrutinise and pass that government's legislation. There is, in other words, a separation of legislative and executive roles at national level, whereas locally they are integrated in the body of the council. Secondly, national government is not, on the whole – and Parliament, of course, not at all – a large-scale provider of services. There are some big exceptions – most obviously the Department of Social Security, the Home Office, and the former Employment Department, now joined with Education – but mostly ministers and their Whitehall-based departments produce *policy, not services*. They decide what services we citizens are to be provided with, by whom, and how they are to be financed; others, in the main, do the actual providing, and throughout the 20th century by far the biggest providers have been local councils.

That still remains the case today, although, as we have seen, things recently have been changing fast. Councils have lost completely some of their former responsibilities. Others have been and continue to be exposed to private sector competition. Sometimes out of choice, sometimes not, councils nowadays find themselves increasingly working alongside a range of other service-providing agencies in their localities. The term sometimes used to distinguish this more fragmented, multi-agency pattern of local government from the earlier 'near-monopolistic council' model is *local* or *community governance*.

Community governance implies a reduced role for local authorities as direct providers. We have entered an era of alternative service delivery systems incorporating local authority, voluntary sector and private sector provision. Partnerships with the non-elected, private and voluntary sectors have become particularly prevalent, one of the best examples being the provision of Community Care. Nevertheless, while service provision at local level is sometimes more complex than it once was, it remains a major role for local authorities, albeit not necessarily through direct employment and in-house management. Midwinter (1995, p. 131) reminds us of the continuing importance of service provision: 'Despite the welter of rhetoric, the image of radical reform, the language of the new public management, the glitz of marketing and public relations, the central role of a local authority remains – municipal provision of services.'

■ Changing roles – from provider to commissioner?

In Chapter 1 we saw how a council could attempt to respond to the needs of its citizens 'either through the direct provision or through the sponsorship, indirect funding, regulation or monitoring' of services (p. 8). In Chapter 2 we added some more roles: licensor, registrar, certificator, facilitator, contractor (p. 25). It is time to bring some order to this lengthening list. Leach and Stewart identify four primary roles for elected local government:

1. *Service Provision*: the planning, resourcing and provision, directly or indirectly, of individual local services.
2. *Regulation*: the regulation of the economic behaviour of individuals or other agencies in the public interest by insisting on their compliance with standards, rules and procedures of various kinds for exchange or provision of goods and services. This is where the licensing, inspection, monitoring, registration and certification come in.
3. *Strategic Planning*: the provision of a longer-term planning framework to influence the activities of internal departments and external organisations in relation to individual service areas or authority-wide issues.
4. *Promotion and Advocacy*: the persuasion of one or more other organisations (e.g. private industry, voluntary bodies) to carry out activities which are likely to benefit the local community (e.g. by loans to small businesses, by grants to voluntary organisations). (Leach and Stewart, 1992b)

Unlike Leach and Stewart, who are academic analysts, David Curry, addressing the House of Commons in July 1994, was speaking as Conservative Minister for Local Government. Not surprisingly, he chose slightly different terminology and a significantly different emphasis:

The first role is that of *regulator* . . . it is clear that that role will remain. The second role is that of *service commissioner* – I use the term deliberately – because local government organises the delivery of a range of services, whether the individual services are delivered directly or through the competitive process. [The] third role is that of a *regenerator*, [something] that will be more relevant in urban areas than in some rural areas. Local government has a role to work more and more with other agencies . . . so as to bring the resources of the community to tackle specific problems.   (*Hansard*, 21 July 1994, Cols. 616–19, our emphases)

For this Conservative minister, then, it was regulation first, then direct service provision and that only as part of a broader service commissioning role. Regeneration, like service commissioning, involves negotiation and partnership with other agencies, and, in the minister's preferred scheme of things, a scaling down of the activity and spending of local authorities themselves. But a scaling down from what?

■ Still big business

It is a cliché, but true nonetheless, that local government in Britain, even after all the constraining legislation of recent years, the transfers of services, the property sales and the enforced competition, is still extremely big business. Its combined current and capital spending in 1996/97 was well over £80 billion, or more than a quarter of all government expenditure. If individual local authorities were listed in terms of their expenditure, almost a hundred would rank alongside the top 500 British companies. To take just one example, Kent County Council in the early 1990s served a population larger than that of 40 member states of the United Nations. With an annual turnover in excess of £1 billion, 50,000 employees and 1,400 service points, it was not only the biggest single employer in Kent, but larger than many national and international companies such as the Beecham Group, Unigate and Burmah Oil (Kent CC/Price Waterhouse, 1992).

Non-metropolitan county councils like Kent are among the biggest of the local government 'businesses', together with the larger unitary authorities: the metropolitan districts, the London boroughs, and some of the new big city unitaries. For these are the authorities that are responsible for either most of the council-provided services in their areas or at least for the most labour-intensive and biggest spending ones: notably education and social services. The detailed division of services between English county and district councils can be seen in Exhibit 6.1.

It is not a hierarchical division. Despite the fact that in our organisation charts in Chapters 4 and 5 the counties and Scottish regions appear above the districts, the two tiers should properly be seen as equal in status, each responsible for the range of services felt to be most appropriately

Exhibit 6.1 *Who does what? English county and district councils*

Activity	County Council	District Councils
County farms	All services	
Education	All services	
Highways and Transportation	Transportation planning Constructing new county roads Maintenance of county roads* Public transport infrastructure and co-ordination Highways and street lighting Public rights of way	Street cleansing Street lighting
Housing		All services
Leisure and Amenities	Libraries Archaeology Archives County parks and picnic sites Grants to village halls, sports, arts, countryside and community projects	Allotments Museums/art galleries Country parks, local parks and open spaces Playing fields, other than schools Swimming pools and sports centres
Planning	Structure plans Minerals control Environment and conservation Economic and tourism development Waste disposal control	Local plans Development control Local land charges Environment and conservation Economic development
Public Protection	Waste regulation and disposal, waste recyclying centres Trading standards Registration of births, deaths and marriages Coroners courts Fire and rescue	Refuse collection Food safety and hygiene Markets Control of pollution Cemeteries/crematoria
Social Services	All services	
Council tax		Collection of own tax, plus precepts for county and parishes

*Some highways functions are undertaken by District Councils on an agency basis.

provided on either a relatively larger or a more localised scale. It is, though, a severely unbalanced division, with the cost of county-provided services likely to be four or five times that of district-provided services in any particular area.

Unitary authorities in principle have responsibility for all those services that in the remaining two-tier parts of the country are split between the counties and districts. In practice, as we saw in Chapter 5, there is also a complex network of joint boards and committees contributing to service provision: bodies composed of councillors not directly elected to them but nominated by their respective councils.

Then in addition there is the welter of other organisations that nowadays are likely to be involved in the governance of a community: none directly elected and some with no elective element at all (Wilson, 1995). These too are very big business indeed, spending on local services well over half of the total spent by elected local government (Democratic Audit, 1994, p. 36). They include:

* 10   *Integrated Regional Offices* (1993–) for the Departments of Trade and Industry, Education and Employment, Environment, Transport and the Regions, each office responsible for a Single Regeneration Budget (SRB);

* 13   *Urban Development Corporations* (UDCs, 1980–): government-appointed and -funded agencies with powers to take over local councils' development control and planning responsibilities to promote market-led urban regeneration (to be wound up by 1998);

* 6   *Housing Action Trusts* (HATs, 1988–): government-appointed and tenant-supported agencies with powers to take over temporary ownership of designated council housing estates, refurbish them, then sell or transfer them to other landlords;

* 2,565   Registered Housing Associations: voluntary bodies, now the main providers of new social housing, funded by private finance and grants from the government-appointed Housing Corporation, or in Wales Tai Cymru (Housing for Wales);

* 81   *Training and Enterprise Councils* (TECs, 1989–): government-approved and private sector-dominated corporations, responsible for assessing and meeting skills and training requirements in their local areas; in Scotland, 23 *Local Enterprise Companies*;

* 91   *Careers Service Pathfinders* (1993–): Partnership companies, usually involving local authority, TEC and Chamber of Commerce, set up to compete for and deliver former council careers services;

* 1,100+   *Grant Maintained Schools* (GMSs, 1988–): schools whose parents have voted to 'opt out' of their respective Local Education Authorities (LEAs) to be funded instead by direct central government grant;
* 15   *City Technology Colleges* (CTCs, 1988–): government- and private sector-funded schools, run by appointed governors, specialising in science, technology and maths;
* 735   *Higher* and *Further Education Funding Corporations* (1988–): the former LEA-run polytechnics, further education and sixth-form colleges, funded by the government-appointed Higher and Further Education Funding Councils for England, Wales and Scotland;
* 43   *Police Authorities* (1995–): formerly council committees (see Chapter 5), now separate and more Home Office-influenced authorities, funded partly by Home Office grant;
*   *City Challenge Boards, City Action Teams, Inner City Task Forces*: various government initiatives in inner city areas designed to develop new alliances between local government, local business and the voluntary sector to stimulate urban regeneration.

As will be noted from their dates, most of these agencies have sprung up since 1980. They determine and control the provision of services that previously were the direct responsibility of elected local authorities. Other appointed bodies have longer histories: notably the NHS structure of District Health Authorities (to which can now be added the large number of NHS trusts).

■ Fragmentation and partnership

The chief outcome of these developments has been the indisputable fragmentation of local service provision and, on the face of it, a corresponding loss of democratic accountability for the spending of billions of pounds of public money. It has certainly made it harder to answer such questions as: Who runs things in this town? Who provides the public services in this area?

You might imagine that, with a so-called unitary council, the local government of a city like Birmingham would be relatively straightforward to describe and comprehend. Not so unfortunately, for, in addition to the City Council, you would have to take account of the new separate police authority, several joint boards, district health authorities, health service trusts, a TEC, boards of further education colleges and grant maintained schools, a UDC, a Housing Action Trust, and a City Challenge Board. Even in Milton Keynes, when it was still just one of five

Buckinghamshire districts, there were found to be over a dozen principal quangos responsible for an annual expenditure of well over £400 million, equivalent to about two-thirds of the Council's total budget. They included four grant maintained schools, the Buckinghamshire Health Authority, family health service authority, General NHS and Ambulance NHS Trusts, a housing association, a parks trust, and a Commission for New Towns (Milton Keynes Liberal Democrats, 1995).

Naturally enough, local authorities have resented what they have tended to see as central government's 'stealing' of their service responsibilities (LGIU, *The Quango File*, No. 9, 1995). That resentment, though, has not prevented many of them working closely and productively in partnership with some of the new quasi-governmental agencies and with private sector and voluntary organisations in their localities. Birmingham Heartlands (see Exhibit 6.2) is a particularly prominent and large-scale example of one such partnership, but there are plenty of others (Bailey, 1995; Atkinson and Moon, 1994; Imrie and Thomas, 1993; Deakin and Edwards, 1993; Campbell, 1990). Local authorities may nowadays be just part of a complex mosaic of agencies operating at the local level, but they remain a uniquely large, pivotal, multi-functional, locally knowledgeable and experienced, and, above all, directly elected part of that mosaic, not easily sidelined by even an antipathetic central government.

■ The extent of local authority discretion

Elected, multi-purpose and multi-functional though they are, local authorities in Britain are also what in Chapter 2 we called 'creatures of statute'. They can do only what the law explicitly allows; all council powers come from Act of Parliament. Local government itself exists only by courtesy of Parliament, which can and frequently does amend the powers and functions of local councils. Should any local authority provide a service or spend money for a purpose not specifically permitted by Parliament, it would be acting illegally or beyond its powers: *ultra vires*, to use the legal term.

Individuals or private sector organisations are able to act in any way they choose, as long as they do not break the law. In many European countries, local authorities have a similar freedom of action, or power of general competence. They can undertake any initiative, or provide any service, that they consider to be in the interests of the citizens of their community, provided that they do not break the law or trespass into the sphere of responsibility of another public body. Indeed, this principle is specifically incorporated in Article 4 of the Council of Europe's 1985 European Charter of Local Self-Government which successive Conservative Governments, along with those of Albania, Latvia, Slovakia and the Ukraine, refused to sign. In June 1997, however, the Labour

---

Exhibit 6.2 *Birmingham Heartlands: a public/private sector partnership*

The site: an exceptionally derelict 1000-hectare (2,350-acre) mixed industrial and residential area of East Birmingham, around Spaghetti Junction.

The partnership: an **Urban Development Agency** set up, with DoE blessing, in 1987. Led by the private sector, its aim was to regenerate and develop the area by bringing together the private sector resources (finance, personnel, management skills) of companies such as Bryant, Galliford, Tarmac, Tilbury-Douglas, Wimpey, and the Birmingham Chamber of Industry and Commerce, who held two-thirds of the shares, and the public sector resources (land, grants, planning expertise, compulsory purchase powers, management skills) of Birmingham City Council who held the other third.

In 1992 the Agency evolved into an **Urban Development Corporation (UDC)**, with a 12-member board consisting of six members from the City Council and six private sector members appointed by the Environment Secretary.

Development achievements:

– creation of a new urban village at Bordesley;
– a greatly improved network of roads and supporting infra-structure, including a new spine road and cross-city rapid transit system;
– a flagship, canal-focused commercial centre, Waterlinks;
– hundreds of new and refurbished homes for sale, share ownership and rent;
– major industrial investment and development;
– new and improved local shops and social and community facilities;
– improved access to jobs, training and childcare.

Government signed this Charter which commits signatory member states to guarantee 'the right and the ability of local authorities to regulate and manage a substantial share of public affairs under their own responsibility'. Signing of this Charter was one of the central recommendations of the Hunt Report (Chapter 7) and was widely seen as an important symbolic gesture by the Blair Government in the context of improved central–local relations. Labour's endorsement of the Charter could be seen as a first step towards a loosening of the shackles of *ultra vires*. For the present, though, British local authorities are still able to do only that for which they have explicit statutory authority.

Currently, even councils' very limited scope for wholly discretionary spending has to have statutory authority – in this case Sections 137 and 83 of the Local Government Act 1972 and the Local Government (Scotland) Act 1973 respectively. These sections permit councils to spend up to a specified amount per local resident 'for any purpose which in the opinion of the council is in the interests of the area of the council or any part thereof', which might include the provision of advisory and other welfare services, local environmental schemes and, potentially most controversially, publicity and promotional campaigns. In 1996/97 county councils and non-metropolitan district councils were permitted to spend up to £1.90 per resident on such discretionary initiatives and the single-tier London boroughs, metropolitan districts and new unitary councils roughly double that amount.

This so-called Section 137/83 discretionary spending, though, is not the main reason why service delivery and spending patterns vary to the considerable extent that they do from council to council. The greater reason is what in Chapter 2 we called the 'discretion factor' built into much of the effectively permissive legislation affecting local government. The relevant legislation permits the spending of money on, for instance, slum clearance, the provision of leisure centres and playing fields, or the support of the arts, leaving councils to decide whether they wish to provide and support these services and to what extent.

It has been calculated that for an average council only between a third and a half of its total spending is likely to be absolutely mandatory – in the sense that, if it did not deliver certain services to certain standards, it would be breaking the law. The rest of its spending, strictly speaking, is discretionary. The council is choosing to provide what it considers to be desirable and necessary services to standards above any minimum levels laid down in law. There may be excellent historic, humanitarian, communitarian and political reasons for continuing to provide such services, but legally they are discretionary.

Additionally, as we saw illustrated in one of the news headlines in Chapter 2, it is open to any local authority to promote a Private Bill through Parliament to extend its powers. While this procedure is both complex and costly, each year a number of mainly larger authorities acquire powers by this means to add to their list of functions. Birmingham, for example, was permitted to run its own municipal bank and more recently, during the 1980s, a Monaco-style Super Prix around a city centre street circuit. In our own City of Westminster example the council is now able to require the immediate closure of unlicensed sex shops and cinemas.

■ A classification of services

We have sought so far in this chapter to re-emphasise the importance of adopting a balanced perspective when assessing local councils' present-day service responsibilities – as we did when introducing our funnel of

---

Exhibit 6.3   *A categorisation of local services*

1.   *Need Services* – e.g. education, personal social services, housing benefit. Services provided for all, regardless of means, and which therefore contribute to the redistribution of resources within the community. Need services account for well over half the total net expenditure on all local government services.
2.   *Protective Services* – e.g. fire and rescue, and, most obviously, the police, until the creation of the new independent police authorities in April 1995. Services provided for the security of people, to national guidelines. Access to them cannot be restricted, and use by one person does not affect availability to others.
3.   *Amenity Services* – e.g. highways, street cleansing, planning, parks and open spaces, environmental health, refuse disposal, consumer protection, economic development. Services provided largely to locally determined standards to meet the needs of each local community.
4.   *Facility Services* – e.g. housing, libraries, museums and art galleries, recreational centres, refuse collection, cemeteries and cremetoria. Services for people to draw upon if they wish, sometimes in competition with private sector provision.

Source: Adapted from Hollis *et al.* (1990).

---

local authority discretion in Chapter 2. It is true that here in Britain local government rests on a constitutionally weaker base than it does in many European countries; also that its scope and freedom of action have been significantly reduced in recent years as the result of national government policy. It is also the case, however, that local authorities are still unusually large, diverse organisations with large budgets, big workforces, and responsibility for literally hundreds of different services. These services – or at least some of the most important – constitute the focus of the remainder of the chapter.

For convenience, we will follow the order of the fourfold classification used by Hollis and his colleagues and summarised in Exhibit 6.3.

☐ Education

Education is still by far the largest council service, accounting for nearly half of all local government revenue expenditure in the early 1990s. But under the Conservatives it shrank substantially. There was an average of at least one Education Act each year during the 1980s and 1990s: enough to justify a funnel of diminishing discretion for education on its own. This legislative onslaught has profoundly altered the role of councils – the English counties, London and metropolitan boroughs, and now the new unitaries – in their capacity as local education authorities (LEAs). They have lost control altogether of polytechnics, Colleges and Institutes of Higher Education, Sixth-Form and Further Education Colleges, which are now financed directly through various funding council quangos.

The management of state (maintained) schools has been radically changed and LEAs are now required to pass on or delegate to the governors of schools at least 85 per cent of their education budget. It is the governors who are responsible for overseeing the running of the school and its financial operation in what is known as the Local Management of Schools (LMS). The same legislation, the massive Education Reform Act 1988, introduced the national curriculum, with its core and foundation subjects and pupil-testing against attainment targets. In addition under the Conservatives, schools were able, through a parental ballot, to vote to opt out of LEA control and become Grant Maintained Schools (GMS), funded directly by central government.

These parental ballots were the chosen instrument for what Prime Minister Margaret Thatcher and some of her ministers anticipated would be an educational revolution, with the vast majority of the country's 24,500 schools voting enthusiastically to sever all connections with their LEAs. As can be seen in Figure 6.1, this was a revolution that never really took off. By April 1997 there had been only 1,188 opt-outs, including 663 secondary, 504 primary and 21 special schools. At this rate, a cynic calculated, it would take nearly half a millennium for former Prime Minister Thatcher's vision to be realised (*The Guardian*, 13 September 1995).

Yet, even with no further opt-outs at all, the role of LEAs has been changed fundamentally. Most of their services are now devolved to their

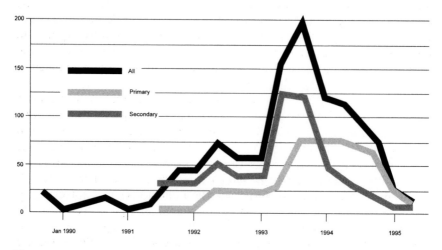

Figure 6.1 *The rise and fall of opting out*

schools who may, if they wish, buy them back from the LEA. This devolution will continue under a Labour Government which, whilst recognising in its manifesto that 'LEAs are closer to schools than central government, and have the authority of being elected', plans at the same time that *their* performance should in future be inspected by OFSTED and the Audit Commission, as well as that of their schools.

☐ *Personal social services*

The important emphasis here is on *services*, for, as noted in Chapter 2, in the UK cash payments to the needy and vulnerable are made not by local government but by local offices of the national Department of Social Security's Benefits Agency. Local authorities, frequently working nowadays with and through voluntary and private organisations, are responsible for services to the elderly, people with learning difficulties, people with mental health problems, children, young people, and families considered to be at risk. Services provided include residential care, day care, help – such as meals, laundry, practical aids – to enable people to remain in their own homes, one-to-one counselling, fostering and adoption, and child protection.

The first of these – residential care – has been and continues to be the single most important, but the emphasis has been gradually shifting towards domiciliary and community care, particularly since the post-1993 implementation of the NHS and Community Care Act 1990. This legislation represents the most striking example in recent years of local authorities having new responsibilities thrust upon them, rather than taken away. Social services departments are now responsible for assessing all requests for residential and nursing home care where public funding is sought, and for assessing people's overall needs and co-ordinating the appropriate service provision. They are also required to produce annual Community Care Plans evaluating how effectively the resources of various organisations and sectors are being used in meeting the diverse needs of local people.

Like teachers, social workers live nowadays with both the continuous pressure imposed by new legislative demands and public expectations and the seemingly inexorable squeeze on available resources. Both groups too have become used to the exceptional case that propels one or two unfortunate individuals, a single institution or department, and indirectly the whole profession, into the glare of national media headlines. For teachers it can be the allegedly 'failing school', singled out by the Secretary of State for Education and Employment as requiring the highly publicised intervention of a government 'hit squad'. For social workers it can be an even more tragic case involving the failure of child protection and the ensuing investigations into either inadequate or misguidedly zealous professional behaviour. Such cases are obviously atypical, which is why they attract the attention they do. But the very depth of their coverage, especially if they result in an official inquiry report, can reveal a great deal about the day-to-day operations of the relevant council departments.

☐ *Police service*

As already noted, the far-reaching Police and Magistrates' Courts Act 1994 changed the role and function of police authorities by establishing them as free-standing authorities, with considerably enhanced powers over their own service provision, and very much more independent of and detached from their respective local councils. We include the service here for two key reasons. First, it serves as a reminder that, in contrast to the practice in many other countries, in Britain it is *local* government that since the 19th century has been responsible for organising the country's policing – the important exception being the Metropolitan Police in London which is currently the direct responsibility of the Home Office.

Secondly, the reduction in local government's involvement in the new authorities, substantial though it has been, is much less than was initially intended by the then Home Secretary (Michael Howard), and the important amendments made, particularly in the House of Lords, represented one of Mr Howard's more embarrassing retreats. His plan was to slim down Police Authorities and to change their composition from two-thirds nominated councillors plus one-third magistrates to one in which there could no longer be a councillor majority. In the event, most authorities now consist of nine council members, three magistrates, and five Home Office nominees: a bare elective majority, but indirectly rather than directly elected, and generally seen as now distinctly the weakest element in the 'tripartite structure' of central government, local government, and Chief Constable (Loveday, 1996).

☐ *Fire and rescue service*

It was not until the late 1930s that fire brigades joined police forces as a statutory arm of local authorities' protective provision. Since then the police have come to prefer us to see them less a force and more as a service, while fire authorities are concerned to emphasise that they do more than fight fires. Understandably enough, for they also nowadays have to deal with road traffic accidents, chemical spillages, and personal (as well as kitty) rescue; they have important emergency planning and fire safety promotional responsibilities; and they contribute to local government's monitoring and regulatory role through their fire certification of shops, offices, factories and hotels.

□ *Highways and traffic management*

This is perhaps the most shared of all public services, covering as it does everything from motorways to bridleways and involving all levels of government from the Department of the Environment, Transport and the Regions to parish councils. The counties, metropolitan districts, London boroughs and, of course, the new unitaries are the designated highway authorities and have responsibility for all but trunk roads, which are overseen by central government. 'Responsibility' in this instance includes design of routes, taking into account cost, environmental impact, residential and industrial needs and safety; road building, improvement and maintenance; highway management, including parking restrictions, speed limits, street lighting, traffic signs, street cleaning and litter collection; winter maintenance and road safety. In practice, as noted in Exhibit 6.1, agency agreements are common and several of the above functions are likely in two-tier areas to be carried out by district councils.

□ *Planning*

This is another responsibility shared, where appropriate, between the different tiers of local government. There are in fact two principal planning roles: strategic planning and development control. Strategic planning is the process through which local authorities decide how they would like their area as a whole to develop. Structure plans are drawn up by county councils, local plans by district councils; elsewhere the two are combined in a unitary plan. These plans allocate areas of land for future housing, industrial and commercial developments, taking into account national and local policies for protecting the environment.

Development control is where local councils make judgements about the desirability of proposed individual developments, granting the applicant planning and building permission if it seems compatible with structure and local plans and refusing it if not.

□ *Environmental health*

This is one of the oldest local government services, yet one that features at least as prominently in our news today as it did a century ago. It involves all those local authority functions of inspection, regulation, registration, licensing and certification that tend to go relatively unnoticed until there is a food contamination crisis, a dangerous dogs scare, or the suspected importation of some infectious disease. It includes the inspection of premises selling and preparing food; investigating outbreaks of infectious diseases and carrying out checks at ports; control of air, water and noise pollution; assessing over-crowding and premises unfit for human habitation; health and safety inspections of commercial and industrial premises; licensing of sex shops, riding stables, kennels, gaming machines, taxis and private hire vehicles; and pest control.

☐ *Economic development*

All local authorities have a permissive power under the Local Government and Housing Act 1989 to promote local economic development. This involves working in partnership with the private sector and other bodies, such as TECs, enterprise agencies, chambers of commerce and trade, to set up or expand businesses, thereby creating and protecting jobs within the local community.

☐ *Housing*

This is another service that has undergone enormous change as the result of government legislation and constraint. It is still the major service provided by district councils and accounts for most of their staff and resources, but the nation's stock of council housing fell from nearly 7 million dwellings in 1980 to well under 5 million in the mid-1990s. Starting with the introduction of tenants' 'right to buy' their homes at discounts of up to 70 per cent, successive Conservative Governments legislated to reduce local councils' housing role from providers to enablers, with the bulk of provision being taken over by housing associations, co-operatives, and private landlords.

Financial controls on councils' investment meant there was very little new building and the Conservative Government sought to speed up the transfer of existing stock through the introduction in the Housing Act 1988 of 'tenants' choice'. This legislation allowed new landlords to take over council housing following a ballot of tenants: a ballot whose rules were weighted firmly against the local authority. But, as with school opt-out ballots, tenants' choice proved less successful than the Government had hoped. Rather than challenge local authorities, housing associations mostly preferred to work with them, as a consequence of which increasing numbers of district councils transferred all or part of their housing stock voluntarily.

Following the implementation of the Local Government and Housing Act 1989, central government control over local housing authorities tightened still further, with the prescription of minimum rent levels and the outlawing of councils' longstanding practice of subsidising rents from other areas of their activity. As councils prepared from 1996 to put their housing management functions out for compulsory competitive tendering (see Chapter 19), their role could be seen as being at a watershed. On the one hand, it was clear that the Conservative Government's original goal of breaking up local authority housing and transferring it to different landlords was going to take a great deal longer than envisaged. On the other hand, there seemed the real prospect of at least some councils being left effectively as 'landlords of last resort' – retaining only the oldest and least attractive parts of their stock, to be made available for the homeless and other households unable to find accommodation elsewhere (Warburton, 1996).

The Labour Government is committed to enabling local councils 'to start building houses again, and an early Local Government Finance (Supplementary Credit Approvals) Bill was introduced to allow local authorities to use up to £5 billion in receipts from the sale of council houses for building new homes and renovating old ones.

☐ *Libraries*

Prompted in part by new regulations enabling them to make charges for some of their specialist services, libraries have been updating their image and encouraging us to see and treat them not just as book-lenders, but as information and resource centres for our various business, learning and leisure requirements. They will therefore publicise their various specialist services for schools, blind persons, hospitals and ethnic minorities, their music, video and spoken word libraries, their reference and research facilities, and their community cultural and arts provision. They are also likely to receive and display details of council services, copies of committee agendas and reports, information on council meeting times and contact numbers and addresses for councillors.

☐ *Leisure, arts and recreation*

These services, like economic development, are very largely discretionary, which means that you can tell a great deal about a council's political, social and cultural priorities from its scale and patterns of expenditure. In two-tier areas they are mainly provided by district councils, but they are obviously closely linked with the library, youth and community services of county councils, many of which, as we saw with Nottinghamshire in Chapter 5, have their own Leisure Services departments.

■ Conclusion – more sharing of the local turf

This inevitably somewhat breathless overview of local authority services rounds off appropriately, we feel, a chapter which began with our emphasising the continuing role of councils as large-scale service providers. Almost all of the services we have mentioned have undergone significant transformation during the past few years. In some cases the council's formerly largely exclusive role is being shared with a range of other providers. Almost everywhere there is greater consciousness of financial constraint and the pressure of government-fostered competition. But in no instance can it really be suggested that councils are no longer playing a leading and central role in service determination and delivery. As Davis puts it, the balance and much of the detail have certainly changed and could change further, but the 'traditional' picture is still recognisable:

> it has never been the case that local authorities have exercised all governmental powers in any particular locality. Others have always been involved but, in the past, local authorities confidently saw themselves as the rightful and undisputed leaders of their communities. Now their position is under challenge as they find themselves sharing the local 'turf' with a whole range of bodies also exercising governmental powers at the local level.   (Davis, 1996, p. 1)

Guide to further reading

Once again, your local council should be able to provide plenty of information about the services that you yourself actually receive, in the form of publicity leaflets and brochures and also the Annual Report. Most textbooks can afford space for only brief overviews of individual services. P. Lloyd (1985), written for and published by the Institute of Chartered Secretaries and Administrators, contains chapters on the major local government services. Young (1989) contains a centennial review of all principal county services. Savage and Robins (1990) looks back at the last decade of that century, the 1980s, and contains several relevant chapters, while Stewart and Stoker (eds) (1995) focus more on the near future. A vigorous defence of the service delivery role of local authorities is provided in A. Midwinter (1995). Leach, Davis and Associates (1996), provide an excellent overview of recent developments.

■ *Chapter 7* ■

Central–Local Government Relations

■ Introduction

This chapter explores the complex area of intergovernmental or central–local relations. It begins by providing an overview of the formal framework within which interactions take place and some of the instruments of central control available to Ministers individually and collectively. Formal frameworks must, however, always be studied alongside actual working relationships – hence the dynamics of central–local relations come under scrutiny next. The third part of the chapter highlights the important role of the newly expanded Department of the Environment Transport and the Regions (DoETR) and the recently created Integrated Regional Offices (IROs). Attention then focuses upon a major House of Lords report on central–local relations published in 1996. Finally a number of theoretical perspectives are considered.

■ The formal framework: eight instruments of potential control

It is necessary at the outset to provide an overview of the *formal* relations between central government departments and local authorities. We do so through an enumeration and brief discussion of eight of the main instruments of control potentially available to Ministers and their departments in their dealings with local authorities.

☐ Legislation

In Chapter 2 we used the term 'partial autonomy' to describe the constitutional status of British local government, and in Chapter 6 we indicated the constraints imposed by the doctrine of *ultra vires*. National governments can, through parliamentary legislation, create, abolish, restructure and amend the powers of local authorities as and when they determine. Local authorities, for their part, 'receive a measure of independence to provide certain services but only within the parameters of a framework of national legislation' (Chandler, 1988, p. 180). Legislation is therefore the most direct instrument of central control of local authorities and one that has in recent years been used with unprecedented frequency and impact. The Conservative governments from 1979 to 1997 produced well over 210 Acts of Parliament affecting local government, at least a third of them in major and far-reaching ways. This mountain of legislation and the associated use of the courts to enforce government intentions contrast strikingly with what Goldsmith (1986c, p. xv) describes as 'the more informal approach generally adopted by central governments in their relations with local authorities in the years up to 1979'.

☐ *Statutory instruments*

Acts of Parliament are often referred to as 'primary legislation'. Many Acts, however, delegate law-making powers to appropriate government ministers in something like the following form of words, known in Whitehall as 'Henry VIII clauses':

> The Secretary of State shall make supplementary, incidental, consequential or transitional provisions as appear to him/her to be necessary or expedient for the general purposes or any other particular purpose of the Act.

The Statutory Instruments Act 1946 requires that all such secondary legislation is published and laid before Parliament. But, with some 3,000 statutory instruments currently issued each year, the detailed scrutiny most of them receive is inevitably limited, and they constitute a significant means by which ministers can 'flesh out' their own primary legislation and thereby stengthen, if they choose, their control over local authorities' actions and activities. Just because statutory instruments tend to have laborious titles and do not make media or even parliamentary headlines does not mean they are unimportant, certainly not for the councils and classes of persons affected by them (see Exhibit 7.1).

☐ *Circulars*

In addition to statutory instruments, government departments will also issue circulars to local authorities containing 'advice' and 'guidance' on how they should exercise their various responsibilities. Such circulars are often perceived as further vehicles for central direction, and indeed they can be. But not all circulars are directive, and some are the product of genuine negotiation with local authority associations and contain useful practical advice.

There were examples of both among the 1996 batch from the then Department of the Environment. DoE Circular 5/96, *Guidance on the conduct of compulsory competitive tendering*, was one of the former. It was

---

Exhibit 7.1   *Statutory Instruments: secondary but still significant*

A small selection of the more than 3000 Statutory Instruments
that passed through Parliament in 1996:

SI 1603   Education (Teachers) (Amendment) Regulations. Exempt from
UK qualification requirements temporarily employed teachers
holding foreign teaching qualifications.

**SI 1648   Adventure Activities (Enforcing Authorities and Licensing
Amendment) Regulations.** Redefine safety enforcement responsi-
bilities of local councils under Adventure Activities Licensing
Regulations 1996.

SI 2086   Nursery Education Regulations. Define authorities and persons to
whom nursery education grants may be made and how funded
nursery education is to be inspected.

**SI 2235   Deregulation (Slaughterhouses Act 1974 and Slaughter of
Animals (Scotland) Act 1980) Order.** Removes powers of local
councils to issue slaughterhouse licences.

SI 2326   Housing Benefit (Permitted Totals) (Amendment) Order. Re-
defines the total amount of money which councils can pay out in
discretionary housing benefit.

SI 2754   Homelessness Regulations. Enable the Environment Secretary to
restrict terms under which immigrants can claim housing
assistance.

**SI 2987   Disability Discrimination Code of Practice (Goods, Services and
Premises) Order.** Set date (December 2, 1996) on which Code of
Practice on disabled access to goods, facilities, services and
premises came into force.

---

the latest in a lengthy series of attempts by government ministers to
tighten up the definition of 'uncompetitive practices' and thereby prevent councils from drawing up contract documents in such a way that
might be disadvantageous to private sector competitors. Circular 13/96,
Planning and affordable housing, was less obviously ideological and offered
detailed advice on how councils might provide affordable housing
through, for instance, the use of 'windfall sites', flats over shops, the
conversion and sub-division of buildings.

☐ *Judicial review*

The period since 1979 has seen an explosion in the number of disputes
between central government and local authorities being settled in the

courts. In 1974 leave for what is known as judicial review was sought 160 times. By 1995 this had increased to 4,400. Loughlin in particular (1996b. p. 61) emphasises the significance of this massive expansion of the formal legal dimension of central–local relations, arguing strongly that the contemporary period has 'been one in which both Parliament and the courts have been brought back into the central–local relationship'. Disputes over such issues as the allocation of pupils to schools, which have not hitherto generally ended up in the courts, are now regularly the subject of judicial review.

The government, of course, is ultimately responsible for the legislation which the judges review and interpret. A favourable judgement confirms its authority, while ministers, unlike local authorities, can attempt to persuade Parliament quickly to make legal what has just been pronounced illegal. But in the short term at least an adverse judgement can prove both embarrassing and a policy setback for a government and there have been plenty of these in the past two decades, the following three being an extremely small sample.

In May 1976 the Conservatives gained control of Tameside Metropolitan Borough Council in Greater Manchester and announced that they would abandon the former Labour administration's planned comprehensive reorganisation of education just weeks before its scheduled introduction. The Labour Secretary of State for Education intervened under Section 68 of the Education Act 1944 and ordered the LEA to proceed with comprehensive reorganisation, on the grounds that not to do so at that late stage would amount to acting unreasonably and thus illegally. Tameside resisted and successfully challenged the minister's intervention in the courts, the House of Lords ruling that in law the LEA's action was not unreasonable.

In 1991 Avon County Council took the Secretary of State for Education to the High Court over his having agreed to allow a Bath comprehensive school to 'opt out' of the local government system. The judge said that John MacGregor, the Secretary of State, had failed to weigh properly the advantages of allowing an 800-pupil boys' school to opt out against the council's plans for the school to become a sixth-form college as part of a city-wide reorganisation of secondary education. He therefore ordered the Secretary of State to reconsider both proposals.

In January 1994 Lancashire and Derbyshire County Councils won judicial reviews, arguing that the Secretary of State for the Environment was wrong to try to steer the deliberations of the Local Government Commission (see Chapter 5) by writing into its guidelines an expectation that status quo or non-unitary solutions would be the exception. The minister accepted the Court's ruling. The courts can and will, then, on occasion back local authorities in their disputes with the centre; governments must abide by, as well as impose, laws.

□ *Default powers*

Contemporary legislation sometimes confers default powers on ministers, so that a minister dissatisfied with the way an authority is providing a particular service can, as a final resort, step in and take it over or transfer responsibility to another local authority or special body. The best known example of default powers being exercised occurred in Clay Cross, Derbyshire, when the local Labour-controlled Urban District Council refused to increase its council house rents to the 'fair rent' level defined in the Housing Finance Act 1972. The Conservative Government sent in a housing commissioner to take over all the Council's housing responsibilities, and eleven Clay Cross councillors were disqualified from holding public office and surcharged £63,000 for the money which would have been obtained had the Act been implemented. In 1981/82 Norwich City Council, accused by ministers of 'going slow' on the sale of council houses under the Housing Act 1980, resolved to take on extra staff to process the backlog rather than face a similar outcome.

The sheer practical difficulties involved in government-appointed officials taking over the running of a whole council service, quite apart from the political and personal animosity they are likely to provoke, mean that such default powers are used only very rarely. Even ministers who feel they are being deliberately frustrated will tend to hold back and seek other solutions. Taking over an individual school, however, is a slightly less daunting proposition. In July 1995 the then Education Secretary, Gillian Shephard, appointed an 'Education Association' – or 'government hit squad', as the media labelled it – to run Hackney Downs Comprehensive School in East London, following a highly critical report the previous year from the Office for Standards in Education (OFSTED). The Association recommended and the Education Secretary accepted that the 119-year-old school be closed from December 1995. Though initially opposed by both the Labour Party and the teaching unions, nationally-prompted intervention is set to become a key policy instrument of Labour's Education Secretary, David Blunkett. The first announcement of his Department's Standards and Effectiveness Unit, emphasising its 'zero tolerance' of poor standards, was of a list of 18 allegedly failing schools that could receive such visitations, from what the Government prefers to call 'help squads'.

□ *Inspection*

Government-appointed inspectors, like those of OFSTED referred to above, are an extensively used means of central supervision of local authority services. Indeed, the use of inspectors goes back to the Poor

Law reform of 1834. Several local authority services are subject to direct oversight by inspectors, notably education and fire. Schools are inspected on a regular basis by OFSTED which is headed by Her Majesty's Chief Inspector of Schools. OFSTED arranges and pays for inspection teams who work to the national standards set down in its *Framework of Inspection* document. Similarly, each local fire service has an annual inspection by Her Majesty's Territorial Inspector (HMI) of the Home Office Fire Service Inspectorate. While inspectors have a duty to ensure that minimum standards of service are maintained at local level, they can also spread examples of good practice from authority to authority. An important communications role is thus served by members of the various inspectorates, although they can sometimes be extremely critical, as in the early 1990s when HM Inspector of Constabulary severely censured Derbyshire CC police force and considered recommending withholding a certificate of efficiency.

☐ *Statutory appeals*

Inspectors act at arm's length from their respective departments. In some circumstances, though, ministers may be keen to be seen acting more personally as arbitrators or defenders of the rights of local citizens. Since many local authority powers can adversely affect the interests of individual citizens – e.g. the closure of a school, the issue of a compulsory purchase or clearance order, the granting of licences, the refusal of planning permission – they may require ministerial confirmation or approval before they can be implemented, and also offer aggrieved citizens a statutory right of appeal to the minister and ultimately to the courts.

☐ *Finance*

Chapters 9 and 10 discuss finance. Here, therefore, we simply note in passing that additional means available to a central government wishing to control local authorities are through, first, regulating the amount of money which they can spend locally and, secondly, scrutinising the way in which that money is spent. The government – by, for example, capping local budgets and vetoing capital investment projects – can and does tightly restrict local spending.

Scrutiny is exercised principally through the *Audit Commission* in England and Wales and the *Accounts Commission* for Scotland, which appoint external auditors for all local authorities, either from their own staff (district auditors) or, increasingly nowadays, from private firms of accountants such as Price Waterhouse, Coopers and Lybrand and

KPMG. The Audit Commission, set up in 1982, is itself appointed by the Environment Secretary after consultation with local authority associations and professional accountancy bodies, and the minister is empowered to issue directives which the Commission must observe. The external auditors check an authority's accounts for:

* *Legality* – did it have the statutory authority to spend the money in the way it did?
* *Reasonableness* – did it act in the way a reasonable body would?
* *Wilful misconduct* – was anyone recklessly indifferent about whether a course of action was illegal?

They must also nowadays audit for value-for-money (VFM) and satisfy themselves that the council is securing the '3Es' – economy, efficiency and effectiveness – in its use of resources. District auditors' reports can be very wide-ranging and very hard-hitting, such as that on Westminster City Council's 'home for votes' affair in 1996 (see p. 30).

The Audit Commission, established by a government anxious to increase effective scrutiny of local authority finances, has nevertheless been far from subservient in practice. It has, regularly and almost from its inception, been outspokenly critical of central government policy when it has deemed it appropriate, and also on occasion strongly supportive of individual councils' spending priorities, when it has judged them to reflect the preferences of the local population. It inevitably remains, however, a creature of central government and in recent years it has been the body responsible for producing the 'league tables' of Performance Indicators (PIs) which enable local authorities, and of course the government, to compare their expenditure and efficiency records with those of all other councils.

■ Working relationships: the full complexity of sub-central government

It is important to move beyond formal legal statements about the respective powers of central and local government and look at actual working relationships. The centre, as we have seen, has plenty of capacity to legislate, regulate, direct and exhort,

> but it does so in the context of a system of sub-central government in which day-to-day control and the scope for innovation and initiative are in the hands of a range of other elected representatives, appointees and full-time officials and managers. The centre may seek to control the system but its influence is limited by the scale and fragmented character of the governmental system it oversees. (Stoker, 1990, p. 127)

In recent years, up until 1997, this inherent complexity was compounded by the political tension resulting from a Conservative Government facing a local government world increasingly dominated by Labour and Liberal Democrat councils.

Working relationships are far from simple; they vary over time, from authority to authority, and from one service area to another. You should by now have come to expect local authorities to differ from one another: to have their own political outlooks and policy agendas, their own service or spending priorities, histories and traditions, and their differing sets of neighbouring councils with whom they compare themselves. The constant danger of seeking to say anything universally generalisable about 'local government' is that there is bound, somewhere, to be an exception.

It is equally important to recognise that, despite the UK's centralist political culture, central government itself is not a single uniform entity either. There are not of course as many central government departments as there are local authorities, but, just like councils, they have their own traditions, cultures, and ways of working, as well as fundamentally different – and sometimes directly conflicting – approaches to local government. The kinds of variations noted by Griffith in the 1960s among central government departments in their interactions with local authorities are just as prevalent today. Some departments tended to be conventionally laissez-faire in their approach, intervening as little as possible; some (e.g. the Home Office, Department of Transport) were more regulatory; and some (e.g. the then Department of Education and Science) promotional.

Today such departmental inclinations are rather more likely than in the 1960s to be overlaid by party political considerations. Thus, Goldsmith and Newton (1986a, p. 103) showed that, while the early Thatcher Government was very directive towards local authorities on council house sales, by contrast it hardly involved itself in environmental health: a reflection of the much lower priority initially given to this policy area. 'Consequently, local authorities have somewhat greater discretion in the environmental health area than they do in relation to council house sales.' By 1990, however, the Government's conversion to 'green' politics as a priority area – expressed, for example, in its Environmental Protection Act and promotion of a Litter Code – was beginning to impose more regulatory functions on local authorities. Hence another warning: observations about specific policy areas are time-bound; new policy priorities can soon introduce new sets of relationships. There is in reality something of an ebb and flow in relationships; a high political profile in a policy area (e.g. local government finance) invariably results in more intensive and interventionist central government activity.

The reality, in truth, is very complex indeed: far more so than is first suggested by the phrase 'central–local government relations'. Not only is there a multiplicity of local authorities, a diversity of central government departments and policy areas, and a constantly changing party political dimension to consider. Account must be taken too of the many other appointed and representative intermediate agencies that go to make up anything approaching a full picture of what is sometimes usefully labelled *'sub-central government'*. It was the term used by Stoker in the quote with which we began this section, but it is particularly associated with Rhodes, who adopted it as the sub-title of his comprehensive analysis of government *Beyond Westminster and Whitehall*, if only, as he puts it, to draw attention to the fact that links between the centre and sub-central units of government are *not* restricted to the relationship between central departments and local authorities (1988, p. 13). Gray does the same in his more recent account of *Government Beyond the Centre* (1994).

Our own 'sketch map' in Figure 7.1 is a considerable simplification of the territory covered by Rhodes and Gray, but it does incorporate the decentralised offices of central government departments, local authority associations, professional associations, pressure groups and the political parties, voluntary sector organisations and the territorially decentralised departments in Edinburgh and Cardiff. It also serves as a reminder of the fragmented character of both 'central' and 'local government' in this context. The broken lines of communication symbolise the myriad relationships that can theoretically exist between each local authority and a range of central government departments. The unbroken lines signify that in practice much of this contact and attempted influence is necessarily channelled through 'umbrella' organisations and other agencies.

■ Increasing central intervention

At one level the scale of central intervention in local authorities' affairs can be relatively easily measured; since 1979, as noted above, there have been well over 200 Acts of Parliament relating either directly or indirectly to local government. With the plethora of regulations, circulars, guidance notes, codes of practice and statutory instruments emerging from Whitehall, the scale of central oversight and intervention is clearly massive. What is rather more difficult to assess, however, is the *nature* of the relationship. In Chapter 10 we identify four key phases of intergovernmental relations over the past quarter-century, progressing – or, some would say, regressing – from consultation, through corporatism, to confrontation and finally control (see Exhibit 10.2). The 'live and let live' relationship of the 1960s and early 1970s gave way to increasingly forceful attempts by national governments of both parties to impose their influence – initially through the incorporation of local authority

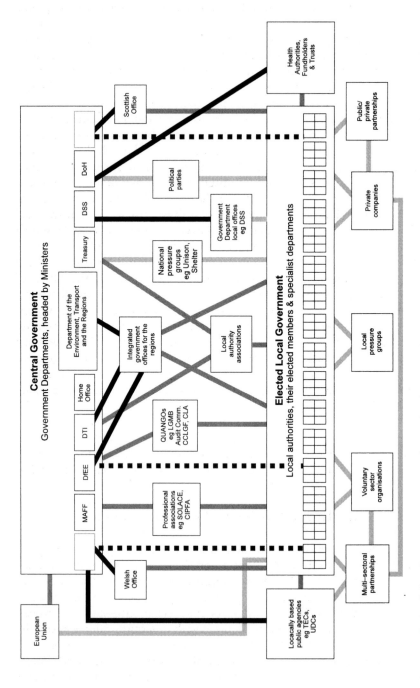

Figure 7.1 *Central–local government networks: a sketch map*

representatives into the policy-making process, then latterly through their deliberate exclusion and the unnegotiated imposition of policy directives.

That schema, designed primarily to characterise changing *financial* relations, can also be applied more generally, though with the qualification that the centre's 'control' over local finance was by the 1990s more direct and comprehensive than over some other policy areas. In the last two decades centralisation has increased greatly and the formal consultative machinery between the centre and local authorities – through such bodies as the local authority associations and the Consultative Council on Local Government Finance (CCLGF) – has been taken far less seriously by ministers and their Whitehall civil servants. There are as a result plenty of observers who would now question Goldsmith's sanguine conclusion in the mid-1980s (1986c, p. xiv) that 'Britain has not become a totally centralised state . . . British local authorities still retain considerable discretion over the way in which they run their services and the level of service they provide.'

There were some signs following the 1992 General Election of the Major Government seeking to re-establish some of the fractured lines of consultation. We noted in the first edition of this book some ministerial talk of there being a 'new spirit abroad in central–local government relationships': of ministers being 'happy to treat local government in an adult way' and being 'ready to co-operate with those of all parties or of none who put the interest of their communities and good local government first' (Wilson and Game, 1994, p. 104). In November 1994 John Major produced a set of 'guidelines' aimed at improving central–local relations. In our judgement, however, and, as we shall see, in that of the House of Lords Select Committee, there has been far too little change in practice, as opposed to rhetoric, to justify our adding a fifth 'C' for Co-operation to Exhibit 10.2. The furthest we would go is to draw attention to our still open-ended 'funnel of local authority discretion' in Figure 2.1.

■ The DoETR: the Whitehall holding company

Local authority working relationships focus in England on the Department of the Environment, Transport and the Regions (DoETR), as it has been since June 1997. Hence its prominence in Figure 7.1, which also, however, details some of the other central departments that deal directly with local authorities in specific policy areas. Some of these departments – Education and Employment, Trade and Industry – together with the DoETR itself, have an additional channel of communication, through 10 Integrated Regional Offices (IROs). Local authorities in Scotland, Wales and Northern Ireland relate largely to their own decentralised Offices of State since all three have substantial – though differing degrees of –

oversight of local government matters in their respective areas, as we shall see in Chapter 8.

The core of the new 'giant' department, the Department of the Environment, was created in 1970, the product of a merger of the former Ministry of Housing and Local Government with the Ministry of Public Building and Works. Like several other so-called 'Whitehall departments', it was not in fact located in Whitehall at all, but was, until 1997, the best part of a mile away at 2, Marsham Street, in three ugly towers designed, in one of those nice quirks of history, by the disgraced architect, John Poulson (see p. 30 above). Local government officers and politicians used to grumble regularly about the frequency and unreasonableness of the latest circular or instruction from 'Marsham Street', and specifically from what they saw as the aptly named 'Local Government *Directorate'*. In 1977, before its merger with the Department of Transport, the DoE moved to a new home in Bressenden Place, around the corner from Victoria Station, which, no doubt, will soon occupy an equally diabolic place in local government folklore. An outline of Labour's first ministerial team can be seen in Figure 7.2, and in Exhibit 7.2 a profile of Permanent Secretary, Andrew Turnbull: the Department's Sir Humphrey Appleby for *Yes, Minister* followers.

Even following its expansion in June 1997, the DoETR's core staff of some 4,400 means that it is only a fraction of the size of the big service-providing departments like the Home Office and DSS with their staffs of 50,000 and 80,000 respectively. The DoETR is not a direct service-provider; rather, as Hennessy described the old DoE, 'a bit like a Whitehall holding company in the range of activities it supervises to a greater or lesser extent at arm's length' (1989, pp. 439–40). 'It is the classic quangoid department', he goes on, operating through a network of often big spending and big employing statutory bodies, such as the New Town Corporations, Urban Development Corporations, the Audit Commission, the Housing Corporation and the Countryside Commission. This mode of operation means that, even before the 1997 merger, the Department's annual budget of over £31 billion, *excluding* local authorities' own spending, put it considerably higher in the Whitehall league table, the great bulk of it passed on to and spent by these other public bodies.

The DoETR is at the centre of extensive formal and informal communications networks in Whitehall relating to local government matters. Numerous central government departments have interests in local government; they are handled through formal and informal civil service meetings, various *ad hoc* groups and committees. While the DoETR provides directives and guidance to individual authorities, it spends much of its time discussing matters with broader representative bodies, known as *local authority associations* (see Chapter 8). From April 1997 a new unified Local Government Association (LGA) took over the functions of the Association of Metropolitan Authorities, the Association

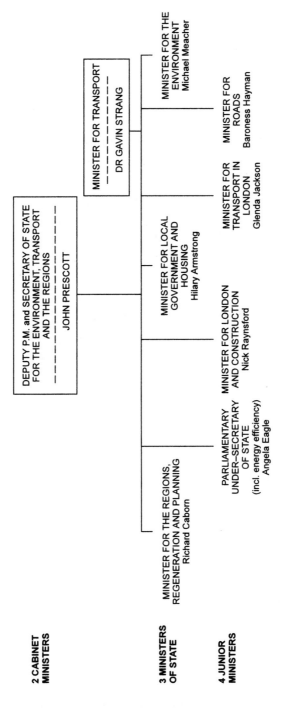

Figure 7.2 *The Department of the Environment, Transport and the Regions (from June 1997)*

Exhibit 7.2 *The top DoETR bureaucrat*	

Andrew Turnbull, Permanent Secretary, DoETR (1994–)

Education:	Enfield G.S.; law degree (with some economics), Cambridge.
Early career:	Economist in Zambia, working on nationalisation of copper industry.
Civil service (1970–):	Treasury posts (1970–94) including: Secondment to International Monetary Fund, Washington; Private Secretary (Economics) to PM Thatcher, at the time of 1984/85 miners' strike; Principal Private Secretary to PMs Thatcher and Major.
Own description of job:	(1) Policy adviser (2) Leader of DoETR management team – responsible for establishing and securing department's objectives (3) Accounting officer – ultimately answerable for department's £40 billion budget (4) Representative of department – meeting and listening to as many people as possible and explaining what DoETR does.
How others see him:	'The key guy who sits alongside the Secretary of State at grant negotiations'; 'much more in touch with modern life than the archetypal civil servant'.
Personal contact with local government:	Wife, Diane – special needs case manager, Wandsworth LBC.
Interests:	Sports, esp. Spurs; runs to keep fit ; Russian opera.
Useful quote:	'I've come to appreciate that local government has a remarkable capacity to cope and survive. You can give it outrageous deadlines – the local government review, get poll tax in, get poll tax out – and local government is resourceful in dealing with it and in the end gets things done.'
Main source:	*Local Government Chronicle*, 29 November, 1996, p. 18.

of County Councils and the Association of District Councils. A Welsh local authority association has been created from the merger of the Council of Welsh Districts and the Assembly of Welsh Counties, operating as a sub-division of the LGA. An Association of London Government was created in 1995. In Scotland, the Convention of Scottish Local Authorities (COSLA) will continue as a separate organisation. A former eight associations have thus been reduced to four, and the hope amongst local authorities is that this less fragmented pattern of interest representation will provide a more potent lobbying force in dealings with central government.

Though several departments have policy responsibilities for services organised and delivered by local authorities, it is the DoETR that has the central responsibility for policy towards local government, including the structure and areas of local authorities, their general powers and rules of procedure, their financial basis and resources. Both headquarters divisions and regional staff are involved, on a day-to-day basis, in extensive communications both with local authorities themselves and with the broader 'umbrella' organisations, including the associations, which represent particular sectors of the world of local government.

The Bressenden Place headquarters office deals with all aspects of policy and legislation, from structural reorganisation to the Citizen's Charter, from European relations to bye-laws for public conveniences. Staff comprise economists, statisticians, lawyers and researchers as well as general administrators, and they are involved in preparing and implementing legislation on matters including government financial support for local authorities, local government structure – such as the implementation of the recent Local Government Review – the conduct of local authority business and, more recently, the council tax. Regional staff play a crucial role in maintaining close contact with the local authorities in their region to ensure that these nationally determined policies and procedures are fully understood and properly implemented locally.

■ Integrated Regional Offices and the Single Regeneration Budget

In 1993 the then Environment Secretary John Gummer announced a new single budget and new integrated regional offices for England (IROs) to take effect from April 1994. Gummer claimed that these innovations would make government programmes and departments 'more responsive to local needs and acceptable to local people'. He also declared that 'this signals an important shift from the centre to the localities'. In practice, however, government announcements have increasingly referred to the ten IROs as 'government offices', thereby apparently emphasising their role as central government's regional outposts rather than local offices in their own right.

The 'integrated' dimension is not assisted by the fact that not all government departments are incorporated into the IROs. They cover only the regional offices of the DoETR, Trade and Industry, and Education and Employment, all of which already had regional structures albeit with some boundary variations. Health is not included, nor is the Department of National Heritage with its focus on broadcasting, sport and tourism. The IROs do not even include the 'Next Steps' agencies of the departments they oversee – so major arms of government like the Employment Service and the Highways Agency are left out too.

Wales and Scotland in this respect represent more of a contrast than a model. As Hogwood notes (1995, p. 11), the Welsh and Scottish Offices 'have acted as integrated regional offices for many years but cover a much wider range of functions. They also have representation in the Cabinet. Of the English regions only London has Cabinet-level representation, but as a side portfolio of the Secretary of State for the Environment.' Each of these structures is now set to change, however, with the Labour Government committed to the creation of a Scottish Parliament, a Welsh Assembly/Senedd, and an elected Greater London Authority.

While the IROs have provided *some* integration at regional level, the truth is that local authorities in England still have to deal with what Hogwood (1995, p. 21) calls 'a multiplicity of government bodies and government-funded agencies, which have a multiplicity of office locations and a multiplicity of boundaries'. Gummer's advertised objective of shifting power from Whitehall to the localities has never fully materialised, although it should be furthered under his successor, John Prescott, with the establishment from April 1999 of Regional Development Agencies.

■ The Hunt Committee: new start needed

In July 1996 an important report was published by an all-party House of Lords Select Committee, chaired by Lord Hunt of Tanworth, a former senior civil servant, on relations between central and local government. Entitled *Rebuilding Trust*, it called for a radical overhaul of central–local relations designed to ensure that local government 'does not wither away through sheer neglect'. Much of the 71-page report took the form of a severe critique of the persistent anti-local government stance taken by the governments of the 1980s and 1990s, which had produced a serious erosion of local government's powers and a profoundly unsatisfactory state of relations between the two tiers of government. Something both far-reaching and urgent needed to be done if local government was to play its proper part as community leader, as enabler, and as provider of services. Accordingly, the report set out a series of key recommendations designed to establish 'a better working partnership', giving local authorities greater freedom to 'breathe and develop'.

The Committee found that the so-called concordat agreed between John Major and local government representatives in 1994 had actually done little to improve relations between local government and Whitehall. It called for its replacement by a comprehensive agreement spelling out the constitutional status of local government and the financial rules underpinning it. The cross-party Committee of peers warned:

> There is a risk of a continued attrition of powers and responsibilities away from local government until nothing is left. We hope this report will help to alert the public to this danger, and lead to a more constructive partnership and the rebuilding of trust.

Exhibit 7.3 sets out in headline form the Committee's key recommendations and alongside them the Conservative Government's White Paper response in November 1996: distinctly positive in some places, rather less so in others. For the Labour Government that replaced it, pledged to removing central government constraints on local decision-making, the recommendations represent a set of inherited benchmarks against which it can expect to be judged.

■ Some conceptual models

In this final section of the chapter we shall outline some of the models that have been applied to the study and interpretation of central–local relations. You should think and make use of these models in much the same way – to use Loughlin's analogy (1996b, p. 53) – as you would maps. For, like maps, they are deliberate simplifications of the real world which should enable us to understand its complexities and find our way through them a little more easily.

□ Agency model

The agency model sees local authorities as having a completely subordinate relationship to central government: as arms or agents of the centre, with little or no discretion in the task of implementing national policies. From the recurring emphasis in recent literature on the increasing marginalisation of local government and growing dominance of the centre, it might be supposed that the agency model is nowadays an accurate characterisation of reality. Bogdanor (1988, p. 7) claimed, for example, that the Conservative Government 'elected in 1979 has been the

---

> **Exhibit 7.3   *The Hunt Report and the Conservative Government's response***
>
> | *Hunt Recommendation* | *The Government Response* |
> |---|---|
> | 1. Sign European Charter of Local Self-Government (see Chapter 6 above) | No |
> | 2. Power of local competence (see Chapter 6 above) | No, but would consider extending s.137 powers |
> | 3. Abolish council tax capping as a general practice | No |
> | 4. Return business rates to local control | No |
> | 5. Relax control over local authority self-financed expenditure | No |
> | 6. Review and simplify CCT | No – compulsion still necessary |
> | 7. Law to allow councils to reform their internal management | Yes – legislation to allow elected mayors and cabinets of councillors to run some councils |
> | 8. More formal central–local concordat for England and Wales | New guidelines promised |
> | 9. Establish permanent committee of MPs to maintain overview of central–local relations | 5-yearly review of relations suggested |
> | 10. Improve Whitehall arrangements for handling big local government issues – e.g. public safety, drugs – which cross departmental boundaries. | Internal review promised |
>
> *Main source: Local Government Chronicle*, 8 November 1996.

most centralist since the Stuart monarchs of the 17th century'. Particularly in the field of local finance, it may seem that, with the introduction of universal council tax capping, local councils are indeed little more than central government's agents.

Such an interpretation, though, ignores the substantial policy diversity that manifestly still exists amongst our local authorities. Central government may exercise increasingly tight financial control, but that control has not produced anything approaching uniform expenditure patterns or policy priorities, as can be clearly seen in any comparison of the financial and other statistics compiled each year by one of those professional associations depicted in Figure 7.1: CIPFA, the Chartered Institute of Public Finance and Accountancy. All councils are required to publish such statistics, enabling their service figures to be compared with those of other councils of the same type and size. We have produced in Exhibit 7.4 an illustrative set of such statistics, of the sort annually compiled by metropolitan district and county councils.

If you are able to find similar service indicators to those in Exhibit 7.4 for a council you know personally, you should find this kind of comparative exercise especially informative, and may feel you can begin to explain some of the variations you will almost certainly observe. All sorts of factors may occur to you: political control, pressure group activity, differences in the geography, economy, and social character of the area, but *not* population size, since all these statistics are *per capita* or the equivalent. You should also remember that expenditure statistics are not performance measures; they tell us simply what is being put into the provision of a service, which may or may not relate to the quality of that service or to the value for money being received by local users and taxpayers.

Trying to explain even these input variations can be a hazardous exercise and one that we do not intend to attempt here. The principal purpose of Exhibit 7.4 is to highlight the extent of expenditure and apparently policy variation that exists among councils with exactly the same statutory responsibilities. Even in the case of a largely statutory service like school education, the percentage variations may strike you as significant. But at the mainly or entirely discretionary end of the service spectrum – museums and economic development – expenditure variations become massive.

You can try the same kind of exercise with the sets of Performance Indicators (PIs) that the Audit Commission now produces each year. All councils have to submit their PI statistics to the Audit Commission and they are also required to publicise them locally – in, for example, a double-page spread in the local paper or a pull-out supplement in the council's own free newspaper. If they make the most of this opportunity, councils can tell their residents what they are shown to be doing well, what services they are prioritising, and even why on some performance measures they appear to be lagging behind other councils of the same type.

Some councils in areas of severe economic and social deprivation clearly face heavier demands on their services and greater pressures on their tight budgets than do those in less stressed areas. Even so, it is difficult to explain away entirely in such fashion the huge differences in, say, average processing times or household waste recycling that are shown in Exhibit 7.5. Councils clearly do vary in efficiency and in the priority they give to different aspects of their service provision. They

Exhibit 7.4 Local authority service statistics, 1994/95: some comparisons

	SECONDARY EDUCATION Budget per pupil (£)	NURSERY EDUCATION Nursery places as % of population under 5	SOCIAL SERVICES Net cost per capita (£)	LIBRARIES Net cost per capita (£)	MUSEUMS GALLERIES THEATRES Net cost per capita (£)	ECONOMIC DEVELOPMENT Net cost per capita (£)
A. Metropolitan Districts						
Manchester	2119	19	147	27	3.7	6.5
Wirral	2342	5	131	12	0.8	4.6
Calderdale	2874	8	120	12	4.2	0.7
Bradford	2010	8	134	10	3.9	n/a
Newcastle upon Tyne	2388	12	152	20	4.8	7.6
Trafford	2229	9	102	12	0.01	n/a
Sheffield	2183	9	n/a	11	6.38	4.0
North Tyneside	n/a	n/a	n/a	11	2.6	13.5
All metropolitan districts	2336	10	130	13	2.91	3.78
% variation between highest and lowest	43	280	49	170	63700	1829

B. English Counties

Kent	2350	1	107	9.1	1.4	2.0
Durham	2082	10	99	9.5	2.6	6.9
Cleveland	2301	12	130	13.5	0.9	5.1
Leicestershire	2177	10	93	10.6	4.3	0.5
Gloucestershire	1941	n/a	93	10.3	0.07	0.8
Hampshire	2406	0.9	85	12.2	1.2	0.6
Hereford and Worcester	2064	3	93	8.9	0.3	0.6
Devon	2212	2	113	9.6	0.04	0.1
All English Counties	2233	4.4	100	10.8	0.9	1.3
% variation between highest and lowest	21	1233	53	52	10650	6800

Note: ☐ signifies highest figure   ◯ signifies lowest figure

n/a not applicable/not available

Source: CIPFA, *Local Government Comparative Statistics, 1995*: CIPFA Statistical Information Service, London, 1995.

Exhibit 7.5 *Some performance indicators, 1994/95*						

	36 Metropolitan Districts only					
	Highest		*Average*	*Lowest*		*% variation*
Total expenditure £ per head p.a.	Manchester	1006	761	Solihull	606	66
Average number of weeks taken to re-let council housing	St Helens	10.4	5.6	Wakefield	1.1	845
% of new council tax benefit claims processed in 14 days	Leeds	98	80	Walsall	52	88
% of household planning applications decided in 8 weeks	Doncaster	92	73	Manchester	50	84
% of household waste recycled	Coventry	9.8	3.1	Liverpool	0.5	1860

Source: Audit Commission, *Local Authority Performance Indicators, 1994–95* (HMSO, 1996).

have, in other words, discretion, which is why we suggest that, on its own, the agency model is a less than fully satisfactory representation of the central–local relationship.

☐ *Power-dependence model*

This is an elaboration of the *partnership model*, which sees central government and local authorities as more or less co-equal partners. The partnership model itself is unsatisfactory in at least two respects. The concept of partnership tends to be left vague and imprecisely defined. It also appears to disregard the constitutional reality of Britain as a unitary state, and local government being necessarily, therefore, a subordinate creation of the national Parliament. To circumvent these criticisms academics have developed an alternative power-dependence model. This model postulates that both central departments and local authorities have *resources* – legal, financial, political, informational, and

---

Exhibit 7.6 *The resources of central and local government*

CENTRAL GOVERNMENT	LOCAL GOVERNMENT
* Controls legislation and delegated powers	* Employs all personnel in local services, far outnumbering civil servants
* Provides and controls the largest proportion of local authorities' current expenditure through the Revenue Support Grant	* Has, through both councillors and officers, detailed local knowledge and expertise
* Controls individual authorities' total expenditure and taxation levels by 'capping'	* Controls the implementation of policy
* Controls the largest proportion of local capital expenditure	* Has limited powers to raise own taxes and set own service charges
* Sets standards for and inspects some services	* Can decide own political priorities and most service standards, and how money should be distributed among services
* Has national electoral mandate	* Has local electoral mandate

Source: Adapted from Rhodes (1988, p. 42).

so on – which each can use against the other and against other organisations as well (see Exhibit 7.6).

It is a model that pays particular attention to *bargaining*; it also argues that, while there are likely to be inequalities in the distribution of resources, they are not necessarily cumulative. Rhodes (1979, pp. 29–31) observes:

> The fact that a local authority or a central department lacks one resource does not mean that it lacks others. One resource could be substituted for another. For example, a central department lacking the constitutional/legal resources to prevent (or encourage) a specific local initiative can attempt to get its way by withholding (or supplying) financial resources. Conversely, a local authority which has been refused financial resources can attempt to reverse this state of affairs by embarrassing the central department. Press and television reports on the adverse consequences of the centre's decision may lead to the decision being reconsidered.

The model thus sees power in relative terms, hingeing upon a process of bargaining and exchange – as in our 'tennis match' over planning gain deals in Exhibit 7.7. Some critics regard the kinds of 'offsite' infrastructure deals being struck by some local authorities as little better than legalised bribery. Others see them as entirely reasonable means of overcoming central government's restrictions on investment, while at the same time ensuring that developers make a needed contribution to the community from which they are seeking to profit. Whatever your view, they offer an instructive illustration of the ways in which councils have exploited their resources of local knowledge and professional expertise, their networking and negotiating skills, and above all their position as the elected and concerned representatives of their communities.

The power-dependence model has generated a good deal of critical interest. It is seen as usefully emphasising, as we have, that neither central nor local government should be seen as monolithic blocs. It has also been criticised (see, e.g., Houlihan, 1988, p. 70; Cochrane, 1993a, p. 25) for understating the superior power of central government, for giving insufficient attention to the internal politics of organisations, and insufficient consideration to the broader (capitalist) economic and political system within which these inter-governmental and inter-organisational relations take place. Such points should not be disregarded; nor are they by Rhodes himself (1986b). The power-dependence model nonetheless remains suggestive and insightful and thus deserving of our attention.

☐ *Stewardship model*

Chandler (1988, p. 180) argues that Britain has not so much a system of local government as a system of local administration. He emphasises the ineffectiveness of agencies representing the world of local government in their dealings with central government. Such assertions suggest advocacy of an agency model, but Chandler argues that the term 'agent' is not entirely appropriate since the centre has always been prepared to allow local authorities a considerable measure of discretion. He maintains (p. 185) that 'stewardship' is a more appropriate metaphor, in the sense that the steward 'is delegated considerable authority by his master to order his estates'. Chandler continues (p. 186):

> The steward will, from time to time, consult with his employer on how best he should manage his estate and may often wish to suggest new policies or point out failures in existing strategies. A capable landlord will listen to the advice of his expert manager and may often be persuaded by his arguments. The master, nevertheless, will always retain the power either to accept or reject the advice. Should the steward fail to obey these orders he will be compelled to change his conduct or, like the councillors of Lambeth, Liverpool and Clay Cross, be removed from office.

Exhibit 7.7	*Planning gain deals: the unfinished central-local tennis match*	

Central government	*Score*	*Local councils*
1980s – Local councils' spending, both current and capital, is subject to increasingly tight central control.	15-love	Individual councils (e.g. S Northamptonshire DC, Plymouth City C) pioneer negotiation of 'planning gain' (p.g.) or 'community benefit' deals with prospective land and property developers seeking planning permission, whereby developers 'agree' to contribute to specified aspects of council's infrastructure – roads, car parking, schools, leisure and recreational facilities, etc.
	15 all	
	15-30	Other councils follow example, with initial encouragement of Ministers, who see p.g. deals as way of deflecting criticism of Government control of local investment
Some developers (e.g. Crest Homes) start to protest and take councils to court, accusing them of imposing an arbitrary 'development tax' and in effect selling planning permission.	30 all	
	30-40	Courts reject developers' case and find nothing legally objectionable in p.g. deals.
Developers take protests to Ministers who issue circulars seeking to limit scope of p.g. deals.	Deuce	
	Advantage councils	Some councils start employing professional p.g. negotiators to help them get best possible deal from developers within government guidelines.
Early 1996 – Environment Department drafts new and tighter policy guidance on p.g. deals.	Deuce	

Principal source: BBC Radio 4, *File on 4*, 27 February 1996.

Chandler, then, provides a variation of the agency model in the same way that Rhodes provides a variation of the partnership model. Numerous other theoretical perspectives abound, however. Two examples will be briefly analysed: those put forward by Cockburn and by Saunders.

☐ *Other perspectives*

In her study of Lambeth, Cockburn (1977) provides a Marxist perspective which sees local government simply as one arm of the capitalist state, providing the conditions for continued capital accumulation and the maintenance of social order. In other words, a general theory of the capitalist state is applied with little modification to what has become known as *The Local State*. Cockburn wrote (1977, p. 47): 'When I refer to Lambeth Borough Council as 'local state' it is to say neither that it is something distinct from 'national state', nor that it alone represents the state locally. It is to indicate that it is part of the whole.'

Saunders (1981) suggests that this approach is inadequate. He argues that the 'local state' is not simply the national state writ small, and that a general theory of the state cannot be applied to the local level. He criticises Cockburn's as 'a surprisingly crass agency model' which reduces local government to a mere agent of central government. In Saunders's view, the 'local state' cannot simply be reduced to a functioning part of the national capitalist state for, within certain constraints, 'non-capitalist interests can win at the local level in a way that is becoming increasingly difficult at national level' (pp. 4, 11). In recent years, for example, there have been 'radical' authorities of the left (e.g. Lambeth, Liverpool) as well as of the right (e.g. Wandsworth, Bradford) which operated with particular local distinctiveness.

Saunders himself produced what he calls the *'dual state thesis'* as a further refinement. Essentially, he argues, there are two spheres of state activity: one at central and regional level, primarily concerned with social investment, where corporatist decision-making is typical; the other at the local level, which is typified by a more competitive and open system of decision-making (Saunders, 1981). There are, therefore, potentially contradictory functions at these different levels of government.

The dual state thesis has itself been criticised (see, e.g., Cawson, 1977; King, 1983), not least for its pluralist characterisation of local politics. But it remains important because, as Houlihan (1988, p. 68) notes, it draws attention to two key issues:

* the need to link the analysis of structures of the state to a consideration of the societal context within which they operate and, by implication, the distributional consequences of state activity;
* the tensions that exist within the state, the sources of these tensions, and how they are resolved.

Like most models, therefore, it has something to offer students of central–local relations. While it largely ignores the policy-making process, it addresses the diversity of political activity at various levels within the state and thereby adds a dimension to our thinking about relationships between central government departments and local authorities. Utilisation of a variety of analytical perspectives is invariably helpful. No single model is able to provide a complete frame of reference for intergovernmental relations.

■ Conclusion

As Bulpitt (1989, p. 57) reminds us, central–local relations used to rank as one of Oakeshott's subjects of 'unimaginable dreariness'. It was also one of no great party political significance. Today the topic is neither dreary nor unimportant. It has become high profile and extremely contentious partly because, as Cochrane points out, the centre has met obstacles in its attempts to exert control. As Cochrane (1993a, p. 44) notes:

> Every change from above seems to have been met by adjustments elsewhere in the system, first to take account of and then to evade the intended consequences of the central legislation. If the relationship between central and local government is a hierarchical one, it is certainly a complex hierarchy. It looks rather more like a constant process of negotiation in which the ground rules are not always clear and may be changed by the centre with often unpredictable consequences.

In a similar vein, Rhodes has argued that the phrase 'policy mess' has characterised the post-1979 period more accurately than 'centralisation'. In other words, centralisation was an unintended by-product of a range of policy initiatives with other primary objectives. It must be recognised, however, that the 1987–97 era witnessed a clearly interventionist strategy in a wide range of areas (e.g. finance, compulsory competitive tendering, education, housing). Intervention became a reality even if control proved to be rather more elusive. The aim was to weaken and bypass local authorities and empower consumers.

The rhetoric of the 1997 Labour manifesto and of the Government's first ministerial team would have us believe that this interventionist era is set to end – New Labour, new stewardship, to use Chandler's metaphor. In an early speech in June 1997, Local Government Minister, Hilary Armstrong, spoke alliteratively of reinvigorating local government, rekindling and reigniting local energy to provide 'energetic local solutions to local problems'. The Hunt Committee's recommendations represent an agenda for achieving precisely such a goal – and a useful checklist against which observers like us, and you, can assess the Government's unfolding record.

Guide to further reading

Amongst the most stimulating contributions to this topic are those by Cochrane (1993a) and, more historically, by Bulpitt (1983). For many years the most insightful book-length treatment of central–local relations was Griffith (1966). It still repays study. More recently the most important single contributor has been Rhodes. In his 'magnum opus' (1988) he reviews the various theories of inter-governmental relations and unravels the maze that is 'sub-central government', as, a few years later, does Gray (1994). Rhodes has also produced commentaries for various edited volumes, including Norton (1991) and Cloke (1992) on the changing nature of the central–local relationship, and with Marsh (1992) the best introduction to policy networks. But by far the most significant addition for several years to the literature on particularly, but not exclusively, the legal dimensions of central–local relations is the work by Loughlin (1996a and 1996b).

■ *Chapter 8* ■

The National Local Government System

■ Introduction – policy influence through networking

This chapter follows on naturally from the previous two, in that it deals in more detail with topics and institutions that we have already at least signposted in, for example, Figure 7.1. It thus serves to reinforce the importance we have attached to looking beyond the traditional and rather narrow focus of Whitehall–(English) local authority relations to the considerably more complex and fragmented but also more lifelike world of sub-central governance or, as we term it here, the national – and supranational – system of UK local government. The chapter focuses on six of the key elements in that system:

1. *Territorial Relationships* – the distinctive patterns of central–local relations which operate in Scotland, Wales and Northern Ireland;
2. *The local authority associations* – the chief 'umbrella' organisations for local government, recently significantly recast;
3. *Professional bodies* – the scores of societies and associations that are the institutional embodiment of the professionalism of local government in the United Kingdom;
4. *The local quangocracy* – the even greater numbers of nominated boards, central government arm's-length agencies, and public–private partnership organisations now operating at local level with their own policy networks;
5. *The Commissioners for Local Administration or Local Ombudsmen* – another set of non-elected officials but in this case working directly on behalf of us, the public;
6. *Europe* – or at least the principal parts of the EU world that impinge upon British local authorities.

In looking at the national local government system, we are studying *policy influence* – the ways in which innovative ideas are communicated, good and bad experiences shared, 'best practice' spread, among the UK's several hundred local authorities and several thousand separate profession-based departments. It is a two-way process: individual authorities learn, but they also teach, as Dunleavy emphasises (1980, p. 105):

Central government policy changes of a substantive or innovative kind, such as the introduction of new standards or methods of service provision, are most frequently generalisations of existing local authority practice or responses to demands produced by local authorities' practical experience, rather than ideas originating with government departments.

One example would be the permissive economic development powers given to local authorities in the Local Government and Housing Act, 1989, which resulted in part from the initiatives already being taken by many authorities using the limited Section 137 funds they were allowed to spend 'in the interests of their area and of its inhabitants'. A more current example would be the way in which the Labour Government, in developing its 'best value' policy to replace CCT, is looking to the direct experience and practice of individual, and not exclusively Labour, authorities.

We are looking, in short, at that activity beloved by modern managers that constitutes the lifeblood of the local government body: *networking* – the meetings of qualified and like-minded experts, the specialist conferences and journals, the production of policy papers and ministerial briefings by representative delegations, the bargaining and negotiation, the wheeling and dealing, even, as Frank Bruno would put it, the 'duckin' and divin', 'arry'. That is what this chapter is about: attempted policy influence through networking.

■ Territorial relationships

In the UK, patterns of central–local relations vary considerably across England, Scotland, Wales and Northern Ireland. Much literature generalises from the English model; this section briefly outlines operational patterns in the other three 'home countries', at least until Labour's devolution proposals are implemented.

□ *Scotland and Wales – different process, similar product*

The Scottish Office, created in the 19th century, is based in Edinburgh; the Welsh Office, a creation of the mid-1960s, is located in Cardiff. The Secretaries of State for Scotland and Wales (and Northern Ireland) are nowadays members of the Cabinet and their offices are responsible for a wide range of policy matters relating to their particular territory – including major services such as housing and education. For local authorities in Scotland and Wales their 'centre' is either Edinburgh or Cardiff. Their 'national local government systems' therefore have a different focus from that in England.

Goldsmith (1986b, pp. 152–3) argues that 'the political networks and processes of intergovernmental relations in the peripheral countries differ markedly from those in England. Relations are more informal, personal and closer between individual local authorities, quangos and their territorial offices at the periphery than is the case in England.' With their very much smaller populations and relatively few authorities, it would be odd if this were not so.

Nor is it really surprising that the Scottish Office, longer established and representing a country with its own distinctive legal and civil institutions, tends to be rather more pro-active in its relations with London than its Welsh counterpart. Goldsmith observes that the Scottish Office will more frequently raise territorial matters on to the Westminster–Whitehall agenda. It will also vary core policy initiatives considerably so that their implementation meets specific Scottish policy needs (1986b, p. 154). Yet Scotland has also on occasion been used as something of a guinea-pig by the Westminster government, both local authority budget capping and the community charge, for example, being 'piloted' in Scotland before being extended to England and Wales (see Figure 2.1).

The Scottish and Welsh Offices, therefore, are in the cross-pressured position of being at the same time agents of 'the centre' and advocates of the interests of particular territories. Ultimately, though, they are more the former than the latter: as depicted in Figure 7.1, they are closer to and more part of Whitehall than they are part of Scotland or Wales. Indeed, Rose goes so far as to describe them as agents of the centre (1983, p. 105). They may lobby on specific issues, but Westminster and Whitehall produce policies and legislation for the whole of the UK and in general terms the task of the territorial ministries is to implement these policies. The point is taken up by Midwinter, who argues that:

> The *structure* and *process* of central–local relations differ from England . . . [But] when one examines the *output* of the process – legislation, policy advice and resource frameworks – there is a remarkable congruity between Scotland and England. This includes, for example, common approaches to financial controls, fiscal systems, the role of public housing, community care in social work, and so on. In short, central–local relations in Scotland are distinctive for how decisions are made, rather than the substantive decisions themselves.   (Midwinter, 1995, pp. 21–2, author's emphasis)

As Midwinter suggests, the persistent attempts by recent Westminister governments to control council spending offer a neat illustration of the important distinction between process and product. In Scotland, as separately in England and Wales, there is a consultative forum on local government finance bringing together government ministers and their civil servants and the representatives and officials of local authorities. In Scotland this forum or working party is chaired by the Scottish Secretary and on the local government side is led by the single local authority association, the Convention of Scottish Local Authorities (COSLA). This Scottish gathering is certainly smaller than the English Consultative

Council on Local Government Finance (CCLGF) and allows for greater informality and more direct – sometimes exceedingly direct – discussion between individual authorities and the Scottish Office on specific issues.

But in each case the process culminates in the announcement of capital allocations and grant levels – maximum permitted levels of respectively longer-term investment and day-to-day spending by each local council for the coming year. There *are* differences: more than cosmetic, but hardly fundamental. Scottish authorities have been allowed a little more flexibility in their capital spending, but they have suffered comparable grant reductions or penalties and, as noted above, they had rate-capping and the poll tax imposed upon them a year earlier than the remainder of Great Britain.

The last Conservative Government's enforced extension of competition through compulsory competitive tendering (CCT) was slightly different: a case where outcomes in Scotland have been more distinctive than the process. In fact, the CCT legislation was the same north and south of the border, but in increasingly Labour-dominated Scotland there were proportionately fewer bids from private contractors, with the result that authorities there have been more successful in retaining their in-house provision of services. Similarly in education: as noted in Chapter 6, there was even less enthusiasm in Scotland for schools 'opting out' of local authority control than in England. In housing, on the other hand, parallel legislation – the Tenants' Rights etc. (Scotland) Act 1980 – giving council tenants the 'right to buy' their houses with discounts, produced sales of a quarter of the nation's municipal housing stock in the subsequent decade: a very similar proportion to that for England and Wales.

By far the greatest difference in *both* process and output came – as we saw in Chapter 5 – with the Conservative Government's structural reorganisation of the 1990s. Though there was to be no English-style Local Government Commission, the then Scottish Secretary, Ian Lang, promised a long consultation process, but one whose starting point would be that 'I regard the two-tier structure as an impediment to strong local government' (Lang, 1992, pp. 2–3), and whose conclusion therefore would be some form of wholly unitary structure. As in Wales, the 'consultation' would be not about the principle, but essentially about the numbers of unitary authorities – the chief difference being the government's enforced, if partial, retreat in Scotland from its initial wish to privatise water and sewerage provision.

The reorganisation process thus serves as a forceful reminder both of where the balance of power in these territorial relationships lies at present and of why there has been substantial support in both Scotland and Wales for further structural change in the form of directly elected Assemblies with, in Scotland at least, the Parliament having legislative and tax-raising powers. Such developments would be consistent with the growing significance of the concept of a 'Europe of the Regions' and

---

Exhibit 8.1   *Regional government in Europe, 1997*

The UK is the only EU country of major size not to
have some form of elected regional government:

		Population (mill.)	Regional authorities
1.	Germany	80	16 Länder
2.	UK	58	–
3.	Italy	57	20 Regioni
4.	France	57	22 Régions
5.	Spain	39	17 Comidades autonomas
Also	Belgium	10	3 Regions
	Austria	8	9 Länder

---

would also be a first step towards ending one of the several ways in
which British local government constitutes an 'exceptional case' within
Western Europe – being the only EU country with a population of over
20 million without some form of elected regional government – see
Exhibit 8.1.

☐ *Northern Ireland*

Central–local government relations in Northern Ireland have been relatively neglected. In some ways this is understandable, but in others
regrettable, for they are reflective of – and therefore offer us a small
glimpse into – the macro-politics of the Province. As previously described in Chapters 4 and 5, the 26 district councils now have relatively
few executive functions: refuse collection and disposal and the provision
of recreation and community services representing their chief items of
expenditure. At the same time, they are, in the absence of a Parliament or
Assembly, the only democratically elected bodies around, and remarkably – since at least five Sinn Fein and Unionist councillors have been
murdered – people have continued literally to risk their lives to serve on
them.

It follows that the range of regular interactions between central
government – in this case the Northern Ireland Office in Belfast – and
local authorities is less than in the rest of the UK. On occasion, though,
council members can find themselves being consulted on functions and
issues outside their immediate responsibility. As in many areas of life,
size *is* important and, with the relatively small number of people
involved, there tends, as Connolly noted (1986, p. 15), to be a great deal
of informal contact with people on first name terms. Connolly continues:

Generally it would be expected that in a system as small as exists in the Province there would be a relatively high quality of communications and knowledge. That in turn enables the centre to exercise more effective control and in the Province the centre probably knows more about each local authority than elsewhere in the UK. The factor of size, combined with the lack of local powers and the tradition of looking to Stormont, means that there is a tendency for the centre to be the dominant influence.

This dominant influence has not, however, produced the same 'policy congruity' that Midwinter noted between Scotland and England. Northern Ireland has been permitted to be more different. Blue-collar CCT, for instance, came into operation only in 1994 – several years after the rest of the UK – and the considerably smaller scale of most districts apparently persuaded the Government that white-collar CCT was hardly worth its while imposing. Similarly, Northern Ireland avoided the upheavals of implementing both the poll tax and council tax. Councils there still depend on domestic rates which provide a remarkable three-quarters of their albeit modest incomes, with less than a quarter coming from central government grant – an almost exact inversion, as we shall see in Chapters 9 and 10, of the position in the rest of the country. Nor is there felt to be any need for the 'capping' of local spending or rates – the Northern Ireland DoETR Ministers and officials relying more civilisedly on their persuasive powers to ensure that councils restrain any unduly profligate tendencies.

In education – one of the services, along with libraries, housing, health and social services, now run by appointed boards – Northern Ireland resisted the widespread introduction of comprehensive secondary schooling in the 1960s and 1970s. More recently, although there is a national curriculum and devolved management of schools, opting out was *not* imposed in the post-1988 package of reforms. The way in which this latter policy came about is instructively recalled by the chief executive of one of the education and library boards at the time:

> We were able to have grant maintained schools rejected because nobody wanted it. Minister Brian Mawhinney consulted widely, found there was no support for it, and managed to win at Cabinet level. He did a good job.   (quoted in Vize, 1994, p. 17)

We have here renewed confirmation of Goldsmith's conclusion from the 1980s that all three territorial offices *can* operate with their varying degrees of discretion *when* their respective Secretaries of State can win concessions in Cabinet. But 'such concessions can only be fought for and won infrequently: otherwise the core will see the periphery as a problem and will take action to deal with it accordingly' (Goldsmith, 1986b, p. 169). There can be no doubt, in other words, where in a unitary system of government the source of power resides.

■ Local authority associations – fewer voices, more influence?

Writing in the 1960s, Griffith (1966, p. 23) argued that:

> Any description of central and local public authorities in Britain would be incomplete without some mention of the role of the local authority associations. It is difficult to exaggerate their importance in influencing legislation, government policies and administration and in acting as co-ordinators and channels of local authority opinion.

Any organisations that meet on average at least daily with government departments and more frequently still with other national bodies are bound to make some impression upon ministerial and official views and evolving legislation. That is what each of the leading three local authority associations did during their last full year of independent operation in 1996/97, and why therefore Griffith's judgement remains at least essentially true thirty years later. These associations have remained significant because governments and their officials will almost always prefer to discuss issues affecting local government with representatives of groups of local authorities than with the authorities themselves individually.

From the reorganisation of local government in the early 1970s until April 1997 there were three major English and Welsh local authority associations: the Association of County Councils (ACC) representing the non-metropolitan counties; the Association of Metropolitan Authorities (AMA) representing the metropolitan districts and London boroughs; and the Association of District Councils (ADC) representing non-metropolitan districts. In Scotland in 1975 a *single* major local authority association was established, the Convention of Scottish Local Authorities (COSLA), which, it was hoped, would be able to speak with a single voice for all Scottish authorities – regions, districts and island unitaries alike – and thus prove stronger and less potentially divisible than the associations in England and Wales. In Northern Ireland there is a separate association of local authorities; likewise in London. Parish, town and community councils can join the National Association of Local Councils (NALC), and there is too a Welsh Association of Community and Town Councils.

The leading associations nowadays are highly partisan organisations, staffed by full-time officials, but governed by councils – or, in the case of the new unified Local Government Association, a general assembly – representing all member authoritites. The councillor delegates are usually senior members of the party or parties that control their own local authorities, which meant, until recently, that the AMA was normally Labour-dominated and the ACC and ADC Conservative-dominated. The fact that by the summer of 1993 Labour controlled all four national local authority associations for the first time ever was as powerful a measure as any of the Conservatives' then unprecedentedly weak position in the country's local government – a position that, as we see in Chapter 14, subsequently became weaker still.

The basic aim of any association is to represent its member authorities and the interests of local government generally as effectively as possible through its dealings with national (and European) government and its contacts with other opinion formers, such as interest groups, the political parties and the media. The kinds of ways in which it will do this are illustrated in Exhibit 8.2, which summarises the mixture of activities – campaigning, negotiating, advising, researching, publicising, supporting – that just one association, the ACC, was involved in during a typical year.

Inevitably, being partisan bodies, the influence of the associations will vary according to their own political complexion and that of the government of the day. There can therefore be little doubt that during the past decade or so their impact on policy development has been less extensive than Griffith observed during the 1960s. Rhodes, however (1988, p. 313), draws an important distinction between the *initiation* and the *implementation* of policy:

> Central government *decides* upon the policy, at least in broad outline. Thereafter, the informational and organizational resources of the associations make them invaluable and influential in the *implementation* of that policy. (our emphasis)

The associations' policy influence, then, tends to be either specialist, technical and low profile, or, on bigger issues, at best shared with various other interested organisations, at worst ignored. In fact, the bigger the issue, the less likely it is that success can be attributed to any single organisation, notwithstanding the hubristic tone of some of the claims made by the ADC in 1994/95:

* secured final recommendations from the Local Government Commission for 50 new district-based unitary authorities;
* lobbied successfully against the Government's proposal to extend CCT to local authority arts and leisure provision;
* lobbied to oppose privatisation of the Post Office;
* ensured a council tax exemption for severely mentally impaired people living alone;
* gained an extra six months for new unitary authorities to prepare for housing management CCT;
* convinced the National Meat Hygiene Service to employ environmental health officers.

These kinds of ongoing, behind-the-scenes, often multi-organisational discussions will go on under any government, because all concerned recognise the expertise and experience that the local government

---

Exhibit 8.2 *Championing the county cause*

Some of the activities and achievements of the
Association of County Councils (ACC) in 1994/95

1. **The Local Government Commission structural review**
   Campaigning to ensure that any proposal for unitary change be tested
   against existing two-tier system for viability and popular support
   Protesting against lack of consultation in the Welsh review
   Arguing for fair procedures – e.g. protection of county staff – in
   implementation of reorganisation
   Helping local authorities to share their information and expertise.

2. **Finance**
   Negotiating, together with other local authority associations, with government officials on annual Grant Settlement
   Collecting evidence from counties about budget cuts, service reductions,
   teacher redundancies etc. in current financial year
   Protesting at 'severest ever' Grant Settlement by the Government, restricting
   most counties to spending increase of ½ per cent
   Publishing consultation document on case for returning business rates to
   local authority control
   Meeting with Home Office officials to develop new funding formula for
   police.

3. **Education**
   Consulting with DFE on detailed implications of Education Act 1993 – on
   'failing schools', religious education and worship, sex education, discipline,
   etc.
   Monitoring impact of new Code of Practice for children with Special
   Educational Needs
   Collating examples from counties of good practice in provision of nursery
   education for DFE Task Force.

4. **Environment**
   Organising, with Association of Metropolitan Authorities, conference on
   Report of Royal Commission on Environmental Pollution
   Producing publication outlining an environmentally responsible approach to
   transport policy
   Working with officials from DoE and Ministry of Agriculture, Fisheries and
   Food (MAFF) on Government's White Paper on the Future of Rural Areas.

5. **Community Safety**
   Submitting evidence to Home Office review of fire safety regulations
   Recommending to Audit Commission study that there be a statutory
   responsibility for fire authorities to promote fire safety
   Advising insurance companies and promoting to counties the concept of risk
   management.

6. **Europe**
   Campaigning at EU Intergovernmental Conference for promotion of the
   constitutional position of British local government.
   Working with UK Delegation to EU Committee of the Regions – especially
   the 11 elected county representatives.

associations can bring to the task of trying to ensure that policy in practice works as effectively and beneficially as possible. The difficult and initially reluctant decision of the three principal English associations to give up their independence and create a new unified Local Government Association was a forceful public statement that they wanted much more than this. They wanted a more politically powerful and persuasive voice for local government as a whole in negotiations about the form and content of legislation as well as its detailed application, about the nature and scale of government grant funding as well as about technical changes at the margin.

The stakes are high, and so are the risks. There are many who remain convinced that the differences between big and small, metropolitan and predominantly rural authorities are greater than their similarities, and it is likely that there will continue within the LGA to be 'clubs' or sub-groups of authorities: the major cities, the shire counties, the seaside towns, and so on. One early sign, though, of the LGA's determination to speak, and be seen to be speaking, with a new and united voice, and to be taken seriously by central government, was its appointment as Finance Director of Neil Kinghan: not one of the obviously professionally qualified candidates from the three existing associations, but someone who just months previously had been sitting on the government's side of the negotiating table (see Exhibit 8.3). Like most bureaucrats, his name is unlikely to feature prominently in the national media, but he will be a key player in the evolving central–local government relationship in the next few years.

One final body that should be included in this section – not least because it owes its existence to the local authority associations – is the Local Government Management Board (LGMB). Created in its present form in 1991, it brought together into a single body the Local Authorities' Conditions of Service Advisory Board (LACSAB) and the Local Government Training Board (LGTB). The LGMB is funded by a combination of subscriptions from local authorities, central government grants and income from its own profit-making activities. The Board itself is made up of current local authority members nominated by the associations.

The LGMB's internal structure reflects its two principal inherited concerns: the negotiation of local government staff pay and conditions and the provision of training. Thus the Employment Affairs Directorate co-ordinates and advises the employers' or local authorities' side in a whole range of salary and wage negotiating bodies – from the Joint Negotiating Committee for Chief Executives to the National Joint Council for Local Authorities' Fire Brigades – the staff or employees' side being of course the recognised and relevant trade unions. The Training and Development Directorate is responsible for identifying and meeting the skills and training needs of the various local government employment sectors. It provides examinations and awards, promotes careers in

---

Exhibit 8.3   *The bureaucrat who swapped sides*

Neil Kinghan
Director, Local Government Finance,
Local Government Association (1997–)

Education:	Brentwood School, Essex – contemporary of Noel Edmonds; Hertford College, Oxford (1969-75) – degrees in Politics, Philosophy and Economics (PPE) and Master's in Chilean politics.
Civil Service (1975–96):	Entirely in DoE, including: Private Secretary to Ministers of Housing; Head of sport and recreation division – dealt with Hillsborough disaster; Head of homelessness policy division – set up Rough Sleepers' Initiative in London; Head of housing, private finance division – dealt with 'right to buy'; Director, Local Government Finance Policy – negotiating grant settlement with local government associations – and from there to . . .
Present job:	A 'brave' – i.e. controversial – appointment, won in competition with ex-local government association, CIPFA-qualified, finance heads; gamekeeper turned poacher.
How others see it:	'We need someone to tell us how to reform local government finance settlements to make them better and fairer; if he does that, he's worth his appointment'; 'he'll have to erect a Chinese Wall from his former DoE colleagues'; 'he's friendly, but innately formal – a quintessential Englishman'.
Interests:	Owner of 'gentle' rottweiler, Henry; cricket.
Useful quote:	'It is very important for one to be able to go out to see what is happening. If I spent all my time in Marsham Street, I'd become blinkered'.

Main source: Local Government Chronicle, 13 December 1996, p. 18

---

local government, provides information on good employment practice, and represents local government's training and education interests to government – in this latter role acting very much like a local authority association.

■ The professional bodies – influence through ACSeS?

Look up 'professional' in a dictionary and you will find several slightly differing definitions. As a noun it can refer to someone following a vocation or calling, preferably one involving advanced and examinable learning. As an adjective it means exhibiting skill, competence and commitment. But it is also used as the opposite of 'amateur' – that is, someone who is engaged in a specific activity as their main paid occupation. In Exhibit 7.2 Andrew Turnbull, the Permanent Secretary of the Department of the Environment, Transport and the Regions, drew attention to the professionalism of local government in the second sense: throw anything at them and they may protest, but they will also get it done with professional competence. Turnbull too is unquestionably professional in this sense, and also in the third sense of being in his case a (very highly) paid full-time civil servant. But neither he nor Neil Kinghan (Exhibit 8.3) are, strictly speaking, professionals in the first sense. They do not owe their positions to having studied for and passed the professional exams of some learned society or having otherwise obtained professional qualifications. Rather, as senior civil servants in our political system, they are *generalist* administrators, occasionally derogatorily referred to as 'amateurs'.

Their counterparts in local government, however, are professionals in all three senses. Senior local government officers may now spend most of their time as managers of sizable departmental organisations, but they are almost all trained and qualified professionals: solicitors, engineers, treasurers, architects, planners, housing managers, education administrators, social workers and so on. Professionalism in this sense is one of the hallmarks of British local government and, as such, a significant force in central–local relations. In its way, through the networks formed by these groups of professionals, it is more influential than, for instance, the local authority associations, for the simple reason that – to use the terminology of the 'power-dependence' model we deployed in Chapter 7 – professionals have more resources at their disposal.

We list, in Exhibit 8.4, a small sample of the dozens of professional bodies involved in local government – some, like SOLACE, SOCPO and ACSeS, almost exclusively; others, like CIPFA and IPR, only partly. In addition to their actual involvement in government, they are, as Rhodes points out (1988, pp. 214–15), 'organised as "learned societies", in which capacity they recruit and train personnel, organise conferences and seminars, produce research and publications and, as with any other organised group, proselytize and lobby for their interests'. They are also 'trade unions and . . . can use working to rule and strikes as a means of influencing the government. In effect, therefore, the professions can have three bites at the cherry of political influence.'

Exhibit 8.4 *Some leading professional bodies: acronym clubs*

---

1. **SOLACE – Society of Local Authority Chief Executives**
   1996 President: Pamela Gordon (Sheffield City Council)
   Membership: 900 predominantly district council chief executives, plus other senior local government managers, reflecting current wish to appear democratic and increase income. But the big county and metro chief executives still stick to their more exclusive Chief Executive Associations.
   Provides, for annual sub. of c.£200, a quarterly journal, other publications and policy papers, conference, training and professional development, recruitment service.

2. **SOCPO – Society of Chief Personnel Officers**
   1997 President: Susan Thomas (Lewisham)
   Membership: 400, also recently extended to senior, as well as chief, officers.
   Provides, for cheapest sub. of £45, practical advice and guidance, publications, conference, plus several specialist working groups.

3. **CIPFA – Chartered Institute of Public Finance and Accountancy** (pron. 'SIPFA')
   Membership: 12,500, nearly half in local government, plus 3,000 students. Open to all passing Institute's education and training scheme.
   Provides, for £200 sub., best staffed and slickest service among local government professional bodies: all usual perks, plus wide range of specialist advisory services and excellent statistical information service.

4. **ACSeS – Association of Council Secretaries and Solicitors**
   Membership: 500. Again you don't actually have to be a CS or S, but just in charge of legal or administration work.
   Provides, for £80 sub., 'best practice' notes and guidance, close links with local ombudsman service, plus obligatory conference and cute acronym.

5. **IPR – Institute of Public Relations**
   Chair, Local Government Group: Lorraine Langham (Hackney LBC)
   Membership: 5,000+, but only 250 in local government, reflecting the profession's continuing struggle for recognition in many traditionally minded councils.
   Provides, for £155 sub., free legal and accountancy service, publications, workshops, seminars, induction training, plus discounts on office equipment, etc.

Main source: R. Wynn Davies, 'Club-wielding power', *Local Government Chronicle*, 13 December 1996, pp. 12–13.

The influence of professionals can thus be considerable, especially within those policy areas where complex technical knowledge is at a premium. Once again, though, we must be cautious of generalising, for some technical professional communities have historically been distinctly more influential than others. Both Dunleavy (1980) and Laffin (1986) contrast the massive influence of local authority highways engineers and surveyors in the development of the motorway programme with the comparatively minor contribution of the still emerging housing management professions to the post-war housing boom, which was led much more by private sector construction interests and a combination of national politicians and civil servants.

Rhodes (1988, pp. 215–21) distinguishes between these more specialised 'technocratic' professions and the 'topocratic' professions of Chief Executives and Treasurers: peculiar to local government and concerned with a whole range of services within a particular geographical area. SOLACE and CIPFA, to take these two examples, have their own elaborate organisational structures and an expertise often required by central government. Flynn (1985, pp. 122 and 132–3) cites as an illustration CIPFA's role in helping to draft some of the legislation on Direct Labour Organisations (DLOs) in the early 1980s:

> Without the detailed work of CIPFA, legislation could not have been implemented. The shift of role of CIPFA was a significant one: from offering guidelines to individual treasurers on how to keep accounts to the imposition of an accounting system.

Communities of senior local authority personnel such as Chief Executives or Treasurers have a good deal of influence across the range of local government policy networks. Even looking at CIPFA, however, one must beware of exaggerating its broad policy influence. As Chandler reminds us (1988, p. 90), its major influence lies in the internal accountancy procedures of local authorities rather than determining how the government should divide its resources: 'Civil servants and ministers are normally only too pleased to leave the issues of internal local authority management to local councillors and the professions.'

Goldsmith and Newton (1986a, p. 104) argue that there is a sense in which 'the phrase "central–local government relations" is a misnomer; what the term really refers to is a set of London-based relations between central government and the national local government community'. Professional groups are an integral part of that community; over the years their contribution to policy-making has been considerable – and, it is most important to note, generally *centralist*. Rhodes (1988, p. 225) explains:

> The consequence of professional influence is the promotion of homogeneous standards, not local diversity. Their locus in policy networks places them in, if

by origin they are not of, the centre. The outcome is centralization by aggregation of interests and nationalization of standards; the source is the professionals employed by sub-central organizations.

■ The local quangocracy – non-elected hierarchies of power

The world of local government, as we have emphasised, comprises much more than simply *elected* local authorities. There is a range of bodies operating at the local level that are *not* directly elected, including many with no elective element at all. Invariably they have been established by the centre to tackle specific tasks locally; as such, they bypass elected local authorities and frequently come into conflict with them. The presence of such agencies not only adds to the complexity of sub-central government, it increases the influence of central government departments at local level – an especially useful device if political control at local level is different from that at the centre.

We have referred in Chapter 6 to many of these bodies that have relatively recently taken over what were previously the responsibilities of elected local councils – urban development corporations, housing action trusts, training and enterprise councils, grant maintained schools, education funding corporations, and so on. Here we have deliberately chosen to label all of them '*quangos*' – Quasi-Autonomous Non-Governmental Organisations, or, as the *Daily Telegraph* and many in local government prefer, Quite Unacceptable And Nasty Government Off-Shoots (Dynes and Walker, 1996, p. 130). Obviously conscious of this pejorative image and keen to avoid accusations of having presided over a massive expansion of unelected and arguably unaccountable government, ministers in the last Conservative Government in particular would challenge our blanket-labelling.

They prefer the term 'Non-Departmental Public Bodies' (NDPBs): bodies which have a role in the process of national government and which, though operating at arm's length from ministers, are at least in principle accountable through them to Parliament. The roles of these 'recognised' NDPBs may be variously *executive*: e.g. UDCs, HATs, the Audit Commission, the Housing Corporation; or *advisory*: e.g. the Local Government Commission, the School Teachers Review Body; or *quasi-judicial*: e.g. child-support tribunals, rent-assessment panels. Many of what we call quangos, therefore, they would describe as new NDPBs, such as UDCs and HATs, which have been created, they would claim, only because they can be demonstrated to be 'the most appropriate and cost-effective solution' to meet government requirements. They are as distinct, this argument goes, from TECs, self-governing schools, and the new police authorities as they are from local authorities, all of which have their own systems of accountability and audit.

As far as local government is concerned, though, this can seem like a distinction without much of a difference. When you have a government that is antagonistic in principle to local authorities and that defines its 'requirements' as being to 'free' services from council control, then one centrally appointed agency taking over your former responsibilities looks similar to another.

Exhibit 8.5, therefore, should be seen as a listing of what are undeniably different kinds of executive bodies, but which share in common the fact that they are effectively agents for central government carrying out government policies, and which collectively have come to be recognised as 'The Local Quango State' or sometimes 'The New Magistracy'.

The 5,200 local quangos identified by the Democratic Audit are run by well over 60,000 mainly ministerially-appointed or self-appointed 'quangocrats': almost three for every councillor, to quote the headline of one of our Chapter 2 news items. The phenomenal increase in these appointed

---

Exhibit 8.5   *The local quango state*

By 1996 there were at least ten times as many unelected
local executive quangos as there were elected councils.

Recognised executive quangos (or NDPBs)	33
incl. Urban Development Corporations	
Housing Action Trusts	
NHS Hospital Trusts	521
'Non-recognised' local executive quangos	
Careers Service Companies	91
City Technology Colleges	15
Further Education Corporations	560
Grant Maintained Schools	1,103
Higher Education Corporations	175
Housing Associations	2,565
Local Enterprise Companies	22
Police Authorities	41
Training and Enterprise Councils	81
Total local quango count	5,207
Estimated expenditure, 1994/95	£5,920 mill

Main source: Hall and Weir (1996b).

agencies has brought about on its own a massive transformation in the nature of local government – or rather, in the policy areas in which it has been carried furthest, almost a transformation *from* local government to local administration. For, as Weir and Hall point out (1994, p. 36):

> the new magistracy does not only sit locally. The boards of major high-spending national authorities – such as the Housing Corporation and its Scottish and Welsh partners, and funding agencies for schools and further education – sit at the apex of non-elected hierarchies of power which take and see through decisions of great importance for local communities. For example, the housing hierarchy in England consists of the Corporation, nine regional offices and [over 2,500] registered housing associations. This hierarchy exercises substantial powers over the provision of social housing in local areas and decides how virtually all the government's investment in public rented homes, as well as substantial private finance, should be allocated. There are similar hierarchies in health . . . further education . . . schools . . . housing in Scotland and Wales . . . and training and enterprise . . . In a comparatively brief period these unelected hierarchies have acquired spending responsibilities which begin to rival the overall expenditure of the United Kingdom's local authorities.

Many issues are raised by the nature, scale and speed of this 'nationalisation' of government at the local level. There is obviously the immense amount of ministerial patronage involved, and a concern about the partisan way in which it can potentially be exercised. There is the linked problem of relative inaccessibility: it is difficult for the public to find out the identity of quangocrats individually or how collectively they come to their decisions about the spending of our money. Since they do not have to stand for election, they do not have to produce any kind of personal or policy statement, or make themselves available to constituents. They may not even have to advertise their meetings, or open them to the public, or even in many cases make publicly available a record of these meetings or produce an annual report.

Even if, as is no doubt generally true, they are bringing valuable experience and expertise to their respective organisations, which in turn are operating with great efficiency and the utmost integrity, it is much harder for us, the public, to check this for ourselves, let alone try to hold them to account for apparent failures of performance, than it was when the same services were run by committees of elected councillors. To adapt Churchill's defence of democracy as a system of government: no one pretends that local democratic accountability is perfect; indeed, it has been said that it is the worst form of accountability . . . except all those other forms that have been tried from time to time. It would be putting words into the great man's mouth to suggest that this would include responsiveness to the market as a *substitute for*, rather than a vital part of, democratic accountability. Better to leave it to the Democratic Audit, who argue (Weir and Hall, 1994, p. 12) that the citizen as consumer is a poor substitute for the citizen as elector: 'who is entitled to choose who runs her or his services, to participate and be consulted in the way they are run, and to know what decisions are being taken in her or his name'.

■ Local ombudsmen – or ombudsmice?

There are, as we have seen, many ways in which local quangos differ from elected councils. We have statutory rights of access to council and committee meetings and to background papers. Councils are obliged to publish locally both auditors' criticisms of their policies and spending and, as we noted in Chapter 7, specified sets of performance indicators. Councils are also, unlike all the 'non-recognised' local quangos in Exhibit 8.5, subject to the scrutiny of, somewhat ironically, another national quango called the Commission for Local Administration (CLA) or, slightly more familiarly, the Local (Government) Ombudsman. It is yet one more body in the national world of British local government.

The CLA and the separate commissions in Wales and Scotland were first appointed in 1974/75, following the creation of a national ombudsman, the Parliamentary Commissioner for Administration, in 1967. It is probably fair to say that neither nationally nor locally have these institutions had as significant an impact on the country's government as their early advocates hoped or as several of their European and especially Scandinavian counterparts have. A 1995 MORI survey revealed, for example, that under one-third of non-white ethnic minority citizens were even aware of the existence of the CLA. The Commission admits its concern that awareness is not higher, and indeed there has recently been serious consideration given to replacing the present form of Commission with a rather less cumbersome system for investigating the undeniably increasing volume of citizens' complaints of council maladministration.

That is what Britain's local ombudsmen do, and that is the limit of their jurisdiction: they investigate written complaints from the public about injustice caused by *maladministration* on the part of their local councils, and also police and fire authorities, joint boards, UDCs and HATs. They do not initiate their own investigations. Nor do they deal with any complaints about the actual policy of a council: if you dislike that, you can complain to the councillors themselves and perhaps try to vote them out of office. The ombudsman is concerned solely with the way in which policy is administered – for example, the speed, efficiency, fairness and propriety with which it was implemented in your particular case.

The ombudsmen will accept such complaints either directly from aggrieved citizens themselves or via their local councillor. If a complaint falls within their jurisdiction, they will normally then get the local authority concerned to respond in detail and do everything possible to bring about some local settlement, before embarking, in only a small minority of cases, on a much more exhaustive investigation resulting in a final report and published judgement of whether or not maladministration and injustice have been found. If so, the ombudsman will look to the local authority for some form of satisfactory action: an apology, financial compensation, a change of procedure in dealing with future cases. Usually acceptable action will be forthcoming, but on occasion a council will continue to dispute and resist the ombudsman's judgement, whereupon the latter is left with little sanction beyond the production of a second critical public report.

There are, then, grounds for suggesting that ultimately we are dealing here with 'Ombudsmice', the fairness of the label depending on whether you attach more weight to the exceptional case than to the generality. It can hardly be disputed that the CLA nowadays does much valuable work. In both 1995 and 1996, for instance, the three English Commissioners alone received over 15,000 complaints – compared with an average of around 1,000 p.a. by the Parliamentary Commisioner – the main subjects, as always, being housing (37.5 per cent) and planning (22 per cent), followed by education and council tax (7 per cent each). In roughly 97 per cent of these complaints investigation was not pursued beyond the stage of obtaining the authority's comments, but the remaining 3 per cent resulted in well over 400 full formal reports each year, with findings like those illustrated in Exhibit 8.6.

A serious problem, though, can be discerned from a study of the reference numbers of the cases summarised in Exhibit 8.6. These reports, all published in 1995/96, dealt with complaints that first reached the ombudsman at least a year previously, and indeed the average waiting period nowadays for a formal investigation decision has risen to some 72 weeks. For an institution employing nearly 200 staff at a cost of £7 million that finds maladministration and injustice in only 3½ per cent of all the cases it handles, and that even then cannot enforce any redress, such delays almost inevitably provoke criticism.

As suggested above, alternative and more streamlined procedures have been proposed, particularly by those who argue that since 1974 councils' own internal complaints systems, their responsiveness to complaints, and their general customer orientation have improved immeasurably and that an ombudsman-quality sledgehammer is no longer needed to crack these proverbial nuts of alleged maladministration. Better, such critics assert, to set up a more localised procedure of investigation, based on councils' own complaint systems and overseen by council-funded but genuinely independent local adjudicators, with a very much smaller-scale Commission acting as a central monitoring body. Another idea, of course, would be to extend its jurisdiction to take in at least some of the proliferating local quangos.

Exhibit 8.6   *Findings of maladministration*

A selection of 1995/96 decisions in which the local ombudsmen found there to have been maladministration and injustice.

Blackburn BC (91/C/3521)
The council failed to inspect a house to see if it was unfit and therefore eligible for a renovation grant. To remedy the injustice the council inspected the property and processed the grant application.

Havant BC (94/B/1895)
The council failed to investigate complaints of a homeless couple that the temporary bed and breakfast accommodation in which they and their baby had been placed was unsuitable. It also failed to notify them of the council's 'damage deposits' scheme which could have helped them find private sector accommodation. The council paid the couple £1,250 compensation and published an advice leaflet for homeless applicants.

Trafford MBC (94/C/1707)
A boy lost the chance of a place at a grammar school through lack of proof of residence which could have been provided, had the council informed his parents that it was necesssary. The council paid £750 compensation and agreed to review its instructions to admissions staff in its education department.

Kirklees MBC (93/C/3209)
The council failed properly to notify a complainant of a planning applicat-ion for a large extension to commercial premises next to his home, and also failed to detect an error in the relative heights of the two buildings in the submitted plans. The complainant was paid £8,500 in recognition of the drop in value of his home, plus £250 for his time and trouble.

Berkshire CC (93/B/2569)
The council failed to obtain a temporary road closure order when it closed a road in order to undertake repairs in a village, thereby denying the complainant the opportunity to object and take action to safeguard his business. The council apologised and paid £300 in compensation.

Newcastle upon Tyne City C (94/C/1209)
A man applied for a loan to help him start a business. The council incorrectly sent him a letter refusing the application when it had in fact been approved, as the result of which the man incurred the expense of a commercial loan. The council paid him £600 compensation.

Source: The Commission for Local Administration in England (1996).

■ The European dimension – more than just funding

This final section differs from the remainder of the chapter in at least two significant ways. Most obviously, we move from the national to the supra-national world of local government. But, in doing so, we are also moving outside the increasingly constrained central–local relationship that has concerned us throughout Chapters 7 and 8. For, as Pycroft suggests (1995, p. 20):

> As local authorities have faced increased restrictions on their activities imposed by the centre, they have started to enjoy greater opportunities presented by the deepening and widening of the European Union.

Inevitably, local authorities' responses to these opportunities have varied enormously. On the one hand, there are still plenty that, notwithstanding the almost daily evidence to the contrary, continue to regard themselves as remote from EU affairs and are disinclined to seek either funding or policy dialogue. But there are also authorities – predominantly the counties and metropolitan districts in the so-called 'assisted areas' – that have long been benefiting financially from European funding, who have a core of both senior officers and members concentrating on European issues, and that are active members of several of the inter-authority networks, partnerships and consortia that have sprung up.

Some of this networking activity derives no doubt from a genuine commitment on the part of those concerned to the ideals of European integration and harmonisation. But the motive force in the great majority of cases is inevitably funding. To paraphrase Bill Clinton's identification of the economy as far and away the most important issue in the 1992 Presidential Election, 'it's the money, stupid!' (see Exhibit 8.7).

Welcome as such funding is, particularly to councils facing tight nationally imposed restrictions on their capital investment programmes, it is but one aspect of the multifaceted impact of the European Single Market and related legislation on British local authorities and their services. Bongers, in his book-length study of *Local Government in the Single European Market* (1992), illustrates with three distinct headings:

1. *Organisational impacts* – those affecting the ways in which local authorities operate as large public sector organisations and employers: e.g. the removal of barriers against competition for public contracts that has enabled French and Spanish firms to compete successfully for some councils' refuse collection and street cleansing contracts; the freedom of movement of people that has enabled councils to recruit teachers, social workers and other scarce professionals from countries such as Germany, the Netherlands and Ireland.

Exhibit 8.7   *European liaison: 'it's the money, stupid'*

Sources and some recent examples of EU funding received by UK local authorities:

A.   Structural Funds

1. European Regional Development Fund (ERDF)
The main structural fund, available to specified geographical regions for projects such as economic regeneration, business support and tourism development.
e.g. Birmingham City C – £3.1 million for city centre development and pedestrianisation programme
Strathclyde Regional C – £16.5 million for assistance to industry, the environment and tourism
Nottingham City C (+ Nottingham Health Authority) – £870,000 for improvement to former general hospital site in city centre.

2. European Social Fund (ESF)
Aimed at reducing unemployment through counselling, training and job creation schemes.
e.g. Cheshire CC – £750,000 for training schemes, including IT programme for young people
Luton/Dunstable – £1 million to council/private sector partnership for training programmes for ethnic minorities, women returners, disabled, homeless and long-term unemployed.

3. Community Initiatives
Designed for specific objectives identified by the EU.
e.g. £1.1 million to public/private Hampshire Business Liaison Group for region hit by reduction in defence spending
Newcastle City C – £375,000 under EMPLOYMENT initiative to establish Newcastle Women's Network.

B.   Non-structural Funds
Generally smaller grants, not geographically restricted, for education, training and exchange, cultural, environmental and social projects.
e.g. Liverpool City C – £500,000 under POVERTY III programme to tackle problems of racism and poverty
Southwark LBC – £204,000 under LIFE innovative environment programme for project to measure pollution generated by car exhaust emissions.

Main source: Local Government Management Board, *Guide to Europe* (1996).

2. *Impacts on specific services* – e.g. the establishment of a system of mutual recognition of professional and training qualifications by member states; the succession of environmental action programmes – including the fifth and latest: *Towards Sustainability, 1993–2000* – taking the form of legislation, directives, financial incentives and public awareness programmes; the series of directives on control of hazardous waste, affecting councils' use of landfill sites for waste disposal; the 'blue flag' award scheme aimed at improving the environmental quality of beaches.

3. *Socio-economic impacts* – the wider effects of European integration upon a local authority's area and people as a result of changes taking place in the area's trade and industry, e.g. the concentration of EU structural funding on objectively defined regions of economic disadvantage and above-average unemployment, such as Northern Ireland, Strathclyde and Central Scotland, the North East of England, etc.

Whatever the UK's future role in the EU, short of complete withdrawal, the European dimension – through its combination of funding, regulation and economic integration – seems destined to assume a steadily more prominent place in the day-to-day workings of local authorities, whether they welcome the prospect or not.

■ Conclusion

This chapter has moved us beyond seeing central–local relationships purely in Whitehall–English local authority terms. The diversity and complexity of the national local government system in the UK have emerged: a system which comprises far more than simply Whitehall-based ministries and elected local authorities, and a system set to become even more diverse with the advent of devolution to both Scotland and Wales. We have seen, indeed, that even the term 'national' local government system is becoming something of a misnomer. As we refocus our attention in the coming chapters on the finances, politics and management of mainly individual authorities, it is important to keep in mind these broader dimensions of local governance.

Guide to further reading

Rhodes must again be counted a chief contributor to our understanding of the workings of the national world of local government (1986a), though 'national' in this instance means exclusively England and Wales. His later volume (1988) on the sub-central governments of Britain, contains useful introductions to the 'territorial ministries' in Scotland, Wales and Northern Ireland. For a fuller account of arrangements in Scotland, see Kellas (1989) and Midwinter *et al.* (1991), and in Northern Ireland Knox (1989) and Connolly (1990). On the local authority associations (and also professionalism) there is the ubiquitous Rhodes (1988) and, for a slightly earlier account, Isaac-Henry (1984). Laffin is wholly or partially responsible for two of the only book-length treatments of professionalism in local government (Laffin, 1986; Laffin and Young, 1990). The local quango explosion since 1990 has produced almost an equal explosion of 'quango-hunt' literature, some of the more noteworthy examples being Hall and Weir's work (1996a) for the Democratic Audit, Stewart *et al.* (1995), and Davis (1996). Bongers, then Director of the Local Government International Bureau, produced what remains a most authoritative guide to the 'European dimension' (Bongers, 1992).

■ *Chapter 9* ■

Finance – The Nuts and Bolts

■ Introduction

In the final two chapters of Part 1 we look in more depth at some of those topics we have so far just mentioned in passing – government grants, the council tax and its predecessors: rates and the community charge, capping – and then set them in comparative and recent historical context. It is a two-part exercise; hence the two chapters.

In this chapter we introduce the basic elements of the local government finance system and the budget-making process. We do so from your perspective: that of an aware, service-receiving, tax-paying citizen. Specifically, we seek to provide you with the information necessary to interpret your own council tax demand and to understand the main decisions that produced it. We shall apply the kind of 'need to know' test that might be used by an American Presidential adviser concerned to protect the President's integrity: if you don't need to know, we won't trouble you with the details. But if there is a risk of your being embarrassed – in your case as either an examinee or local taxpayer – our information should help you avoid it.

In Chapter 10 we look back at the immediate past and at how some other countries run their local government finance, and we relax slightly our 'need to know' test. It may not be absolutely imperative for you to know about abandoned, abolished and alternative ways of financing local government. But the recent history of local financial reform has been so exceptional, so dramatic, and of such national political significance, that it demands more than merely fleeting acknowledgement. The poll tax* alone – arguably British government's single biggest policy disaster of the past 50 years:

> contributed to an exchange of Prime Ministers;
> introduced a culture of non-payment not seen before;
> split society in its evenhandedness towards duke and dustman;
> wasted billions of public £s and months of council work;
> clogged the courts; and caused widespread civil unrest.
> (*Local Government Chronicle*, 2 April 1993)

---

* In these two finance chapters, as elsewhere in the book, we refer sometimes to the community charge by its official name and sometimes, where it seems more appropriate, to the name by which it came almost universally to be known: the poll tax.

A phenomenon of this political, economic, social, fiscal and judicial magnitude merits its own chronicle, and receives it in Chapter 10.

■ Your own tax bill

It is with the council tax – introduced in April 1993 – that we start this chapter. Specifically, we suggest you look at your own council tax bill and at the accompanying explanatory information sent out by your local council – particularly the details of the council's budget. If, perhaps as a student, you have no tax bill of your own, try to borrow one. Alternatively, if, as we suggested in Chapter 1, you have been able to obtain a copy of your council's Annual Report, you should find it contains a summary of the annual accounts and budget – though in this case it will be the budget for the previous financial year, not the current one.

At the foot of your tax bill – the bottom line figure – will be the amount that you personally or your household are required to pay. In this chapter we shall explain, using Birmingham City Council's 1996/97 budget for illustration, how that bottom line figure has been calculated. You will find, though, that your council has already provided its own explanation, in the various additional leaflets it sent out with the bill. These may include:

* the budget and spending plans of the council that actually sent you the bill (the 'billing authority') – district, borough and unitary councils;
* the separate budgets and spending plans of councils entitled to have the billing authority collect tax monies on their behalf ('precepting authorities') – counties and possibly parish, town and community councils;
* the separate budgets and spending plans of other authorities entitled to have the billing authority collect tax monies on their behalf – the police authorities and metropolitan joint fire and civil defence and passenger transport authorities;
* Explanatory Notes from the Treasurer's or Finance Department of the billing authority, detailing possible methods of payment, appeal procedures, discounts and benefit entitlements – often translated into relevant foreign languages.

If you cannot recall having received such literature about the government's spending plans last time the Inland Revenue sent you an Income Tax Return, that is understandable, for you will not have done. It is one of the many ways in which local authorities are considerably more open and accountable than central government chooses to be.

■ Capital and current spending

If we turn first not to the tax bill itself but to the accompanying budget leaflet, it will be clear that we need to start with one or two basic definitions.

> *BUDGET* – a statement defining a council's policies over a specified period of time in terms of finance.

The reference to a 'specified period of time' is obviously crucial. We instinctively think of budgets as annual events, but an organisation like a local authority, spending perhaps several hundred million pounds each year, cannot possibly afford to think only of the short term. It must try, as best it can, to forecast the future and plan ahead. The first thing to note, therefore, about any council's budget is its division into *current* and *capital* expenditure.

Far more of local government's spending goes on current running costs than on capital investment: about eight times as much nowadays, as can be seen in Exhibit 9.1. This gap has widened in recent years, chiefly as the result of central government's steady pressure on local authorities to limit their capital spending.

> *CURRENT (also known as revenue) EXPENDITURE* – the day-to-day spending needed to keep services running: staff wages and salaries, books for schools, office equipment, petrol for refuse collection vehicles, heating bills in children's homes, etc.
>
> *CAPITAL EXPENDITURE* – spending which produces longer-term assets, often expensive, but whose benefits will last beyond the next financial year: purchase of land, construction of buildings and roads, major items of equipment.

The total expenditure figures at the foot of Exhibit 9.1 give an indication of the scale and national economic significance of local government in the mid-1990s. The £75 billion service expenditure represented roughly a quarter of the country's total government spending of nearly £300 billion, about 11p in every £ of its £700 billion Gross Domestic Product, and some £1,340 for every single resident. In Scotland especially, and also in Wales, that last per capita figure would be even higher; in Northern Ireland much, much lower, since the Northern Ireland Office, a central government department, is directly responsible for many of the functions carried out by local authorities elsewhere in Great Britain.

	Capital (%)	Current (%)	Total (%)
Exhibit 9.1 *Local authority spending 1995/96: capital vs. current*			
Education (inc. school catering)	10	35	33
Housing (inc. rent rebates)	42	16	18
Local environmental services (inc. refuse collection and disposal, environmental health, planning and economic development, etc.)	11	16	16
Law, order and protective services	5	13	12
Personal social services	3	11	11
Transport and roads	20	5	7
Sport and recreation	2	1	1
Arts and libraries	1	1	1
Other services	6	2	2
Total UK (£ billion, 1995/96)	£67 bn	£8 bn	£75 bn

Source: DoE (1996), p. 10.

The percentage figures in Exhibit 9.1 demonstrate the still dominant positions of education and housing in the authorities that have responsibility for these services, though that dominance declined under the Conservatives as schools opted for grant maintained status (GMS) and direct central government funding, and council housing has been transferred to private ownership and housing association or private sector management. The contrasting character of these two major services can be seen in the first two columns of Exhibit 9.1: education being labour intensive and housing exceptionally capital intensive.

The current spending of local authorities understandably receives the bulk of both councillors' and citizens' attention. It will be our chief concern too for most of the remainder of this chapter. But we should look first at councils' capital spending programmes, for they are the embodiment of any council's longer-term political and strategic objectives. They necessarily have to be financed in very different ways from current spending; and, once started, they can have major implications for subsequent years' current budgets.

■ Financing capital spending

We mentioned above how central government has sought, especially in recent years, to regulate local authorities' capital spending. The precise form of that regulation has changed frequently, the present system being essentially the one introduced in the Local Government and Housing Act 1989. It is based on the tough but familiar principle of *credit control*, the aim being to control all local authority capital expenditure financed by credit in one form or another. To appreciate the comprehensiveness of the system we should bear in mind that there are in fact four main methods of capital financing, three of which are directly subject to central government control.

☐ *Borrowing up to a prescribed credit ceiling*

Each year, every local council is given by the government a permission to borrow, or *Basic Credit Approval* (BCA). The BCA specifies the *maximum sum* the council can borrow to finance capital projects in education, housing, social services and various other services. In addition, a council may be given a *Supplementary Credit Approval* (SCA) for specific, government-approved projects and initiatives concerning, for example, magistrates courts, roads, rural housing and homelessness.

These credit approvals (known as net capital allocations in Scotland) account nowadays for well over half of all local authority capital investment. They permit a council to borrow from any of several available sources: from a government agency like the Public Works Loan Board (PWLB), from a British or European bank, or by issuing stocks, bonds and annuities. So a local authority may have more borrowing options open to it than we do as private citizens, but it too will have to pay the going rate of interest and repay any loan by its expiry date.

☐ *Using capital receipts*

Councils may supplement their BCAs and SCAs by using money they raise by selling assets such as land, buildings and housing. Again, though, there are usually government-prescribed limits. For most of the 1990s councils were able to use for new investment a maximum of:

* 25 per cent of receipts from housing sales, and
* 50 per cent of receipts from the disposal of other assets.

Remaining receipts, said the Conservative Government, were to be used to pay off outstanding debts. One of the Blair Government's first bills, however, the Local Government Finance (Supplementary Credit Approvals) Bill, promised greater flexibility by allowing local authorities to reinvest up to £5 billion of their accumulated receipts from council house sales in building new homes and renovating old ones.

☐ *Through capital grants*

The government, chiefly through its inner city Urban Programme, and the European Union, through, for example, the European Regional Development Fund, give grants towards the financing of specific projects. These grants can be substantial and crucial to the viability of major developments – such as Birmingham's new £180 million International Convention Centre and Symphony Hall, some £50 million of which came from the EU. But here too there are likely to be conditions: receipt of certain grants may simply lead to the government reducing a council's credit approval by an equivalent amount.

☐ *Using current (revenue) income*

The one source of capital finance available to a council which is not subject to direct government control is its own revenue income – from local taxes, rents, and other charges. But in a period of financial constraint that freedom may seem like the freedom we all have to dine at the Ritz: the many more immediate calls on a council's government-capped revenue budget are likely to appear more practically and politically insistent.

■ The capital budget

In summary, then, a local authority's capital spending will be shaped by the following formula:

> Its Basic Credit Approved spending,
> *plus* any Supplementary Credit Approved spending,
> *plus* the usable parts of its capital receipts,
> *plus* any capital grants,
> *plus* any revenue-financed spending.

As we have seen, the government now sets most of the effective *ceilings*. But councils must choose for themselves whether to spend up to the limit of their credit approval, and whether to top that limit up with other permitted sources of finance. Capital budget profiles will accordingly vary considerably from council to council, and also from one year to the next. Biggest spending heads, depending on your council's location, size and responsibilities, are likely to be housing and urban renewal – improvements to its own housing stock plus grants for private sector renovations and improvements – followed, usually some way behind, by highways, education, leisure and social services. Details of your own council's main capital projects should be itemised in its budget; also its principal sources of capital finance (see Exhibit 9.2). So you should be

---

Exhibit 9.2 *Birmingham City Council's capital budget, 1996/97*

Major projects

HOUSING/URBAN RENEWAL (£73 million)
* £23 million on major council estate revitalisation (Estate Action) programmes
* £16 million to provide central heating and replacement windows in council homes
* £6 million for grants to individuals to improve unfit housing
* £2 million for grants to provide aids and adaptations in the homes of people with disabilities

HIGHWAYS (£40 million)
* £21 million on the new Heartlands Spine Road (see Exhibit 6.2)
* £4 million on new schemes for strengthening roads

EDUCATION (£9 million)
* £9 million, mainly on school improvements and extensions

OTHER (£32 million)
* £7 million for major improvements to the Victoria Law Courts

Major sources of funding

* £55 m (36%) Borrowing
* £53 m (34%) Capital grants
* £31 m (20%) Council's own revenue and reserves
* £15 m (10%) Capital receipts and other contributions

---

able to compare for yourself the probably very limited funding by local taxation with the figures for borrowing under credit approval and for types of capital grants.

■ Current or revenue spending

How much is to be spent? On what? Where is the money coming from? The three fundamental questions we have just asked of our council's capital budget are similarly applicable to its considerably larger current or revenue budget. In fact, the answers should be more easily obtainable, for the main purpose of the tax demand literature is to set out and explain the council's revenue budget: its planned expenditure on the day-to-day provision of services for the coming financial year. Yours may be one of the enterprising councils which nowadays seek to present such information in as eye-catching a manner as possible, with an imaginative use of illustrative diagrams and graphics.

But, however they are presented, you should encounter some figures set out under service or committee headings that will resemble those of Birmingham City Council in Exhibit 9.3, even if the figures themselves are on a very different scale. In order to interpret them, two further definitions are immediately required.

GROSS SPENDING – the total cost of providing the council's services, *before* taking into account rents, fees and charges for services, and income from government grants.

NET SPENDING – gross spending *minus* income from rents, fees and charges and from *specific* government grants for particular projects or services – e.g. towards rent rebates and allowances, mandatory student awards.

We can see from the first column of Exhibit 9.3 that Birmingham City Council proposed to spend a total of £1.8 billion on its day-to-day service provision in 1996/97. Even after the transfer of further education and sixth form colleges out of local authority control and the opting-out of some of its secondary schools, almost a third of the council's *gross* spending and half of its net spending goes on education, with roughly 60 per cent of that sum on teachers' salaries. Next biggest net spender, similarly labour intensive, is social services, with a clientele in Birmingham of over 50,000 children, elderly and disabled people. These services derive respectively about one-eighth and one-fifth of their income from service charges and specific grants for designated purposes, such as student grants, social services training, the treatment of mental illness and AIDS.

By comparison, nearly 95 per cent of Birmingham's housing expenditure is met by income, much of it from rents on the council's massive housing stock of over 100,000 dwellings. But the council also receives sizeable specific grants from the government for administering on its behalf what is essentially a national housing subsidy scheme: similar to the provision of LEA mandatory student grants, though in this case the payment takes the form of rent rebates and allowances to low-income tenants. As a result of these two major sources of income – rents and government subsidies – Birmingham's *net* revenue spending on housing is lower than might be expected of what used – before smallness became beautiful and bigness unfashionable – to proclaim itself Western Europe's largest landlord.

Exhibit 9.3 Birmingham City Council's revenue budget, 1996/97

MAJOR SERVICES (by Committee)	GROSS EXPENDITURE		INCOME	NET EXPENDITURE		
	1996/97 (£m)	% of total	from charges and specific grants	1996/97 (£m)	Change from 1995/96 (£m)	% of total
EDUCATION (150,000 pupils, 400+ Schools)	562	31	69	493	+12	50
SOCIAL SERVICES	236	13	48	188	+11	19
FINANCE AND MANAGEMENT (central services – finance, procurement, personnel, PR, IT)	164	9	88	76	+7	8
LEISURE SERVICES (swimming pools, parks, leisure centres, libraries)	74	4	9	65	–3	7
TRANSPORTATION AND TECHNICAL SERVICES (road maintenance, street lighting, traffic planning)	72	4	10	62	+1	7
ENVIRONMENTAL SERVICES (street cleaning, public health, trading standards)	37	2	11	26	–1	3
HOUSING AND URBAN RENEWAL	474	26	450	24	–3	2
PLANNING AND ECONOMIC DEVELOPMENT (controlling development, attracting investment)	45	3	26	19	–2	2
OTHER SERVICES (inc. NEC/ICC, General Purposes)	136	8	111	25	+17	2
Plus: contingency	3			3		
TOTAL EXPENDITURE	1803	100	822	981	+39	100
Less: contribution from balances				(10)		
COUNCIL'S NET BUDGET REQUIREMENT				971		

■ Levies and precepts

Identifying the council's net spending requirements is but the first step in the determination of an individual's local tax bill. To the services listed in Exhibit 9.3, provided by the City Council itself, must be added those services provided for Birmingham residents by bodies that cannot themselves directly demand and collect local taxes. In Birmingham – and the other six districts in the former West Midlands Metropolitan County Council area – there are three such bodies:

1. *The West Midlands Police Authority* – formerly a joint board, but now a separate Authority, half of whose members are councillors nominated by the West Midlands district councils and the other half local magistrates and nominees of the Home Secretary. As do all police authorities, it receives a direct central government grant equivalent to half of its net revenue expenditure.
2. *The West Midlands Fire and Civil Defence Authority* – like the Passenger Transport Authority, a joint board of nominated district councillors.
3. *The West Midlands Passenger Transport Authority* – the largest slice of whose revenue budget provides free bus and rail travel for senior citizens and concessionary fares for children and school students.

Just like the City Council, all these bodies have their own capital and revenue budgets, funded in part through a combination of loans, grants, capital receipts and revenue income. But they also finance some of their revenue expenditure by means of a *precept* or *levy* on their tax-collecting district authorities, divided amongst them according to their population size. These latter councils are thus required to collect from their local taxpayers, in addition to their own tax demands, these other monies and then hand them straight over to the various precepting and levying authorities.

Birmingham's *total* net revenue requirement consequently includes over £60 million which it has to collect but over which it has no direct control. As may be imagined, this obligation can be distinctly irritating to city councillors, who have to take the political responsibility and blame for a tax level, part of which they can hardly even indirectly influence. But their irritation is mild compared to that of some of their shire district council colleagues, who have to collect a county council precept that may amount to almost 90 per cent of their total tax demands, plus, in some cases, an additional few pounds in parish council precepts which, just to add to their frustration, are not even capped.

One of the sources of tension in our present two-tier system of local government is that in non-metropolitan England and Wales it is not the counties – with their bigger spending education, social services and transport responsibilities – that are designated billing and tax-collecting authorities, but the much smaller and inevitably lower spending district councils (see Exhibit 6.1). This position, you may be sure, will be emphasised by district councils in their explanatory budget literature. Just look, they will say, at all the housing, leisure, environmental and community services we provide to enhance your quality of life, and all for perhaps £50 per person or under £1 per week.

■ Financing current spending

There are two final 'technical' adjustments to be made to the spending side of our council's current account. It has to be decided how much to set aside for any unforeseen items of expenditure, known as 'contingencies', and how much to keep as balances or reserves. With those adjustments made, Birmingham City Council's total net spending requirement for 1996/97 amounted to a formidable £971 million: not far short of £1,000 per resident. The obvious next question: how is it to be found?

There is a certain symmetry to British local government finance. Just as there are four main methods of raising capital finance, there are four main ways of financing current or revenue expenditure.

□ *Charges*

Local authorities have always set fees and charges for the use of some of their services – passenger transport, car parks, home helps, school meals, swimming baths and other leisure facilities. They also, as noted above, collect council rents. In Birmingham's case these charges, taken together, meet over a fifth (21 per cent) of the council's gross current expenditure. Since the Local Government and Housing Act 1989, councils have been able, if they wish, to introduce charges for any of their services except for education, the police and fire services, elections, and library book borrowing. This extension of charging was a key element in the Conservative Government's programme to increase local accountability by making consumers more directly aware of the cost and value of the services they receive.

Most charges are discretionary, councils deciding for themselves what they wish to charge or what they feel the market will bear. They can try to encourage the use of a service, like adult education classes or day nurseries, by setting a *social* charge, below the full cost of provision. They can just cover the provision cost; impose a *means-related* charge based on ability to pay, as for some residential homes; or a *market* charge to maximise profit. Finally, they can try to limit the use of certain services, such as city centre car parks or cemetery burials, by imposing a *deterrent* charge.

Such decisions – whether or not to subsidise a particular service, by how much and in what way, or whether to try to maximise profit – raise some of the most fundamental of all political questions, and they offer councillors a ready-made subject for debate whenever charges and a council's charging policy come up for review. Different economic, social and political objectives will be argued, and sometimes intriguing policy decisions taken, as can be seen in Exhibit 9.4.

It is always enlightening to compare your own personal experience – the cost of your LEA's school meals, for example – with that of others. You might also question why it should be that Kent's meals-on-wheels service recently cost twice as much as Staffordshire's and over four times that in Derbyshire; why the hire of a squash court should have been twice as expensive in Castle Point as in neighbouring Basildon; and, without being too morbid, how and why a burial in Brent could be

---

Exhibit 9.4   *Examples of local authority discretionary charges*

Meals on Wheels		*Hire of squash court*		*Cemetery burials*	
Standard charge per meal – County Councils		Charge per hour – District Councils		Charge for adult interment – London Boroughs and Metropolitan District Councils	
	(£)		(£)		(£)
Kent	1.50	Ellesmere Port (Cheshire)	8.70	Lambeth	300
Hampshire	1.30	Castle Point (Essex)	7.35	Bexley	283
West Sussex	1.30	Dartford (Kent)	7.80	Barnet	198
Notts	0.80	Basildon (Essex)	3.10	Enfield	58
Staffs	0.75	Forest of Dean (Gloucs)	3.00	Knowsley	39
Derbyshire	0.35	Bolsover (Derbys)	2.20	Brent	27

Source: CIPFA (Chartered Institute of Public Finance and Accountancy), *Statistical Information Service*.

'undertaken' at a fourteenth of the cost of one in Lambeth. The differences in these completely discretionary service charges are, as you might expect, at least as great as the substantial variations in per capita expenditure and performance that we noted in Exhibits 7.4 and 7.5. No matter what possible explanations you come up with, it is difficult to argue from these figures at least that local councils have been stripped of all their powers of decision and discretion.

☐ *Government grants*

Grants, like charges, have long been an integral and indispensable feature of local government finance, although, as we shall see in Chapter 10, their nature, role and scale have all changed significantly in recent years. Focusing on the budget process, we shall be concentrating mainly on one particular grant: the Revenue Support Grant (RSG). There are, however, numerous other grants paid by central government to local authorities, and almost as many different reasons for paying them. The two most fundamental purposes of grants, though, are compensation and persuasion.

Compensation takes a variety of forms: compensation to local councils, for instance, for providing certain basic services that are acknowledged to be in the public interest and for which, therefore, local taxpayers should not be required to foot the whole bill, such as LEA-administered mandatory student grants.

Councils may be compensated too for their varying spending needs and taxable resources. The rationale behind the Revenue Support Grant is that local authorities should be able, and be given grant incentives, to provide a common standard of service at broadly the same cost to local taxpayers across the whole country. Another example of a compensatory grant was provided by the Community Charge Reduction Scheme, which from 1991 transferred part of the burden of the charge – both fiscal and political – from local to national taxpayers.

The *persuasion* motive for grants can be seen as a straightforward wish by central government to influence or control some aspect of local council spending – in accordance with the principle that she or he who pays the piper expects to call the tune. Grants can be used to promote spending on certain services, to enforce minimum standards, to encourage councils to implement central government policy initiatives, and generally to push them in directions in which they would not necessarily otherwise go.

It ought to be the case that the principal purpose of a grant will suggest its most efficient form, and that a grant's form will imply its purpose. We need therefore to distinguish between the two basic forms of grant – specific and general – to match our two fundamental purposes.

SPECIFIC GRANTS (also sometimes known as *selective* or *conditional grants*) – government grants to local authorities whose proceeds must be spent on some specified project or service – e.g. social services training grant, Welsh language education grant. In 1996/97 specific grants in total accounted for nearly 30 per cent of central government support for local government.

GENERAL GRANTS (also known as *non-selective* or *unconditional grants*) – grants whose proceeds may be spent at the discretion of the grantees, local councils themselves. The general grant to local government – now known as the Revenue Support Grant – was over £22 billion in 1996/97, equivalent to nearly 40 per cent of total central government support.

The distinction between the two grant forms is important, to both central government grantor and local authority grantee. If persuasion and influence are the government's objectives, it will presumably opt for a specific grant, and define its purpose as precisely as possible. If compensation is the objective, or the retention of the maximum degree of local financial discretion, then a general grant is the logical choice. The specific:general grant ratio can thus serve as a rough and ready indicator of central government financial control. That we have seen a steady trend in recent years towards specific grants is not, as we shall argue in the next chapter, coincidental.

You will recall from Exhibit 9.3 that, together with its income from fees and charges, the *specific* grants received by Birmingham City Council were taken into account in translating the city's gross spending to a net spending requirement. We come now, therefore, to the council's single largest source of current income: a general grant known since 1990 as the *Revenue Support Grant* (RSG).

The annual RSG distribution process takes the public form of a series of government announcements, concentrated nowadays in the late autumn at the time of the Chancellor of the Exchequer's budget speech, or less than six months before the start of the new financial year. First, the government decides how much money in total local authorities will be permitted to spend during the coming year – their *Total Standard Spending* (TSS). Secondly, it declares the proportion of that total spending that it will finance through national taxation, or *Aggregate External Finance* (AEF), (just under 80 per cent in 1996/97), and, by implication, the proportion that local authorities collectively will have to find for themselves (roughly 20 per cent in 1996/97).

The government then turns its attention from the aggregate to the individual authority level. It produces an assessment of what it feels each authority needs to spend – both in total and in each of seven principal service areas – in order to provide what it defines as a 'standard level of service'. These figures constitute a council's *Standard Spending Assessment* (SSA) and are absolutely critical in determining the level of grant it will receive. The government bases its calculations on a limited range of indicators, such as the total residential population of the council area, the number of people aged over 65 living alone, the number of school children aged 5–10. If it over-estimates a council's spending needs, the council will receive in effect a grant subsidy; if it under-estimates, council tax bills must rise or services be cut.

From the council's total SSA two deductions are made: first for the total income the government estimates the authority should receive, were it to set its council tax at a specified standard level – the *Council Tax at Standard Spending* (CTSS); secondly, for the income it will receive from the government-set *National Non-Domestic Rate* (NNDR). A council's Revenue Support Grant is the figure remaining after these deductions.

Expressed as a formula:

$$RSG = SSA - (CTSS + NNDR)$$

where   SSA   is the government's aggregated assessment of a council's spending needs;

        CTSS   is the government's assessment of a council's income from its council tax payers at a specified standard tax level;

and   NNDR   is a council's population-based income from its National Non-Domestic Ratepayers at a government-set rate.

Clearly, this grant distribution process incorporates both of the fundamental purposes of grants. It seeks to compensate authorities with above average spending needs, but within a system based on the government imposing its judgement of what these authorities ought to be doing and how much of it they should be doing.

For their part, local authorities – of all political complexions – protest and plead. They protest at the presumption of ministers and their Whitehall civil servants claiming to know better than do they themselves and their local electorates what should be spent on different services. They protest at the government's methodology – its choice of indicators, its use of unreliable and outdated information – and at the consequential anomalies. Could it really have been the case, to pick one notorious example, that there was more snow on the ground at 9.00 a.m. for more days each year – and thus higher winter road maintenance costs – in Brent than in Cumbria, and in Camden than in Lancashire? (LGIU, 1993, p. 37).

Councils protest too at the distribution of grant: that the total is inadequate and fails fully to take account of the prevailing inflation rate; that the whole process is political; and that the wrong authorities have gained and lost. And they will plead – though rarely with marked success – their exceptional local circumstances which, they claim, the government's formulae fail to recognise and which merit special treatment.

Cornwall is a typical protester; that is, it is typical in its protestations that it is *not* typical of, for instance, the other English county councils with which it feels central government tries to compare it (see Exhibit 9.5).

Your own local authority may not be blessed or cursed with Cornwall's peninsular form and indented coastlines, but it will invariably point to its own exceptional features which require higher spending and thus deserve more grant recognition.

Exhibit 9.5   'Why Cornwall is different'

Cornwall has above average spending needs

We know that Cornwall is different. Why else would over three million visitors be attracted to Cornwall every year? But what statistical evidence is there that these differences create a need to spend more than the average on local government services?

* Cornwall has more school pupils per 1,000 population than the average.
* Cornwall has to maintain 116 per cent more kilometres of road than the English county average.
* Cornwall is one of the most rural counties in England. The sparsity of population means that the County Council needs to spend more on transport for most services, but particularly on buses and coaches to transport pupils and students to schools and colleges.
* Cornwall has one of the worst records for unemployment. This creates an additional need to spend: directly on Economic Development, and indirectly on additional free meals or higher discretionary grants to college students.
* The geography of Cornwall is unique in its peninsular form, linear communications and indented coastlines. The predominance of small towns, many of which are coastal, directly results in more fire stations being required than in other English counties with a similar population.

Source: Cornwall County, *Cornwall Compared: Key Service Statistics, 1990–91* (Cornwall County Council).

☐ *National Non-Domestic Rate/Uniform Business Rate*

The third source of current income available to local authorities is one we just touched on in describing the calculation of grant: the National Non-Domestic Rate (NNDR) or, as it is almost equally commonly known, the Uniform Business Rate (UBR). It came into operation at the same time as the community charge, though without anything like the same attendant public outcry, despite being in some ways the more constitutionally significant of the two tax reforms.

For almost four hundred years prior to 1989/90 the one source of local taxation available to local authorities in this country was a property tax, known as the *rates*. Its principles were administratively simple, which is one reason why a property tax of some kind is to be found in most developed systems of local government. Every property in the area – houses, flats, shops, offices, factories – was given a valuation: its *Rateable Value*. Then each year the local council would calculate how much, in addition to the grant it would receive, it needed to collect to pay for the services it wished to provide, and would set an appropriate *Rate Poundage*: so much to be paid per £ of each property's rateable value. Domestic ratepayers used to pay a slightly lower rate poundage than non-domestic ratepayers because the government would pay a compensating subsidy to the local council.

In 1989 in Scotland and 1990 in England and Wales this whole system changed. Domestic rates were abolished, replaced by the community charge. Northern Ireland alone retained its rating system, no doubt to many people's relief – in both senses of the word, since, as formerly in Great Britain, a large proportion of the population is entitled to rate rebates.

The non-domestic rate was not abolished, but nationalised: hence the National Non-Domestic Rate. In future, central government would set each year a standard or uniform rate poundage for *all* non-domestic properties in England, and similarly in Wales – though not in Scotland, where existing rate poundages were retained. Local councils continue to send out the bills and collect the rates, but these are now paid into a national fund and redistributed back to the councils in proportion to their populations. The NNDR has become in effect part of the central government grant – its more than £14 billion in 1996/97 amounting to about a quarter of total central government support. Previously local ratepayers have become national taxpayers, and there is no longer any financial link between businesses and local authorities.

In 1989/90 non-domestic rates had provided over a quarter of local government current income: more than that from domestic rates. At a stroke, therefore, the proportion of their income controlled by local councils fell from over a half to barely a quarter: a fraction that, as we shall see, has since declined even further.

☐ *Local taxation*

It will be obvious by now that the final source of local authorities' current income is their own local taxation: traditionally the rates, then the community charge, now the council tax. We deal in Chapter 10 with the respective merits and deficiencies of these and other possible forms of local taxation. For the present, we need only remind ourselves that, whereas rates were a tax on property, the community charge/poll tax was a tax on the individual: a flat-rate tax payable by most adults over the age of 18. The council tax is a combination of the two. It is a domestic property tax, but with the size of the bill depending in part on the number of residents as well as on the property's value, since taxpayers living alone get at least a 25 per cent reduction, regardless of their income. It is also very different from the old rating system, with each home assigned to one of eight property bands (Figure 9.1). As a completely new tax, and one that has already lasted longer than the community charge, it is worth setting out the essential features of the council tax (see Exhibit 9.6).

To us, as individual local taxpayers, this most recent tax change may well have made a substantial difference to our personal finances. Employed single persons, for instance, are likely to pay more now than they did in

Figure 9.1 *Cartoon: Council Tax assessment*

Source: Local Government Information Unit, *LGIU Briefing*, No. 55, December 1991.

Exhibit 9.6	***The council tax: key features***

WHAT IS IT? — *A tax on domestic property,* not people, but with a personal element. There is *one bill per household,* with a 25% discount for single-person households and certain other property.

HOW MUCH? — Will depend first on the *Inland Revenue's valuation of your property.* All domestic properties were placed in 1993 in one of 8 bands, A to H, which are in a fixed proportional relationship with each other.
Band A, the bottom band, is for properties valued in 1993 at under £40,000 in England, under £27,000 in Scotland, and under £30,000 in Wales. Band H, the top band, is for properties over, respectively, £320,000 (England), £212,000 (Scotland), and £240,000 (Wales).

WHO SETS IT? — *Each local authority,* though in two-tier non-metropolitan England billing and collection are the responsibility of the district alone.

EXEMPTIONS? — Can apply only to property. Most significant addition to property types previously exempt from the community charge: *halls of residence,* flats and houses occupied solely by students.

DISCOUNTS? — Relate to the numbers and types of people occupying the property, *not* to ability to pay. 25% discounts for all single householders. 50% discounts for those under 18, full-time students, the 'severely mentally impaired', and some carers for disabled people.

REBATES? — *Up to 100%* available for taxpayers on low incomes.

STUDENTS? — *Do not* pay, if you are a full-time student in a hall of residence, hostel, or other *exclusively* student accommodation.

WHO IS LIABLE? — The resident, over 18, with the strongest legal interest in the property.

NON-PAYMENT? — Dealt with in essentially the same way as poll tax non-payment: summons to appear in magistrates' court, liability order issued by court, attempted recovery of money by council, imprisonment for up to 3 months (except in Scotland).

REGISTERS? — No specific register for council tax. Community charge registers retained by some councils, to enable recovery of outstanding debt.

CAPPING? — Ministerial capping powers *retained* and used more extensively.

NON-DOMESTIC RATES? — No change to the 'nationalised' system introduced in 1989/90.

THE FUTURE? — Most basic aspects of the tax – the bands, discount systems – can be changed substantially by Parliamentary Order, without the need for further legislation. More fundamentally, Labour is committed to returning non-domestic rates to local council control and to making the council tax 'fairer' – possibly by introducing new tax bands at the top end of the scale and updating and regionalising valuations.

poll tax; pensioners, single parents, the unemployed, especially those with children, mostly pay less than they would have done. For those local council officials responsible for its collection, the council tax also brought, for what was the second time in four years, major changes – not least because the number of tax bills sent out was roughly halved. But from the point of view of those involved in a council's annual budget process, the key decisions remain essentially the same as ever.

The tax levied is still the final residual outcome of a process in which all the other elements are now known: your own council's spending plans, those of any precepting authorities, the amount you will receive in specific grants, fees and charges, the income you will get from the NNDR pool, your RSG. The sum still outstanding has to come from the council's own local council taxpayers since, unlike their counterparts in most other countries, British local authorities have access to only the one local tax.

The last point is important, especially when considering, as we are, the budgetary discretion of local authorities. Common sense suggests that an authority with access to several different local taxes, paid by different groups of taxpayers, has more options at its disposal than one forced to rely on a single tax, the burden of which falls on a single group of taxpayers.

In Belgium, to pick one particularly vivid example, they do things very differently. Their relatively small municipalities choose, as well as set, their own taxes, and have a list of more than 130 types of local taxation from which to make their selection. The list ranges from the conventional – income and property taxes – to the arcane – taxes on advertising hoardings, vehicle taxes on boats, bicycles and horses. Indeed,

> some municipalities even tax pigeon keeping. Anything is permitted as long as it is fair and in the public interest.   (Gasson, 1992, p. 20)

The details, though, are less important than the principle, which is that Belgian local authorities, like most of their European counterparts, have a range of tax choices they can make which are simply not available to British councils.

In fact, it could be argued that significant local tax choice has now been removed from British councils altogether. Since the Rates Act 1984, local authorities' previously limited discretion has been curtailed still further through the process known as *capping*. The term tends to be used slightly misleadingly: 'rate-capping', 'charge-capping' and 'council tax-capping', instead of what would be strictly more accurate, which is *budget-capping*. Since 1984, successive Secretaries of State for the Environment have had the power to cap, or impose a statutory ceiling on, the planned budget of any local authority which is, in their view, excessive. The effect is essentially the same as if the cap were placed directly on the council tax. For, with only the one local tax, that tax has to be reduced on a £ for £ basis to reflect the cut in spending demanded by the Minister.

Initially, until the end of the 1980s, Ministers used their newly acquired power *selectively*, devising criteria each year that would enable them to pick out usually between 12 and 20 councils – almost all Labour ⟶ whose proposed budgets and rates they would then reduce. With the advent of the poll tax, though, capping rapidly moved from selective to *universal*, and since 1992/93 it has applied to all councils except parishes. If the system sounds centralist and dictatorial, that is because it was designed to be so. It is also quite simple to understand. The coming financial year's capping criteria – maximum percentage budget increases – are announced in November along with the other RSG details. Each council thus knows, before it makes any of its key budget decisions, exactly how much it will be permitted to spend and to raise from its own local residents in tax. Many, indeed most nowadays, then use those figures in effect as guidelines and spend and tax at their government-determined levels.

To local authorities of all political colours, if not to the general public, this introduction of universal capping is probably more offensive than was the imposition of the community charge. It amounts to the government's setting a spending ceiling for every council in the country, leaving locally elected politicians in the position of having the framework of their budgets, if not their detailed content, determined for them. As Jones and Stewart describe, there has been a serious weakening of local financial responsibility and accountability:

> Most authorities now cap themselves. Once the government announces the criteria, they keep within them to avoid the uncertainties of the capping process. Balancing the need for expenditure against the costs of local taxation has always been a key local choice. Now the issue is how to reduce expenditure to the capping level.   (Jones and Stewart, 1993b, p. 15)

In 1996/97 over three-quarters of all authorities (77 per cent) capped themselves in this sense of setting their budgets at the government's imposed cap limit. Just six endeavoured to challenge their caps, most either very marginally or to give themselves an additional chance of arguing a detailed technical case to the minister. In the end only two were required actually to reduce their budgets, the not obviously revolutionary county councils of Oxfordshire and Cambridgeshire.

■ The caged parrot: local budgeting, centrally controlled

What we have described, in outlining the basic elements of the local financial system, is a process of local budgeting within a tightly controlled central government framework. For those familiar with the famous *Monty Python* sketch, a council's budget in the mid-1990s can be likened to a caged and injured parrot: not, like John Cleese's bird, dead, or nailed to its perch, or actually inert, but very far from healthy and very definitely confined. Its former freedom of movement has been steadily constrained by a government that, through its policies of grant restriction and increasing central control, could be said to have clipped its wings, reduced the size of its cage, and finally, with universal capping, to have securely closed the door. The choices still available to the parrot are limited: it can fly around, making the most of the space available, equivalent to a council spending right up to its permitted limit. Or it can sit on its perch, or on the cage floor, like the minority of authorities choosing to budget below their caps. The one thing that neither bird nor council can do is to escape from their respective cages.

Less metaphorically, and from the perspective of the local councillors and officers involved, local budgeting could be described as 'managing the margins', to quote the sub-title of the most readable recent account of the subject (Elcock *et al.*, 1989). In fact, the authors' use of their sub-title is intended to emphasise the almost inevitable *incremental* or marginal nature of most local budgetary decisions: adding relatively small increments to, or cutting them from, a largely unquestioned and untouched budgetary base. But it could equally be interpreted to suggest the management of the increasingly tightly defined and delimited margins left to local councils' discretion, once government ministers have taken and announced all the major decisions on total spending, grant distribution, the NNDR poundage, and capping criteria.

Either way, there may be the temptation to see the role of 'managing the margins' as insignificant, even demeaning. The temptation should be resisted, by those in local government and by us as observers. As we have emphasised both at the start of this chapter and elsewhere in the book, the size, employing and spending power of local authorities are such that even their marginal budgetary decisions can have a major local impact. The government may define the budgetary cage by setting its spending and tax limits, but there is still plenty of scope *within* that cage for councils to respond to particular local needs and for councillors to pursue their political objectives.

To illustrate, let us return to Birmingham's 1996/97 revenue budget, as set out in Exhibit 9.3, and complete the story of the setting of that city's council tax. As noted before, while the scale of Birmingham's budget may be exceptional, the basic decisions underpinning it are essentially similar and comparable to those required of your own council.

The effective starting point in both cases will have been the Government's Revenue Support Grant Settlement at the very end of November 1995. The information that Birmingham derived from that settlement included first its Standard Spending Assessment (SSA) – what the Government felt it should be spending to provide a standard level of service; secondly, the Government's proposed capping rules, what was to be its maximum permitted budget. In Birmingham's case the key figures were an SSA of £920 million and a maximum budget of £971, which, the council claimed, was at least £50 million less than was needed to maintain services at their existing level and fully to take account of inflation and increased pension fund contributions, and of government-instigated changes in responsibilities through, for example, the transfer of community care to the City Council. To stay within the capping limit, service cuts would have to be made and jobs would almost certainly be lost from the council workforce of just over 50,000.

The Government's under-assessment of what the council saw as its spending need meant that Birmingham's share of the Revenue Support Grant also fell short of what it felt to be its entitlement: some £30 million short. Like many other councils, therefore, Birmingham appealed against its grant allocation – principally on the grounds that the Government's grant distribution formula was biased in favour of what Labour Leader Teresa Stewart termed the 'so-called higher costs' in the south-east. To no one's great surprise, the council's appeal fell on deaf, or at least unresponsive, ears – Environment Department Ministers no doubt reminding the council delegation that, if the Treasury had its way, the whole RSG, including Birmingham's share, would have been a good deal smaller still – see Figure 9.2.

In the absence of any reassessment, the vital figure of £971 million, calculated by Whitehall civil servants and imposed by ministers, effectively determined the council's budget strategy. A glance at Exhibit 9.3 will show immediately that Birmingham became one of the many councils deciding in effect to cap itself, by spending right up to its capping limit. Cost savings of some £48 million would still need to be found, the key policy questions for councillors to address – and, in

Figure 9.2 *Cartoon: Differing perspectives*

Source: Local Government Chronicle, 10 July 1992

Birmingham's case for its majority group of Labour councillors in particular – being:

* How and where should the savings be made?
* Which services should be prioritised and protected from cuts and perhaps even allocated extra resources?

Initially, as a distinctly chastening exercise, all service committees were instructed by the Labour leadership to identify and examine the effects of cuts of 5 per cent, 10 per cent and 15 per cent. It is these exercises that invariably produce the early January scare stories in the local media: in this case, the possibility of up to 18 branch libraries having to be closed by Leisure Services, residential homes closed by Social Services, and so on. Eventually, though, after much heated and protracted debate, including what for Birmingham was an unprecedented series of public consultation meetings, the following major policy decisions were taken and formed the basis of the council's own contribution to its budget-making process:

* Cost savings and any staffing cuts were to be concentrated as much as possible in 'non-frontline' service areas, with closures and complete withdrawal of services kept to a minimum.
* Specifically, the council's education budget would be increased, with an additional £17 million going to schools, the only major service earmarked for growth in 1996/97. Much of this extra funding, though, would have to come from the department's non-schools budget, with reduced training for non-teaching staff and savings in support services.
* Social services was to be the other principal protected area, with more money going to community care in the form of home care or nursing home places and also to the employment of extra occupational therapy staff, but at the cost of cuts in staffing and in grants to voluntary organisations.
* Leisure and Community Services were committed to a 'no closures' policy, but had to find over £5 million of savings through cutting back on library books, restricting leisure centre opening hours and, again, reducing grants to voluntary groups. Support for the arts was cut by 15 per cent.
* Environmental Services cuts included a halving of the number of recycling sites and less frequent grass cutting in parks and other public areas.
* There would be a 'wide-reaching' review of the city's 10-year-old network of 43 neighbourhood offices, some of which would almost certainly be closed.
* 'Efficiency savings', through improvements in working practices, were to be found in all services, and an estimated 727 full-time jobs would be lost, of which 150 could be compulsory redundancies.

There is a sense in which such policy decisions can be regarded as 'marginal'. Even the most prioritised services would have their budgets increased by only a few percentage points. Similarly, the most harshly affected departments would lose only a small proportion of their staffs, and those mostly by voluntary, rather than enforced, redundancy. The great bulk of the council's budget and all its major services would remain intact.

Marginal they may have been; trivial they were not. All these decisions and the dozens of others linked to them, had costs and consequences for those involved in and affected by them. They were not inevitable; they were not made by central government; they were politically, even socially, contentious, and were the subject of much political debate, both across and within the parties represented on the council.

The fact remains, however, that it was not these policy decisions by locally elected politicians that played the *crucial* part in determining Birmingham's overall level of spending and service provision, its overall level of council tax, or the amount to be paid by the city's householders. These decisions, once the responsibility of local councillors and their electorates, were in 1996 all effectively settled by national politicians and civil servants in London. As can be seen in Exhibit 9.7, local taxpayers – in Birmingham as across the country as a whole – now contribute under one-fifth of their councils' net expenditure. Moreover, under a regime of tough grant settlements and universal capping, it must be debatable whether, as voters, they can properly hold their councillors accountable for even that modest proportion.

Exhibit 9.7 *Birmingham's council tax, 1996/97*		
City Council's 1996/97 Net Budget Requirement (set at limit determined by government)		£971 million
Less Revenue Support Grant (determined by government)		550=52%
Less Redistributed National Non-Domestic Rate (collected at uniform poundage set by government)		237=24%
Leaves Budget Requirement to be financed by council tax		**184=19%**
	(£)	
Which represents for a Birmingham property in *Band A* a council tax of	500	
Which equals $\frac{2}{3}$ of the tax for a property in *Band D*	750	
And $\frac{1}{3}$ of the tax for a property in *Band H*	1,500	
And an *average* council tax per Birmingham household of	**609**	

■ Conclusion

We have in this chapter defined and described the basic elements of the local government finance system. We have also outlined the contemporary budget-making process and familiarised you with some of its vocabulary: credit ceilings and the use of capital receipts, standard spending assessments, capping limits, the uniform business rate, the protection of frontline services. You should now be able to 'read' your own council tax demand, or the budget summary in your council's Annual Report, and understand how at least the major figures have been determined. The advent of a Labour Government in 1997 promised some changes. The Party's manifesto noted, 'Although crude and universal council tax capping should go, we will retain reserve powers to control excessive council tax rises.' It also argued that there 'are sound democratic reasons why, in principle, the business rate should be set locally, not nationally'. The impact of any such change will need careful evaluation. In Chapter 10 we explain how the system we have described has recently evolved and specifically how we come to have something called the council tax.

Guide to further reading

Our first recommendation will be obvious from the content of the chapter itself: get what information you can from your own local councils. Apart from its interest to you personally, it is bound to be more up-to-date than any book can be. The best textbook introduction to local finance used to be Hepworth (1984) but, not having been revised for so long, it is now distinctly dated. So, too, though still essential for the most specialist reader, is Foster *et al.* (1980). By far the best starting point for the general reader is the *Guide to Local Government Finance* produced by the Local Government Information Unit (LGIU), who also publish regular bulletins of 'Facts' on the Council Tax and other topics. CIPFA too produce a *Guide to Local Government Finance* which they regularly update. From here a natural progression, especially for local government practitioners, might be Rawlinson and Tanner (1990). More specifically on local government budgeting, Elcock has co-edited two comparative accounts (Elcock and Jordan, 1987; Elcock, Jordan and Midwinter, 1989).

■ *Chapter 10* ■

Finance – The Recent Story

■ Introduction

In Chapter 9 we outlined what we labelled the nuts and bolts of local government finance – grants, taxes, fees and charges – and looked in detail at the budget process in one particular local authority. In this chapter we take several steps back, so that we can view the whole system of local government finance and the way it has changed over the past two decades.

Specifically, and in a more truncated form than in the first edition of the book, we tell the story of the community charge or poll tax which, though now abolished, warrants our detailed attention for at least three reasons. First, while officially dead since 1993, its consequences have remained with us, as non-payers have been pursued by council treasurers grappling with the 'non-payment culture' that the tax fostered. Secondly, it represents a fascinating case study of intergovernmental relations, described in more general terms in Chapter 7. Thirdly, it is quite simply too important to by-pass: arguably the biggest single policy disaster since the Second World War. As finance expert Tony Travers has observed: 'for all the good it did, you might as well have taken £1½ billion to Hyde Park and burned the lot'. We need to know how and why such things happen.

In this chapter, therefore, the kinds of questions we shall address are:

* How does Britain's approach to the financing of local government compare with those of other countries?
* Why was the totally novel and highly controversial community charge introduced and then so swiftly abolished?
* How, in less than 20 years of central–local government relations, have local authorities gone – in Paul Cook's vivid phrase – from being financially cosseted to financially corseted? (Cook, 1992 – see Figure 10.1)

■ The historical context

We could go back to the 13th century, or at least to the 1601 Poor Law, to trace the origins of the rating system; to 1835 for the evolution of central

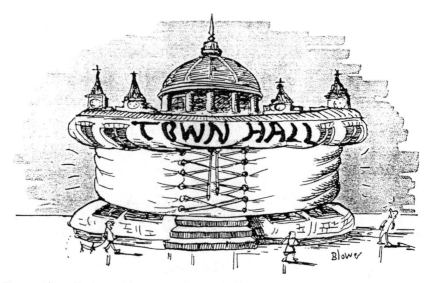

Figure 10.1   *Cartoon: The corseted town hall*

Source: *Local Government Chronicle*, 20 March 1992.

government grants. But others have done that more than adequately (Foster *et al.*, 1980; Travers, 1986). We shall cut a long story short and look only at very recent history, starting with the local government reorganisation, outside London, of 1974.

If ever there was a time at which local government could be described as 'cosseted', this perhaps was it. Local government spending, which since at least 1890 had been growing steadily and faster than the economy as a whole, had positively surged ahead during the 1950s and 1960s: an 11-fold increase in 25 years (Layfield, 1976, p. 15), during which time the service responsibilities of local authorities had remained fairly constant. The bulk of this new spending, moreover, was met not by councils themselves, but by central government grants, and particularly the Rate Support Grant: a general or 'block' grant, which recipient authorities could use substantially at their own discretion. There were rate increases too – for both domestic and non-domestic ratepayers – but, as can be seen in Figure 10.2(a), theirs was a minority contribution at this time.

In the following 15 years the wheel can be said to have turned rather more than a full circle. We see in Figure 10.2(d) that, once more, only a small fraction of local net spending comes from local domestic taxpayers, and we saw in Chapter 9 how even this is subject to capping. The remainder is under the direct control of central government. The turn of that wheel is this chapter's story, but first we need to return to an important topic we raised in passing in Chapter 9.

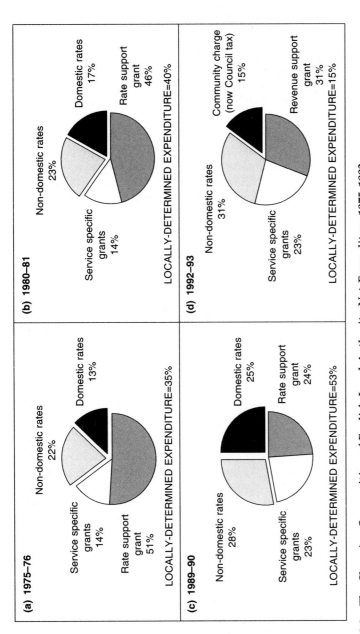

Figure 10.2 *The Changing Composition of English Local Authority Net Expenditure 1975–1993*

Notes: These *net* figures exclude, by definition, income from rents, fees and charges. Some percentages have been standardised and rounded for the purpose of producing these pie charts.

Sources: Department of the Environment, *Local Government Financial Statistics* (London: HMSO); Local Government Information Unit, *The Review of Local Government Finance and Structure*, LGIU Special Briefing, 35 (May 1991).

■ The comparative context

In commenting on Exhibit 9.1, we noted that local government accounted for roughly a quarter of the country's total government spending and over one-tenth of the total Gross Domestic Product. It sounds – and obviously is – a lot, and it explains why, in any local authority area, the council itself will be one of the largest employers and spenders, and frequently *the* largest.

Compared with other Western systems of local government, though, the UK is, in football parlance, in the lower reaches of the second division. The Premiership comprises the Scandinavian 'welfare democracies' and the federal systems of Canada, Switzerland and Germany, whose regional/provincial and local governments account for at least 16 per cent, and in Canada and Denmark over 30 per cent, of their respective GDPs. In all these countries too, state and local governments account for significantly higher proportions of their countries' total tax burdens than in most other Western European countries, and certainly than in Britain (see Figure 10.3). In tax terms, British local government can be seen as contributing a very small slice to a not particularly large national cake. We are, despite what national politicians would sometimes have us believe, a comparatively modestly taxed country, and less than £1 of every £20 of tax that we pay goes direct to our local councils.

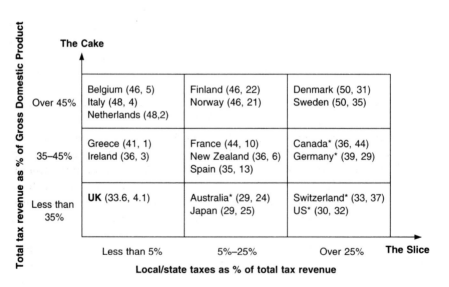

Figure 10.3 *Britain's Council Tax: a small slice of a modest cake*

Notes: First figure for each country is tax revenue as % of GDP; second is local tax as % of total tax revenue. For federal countries (*) the second figure = state + local taxes

Source: OECD, *Revenue Statistics of OECD Member Countries, 1965–94* (OECD, 1995).

		Income and profits (%)	Property (%)	Goods and services (%)	Other (%)
Federal countries					
Canada	State	50	6	44	–
	Local	–	85	2	13
US	State	39	4	57	–
	Local	6	75	9	–
Germany	State	57	6	37	–
	Local	81	18	1	–
Unitary countries					
Belgium		73	–	22	5
Denmark		92	8	–	–
Finland		95	5	–	–
France		13	34	12	41
Italy		30	23	29	18
Japan		58	28	13	1
Netherlands		–	67	33	–
Norway		88	9	1	2
Spain		17	36	43	4
Sweden		100	–	–	–
UK pre-1989		–	100	–	–
1990–1993		–	–	–	100
1993–		–	100	–	–

Exhibit 10.1 *Composition of state/local tax revenues*

Source: OECD, *Revenue Statistics of OECD Member Countries, 1965–1994* (Paris: OECD, 1995), tables 126 and 128.

It is true that some of Britain's other EU partners have markedly smaller local government sectors than we do – notably those countries in which teachers are employed by central, rather than local, government. But, following the post-1988 reforms that we shall be describing, there are no longer many countries in which local government has apparently less financial discretion. The key to that situation lies, we suggest, in Exhibit 10.1.

The detailed figures in Exhibit 10.1 are in some ways less important than the evident message:

* In very few Western countries are local authorities forced to rely on only one source of local taxation.
* In most countries local authorities can levy a variety of taxes on different groups of taxpayers and service users.

* The few exceptions are those mainly Scandinavian countries that rely very heavily on a broad-based and progressive direct tax: a local income tax.
* Britain has been unique in placing such a concentrated burden on *either* a property tax *or* a flat-rate personal tax.

That steadily growing and increasingly resented burden opens our post-reorganisation story.

■ 'We shall abolish the rates'

'No tax has ever been more unpopular than the local rate', wrote Richards (1988, p. 25) at the time of its impending abolition. A slight exaggeration perhaps, but this originally medieval tax, the principles of which we outlined in Chapter 9, was certainly bitterly criticised over the years – by the heads of households to whom the bills were sent, by the members of those households, and, increasingly, by governments. The criticisms, of which a selection are itemised in Exhibit 10.2, were varied, both in content and defensibility.

No tax, however, can survive for as long as the rates did without having also a number of merits. They were sympathetically enumerated by the Layfield Committee of Enquiry into Local Government Finance in the mid-1970s, in what was by far the most systematic and authoritative examination of the subject in recent years. Again, a selection are summarised in Exhibit 10.2.

So, flawed though the rates undoubtedly were, particularly as the sole source of local taxation, it still required there to be an exceptional combination of circumstances for their abolition to become a popular political cause. The 1974/75 financial year produced such a combination of circumstances: increased local spending, especially in the wake of local government reorganisation; the first rating revaluation for ten years; and near-record levels of inflation – 19 per cent at the end of 1974, eventually peaking at 27 per cent in August 1975.

The Conservatives, or more precisely the Opposition Spokesperson for the Environment – one Margaret Thatcher – produced a manifesto pledge for the October 1974 General Election that:

> within the lifetime of a Parliament we shall abolish the domestic rating system and replace it by taxes more broadly based and *related to people's ability to pay*.
> (*Putting Britain First* – Conservative Party manifesto, October 1974, our emphasis)

■ The Layfield Committee

The 1974 Labour Government, for its part, set up the Layfield Committee on Local Government Finance – to review the whole system of local

---

Exhibit 10.2 *The pros and cons of domestic rates*

Accusations and criticisms

* **Unfair** – unrelated to number of occupants, their local service usage, or ability to pay
* **Regressive** – took relatively larger share of income of poorer households
* **Inconsistent** – both between and within areas
* **Incomprehensible** – even to ratepayers, more so to ordinary voters
* **Unbuoyant** – yield did not automatically rise in line with costs
* **Limited accountability** – no direct relationship between rate bill and local service standards
* **Encouraged 'freeloading'** – non-payers could vote for services without facing financial implications

Merits

* **Reasonable** – most countries part-fund local services through property taxation because of its common-sense acceptability
* **Fair** – especially with rebates, there is a broad relationship between property value and personal wealth
* **Efficient** – easy and relatively cheap to administer, difficult to evade
* **Predictable** – yield is predictable, aiding a council's budget calculations
* **Visible** – ratepayers knew how much they were paying and what for . . . .
* **Accountable** . . . . and therefore (in principle) who to blame, and to vote for or against.

Note: for more details on these points, see Wilson and Game, 1994, pp. 164–67; also Layfield Committee, 1976.

---

government finance and to make recommendations. This it did, meticulously, authoritatively and, from local government's viewpoint, supportively.

The Layfield Report expressed concern at the extent to which local government had come to be funded by central government grants. Such a situation confused and contorted what should be a clearly identifiable *chain of accountability* – from a local council deciding its level of service provision, translating that provision into a demand on local taxpayers, who then, as voters, would be able to approve or protest. But, with grant funding up to two-thirds of local spending, and its impact on a council's finances varying from year to year, whom should a disgruntled ratepayer properly blame: the council or the national government?

That national government, Layfield argued, had a vital choice to make – between a continuing and accelerating drift towards further centralisation or a reaffirmation of local responsibility: providing local government with a more extensive and robust tax base, so that it could begin to assume proper electoral accountability for its spending decisions. This preferred option necessitated, in the Committee's view, a local income tax (LIT) on personal incomes, to supplement rates.

The Labour Government's Green Paper response to Layfield rejected both the Committee's analysis and all its main recommendations, including LIT. The Government was, by this time, well into what in Exhibit 10.3 we have described as the 'corporatist' phase of intergovernmental relations. General economic difficulties had forced the Government to seek a substantial loan from the International Monetary Fund, the conditions of which included a significant reduction in public expenditure. In the case of local government spending, this reduction was most swiftly achieved through cutting back the Rate Support Grant and, through the medium of the Consultative Council on Local Government Finance (CCLGF), hoping to persuade local authorities of the virtues of restraint.

In a sense, therefore, the Labour Government, like its Conservative successors, could be said to have accepted one strand of the Layfield prescription, but not what the Committee considered to be the linked and equally essential second strand. Local dependence on government grant was reduced, simply by giving councils less of it; but, having no additional taxes with which to meet and spread their growing financial burden, these councils became more heavily reliant than ever on their hard-pressed ratepayers.

The Conservatives who came into government in 1979, however, were still committed to rating abolition and reform. The Government's priority, in this new and manifestly more confrontational phase of intergovernmental relations (see Exhibit 10.3), was to gain control over council spending. Starting with the 1980 Local Government, Planning and Land Act which, among a great many other initiatives, fundamentally reformed the central government grant machinery, there were no fewer than 11 changes in the local government financial system during the first two Thatcher administrations. Almost all of these changes were aimed at tightening and sharpening the government's control over the grant distribution system, thereby constraining the expenditure of local government as a whole and of what government ministers referred to as 'overspending' councils in particular. The predictable enough response of many, especially Labour, councils to this attack on their financial discretion and integrity was to seek to maintain their existing service levels and spending plans by raising their domestic and business rates to compensate for their lost grant revenues. Domestic rates, therefore, began to rise again by almost 1974/75 percentages: 27 per cent on average in 1980/81, 19.4 per cent in 1981/82.

Exhibit 10.3 Four key phases of intergovernmental financial relations, 1960s-1990s

	CHARACTER OF THE PERIOD	INTERGOVERNMENTAL FINANCIAL RELATIONS
CONSULTATION 1960s and early 1970s	Increasing local service spending and employment, much of it encouraged and financed by central government.	*Live and let live* Considerable local discretion permitted by general (i.e. non-specific) grant funding; central direction and intervention (e.g. imposition of council housing rent increases, 1972) more the exception than the rule.
CORPORATISM late 1970s	Accelerating economic decline; inflation – partly through oil price rises – necessitating loan from International Monetary Fund and tough public expenditure cuts.	*Influence through incorporation* Labour Government incorporation of local authority representative associations into policy-making – notably the Consultative Council on Local Government Finance (CCLGF) – to try to secure councils' voluntary expenditure restraint, reinforced by successive cuts in grant funding.
CONFRONTATION early 1980s	Conservative Government search for means to control local, and thereby overall public, expenditure – mainly through manipulation of grant system.	*Central direction, local defiance* Consultation replaced by unilateral Ministerial decision-making; CCLGF turned into forum for government announcements of further block grant reductions, accompanied by new detailed spending 'guidelines' for every council and grant penalties for 'overspending' these guidelines, even if using their own tax revenues; increasing use of specific grants and directive legislation.
CONTROL mid-1980s onwards	Government recognition that local current spending only fully controllable through statutory limitation of rates and their eventual abolition.	*If you can't persuade, abolish* Abolition of 'high-spending' GLC and MCCs; introduction of selective and potentially general rate/tax- and expenditure-capping; replacement of domestic rates with first community charge, then council tax; further use of specific grants, and additional legislation to reduce responsibilities and discretion of local authorities.

Sources: Dunleavy and Rhodes (1983, 1985); Rhodes (1992).

■ First sighting of the poll tax

Thus it was that rating reform reasserted itself as a government priority and prompted, in December 1981, the publication of another Green Paper, *Alternatives to Domestic Rates* (DoE, 1981). In many ways a negative document, the Green Paper reviewed and rejected once more on the grounds of practicability many of the supposed alternatives to rates: local sales taxes; petrol, alcohol and tobacco duties; a charge for licences for the sale of alcohol and petrol; and a local payroll tax. LIT too was dismissed, principally on the grounds that it would run counter to the government's stated policy of switching taxation away from income and on to expenditure and could limit the Chancellor of the Exchequer's freedom of manoeuvre.

There are two features of particular interest in the 1981 Green Paper. The first was its discussion of the feasibility of a poll tax (pp. 37–9), which can be summarised as follows:

* A poll tax of *about £120 per head* on average would be required to replace the roughly £5 billion raised at the time by domestic rates.
* If, instead of all adults being liable, only those with incomes were to pay, the average poll tax rate would have to be doubled to *about £240 per head.*
* A flat-rate annual capitation charge of this magnitude would *almost certainly not be a practical proposition.*
* The most practical proposition would be to use a flat-rate poll tax *only to supplement a major revenue-raising tax,* thereby lowering the annual charge to, say, *£25–£30 a head a year,* which would raise just over £1 billion   (DoE, 1981, pp. 37–9, our emphasis).

Also recognised were many of the other objections that would eventually undermine the acceptability of the community charge, which, when first introduced in England and Wales in 1990/91, averaged some *fourteen times higher* than the level regarded as reasonable in the Green Paper:

* A flat-rate annual capitation charge 'could be interpreted as *paying for the right to vote'.*
* *Evasion and mobility would present difficulties* if a separate poll tax roll were to be compiled.
* *A separate roll or register* would cost 'probably a good deal more' to compile and maintain than did the electoral register.
* *A new statutory code of enforcement and penalties* would be required.
* The various registration and enforcement costs alone would probably make the tax *at least as expensive as domestic rates* to collect.
* *It would inevitably be regressive,* taking a greater proportion of a lower income than of a higher one.

As the Biblical phrase goes, so these things would come to pass! The second noteworthy contribution of the 1981 Green Paper was its enumeration of what the government considered to be the main requirements of a local tax. They constitute, as set out in Exhibit 10.4 a useful checklist of questions that may be asked of *any* actual or envisaged local tax.

Exhibit 10.4   *Local Tax Criteria*

A series of questions that may be asked of any existing or proposed local tax.

1. *PRACTICABILITY*
   Could it produce a substantial yield
   (a)   on its own?
   (b)   in combination with other taxes?

2. *COMPREHENSIBILITY*
   Is it relatively easy to understand?

3. *FAIRNESS*
   (a)   Does it relate to people's ability to pay?
   (b)   Is it fair between people of similar means living in different areas?

4. *ACCEPTABILITY*
   Would it command broad public support?

5. *PERCEPTIBILITY*
   Would it be clearly perceptible to local taxpayers and electors?

6. *ACCOUNTABILITY*
   Would it be paid directly by most people who benefit from the services provided?

7. *COST-EFFECTIVENESS*
   Could the costs of administration and collection be kept within reasonable limits?

8. *EFFICIENCY*
   Would it be difficult to evade, and so produce a high percentage collection rate?

9. *PREDICTABILITY*
   Would the yield be predictable for local authorities needing to plan their budgets?

10. *BUOYANCY*
    Would the tax yield keep pace with rising costs and incomes without needing to change the tax rate?

11. *SUITABILITY*
    Would it be suitable for all tiers of local government?

■ Rate capping

Though rejected by the Green Paper, the principle of a local income tax found favour in the only serious parliamentary examination of local government finance in recent years: by the House of Commons Select Committee on the Environment in 1981/82. This Committee's deliberations, however, had little impact upon a government whose assault on local spending had by this time changed its focus to rate capping. If grant cuts and penalties produced merely compensatory rate increases, and if there was no obviously suitable alternative local tax available, the only remaining course of action, concluded the government, was to take direct control over rate levels and thereby protect ratepayers from the alleged profligacy of their own councils.

Hence the form of the Conservatives' 1983 General Election manifesto, in which the promise to abolish the rates had disappeared altogether, supplanted by a commitment 'to legislate to curb excessive and irresponsible rate increases by high-spending councils'. As was to happen again over the introduction of the community charge, this attempt to seek an electoral mandate came rather late in the day for Scottish authorities, for whom capping powers had already been introduced in the Local Government and Planning (Scotland) Act 1982. For English and Welsh authorities, the commitment was swiftly confirmed in the government's post-election *Rates* White Paper and translated into the 1984 Rates Act.

Giving, as it did, central government complete control for the first time over the spending and taxing policies of some and potentially all local authorities, the Rates Act had a fundamental constitutional significance – more fundamental, it might be argued, than the government's abolition the following year of the GLC and the Metropolitan County Councils.

Each year from 1985/86 to 1990/91 a limited number of usually between 12 and 20 English councils were picked out for selective capping. Capping criteria would be announced by the Secretary of State for the Environment, followed by the select, and always heavily Labour-dominated, list of councils that had fallen victims of the criteria. These councils, which had been planning to spend more than the government's permitted percentage increase over last year's expenditure, would then have to cut their projected spending and rate levels swiftly and sometimes savagely. All other councils remained free, however, for that year at least, to spend and tax as they chose, and the impact of selective capping on the *overall* level of local spending that the government was seeking to control was negligible. Local current expenditure continued to *rise* in real terms (i.e. controlling for inflation) throughout the 1980s, and, expressed as a proportion of total public spending, stayed remarkably constant at just under a quarter: 23.5 per cent in 1979/80; 23.8 per cent in 1991/92 (Travers, 1992).

■ The community charge

Even if capping *had* had the same direct effect on aggregate local spending that it obviously did on the finances of the individual capped authorities, the government would still have had on its hands a tax that they were politically committed to abolish. In the autumn of 1984, therefore, a further study of local government finance was set in motion, this one to be carried out internally by Environment Department ministers and civil servants. This DoE group in January 1986 produced the Green Paper, *Paying for Local Government*, in which were outlined 'proposals for the most radical reform of local government finance in Britain this century' (DoE, 1986, p. 76) – one government claim that no one now dismisses as hyperbole.

That the 1986 Green Paper proposals took as radical a form as they did – after the 1983 manifesto omission of any explicit commitment to rating abolition – is largely attributable to two factors.

□ *The Scottish revaluation*

The first of these factors was that, although the last two scheduled rating revaluations in England and Wales – those due in 1978 and 1983 – had been postponed, the Government had been statutorily required to undertake a revaluation in Scotland. The main impact of the revaluation, which came into effect in 1985/86, was felt by Scottish domestic ratepayers, many of whom – especially in the more prosperous and Conservative-voting areas – faced individual rate increases in excess of 30 per cent. The government's swift political response was to assure its protesting supporters that, in Scotland at least, substantial reform legislation would be introduced *before* the next General Election; and to dismiss the very idea of any comparable revaluation in England and Wales as out of the question.

□ *Intellectual respectability*

The second development was that, since the government's distinctly unenthusiastic treatment of the poll tax in its 1981 Green Paper, the idea of a flat-rate per capita tax had acquired, within Conservative circles, a certain intellectual respectability. One of the several key figures was Douglas Mason, a Scottish academic, local politician, and a policy adviser to the right-wing 'think tank', the Adam Smith Institute. Mason argued that:

> a *per capita* tax would have the enormous advantage over all other forms of taxes, in that it would involve everyone in paying for the services they had chosen through the ballot box. The two-thirds of the voters who currently enjoy immunity from the consequences of their electoral actions would no longer be able to exploit the ratepaying minority.
>
> If every adult over the age of eighteen were required to pay . . . their share of the money currently being raised from domestic rates, each would have to pay on average just under £180.   (Mason, 1985, pp. 23–5).

There was sufficiently widespread Cabinet acceptance of such arguments for the then Environment Secretary, Kenneth Baker, to feel able to make a universal flat-rate poll tax – or community charge, as it was carefully christened – the centrepiece of the 1986 Green Paper.

There were, as we saw in Chapter 9, two main strands to the government's proposed fundamental restructuring of local taxation:

1. *Domestic rates* would be abolished, and replaced with a Community Charge, payable by all adults aged 18 and over at a level to be set by individual local authorities as a flat-rate payment.
2. *Non-domestic rates* would be 'nationalised' – that is, set in future by *central* government, following a revaluation of non-domestic properties, at a uniform rate across the whole country.

These reforms were designed to address the two main existing shortcomings identified in the Green Paper as weakening local accountability:

1. *The mismatch between ratepayers, service users, and voters* – from the Government's viewpoint, probably the most telling assertion in the whole Green Paper was that, of the 35 million English electors, only 18 million (51 per cent) were *personally* liable as householders for the payment of rates, and 6 million of these were eligible for either full or partial rebates. This left just 12 million electors (34 per cent) paying full rates, the other two-thirds being able to vote for higher services while, as Douglas Mason had put it, 'enjoying immunity from the consequences of their electoral actions'.
2. *The burden on non-domestic ratepayers* – local councils had little incentive to economise, it was argued, if they could increase their spending substantially at the expense of the non-voting non-domestic ratepayer.

The operational difficulties associated with the community charge – the compilation of a rolling register, the difficulties of enforcement – were pronounced to be 'not insuperable'. The new tax would significantly affect individuals' personal finances – single-adult households gaining at the expense of multi-adult households – so it should, the Green Paper argued, be *introduced at a low level (perhaps £50 per adult) and gradually increased* as rates were phased out over a ten-year period in England and Wales and a four-year period in Scotland.

Here, for sure, was one commitment which should never have been subjected to second ministerial thoughts. Neither the community charge itself nor its flat-rate principle would ever have been popular; but then no tax is. There would still have been sceptics among government ministers, Conservative MPs, and throughout the local government world, who recognised – and seriously questioned – the unique and revolutionary nature of the proposed community charge. But, sceptics notwithstanding, phased in over a decade, from an initial £50 a head, the government might just conceivably have got away with the community charge, at least until the next General Election.

■ **The big bang**

With the benefit of hindsight, it looks as if about the single most crucial decision in the whole community charge saga was that it should be introduced 'at a single stroke', rather than phased in over a number of years. It was a Cabinet decision, but one influenced to an unusual extent – certainly in the Conservative Party – by the evident wishes of party activists, voiced at the 1987 annual Conservative Party Conference. 'There are bound to be difficulties, so let's get them over and done with quickly', was the clear Conference message, to which ministers immediately responded. Domestic rates would be abolished completely on 31 March 1989 in Scotland and a year later in England and Wales.

This timetable change represented by far the biggest difference between the community charge as proposed in the 1986 Green Paper and as eventually introduced. Vigorous efforts were made, at each key stage of the Local Government Finance Bill's passage through Parliament, by Conservative MPs and Peers to amend the charge to a graduated 'three-band tax' based on income levels. By this time, however, it had acquired the status of Mrs Thatcher's 'flagship' policy of her third term of office, and the Government, with its Commons majority of 100, remained firmly committed to the flat-rate principle. The tax was duly enacted and implemented with effect from 1 April 1989 in Scotland and 1 April 1990 in England and Wales as summarised in this book's previous edition (Wilson and Game, 1994, Exhibit 10.3, p. 177).

No predominantly financial review, however, can come near to capturing the real flavour and social historical significance of this extraordinary episode in our contemporary history. If it had been suggested to a previous generation of readers that that seemingly dullest of subjects – local government finance – would come to dominate, for months on end, the *national* media headlines and change the lives of millions of the country's citizens, they would reasonably enough have dismissed the very notion as surreal or Pythonesque. But for once the dust cover blurbs of the left-wing books and pamphlets ring true. The 'poll tax rebellion' may well qualify as 'the biggest mass movement in British history'. There surely has 'never been a campaign of resistance in Britain which involved so many people in direct confrontation with the law' (Burns, 1992).

Exhibit 10.5   *The community charge: key facts*

1.   Costs to central government of the community charge, over and above those involved if rates had not been abolished, amounted in 1991/92 alone to some £7½ billion – equivalent to a 4p cut in income tax.

2.   Local councils had to employ more than 15,000 additional staff to administer the tax.

3.   By November 1989, over 1,000 local Anti-Poll Tax Unions had been formed throughout Great Britain, the largest with up to 500 members.

4.   In England, after the first year of the community charge, £1 billion out of a total of £12 billion remained uncollected; in Scotland, after three years £500 million (over 18 per cent) was still outstanding.

5.   In just the first six months of 1992/93, nearly 4 million people in England and Wales received court summonses for non-payment; in addition 2.6 million defaulters were issued with liability orders.

6.   Costs to the taxpayer of the 2-month prison sentences served by the Liverpool MP, Terry Fields, and his fellow 'convicts' were over £500 a week for an average non-payment of around £500.

7.   More than a million potential voters have 'disappeared' from the electoral register since the introduction of the community charge. Almost 2 million people were added to the 1991 Census count, partly to compensate for a suspected 'poll tax effect'.

8.   By 1992 chargepayers were being required to pay an average surcharge of £14 per head to make up for others' late or non-payment. In metropolitan districts this average was £32 per head, in London £28, and individual boroughs levied surcharges of up to £150 (Lambeth).

9.   Long after its abolition unpaid poll tax remained councils' biggest single debt problem, with some £1½ billion still outstanding at the end of 1995.

10. By the time of the abolition of the charge, the proportion of locally-determined net revenue expenditure had been reduced to about 15 per cent.

Exhibit 10.5 provides a summary of key facts related to the community charge, several of which serve as reminders that, though officially dead, the consequences of the community charge will remain with us until at least the end of the decade. The property-based council tax is politically more acceptable, simpler to administer, and harder to evade, but few councils have yet managed to get back to the 98 per cent and 99 per cent collection levels that were commonplace for domestic rates.

■ Conclusion: a command economy control system

The most profound legacy of the post-1988 tax reforms, though, must be their impact on the whole system of local government finance. Returning to the points we emphasised at the start of this chapter, British local authorities are still in the almost unique position of having access to just one source of local taxation. Not for them the 'sin taxes' on alcohol and tobacco available to many US municipalities, the French and German business taxes, the Norwegian wealth tax, or the Dutch second house tax – let alone most of these countries' substantial state or local income taxes.

Moreover, as we saw in Figure 10.2(d), the single British tax now accounts for under 20 per cent of local government's net expenditure in England and a mere 8 per cent in Wales. Local authorities thus control little more than a third of the 53 per cent of their local expenditure that they had as recently as 1989/90, and little more than a half of the 35 per cent they had in those 'cosseted' years of the early 1970s. With specific grants having increased, and the government's practice of publishing service-by-service spending guidelines to which councils are expected to adhere, they now have significantly less discretion too over how they spend their grant income. The laces of the financial corset, in short, have been pulled steadily tighter.

Tony Travers' description is vivid but hardly exaggerated:

> The annual ritual of the RSG settlement . . . is a spectacular example of a command economy control system in operation. The former Soviet Bloc never managed this kind of all-embracing and intricate control. A computer in London SW1 dictates the fate of a primary school roof repair in Wirral or a secondary school's music teacher in Cornwall. (*The Guardian*, 3 December 1996)

In two decades local government finance has undoubtedly come a long way, but not, it would seem, along that road towards greater local accountability on which it was constantly being told it should embark back in the 1970s.

Guide to further reading

A 'must' for anyone seriously interested in the reform of local government finance is still the Layfield Committee Report (1976). The various Green and White Papers which followed it are cited in the text, and the early part of the 'poll tax story' is recounted in detail in Travers (1986). The whole story is now available in an immensely readable and self-explanatorily titled paperback by David Butler and colleagues, *Failure in British Government: The Politics of the Poll Tax* (1994). It is a kind of pathological study of modern British government, but it also incorporates some of the more specialist literature on the subject, including Bailey and Paddison (1988), Paddison and Bailey (1988), and Gibson (1990). Worth singling out for special mention are the instructive, and massively contrasting, contributions by the former Chancellor of the Exchequer, Nigel Lawson (1992) and by Danny Burns (1992), secretary of the Avon Federation of Anti-Poll Tax Unions.

PART 2

THE POLITICS AND PEOPLE OF LOCAL GOVERNMENT

■ *Chapter 11* ■

Local Elections

■ Introduction

There are, as we saw in Chapter 2, several characteristics which distinguish local authorities from other institutions of public administration.
One – the most fundamental of all – is the fact of their election, aspects of
which provide the content of the next two chapters. Chapter 12 focuses
on the products of the electoral process: the councillors. This chapter
deals with the process itself: how local elections are conducted, who
turns out to vote in them, and how those votes are cast.

■ But why are we bothering?

To hear some people talk, you might wonder why we include a separate
chapter on local elections. Is it not the case that local elections constitute
little more than an 'annual general election', to quote Newton's portrayal
of Birmingham politics in the 1960s (Newton, 1976, ch. 2)? Are not
Government Ministers – real, as well as fictitious ones like *Yes, Minister*'s
Jim Hacker – right when they suggest that:

> Local democracy is a farce. . . Most people don't even vote in local elections,
> and the ones who do just treat it as a popularity poll on government in
> Westminster?   (Lynn and Jay, 1983, p. 45)

Certainly local elections do not seem to be accorded very much importance in their own right in our national political life. Their results are
analysed mainly for what they would mean *if* they had been produced in
a General Election rather than for what they *actually* mean: namely,
councils changing political control, policies altering, councillors winning
and losing seats. One senior Cabinet Minister in the 1960s, Richard
Crossman, even admitted forgetting about them altogether – after he
had chosen the Monday of local elections week on which to announce a
highly unpopular and electorally damaging 25 per cent increase in health
service charges (Crossman, 1977, p. 47).
 So why are we bothering? The answer is simple. We do not believe –
even, indeed, *especially*, when, as in 1979 and 1997, they are held on the
same day – that local elections can or should be dismissed as merely a

General Election writ small. They are much more complex, and much more important, than a national popularity poll, or, as Margaret Thatcher seemed to regard them in 1983 and 1987, a handy aid for Prime Ministers seeking tactically advantageous election dates. Our view of what local elections are and are not about can be summed up in the kind of 'before and after' editorials regularly produced by our more serious national newspapers – in this instance, *The Times* in May 1990. On polling day itself, Thursday 3 May, editorial readers were instructed:

> Today's local elections are about the running of Britain's cities, towns and county districts. They are not a public opinion poll. They are not meant to be a judgement on Mrs Thatcher, on her government at Westminster, or on the vexed matter of the poll tax. They are to select the men and women who are to run local administration. Those of all political persuasions who treat local elections as surrogate general elections are merely playing the centralist game. They are enemies of local democracy.

Odd, then, and disappointing, that just two days later the same paper's editorial column should choose to play its own 'centralist game':

> Yesterday's election results showed, as predicted, that the public does not like the poll tax . . . The swing to Labour on a high turnout would be enough to give Mr. Kinnock a good parliamentary majority.

Setting aside the fact that many voters demonstrably did like the poll tax and voted accordingly, what happened to all those men and women running our cities, towns and county districts? The assumption is being made that national and local elections are interchangeable. A principal message of this chapter is that *they are not*, and should not be so regarded. Local elections are local political events and a great many voters, if not political commentators, clearly treat them as such. Far fewer of them actually use their votes than in parliamentary elections, but many of those doing so *consistently vote differently* in the two types of election.

They will vote on the basis of local, rather than national issues, and for or against the records or personalities of particular candidates, regardless of their party. We shall introduce some specific examples at the end of the chapter, but first we must outline how British local elections are actually conducted – see Exhibit 11.1.

■ Local elections – see how they're run

There can be no doubt that some aspects of present local electoral arrangements, the product largely of historical accident, are complex and confusing – particularly for those living in parts of non-metropolitan England, who may well have to contact their local electoral registration office to find out whether theirs is a 'by thirds' or 'all out' council and when they will therefore have their next chance to vote. While there are many areas of life in which variety of local practice is to be thoroughly welcomed, it is not self-evident that the organisation of elections should be one of them. Surely the Widdicombe Committee was right in arguing for a uniform system, even if not necessarily the 'county' system of the single-member wards and whole council elections that it favoured itself?

There are arguments for and against the 'Widdicombe' solution (Game, 1991a). *Single-member wards* are smaller, provide the strongest link between councillors and their constituents, and may encourage higher turnouts. On the other hand, they limit voters' choice of candidates, may leave them feeling inadequately represented if 'their' candidate is defeated, and they may discourage party selection committees from picking women and ethnic minority candidates.

'*Whole council*' *elections*, by giving councils a clear breathing space between elections, may encourage policy consistency, forward planning, and reduce the temptation to defer politically difficult decisions, such as school closures, tax increases, the siting of roads. They can certainly lead to sudden and dramatic changes in political control, producing large and sudden influxes of new and inexperienced councillors. But, perhaps above all, they dilute the political accountability that comes from politicians having regularly to explain and defend their policies and actions to the electorate. For this reason – 'to ensure greater accountability' – the 1997 Labour manifesto pledged that 'a proportion of councillors in each locality will be elected annually'.

■ The electoral system

However, the greatest controversy about current electoral practice is generated not by the mechanics of ward representation and the frequency of council elections but by the system itself: the *simple plurality* or *first-past-the-post* (FPTP) method of election. It is a longstanding and easily understood system, familiar to almost everyone through its use in all our governmental elections in mainland Britain. Yet there is also increasingly widespread resentment of its obvious deficiencies and biases and, some would argue, a gradually emerging consensus across the political spectrum in favour of some kind of electoral reform. The main arguments for and against the existing system are summarised in Exhibit 11.2.

It is easy to see what Rallings and Thrasher (1991, p. 5) mean when they suggest that 'all the evidence is that local voters are poorly served by existing methods of electing councils'. It is not our intention here to add greatly to the proliferating literature on electoral reform, but it may be appropriate, given the confusion which manifestly exists even among would-be reformers themselves, to make one or two fundamental points.

Exhibit 11.1   *The who, when, how and why of local elections*

1. When are local elections held?
Every May, normally on the first Thursday of the month. *Not,* as in many countries, at weekends or on a declared public holiday, although the Labour Government is considering the possibility.

2. Can I vote?
Almost certainly, yes – if you are 18 or over, a citizen of Britain, Ireland or the Commonwealth, and not a convicted prisoner.

3. Must I register first?
Yes, as for Parliamentary elections. Unlike some countries, the UK has an annually compiled, rather than a continuously maintained, electoral register. The register, like all other aspects of electoral administration, is the responsibility of your local district or unitary council, and specifically of the Electoral Registration Officer, who should require you to complete a registration form confirming *your residence in the electoral area* on the qualifying date, 10 October. The new register comes into operation in the following February. Non-registration is an offence and, as former East 17 singer and Epping Forest resident Brian Harvey discovered, can lead to prosecution and a £150 fine.

4. Isn't there also a property qualification?
Not any longer. Non-residents used to be able to vote and stand as candidates if they occupied land or property in an area, but this plural voting was abolished in 1969, except in the City of London.

5. So can I vote every year?
Maybe, maybe not. It depends where you live.
  Most councils are now elected *en bloc* every 4 years:

  e.g.   English and Welsh Counties (1993, 1997, 2001)
         London Boroughs (1994, 1998, 2002)
         Scottish and Welsh Unitaries (1995, 1999, 2003)
         Northern Ireland Districts (1993, 1997, 2001)

But Metropolitan Districts are elected '*by thirds*', one-third of councillors standing for re-election in each of the non-county years: i.e. (1995, 1996, 1998, 1999, 2000, 2002).
  Some – English Unitaries and non-metropolitan Districts – may *choose*. Just over a third of the mainly more urban authorities have chosen election by thirds, like the metropolitan districts; the remainder have whole council elections every four years (1995, 1999, 2003)

6. Whom do I elect?
The councillor(s) representing the particular area in which you live.
  All councils are divided into single-member electoral *divisions* (counties, regions and islands) or single- or multi- member *wards* (districts and boroughs), each returning one, two or three councillors for *4-year terms* of office.
  There is at present no separate political executive in British local government, so you do not elect the Mayor or Leader of the Council.

7. When and where do I do it?
On *election day itself,* in your designated local polling station, between 7.00 a.m. and 9.00 p.m. – though, if you would find it difficult or impossible to vote in person, you may be eligible to apply for a postal or proxy vote. We do not in Britain do much to encourage turnout by, for instance, holding elections over more than one day (as in Norway, Finland, Italy, Switzerland), allowing voting in advance of polling day (as in Sweden, Canada, New Zealand), or setting up special polling stations in shopping malls and other places likely to attract large populations.

Exhibit 11.1   *(cont.)*

8. Is voting easy?

Yes – once you get to your polling station, it could hardly be easier. In England, Wales and Scotland the same *simple plurality* or *first-past-the-post* system is used as in Parliamentary elections. You simply mark an 'X' against your preferred candidate (or candidates if you are voting in a multi-member ward), and whoever gets the most votes wins the seat. There is no need, or opportunity, to rank the candidates in order of preference, unless you are voting in Northern Ireland, where the *Single Transferable Vote* is used.

Counting the votes is similarly straightforward, and the complete results for many councils are often available nowadays by 1.00 a.m. the following morning.

9. Will I recognise the candidates' names?

Not necessarily – though you may recognise your existing councillor if s/he is standing for re-election. Your ward may consist of between 1,000 and 20,000 registered electors, so even the most diligent candidate may not have been able to visit you in person. But the candidates should have delivered to your residence at least a brief 'election address', describing themselves and the policies they support. They may also describe themselves, in not more than six words, on the ballot paper itself, which will usually consist of their party affiliation.

10. Could I stand as a candidate?

Probably – provided you are over 21, a British or Irish citizen, and you have lived or worked in the local authority area for at least 12 months prior to your nomination. But there are disqualifications – for convictions, bankruptcy, etc. – the most important and controversial being that, if you are a paid employee of a local authority, you cannot also be elected to it, though you may be eligible to stand for another authority. This last disqualification was extended in 1989 to prevent senior local government officers and those in 'politically sensitive' posts standing for election at all.

11. Would I have to be nominated?

Yes, again as for Parliamentary elections – by 10 electors for the ward concerned.

12. Is it expensive?

Not terribly. It is cheaper to do badly than in Parliamentary elections, since there is no forfeitable deposit required. There is also a strictly enforced limit on each candidate's election expenditure – which in 1996 was £144 for the first 500 electors and 2.9p for each additional elector – though very few candidates report spending up to anywhere near their permitted limit.

13. Why is the system unnecessarily complicated?

Good question – also raised by the Widdicombe Committee:

'a system which is as complex and inconsistent as the present one is hardly calculated to encourage electoral participation. Citizens have a reasonable expectation that, when they move from one area to another, the electoral arrangements should be the same.' (Widdicombe Report, 1986, para. 7.15, p. 167)

The Committee's recommendation of a uniform system of single-member wards and whole council elections was rejected by the Government. For the present, therefore, it remains one of the idiosyncracies of British local government!

**Exhibit 11.2   *The case for and against 'first-past-the-post' (FPTP)
in local elections***

For FPTP

* *Maximises chance of decisive electoral outcome,* with a single party having full power to carry out its programme. Conversely, minimises the likelihood of coalition or minority government, and of protracted post-election inter-party bargaining.
* *Provides for a direct and personal councillor – constituent relationship,* unlike some systems of proportional representation in which representatives may not be directly linked to any geographical constituency.

* *Encourages parties to be broad-based, tolerant and moderate,* and discourages the creation and proliferation of new parties to represent new interests and arguments.
* *Reduces impact of extremist parties and views.*
* *Is the easiest system,* both to understand and to administer.
* *There is no alternative system* on which there is widespread agreement.

Against FPTP

* *Distorts,* often grossly and even more than in Parliamentary elections, the relationship between votes cast and seats won. Parties regularly win overwhelming control of councils on either bare majority, or even minority, votes. In other instances, a party gaining most votes may win fewer seats than rival parties with fewer votes.
* *Can effectively eliminate opposition,* producing councils on which opposition representation is either non-existent or too small perhaps even to be able to fill available committee places.
* *Wastes more votes* – in the sense of their going either to losing candidates or to build up needlessly large winning majorities – than almost any other system.
* *Reduces incentive to vote,* by reducing the proportion of potential voters who feel they can affect the result, either in their own ward or in the council as a whole.
* *Undermines perceived legitimacy of councillors,* since many, like MPs,

are elected on minority votes – and usually on smaller turnouts than MPs.
* *Is electorally inefficient,* using only voters' first preferences and giving them no opportunity to express their political opinions in greater detail.
* *Is socially and geographically divisive,* benefiting the two major parties in areas in which they are already strong.
* *Is politically divisive,* encouraging adversarial politics, with more attention given to demolishing the opposition than to fostering inter-party understanding. Can make post-election negotiation and co-operation on a hung council even more difficult than it would be anyway.
* *May discriminate against women and ethnic minorities,* by making it harder for them to be selected and thus elected, though in fact female representation in British local government is higher than in at least some countries with PR systems.

Exhibit 11.3 *Basic types of electoral system*

1. *Plurality (or first-past-the-post, FPTP) systems*
   The candidate with the most votes wins.

2. *Majority systems* – e.g. the Alternative Vote, double ballot
   These are *preferential* systems, usually in single-member constituencies, the main object of which is not proportionality, but to eliminate the possibility of a candidate winning a constituency on a minority vote.

3. *Proportional systems*
   Any system, *necessarily* based on multi-member constituencies, which has as its aim the achievement of proportionality between votes cast and seats won.
   There are two main sub-types of proportional system:
   (a) Party List systems – which aim to represent *parties* in relation to their popular support, and in which any vote for an individual candidate is, at best, secondary to the vote for the party.
   (b) The Single Transferable Vote (STV) – a system of preferential voting in multi-member constituencies, whose key objective is to provide voters with a choice of candidates *within* as well as between parties.

4. *Additional Member systems*
   Hybrid systems, usually based on FPTP, but with some amendment or 'top up' to achieve proportionality in the elected body as a whole.

First, it can hardly be emphasised too forcefully that the choice of electoral systems, locally or nationally, is not simply between *either* FPTP *or* proportional representation (PR). It is probably most useful to think of there being four basic types of system, as outlined in Exhibit 11.3.

Second, *if* it were felt that PR should be a prime objective in local elections – more important, for instance, than electors being represented by a single ward member, or than maximising the chances of a council being under single party majority control – then there are several arguments that could be made for the Single Transferable Vote (STV), in preference to some variant of the party list system:

* it is already in use in Northern Ireland – in all elections, including local elections, except those to the House of Commons – and has been found to be both readily comprehensible and widely acceptable;
* it could be comparatively easily introduced in the rest of the UK, since there are already many multi-member wards and divisions;
* it can offer voters a choice between candidates of the same party, enabling them to differentiate – as those in multi-member wards can

and do already – between effective and less effective councillors, or between candidates of contrasting backgrounds or political views;
* it would probably give independent and minority party candidates a better chance of election.

An inevitable outcome of the introduction of any form of PR into local government would be a substantial increase in the already sizeable proportion of hung or 'balanced' councils: 30 per cent, or 134 out of Great Britain's 441 in 1997/98 (see Exhibit 14.3). Whether or not you feel this outcome to be desirable depends on your personal political views, but there is plenty of evidence that hung councils *can* be made to work eminently satisfactorily and *may* 'foster a more open and democratic form of local government than that typically found in majority controlled authorities' (Leach and Game, 1992, p. 152; also Leach and Game, 1989; Leach and Stewart, 1992a).

■ Turnout and party competition

The one thing that everyone thinks they know about local elections is that not a lot of people vote in them. It cannot be denied. As Goldsmith and Newton note (1986b, p. 146):

> local election turnout in Great Britain is almost at the bottom of the international league table. Setting aside those nations in which voting is technically or actually compulsory (Italy and parts of Australia), turnout ranges, for the most part, between 60 per cent and 80 per cent.

For Great Britain the range that Goldsmith and Newton record is 20 per cent to 60 per cent, with a mean of 40 per cent – barely half of that of countries 'such as Sweden, Norway and Denmark, where great stress is laid upon local government as an important government institution, and where the continued independence of local authorities is valued', and on a par only with 'Canada and the cities of the United States in which local government is even less significant' (Goldsmith and Newton, 1986b, p. 147).

□ *A consistent 40 to 45 per cent, but falling*

The detailed turnout figures for the different types of local authority can be seen in Exhibit 11.4. Certain tentative conclusions can be discerned, but one's first impression is likely to be of an overall consistency. Only rarely in the past 15 years has turnout risen above 45 per cent and in only two instances (both in Wales) above 50 per cent. Yet equally rarely – until recent years – was it under 40 per cent.

Exhibit 11.4 Local election turnouts, 1981–96

Date, type and timing of local elections	COUNTIES, REGIONS & ISLANDS + UNITARIES (U)			NON-METROPOLITAN DISTRICTS			MET DISTRICTS	LONDON BOROUGHS
	England (%)	Wales (%)	Scotland (%)	England (%)	Wales (%)	Scotland (%)	(%)	(%)
1981	44	49	–	–	–	–	–	–
1982 (thirds)	–	–	43	42	46	–	39	44
1983 (all-out; anticipated Gen. Election?)	–	–	–	46	–	–	42	–
1984 (thirds)	–	–	–	40	43	45	40	–
1985	42	45	–	–	–	–	–	–
1986 (thirds)	–	–	46	42	40	–	40	45
1987 (all-out; anticipated Gen. Election?)	–	–	–	50	51	–	45	–
1988 (thirds)	–	–	–	42	41	46	40	–
1989	39	44	–	–	–	–	–	–
1990 (thirds; verdict on poll tax?)	–	–	46	{ 49 (England & Wales) }		–	46	48
1991 (all-out; anticipated Gen. Election?)	–	–	–	48	53	–	41	–
1992 (thirds; post-Gen. Election)	–	–	–	{ 38 (England & Wales) }		41	33	–
1993	37	39	–	–	–	–	–	–
1994 (thirds)	–	–	45	{ 43 (England & Wales) }		–	39	46
1995 (all-out)	40 (U)	49 (U)	46 (U)	42	49	45	34	–
1996 (thirds)	35 (U)	–	–	37	–	–	31	–

Source: Rallings and Thrasher, *Local Elections Handbooks* (annual).

Rallings and Thrasher (1992b, p. 2) have suggested that 'turnout levels are higher in district council elections than in county council ones', and the figures in Exhibit 11.4 lend them some limited support. But the statistical differences are not great and at least some are more probably the product of heightened voter interest and turnouts in certain sets of elections because of external factors: the anticipated announcement of a General Election – correctly anticipated in 1983 and 1987, incorrectly in 1991 – and the additional controversy generated by the launching of the community charge in 1990.

Where there does appear to be a more genuine contrast is between the figures for the 'whole council' London Borough elections and those for the metropolitan districts held on the same day. Moreover, as Rallings and Thrasher note, this contrast can also be found *among* district councils:

> In 1991 the average turnout in wards where elections were taking place for the first time since 1987 was 51.5 per cent, whereas it was only 44.6 per cent in those wards which had had elections in 1990 . . . The evidence suggests that the electorate is keener to vote when the party control of the whole council is at stake, rather than if only a proportion of seats are up for grabs and political change is less likely.   (Rallings and Thrasher, 1992b, pp. 2, 8)

Ward size can also make a difference. Large wards – that is, those with electorates of significantly more than 6,000 – may 'discourage participation by producing too great a distance between elector and councillor' (Rallings and Thrasher, 1992b, p. 3). This proposition, however, has to be weighed against the fact that the wards with the smallest electorates, while producing high average turnouts, are also precisely those that most frequently produce no turnouts at all, in that they go uncontested. Far fewer councillors nowadays are elected unopposed than used to be the case, but they are commonest in the electorally smaller – though often geographically extremely large – wards in the more rural and least partisan district councils.

☐ *More contests, more candidates*

Turnout figures themselves may not have risen markedly in the past 20 years or so, but the proportions of voters having the opportunity to turn out most definitely has. The 50 per cent or more of today's potential electors who may fail to vote in any particular set of local elections are mainly doing so *out of choice*. In the past, for millions of them, that choice would not have existed. Right up to the 1972–4 reorganisation of local government, thousands of councillors were elected, frequently term after term, without having had to fight a contested election. They were the only nominated candidates, and they were therefore returned unopposed, without necessarily having to produce an election address or ask a single voter for their support.

Harrison and Norton, in their research for the Maud Committee in the 1960s, found that:

> Of 40,859 seats for councillors above parish level which fell vacant in the three-year cycle 1962 to 1964, members were returned for 16,743 (41 per cent) without having to contest elections . . . It seems likely that about one in three county councillors and about one in two of rural district councillors had never had to fight an election.   (Maud Committee, vol. 5,1967, pp. 48–9)

These figures did not change noticeably in the following decade, so that in the last major sets of elections to the pre-reorganisation authorities in the early 1970s:

* 50 per cent of the nearly 20,000 councillors 'elected' in England in 1970 were returned unopposed, including 52 per cent of all county councillors and 70 per cent of rural district councillors;
* 56 per cent of the 3,000 councillors 'elected' in Wales were unopposed, including 67 per cent of county and 65 per cent of rural district members;
* 62 per cent of the 3,100 councillors 'elected' in Scotland were unopposed, including 78 per cent of county and 87 per cent of district councillors   (Craig, 1989, p. 141).

Reorganisation brought the disappearance of almost all smaller urban and rural district councils, and many of their councillors. Previously non-partisan authorities were frequently merged with more overtly party political neighbours, and there began the long-term squeeze on Independent councils and councillors which continues through to the present day. At the same time – and with a direct causal linkage – the proportion of uncontested council seats fell immediately and dramatically from over 40 per cent to around 10 per cent. In the ensuing 20 years it continued to decline, so that, as Rallings and Thrasher note in their 1992 'audit of the health of local democracy':

> The conventional view that local elections produce a large number of uncontested seats is now almost wholly without foundation, *at least in England.* In London, the metropolitan boroughs, the counties, and *those districts with annual elections* fewer than 5% of current members were returned unopposed. (Rallings and Thrasher, 1992a, pp. 20–1, our emphasis)

The general point is a vital one to keep in mind, but so too are our added emphases. In Wales especially, and also in several of the smaller, more rural and less partisan English districts – that is, those who mostly have whole council elections every four years – there are still significant numbers of uncontested seats. In the 'all out' elections in 1995, for example, roughly 8 per cent of just over 10,000 English district councillors were returned unopposed and almost a quarter of the 1,272 members of the new Welsh unitaries: a marked improvement on the figures of 20 years earlier, but at the same time hardly meriting a very robust rating in any audit of local democratic health.

□ *Ways of increasing turnout*

Britain is not – either in local or national elections – a high voting nation. It may be regrettable; on the other hand, it may be seen as a measure of at least tolerable satisfaction with the performance of our governmental institutions. The fact is that, for most of the time, our comparative electoral apathy appears not to worry us unduly. If it did, then there are several ways in which turnout could almost certainly be increased.

We could make it physically easier for people to vote, in some of the ways proposed by the Labour Party's Plant Committee for general elections: by having more, and more accessible, polling stations in, for example, post offices, university campuses, shopping and DIY centres; by extending voting hours; by holding elections at weekends or declaring them public holidays. Or, if it really mattered to us, we could make voting compulsory and non-voting punishable by a fine, as in Australia, Belgium, Greece and Luxembourg. Perhaps more appealingly we could make much more extensive provision for postal voting, as recently happened in New Zealand, with an immediate doubling of many local turnouts from barely 30 per cent to over 60 per cent (Hedley, 1991, p. 18).

If we were really exercised by our electoral apathy, we could even – thinking back to our previous discussion – change the whole electoral system. While there can be no certainty that the introduction of some form of PR in local government elections would significantly improve turnout figures, there is evidence which appears to point in that direction. A survey by Blais and Carty (1990, p. 179) looked at over 500 national elections in 20 countries and found that:

> Everything else being equal, turnout is seven percentage points lower in a plurality system, and five percentage points lower in a majority system, compared with PR.

□ *Party competition*

The intervening factor at work in any proven relationship between PR and local turnouts would presumably be the enhancement of party competition.

If we were to take Exhibit 11.4 a little further and produce league tables of individual authority turnouts, we would find some strikingly consistent patterns of the same councils, year after year, appearing at either the very top or very bottom of the tables. Among the shire districts, for instance, Bath, Exeter and Winchester City Councils, all politically balanced, almost always feature in the top ten, with the overwhelmingly Labour-controlled Kingston-upon-Hull, Stoke-on-Trent and Halton invariably in what would be the 'relegation zone', were one to exist. As Rallings and Thrasher (1992a, p. 20) note:

> Similar consistent variations can be found between Bury and Stockport MBCs (high) and Knowsley and Rotherham MBCs (low) in the metropolitan areas, and between Richmond upon Thames LBC (high) and Barking and Dagenham (low) in London.

The lists could easily be extended. Indeed, you might care to find out where your own councils would be placed in such league tables. The basic message is clear enough: the more politically safe the council, the lower is going to be the incentive for the parties to campaign and for electors to stir themselves on election day. Conversely, the more marginal or evenly balanced a council's control, the stronger is going to be the incentive for the parties and their candidates to battle for every available vote, the greater should be the awareness and interest of the electorate, and the higher the eventual turnout. By increasing the numbers of hung councils, and thereby reducing the proportions of safe seats and 'wasted votes', the introduction of a form of PR would appear likely to have a positive impact on local turnouts.

■ Local votes

As we saw when discussing the Single Transferable Vote, certain measures of electoral reform could have the effect of increasing the 'localism' of local elections. Independent, local or minority party candidacies can be encouraged, and electors given more opportunity to vote on local issues, on the merits or otherwise of the candidates, and generally to play a more involved part in influencing election outcomes. But, while an extension of these practices is always possible, they all happen *already*. Many voters require no reminders from the editor of *The Times* of the dangers of playing the 'centralist game' and of the importance of treating local elections as genuinely local events.

□ Local issues, local candidates

This section of the chapter returns to our starting point by introducing some actual illustrations of local voting behaviour. The most comprehensive recent study of the subject is Miller's provocatively entitled *Irrelevant Elections?* (1988), based in part on a national survey of electors' attitudes conducted for the Widdicombe Committee in 1985. Miller found that, for a great many voters, local elections were far from irrelevant:

* 56 per cent of all respondents claimed to be influenced in local elections *more by local than by national issues;*
* 39 per cent of all respondents claimed to vote *more for the individual candidate* in a local election than for the party;
* 20 per cent of all respondents had *local party preferences different* from their current national party identification, a figure which rose to 34 per cent among those who 'voted for the candidate' in local elections.

In summary, roughly one-fifth of electors claimed to vote for *candidates of different parties* in local and parliamentary elections. To this figure, moreover, should be added the many more who may end up supporting candidates of the same party in the two sets of elections, but on the basis of different considerations.

☐ *Split-voting evidence*

A certain proportion of this differential voting behaviour will inevitably be self-cancelling; some voters preferring Party A's candidate locally and Party B's nationally, while others do precisely the reverse. There has, though, been a perceptible bias over the past decade or so, towards the Conservatives in parliamentary elections and to the non-Conservative parties locally, with the Liberal Democrats especially polling consistently higher locally than nationally.

The most conclusive evidence of people's readiness to vote differently in parliamentary and local elections was provided fortuitously in the so-called 'synchro-elections' in 1979 and 1997, when Prime Ministers Callaghan and Major respectively were forced and chose to call General Elections on the day already fixed for the year's local elections. Millions of voters found themselves with two votes to cast: one for their MP and one for a local councillor.

Exhibit 11.5 shows the extent to which people chose to split their votes, supporting candidates of different parties in the two different elections. The small samples of towns were deliberately selected *not* for any exceptional evidence they showed of split-voting, but for the particularly close comparability of their general and local election results, since virtually all their wards were contested by all three major parties, with very few distorting intrusions from minor party candidates. The Exhibit shows not only that many thousands of electors did indeed split their parliamentary and local votes in both election years, but that the net effect of their doing so was that the leading party nationally fared considerably better in the General Elections, while the Liberals and Liberal Democrats did very much better locally.

	FOUR TOWNS, 1979 (Cambridge, Gillingham, Gloucester, Watford)		THREE TOWNS, 1997 (Gloucester, Redditch, Worcester)	
Exhibit 11.5 *Split-voting, 1979 and 1997*	General Election votes ('000)	Local Election votes ('000)	General Election votes ('000)	Local Election votes ('000)
Conservative	99	88	55	55
Labour	74	71	77	65
Liberal/Liberal Democrats	28	36	17	32

☐ *National inconsistency, local rationality*

If you happen to live in one of the areas of England that had either county or unitary council elections on 1 May 1997, you might well be able to replicate the exercise in Exhibit 11.5. Just compare the percentage vote for your MP with the total percentage for the various council candidates of the same party in the wards/divisions that make up that constituency, and you may well be able to find your own examples of split-voting.

You do not actually need synchro-elections, though. It is possible to find plenty of evidence of the impact of local electoral influences through a careful study of almost any set of local results. Immediately you start digging beneath the headlines and the aggregated figures, you are almost sure to be struck by the immense diversity and apparent inconsistency of the detailed ward-by-ward results. One ward is gained by the Conservative candidate, while an adjacent, previously Conservative-held ward is lost. Labour win control of one council but lose control of several others. Third and minority party candidates and Independents win seats and even whole councils against all other parties.

One famous example, albeit exceptional, is Epsom and Ewell Borough Council in Surrey, where you might imagine Conservative votes would be weighed rather than counted, but which has not in fact had a Conservative councillor for a quarter of a century. The town hall is run today, as it has been since 1936, by the Borough's 13 residents' associations, whose representatives consistently defeat candidates from all the 'conventional' political parties. While certainly unusual, such results should not be thought of as inconsistencies. They are the visible effects of voters' recognition that, on this occasion, it was not an MP they were being asked to elect, or a national government, but a local council to carry out local policies and provide local services.

☐ *The poll tax and other local issues*

Our own illustrations of local electoral influences are from the particularly noteworthy district council and London borough elections of May 1990: those that followed English and Welsh councils' announcements of their first poll tax rates. Nationally, Labour declared itself to have been the overall 'winner' of these elections. But a closer look showed that, while they did gain over 400 seats, they also lost 137 which they had previously held, as well as their controlling majorities on the two London boroughs of Brent and Ealing.

The Conservatives, as *The Times'* editorial quoted at the start of this chapter pointed out, were nationally the losers in these elections. Yet they partially compensated for their 360 lost seats and 13 lost councils by winning 164 seats and four councils previously held by other parties. In particular, they won 29 seats from Labour alone in their two 'flagship' London boroughs of Wandsworth and Westminster with their exceptionally low and highly publicised poll taxes. They won seats too in several other Labour-held, high-taxing boroughs, but lost even more in the two lowest-taxing Labour strongholds of Lewisham and Barking and Dagenham, and in some of their own relatively higher-taxing boroughs. As a national issue there was no doubting the unpopularity of the Government's community charge, but there were plenty of signs even in those 1990 elections that it could attract votes in individual local contests, as well as increasing the propensity to vote.

In the shire districts the potential impact of the poll tax as an election issue was inevitably reduced by the way in which, in a two-tier system of local government, each person's tax level is the shared responsibility of at least two councils (county and district), making it harder for the voter to apportion electoral blame or reward. But there were, as ever, plenty of other issues and influences at work in different parts of the country. Voters in some Kent districts were concerned about the Channel Tunnel and its associated rail link; in Richmond upon Thames it was the future, or lack of it, of that London borough's world-famous ice rink; in Conservative marginal Rochford it was the attempted closure of the local fire station, and in nearby Basildon a key concern was town centre shopping, threatened by the controversial growth of out-of-town superstores and retail warehouses.

In the Midlands there was a Wolves Party, trying to persuade Wolverhampton Council to develop Molineux football ground; while in Greenwich there was the considerably more successful Valley Party, formed by Charlton Athletic football supporters to campaign for their club's return to its former home ground at The Valley. The new single-issue party fielded 60 candidates, won 15,000 votes, and helped defeat the chairman of Greenwich Council's planning committee, who had rejected the club's planning application to redevelop the ground and was reported to think that the issue would not be electorally 'relevant'! A year later the club was granted its planning permission, and in December 1992 played its first home game at The Valley for five years: a small but forceful reminder of the kind of local issues and personalities that local elections arguably should be about and still very often are.

■ Conclusion

This chapter has focused on the conduct of local elections, turnout patterns and differential voting. It has emphasised the 'localness' of such elections and provided a range of examples to show that local elections are not simply General Elections writ small. Local issues and local personalities are far from irrelevant in council elections, although their salience clearly varies from locality to locality. Local elections are, of course, a means to an end – namely choosing councillors to run local authorities. The next chapter focuses on the diverse roles of these democratically elected councillors.

Guide to further reading

For a clear and comprehensive general introduction to elections and voting behaviour see M. Harrop and W. L. Miller, *Elections and Voters: A Comparative Introduction* (Macmillan, 1987). Miller was also responsible for the first book-length statistical study of local elections (1988), which itself was an expansion of the author's work for the Widdicombe Committee (Widdicombe, 1986d). Sharpe (1967) is still about the only comparative study of the actual conduct of local elections. Finally, no reference to local elections would be complete without a mention of the continuingly impressive work of Colin Rallings and Michael Thrasher at Plymouth University's Local Government Chronicle Elections Centre and also of John and Hugh Bochel and David Denver in producing their respective compendia of detailed local results for England/Wales and Scotland – unrivalled sources of fascinating raw material! Between them, they have filled a serious gap left by a national government that saw as unimportant the compilation of any official and comprehensive record of local election returns, and we should all be duly grateful. The product of this work is available to the general reader in Rallings and Thrasher (1997).

■ *Chapter 12* ■

Councillors – The Voice of Choice

■ Introduction: beware of generalisations

This chapter explores who councillors are, what they do, why they do it and how they might do it better. First, though, try to talk to one or two councillors yourself. Find out at first hand how they spend their time and how they justify their elective existences. They will not be 'typical', but part of the message of this chapter is the unhelpfulness of thinking exclusively of typical roles and behaviours. Others may generalise – like the former Conservative Welsh Office Minister, Rod Richards, whose most memorable contribution to central–local government harmony was publicly to label Labour councillors as 'fat, slimy and fundamentally corrupt' (*Local Government Chronicle*, 6 January 1995, p. 7). You should aim for a little more subtlety and sophistication in your own analysis, and you will probably find that your councillors differ one from another just as much as do our own small castlist, to which we shall now introduce you.

■ Five pen portraits

□ *Maureen*

Maureen has been a councillor for some 15 years: a Labour member on the Labour-controlled borough council of one of the old East Lancashire textile towns. She is in her 40s, now a single parent with three school-aged children to bring up. From a Labour-voting family, she joined the party soon after leaving school and worked her way steadily up through its local hierarchy.

She was originally selected and elected for a fairly safe Labour seat, and was quickly rewarded with the 'apprentice' post of Vice-Chair of the Allotments Sub-Committee. She has since served for several years as Chair of Housing, politically responsible for the council's stock of 12,000 houses and flats. She became effectively a full-time councillor, living off income support, spending most evenings as well as daytimes at the town hall, conscious that she was seeing less of her children, and 'bribing them' with money for chips. She then started some employment training, of which politically she disapproved but it brought in an extra £10 a week. It also meant, however, that she had to fit as much of her council work as possible into her lunch hour – 'when officers are never available, unless I absolutely insist on it'.

As Housing Chair she saw through to completion a large town centre clearance programme, negotiated with a housing association the provision of good quality rented housing, and significantly reduced the council's empty properties and rent arrears. But she is prouder still of the fact that:

> with any improvement that now goes on in our council houses, people have choices. We give people budgets and they go out and choose from a range.

She explains her personal contribution to both the development and implementation of this policy:

> The single most important policy I delivered as Chair of Housing, believe it or not, was to allow our tenants the choice of colour of their front door. I could remember, as a tenant myself, the people from the council going down the street on our estate, and they used to have so many colours which they used in turn. One of the colours in my particular street was a purple and I remember counting the houses and being relieved that I just missed getting this awful purple. I didn't want the yellow I got, but I really hated that purple. So, when I was Chair, I said to officers that they had to give a choice of colour. They couldn't seem to understand at first the importance of going to someone's door and asking them what colour, of having contact with them *as tenants*, and *not* because they'd done something wrong. It's a small thing, but it gives everyone a good feeling.

Working to get the small, detailed things right is, to Maureen, much of what being a councillor is about – just as much as contributing to the large-scale policy decisions.

☐ Richard

Richard, like Maureen, has been a senior, virtually full-time councillor, personally and politically concerned with issues of customer service. In most other respects, though, the two could scarcely offer more of a contrast.

Richard was one of 99 Kent County Councillors: a now retired but still pinstripe-suited Conservative businessman on what he hopes was seen, before it became 'hung' in the 1990s, as a businesslike Conservative council. His principal contribution was as Chairman of the County's Police Authority, in which capacity he provided the political drive behind the Constabulary's innovative Policing Charter: one of the first local government schemes to be awarded a Charter Mark by Prime Minister John Major, 'for the raising of public service standards without increasing the cost to the taxpayer or the consumer'.

As a longstanding Conservative Party member and office-holder, it had been Richard's vague intention to 'go into local government' at the age of about 60, when his company required all directors to retire. This plan was thwarted by the Conservatives' success in the 1979 General Election. The sitting Conservative councillor for Richard's home area was elected to Parliament and resigned his council seat, and Richard was, initially with some reluctance, prevailed upon to take his place in what was about the safest Conservative seat in the county. As he himself concedes, for his first four-year term of office, while he was still working full-time, he contributed little to the Council and was very much 'learning the ropes'. After retirement he took on a series of increasingly responsible and time-consuming positions, culminating in his four years as Chairman of the Police Authority.

He did not stand for re-election in 1993. By that time he had 'spent twelve years putting something back into the community' – years which provided genuine job satisfaction but also, for a former businessman, had their definite frustrations. He resented the mainly Government-imposed constraints under which local councils must nowadays operate – 'like having not one hand, but one and a half hands, tied behind your back' – and in particular their ability to raise so little of their expenditure from their own local taxpayers.

□ *Joan*

In Lambeth, by contrast, when Labour councillors in 1985 tried to break free of the Government restraint of rate-capping, their hands were not so much tied behind their backs as metaphorically cut off. Found guilty of failing to set a legal rate, the rebel Labour councillors were ordered to pay £250,000 in surcharges and legal costs and banned from public office – to be replaced by, in many cases, totally supportive and equally radical successors, like Joan.

Joan's political career, much more than those of Maureen or Richard, has been shaped and driven by issues, rather than party. Her earliest involvement in politics was as a single parent with a young child, fighting the social security system, with the help of the local Claimants' Union, for her own and other people's benefit rights:

> I found I was much better arguing other people's cases than my own! But to get even the most simple thing out of social security usually meant occupying their offices with lots of children and forcing the issue.

Later on, as a mature student at university and with her son now at school, she again found herself drawn into campaigns and protests – for the provision of half-term playgroups, against increases in overseas students' fees – and using her personal experience to help other students with their grant and benefit claims.

Only after university, when she moved to London and obtained a council flat in Lambeth, did she actually join the Labour Party. She became constituency party secretary; then, in quick succession, as the disqualified councillors were removed from office, prospective candidate, elected councillor, and, straightaway, her party group's Chief Whip – in which responsible capacity she attended her very first council meeting.

☐ *Joyce*

Joyce is another councillor who came relatively late to party politics. Her first significant contact with her council was also as a protester, and she, too, had never attended a council meeting before being elected.

Like Joan, Joyce was activated by a public issue with a personal impact: the threatened closure of her daughter's primary school by the Labour-controlled metropolitan borough council. She tried to galvanise other parents into action, but without success: the school was closed.

Shortly afterwards she was contacted by the local Liberal Democrat leader, who said how impressed he had been with her activity, and would she be interested in standing as the party's ward candidate at the following May elections? While previously a Lib Dem voter, she had never contemplated becoming a councillor. But, having given up her career as a civil servant and with her children now at school, she agreed to let her name go forward and was elected with a large majority.

From Joyce's viewpoint the Lib Dem-held ward must seem like a small yellow island in an otherwise largely red Labour sea. She feels fortunate in having been put on to the committees in which she was most interested – education, schools, and environment – but is increasingly frustrated at always being in a minority of either one or two. Almost inevitably, therefore, she finds herself spending most of her time on the representational or ward-based part of her councillor role: dealing with electors' problems.

☐ *Keith*

There are thousands of councillors who could identify with both the positive and negative aspects of Joyce's position, but none better than Keith. For, several years ago, that was precisely his position; same council, same ward and same minority party.

Keith was similarly approached about standing as a Lib Dem candidate after playing a leading role in a local community protest: against the council's erection of an unwanted fence around a local housing estate. He, like Joyce a few years later, was elected at his first attempt. But disillusion swiftly set in:

> I was naive. I thought that, being a councillor, I could actually assist people in my area . . . but not as a Liberal Democrat I couldn't. My time is precious. If I was going to put 100 per cent effort in, I wanted to see results.

That, he concluded, on his perpetually Labour council, meant switching parties. So he left the Lib Dems, first becoming an Independent, and then agreeing to 'cross the floor' and join the Labour group. He was, hardly surprisingly, viewed with much suspicion, but at the same time was 'rewarded' at the next Annual Meeting with the Chair of Further Education, 'which sounds exalted, but in fact no one else wanted it'.

With his sole GCE O-level in Biology, his knowledge of further education was minimal – though, as he says, 'that's what the officers are there for'. What he knew about and was genuinely interested in was the youth and community part of his committee's responsibilities. So, for three years he threw himself into the job. He was heavily involved in the council's planned reorganisation of secondary education, and was able, at the same time, to do something for his own ward: bringing together, with the help of council officers, all the local voluntary organisations and forming a community association which now has its own Community Centre . . . in the very building that used to be Joyce's daughter's school!

Here, then, is our own small cast, to which we hope you will be able to add one or two of your own pen portraits. Three women, two men; a county councillor, a London borough councillor, one shire and two metropolitan district councillors; one Conservative, two Labour, one Liberal Democrat, and one Lib Dem-Lab switcher; two longstanding party members, three much more recent joiners; two in powerful policy-making positions, one very active ward representative, one instinctive issues campaigner, and one community politician. Plenty of labels and contrasts, but what do they have in common – amongst themselves and with the other 23,000 councillors across the country?

■ Elected local politicians – the voice of choice

To start with – and, as we shall see, it is not such an obvious statement as it may appear – they are all, all 23,000 of them, elected local politicians. Let us briefly examine the three parts of that description in turn.

There used to be a time, before the reorganisation of local government in the early 1970s, when the majority of members on many councils were unelected. Part of the reason was the existence of *aldermen*. These were usually, though not necessarily, senior and experienced councillors, who were appointed by the elected councillors to bolster their numbers by up to an additional third, and to add expertise and continuity. Their appointments were for six years – compared to councillors' then three-year term of office (now four years); they tended to take disproportionate numbers of committee chairs and vice-chairs; and they never had to seek the support of or face the prospect of defeat from a fickle electorate. They provided continuity, and most councils were able to provide examples of aldermanic members of 30, 40 or even 50 years' standing. They were undemocratic, but they unaccountably – in every sense of the word – lived on until, apart from in Northern Ireland, they and their Scottish near-equivalents, *bailies*, were finally abolished in the 1970s.

The unelected position of aldermen would have been seen as even more anachronistic than it was, had not many councillors themselves also never had to face an election. For, as we saw in Chapter 11, the sorry truth is that, throughout most of the history of UK local government, thousands of council seats at each annual set of elections were filled by unopposed returns, 40 per cent or more councillors by the 1960s winning or retaining their council memberships unchallenged.

There thus existed a kind of double democratic deficit – up to a quarter of council members who did not have to be elected and large numbers who should have been but were not. This is one local government deficit that has, since the 1972–4 reorganisation, been virtually eliminated. With over 95 per cent of seats in most parts of the country now subject to two- or three-party contests, councillors individually and councils collectively can claim with far greater legitimacy to be speaking as their community's 'voice of choice' – as the instruments through which the residents of a particular geographical area have expressed their preferences for one set of candidates, policies, service standards and tax levels, rather than another.

■ Politicians all

Choice, preference, priorities . . . they are the currency of politics, and those who translate them into practical policies are politicians. The third attribute of all our councillors – in addition to being at least nominally elected and representing specific geographical localities – is that they are politicians. All of them – even the self-styled 'non-partisans' and 'In-dependents' – perform what the late Sir Lawrence Boyle, a key member of the Widdicombe Committee, termed the 'political function':

all governments, be they central or local, have a two-fold function to perform. They have the *service function* and the political function. The service function consists of the provision of those goods and services which for one reason or another are supplied through the public sector. The political function, on the other hand, is the management and reduction of the conflict which arises out of the issues involved in the public provision of goods and services. It embraces such questions as *the scope, the scale and the quality of the public services and the manner in which their costs should be met.* And it should be noted that it is easier in fact to remove the service function from local government than it is to remove the political function. Because the service function, as we know, can always be privatised, but *the political function cannot and should not be delegated. If the political function is removed from local government, it ceases to be local government.* (Boyle, 1986, p. 33, our emphasis)

That, surely, is what we expect of our elected representatives, national and local alike: that they debate and determine *themselves* – not delegate to unelected officials – the distribution of our society's resources. We, as electors, delegate the political function to them: to take on our behalf decisions about the building of houses, schools and roads, about levels of service provision and rates of taxation. That is their role and responsibility, whether or not they happen to have been elected under a party label.

■ Representatives, not reflections

Councillors, then, share in common the fact that they are all local elected politicians. But what *kinds* of people are they, who have the apparent arrogance or presumption to wish to exercise *their* political will on our behalf, yet who are, at the same time, prepared to plead for our votes and to risk our ridicule and rejection? How like us are they, or how different? The standard way of responding to this question tends to be by reference to councillors' personal and socioeconomic characteristics, as in Exhibit 12.1. There is nothing intrinsically wrong with such data. They are relatively easily collected and categorised; they have over the years been reasonably regularly updated – most recently in a survey conducted for the Widdicombe Committee in 1985 – thus providing comparisons across time; and they furnish us with numerical measures of the extent to which certain social groups are over- or under-represented in the population of councillors.

It is, for instance, worth knowing – as opposed to merely suspecting – that only about a quarter of this country's councillors are women; that the proportion of councillors over conventional retirement age has scarcely changed since the mid-1960s; and that only 10 per cent of councillors have current first-hand experience of the housing that they themselves are responsible for managing.

Exhibit 12.1 *Personal characteristics of councillors*

	ALL COUNCILLORS		ADULT POPULATION
	1964 (%)	1985 (%)	1985 (%)
GENDER			
Male	88	81	49
Female	12	19 (a)	51
ETHNIC MINORITY	*	1 (b)	5
AGE			
Up to 34	5	7	29
35–44	16	19	19
45–54	26	25	15
55–64	31	27	16
65–74	18	19	12
75 and over	4	3	9
EDUCATION – HIGHEST QUALIFICATIONS			
Degree or equivalent	8	22 (c)	5
Above GCE O level	18	22 (c)	15
Up to GCE O level	25	33	32
No formal qualifications	49	23 (d)	48
HOUSING TENURE			
Owner occupier	66	85	57
Rented from council	16	10	32
Rented privately	18	4	11
SOCIO-ECONOMIC GROUP			
Professional	8	9	3
Employers and managers (inc. farmers)	45	32	11
Intermediate non-manual	8	18	9
Lower-level non-manual	9	10	18
Skilled/supervisory manual	19	16	23
Semi-skilled manual	5	1	6
Other	5	10	12

Notes:
Emphasised figures = significant over-representation
* = less than 1 per cent.
(a) Since about 1995 this figure has been *over 25%*, and in 1996/97 women comprised about 28% of the membership of London Borough and English shire district councils, about 25% on metropolitan borough councils, 23% on Scottish unitaries and 19% on Welsh unitaries (Rallings and Thrasher, *Local Elections Handbooks*, annual).
(b) By 1996/97 this figure had increased to *between 2.5 and 3%* – i.e. a national total of some 600 Black councillors, of whom up to a half are in London, roughly two–thirds Asian, a quarter African–Caribbean, and an overwhelming proportion Labour (Sophal and Muir, 1996).
(c) & (d) These figures too will have changed since 1985. In an albeit non–random national sample survey in 1992, for example, 36% of the councillor respondents had a degree and a further 27% had qualifications above GCE O-level, while only 14% had no formal qualifications (Rao, 1994).

Main source: Widdicombe (1986c, ch. 2).

Such data, though, have their pitfalls and limitations. They can prompt unwarranted and misleading generalisations. They may obscure real and significant contrasts among councillors in different parts of the country, on different types of councils, and from different parties. They can also be seen as implying that 'representative government' is more about trying to produce, like President Clinton's first 'Mirror on America' Cabinet, a socioeconomic cross-section or statistical reflection of the electorate, rather than the representation of ideas and ideals. With these reservations in mind, we draw out a few key distinctions and implications – in the hope of *discouraging* the idea that there is a 'typical councillor'.

☐ Gender

Most readers will surely find the gender figures in Exhibit 12.1 dispiriting, even if the proportion of women councillors has at least doubled in the past 30 years and, as ever, is substantially higher than the figure for Parliament, even after the record influx of overwhelmingly Labour women MPs in May 1997. There are also more women *councillors* in the most senior positions in local government than there are women officers: more women leaders than chief executives, more women committee chairs than directors of departments.

Does such gender distortion matter, or make a difference? Inevitably, yes. It is difficult to claim that councils on which 75 per cent of members are men pursue the same priorities and arrive in the same way at the same decisions as would councils on which even 40 per cent, let alone 75 per cent, of members were female. The illustration usually given is that more women members would mean better child care facilities and fewer municipal golf courses. But there is much more to it than that. Women are the main users of council services. They make an estimated three-quarters of all calls to council departments. They are the majority of tenants, the family members who make most use of swimming pools and libraries, who are most likely to put the bins out for collection, and who are most conscious of and affected by the quality of the local environment – inadequate street cleansing, poor lighting, dog fouling, pot-holed roads and pavements, inadequate public transport and street crime. They are likely to have distinctive priorities and agendas. If you still have doubts, try this simple question: why is it that public buildings invariably have far fewer female than male toilets, instead of recognising that roughly three times as much space should properly be allowed for women as for men?

☐ Ethnic minorities

An equivalent argument can be directed at the under-representation on our local councils of ethnic minorities. These groups also fare a little better locally than nationally and, as noted in Exhibit 12.1, the numbers of Black councillors have risen significantly during the past decade.

But aggregate figures in this instance are singularly unhelpful. What we want to know are levels of representation in those areas with sizeable ethnic minority populations; even here interpretation can be difficult. In Birmingham, for example, there are some 20 ethnic minority members on the 117-seat City Council. This 17 per cent might seem like a not unreasonable representation of the city's approximately 25 per cent ethnic minority population – until you consider the sheer diversity of that population: the African-Caribbeans; the Kashmiri restaurant owners, taxi drivers and textile industry outworkers; the Punjabi Sikhs, with their prominent role in the local economy; the small business-owning Gujuratis from both India and East Africa; the smaller Chinese and Vietnamese communities. Several of these groups are bound to regard themselves as unrepresented – not merely under-represented – on the City Council in any direct racial, religious or cultural sense, and if this is true in Birmingham, it is even more so in most other towns and cities.

☐ *Age*

The world of councillors is a predominantly middle-aged and elderly one, though there are significant differences across the parties. Virtually half of the then Liberals in the 1985 Widdicombe survey were under 45, compared with 33 per cent of Labour members, 19 per cent of Conservatives, and just 11 per cent of Independents. Conversely, over half of all Independents (52 per cent) were over 60, but 'only' 37 per cent of Conservatives, 32 per cent of Labour and 22 per cent of Liberal members. In aggregate terms, while the average age of MPs has been falling in recent years – to well below 50 – that of councillors remains at around 55. On English County and particularly Welsh councils that average is considerably higher, balanced out by the perceptibly increasing numbers of relatively younger members in the metropolitan districts and London boroughs. But even these councils still have some way to go, as Joyce recalls thinking at her first council meeting:

> I was really surprised by the number of elderly gentlemen. There were only about five councillors in my age group (mid-30s), and I'm the only lady councillor with young children. I'm probably the only one who has to organise arrangements for looking after their children while they're at council meetings.

Regrettable, it might be felt, for a council whose responsibilities include childminding, children's centres, creches, day nurseries, play centres, parent and toddler groups, pre-school playgroups, toy libraries and nursery schools.

☐ *Education*

The older the age group, the less likely its members are to have formal educational qualifications. The unmistakable evidence from all surveys of the relatively high levels of councillors' educational attainments is particularly striking. Nearly two-thirds (62 per cent) of councillors in the 1985 Widdicombe sample had stayed on at school till 16, and almost a quarter (24 per cent) until 18 or over, compared to 37 per cent and 5 per cent respectively of the adult population. As can be seen in Exhibit 12.1, councillors are substantially more likely to have formal educational qualifications: not in itself any measure of fitness or aptitude for government, but one characteristic at least on which presumably most of us would be happy to see our elected representatives not perfectly reflective of the population at large.

☐ *Housing tenure*

Owner occupation has increased markedly since the 1960s, and especially rapidly since the Conservative Government's introduction of the 'right to buy' in 1980. Owner occupation amongst councillors has more than kept pace with this national increase, with the result that on some councils, if tenants are to be directly represented on housing committees, it would have to be mainly through the process of co-option, rather than by their elected councillors.

☐ *Occupation*

Given their higher educational qualifications, it is not surprising to find councillors coming disproportionately from non-manual backgrounds in general and from the professional and managerial groups in particular. This is especially true of London borough and English shire district members, only 8 per cent and 19 per cent respectively of whom described themselves in 1985 as having manual occupations. There is a similarly low proportion of manual workers among Conservative and Liberal members (13 per cent), and on this specific occupational indicator Labour can claim to be the party most reflective of its electorate.

☐ *Twin-tracking or cross-employment*

Despite their greater statistical representativeness, it is Labour members whose occupational backgrounds have come under most critical scrutiny in recent years. In the early 1980s allegations began to appear about the emergence of a new 'public service class' of councillors, with personal occupational, as well as political, interests in the maintenance of high levels of local government services, employment and expenditure:

A growing proportion of councillors depend for their livelihood on municipal employment in one form or another: they work as social workers, teachers, or a growing category, as 'professional councillors', living off the subsistence and attendance allowances paid. (Walker, 1983, p. 94)

The Widdicombe Committee research investigated these concerns and found that approximately 10 per cent of all councillors or 16 per cent of those in employment were local government employees – hardly disproportionate figures for a sector then employing some 3 million people or 14 per cent of the workforce. Over half of the 10 per cent were teachers or college lecturers, 16 per cent professionals – e.g. housing officers, planners, accountants, social workers – 14 per cent administrators, and the remaining 12 per cent in manual or other types of employment.

The Committee found very few instances of what was labelled 'twin-tracking', or the cross-employment of a councillor in one authority as officer in another, that caused difficulties for either the individuals or the councils involved. Nevertheless, the Local Government and Housing Act 1989 introduced a limited, though still significant, ban on the practice as part of a broader package of political restrictions on council employees.

These restrictions were intended to apply to more senior council officers – defined as those earning now more than approximately £24,000 p.a. – plus those in particularly politically sensitive jobs, such as press or public relations officers. These people would in future be banned from any party-associated public political activity, including standing for election as a councillor, MP or MEP. As a result, a considerable number of officer-councillors, particularly in London, have had to make the often difficult choice between their professional and political careers: a choice which, if financial considerations play any prominent part, must almost always favour the former.

■ The councillor's job description

We now know something about who councillors are. They can and do come from all kinds of backgrounds and walks of life. It is neither very easy nor helpful to talk of there being a 'typical' councillor.

So does it follow that there is no such thing as a typical councillor's job? Yes, it does. Different councillors will have their differing interests, motivations, skills, aptitudes and opportunities, and they will at least endeavour to spend their inevitably limited time in differing ways. There is no clearly defined 'job spec.' to which a newly elected member can turn. We can, though, offer a composite job description, of the type that councils and councillors are increasingly trying to work out for themselves. The aims and purposes of the job of councillor might be said to be:

to represent and be accountable to the electorate . . .
in formulating policies and practices for the Authority . . .
and monitoring their effectiveness . . .
and providing leadership for the community.

We are not proposing this definition as uniquely authoritative or unimprovable. However, it has three considerable virtues. First, it is a neat distillation of what might otherwise be a lengthy list of more specific councillor duties and responsibilities.

Second, our definition takes us way beyond the traditional and apparently almost unthinking textbook distinctions that used to be made between 'policy' and 'administration': that councillors made policy and officers implemented and administered it, and ne'er the twain should meet. The sheer lack of realism underpinning this 'formal model', as we term it in Chapter 15, grated most with local government practitioners. Was it seriously imagined, on the one hand, that a group of part-time, amateur councillors had the capacity – or even the inclination – to produce a 'policy' for every aspect of every council service *without* there being a necessarily substantial contribution from the numerous highly trained, experienced, and highly paid officers whom they themselves employed? Similarly, were councillors really supposed, having delivered their policy pronouncements like proverbial tablets of stone, to stand aside and pay no attention to how the policy was delivered and to its impact on their own local residents and electors? As Maureen might say, that is a recipe for dreadful purple doors!

This thought brings us to the third virtue of our proposed definition, which is that it is expressed in language that makes sense to councillors themselves. Councillor roles and 'role orientations' have been a favourite topic of academic investigation over the years, and some insightful studies have resulted (Budge *et al.*, 1972; Corina, 1974; Dearlove, 1973; Hampton, 1970; Heclo, 1969; Jennings, 1982; Lee, 1963; Jones, 1973; Newton, 1976; Gyford, 1984). But so too has a positive lexicon of role labels: politico, delegate, trustee, representative, broad policy-maker, tribune, statesman, ministerialist, parochial, people's agent, policy advocate, policy spokesman, policy broker, party politician, ideologist, partyist, facilitator, resister, politico-administrator, communicator, populist, conventional politician, community politician.

For the reader, such a proliferation of labels can produce confusion as well as enlightenment. From most councillors, though, the response is more likely to be cynicism. Even if they recognise the actual words, they would not naturally think of using most of them to describe the behaviour of either themselves or their councillor colleagues. They would, on the other hand, recognise and identify with the language of representation and accountability, policy formulation, performance monitoring and community leadership.

Indeed, councillors tend to use these terms and ideas themselves. Maureen is acutely conscious that, as Chair of Housing, she was both responsible and accountable for the formulation of policy across the whole of her borough, and, as she emphasised, for monitoring the effectiveness of that policy and of the overall performance of the housing department. She no longer lives in the ward she represents, and so will reluctantly acknowledge that she cannot be the almost full-time resident representative that someone like Joyce is. Keith, you will recall, went to the lengths of changing parties to give himself more of a policy-making role and thereby play a more effective leadership role in his local community.

The councillor's job description thus embraces a wide variety of potential roles and responsibilities – as representative, policy-maker, manager, progress chaser, and politician – some of which are shared by all councillors, and all of which will be exercised by some. We shall look briefly at each in turn.

☐ *Representative – on the grand scale*

We start with the most fundamental role of all, yet, as we shall see, in some ways one of the most overlooked. Under our system of local government every councillor is elected by, and is accountable to, the residents of a defined geographical area. It is a much larger residential population than would be represented by most local politicians in Western Europe, as can be seen in Exhibit 12.2.

We have referred before to the exceptional scale of British local government: fewer and larger 'local' authorities than in almost any other Western country, and even fewer and even larger following reorganisation. Corollaries of this scale are that we citizens have fewer councillors to represent us, and we are less likely to know or be known by them. From the councillor's viewpoint, the ratios in Exhibit 12.2 understate the scale of their task. When our two-tier system and many districts' multi-member wards are taken into account, the reality is that an average English district councillor will have an *electorate* of between 3,000 and 5,000, a county councillor one of up to 10,000, and a metropolitan district or London borough councillor one larger still. Multiply these figures by, say, 1.5 for total residential populations, and the reality is, in a city such as Birmingham, that many councillors represent wards of around 25,000 people.

Like all other aspects of the councillor's job, they do not *have* to hold surgeries or advice bureaux, or publicise their availability to deal with constituents' problems, complaints, queries and representations. Most councillors, though, do choose to do these things, many of them finding that the 'casework' part of the job is the one that brings them their greatest satisfaction (Barron *et al.*, 1987, pp. 73 ff).

	Inhabitants per elected member	Average population per council
France	116	1,580
Iceland	194	1,330
Germany	250	4,925
Italy	397	7,130
Norway	515	9,000
Spain	597	4,930
Sweden	667	30,040
Belgium	783	16,960
Denmark	1,084	18,760
Portugal	1,125	32,300
UK	**2,605**	**118,400**

Exhibit 12.2   *Britain's large-scale local government*

Source: Council of Europe, *Local and Regional Authorities in Europe, No. 56* (1996).

Note: To enable realistic comparison with other countries' local and commune councillors, these Council of Europe figures include only councillors of principal authorities – i.e. *not* the approximately 80,000 members of parish, town and community councils, which are not universal and are mostly very small with very limited service responsibilities.

A few even go to the lengths of keeping systematic records. Thus, John Gyford, a Braintree District councillor as well as an academic observer of local government, reports dealing with a total of 172 cases between 1983 and 1987: almost half of which involved housing allocations or repairs, followed by planning, transport, and amenities – footpaths, factory noise, streetlights, street sweeping and grass cutting (Gyford, 1988).

☐ *Policy-maker*

Next there is the policy-making role of councillors – their work in committees, sub-committees and panels in developing policy, both for the authority as a whole and for particular services. They will be assisted, informed, advised, and maybe even steered by their officers, but they constitutionally have the responsibility for giving strategic direction to the authority and for determining its policy priorities.

This role, like that of representative, is shared by all councillors, though again the nature and impact of their contribution will vary enormously – from the longserving and experienced committee chair, seemingly as conversant with the technical details of departmental policy as most of the professional officers, to the neophyte and perhaps minority party backbencher, still trying to become familiar with the procedure of the committee, not to mention its agenda.

All councils organise their work through committees, and all council-lors therefore will find themselves appointed to at least one or two. Most committees, as we saw in Chapter 5, relate to *particular statutory council services* – education, housing, social services and planning. Then there will usually also be some version of a Policy and Resources Committee, probably dominated by the more senior councillors, which focuses on the *overall policy* of the authority and on the allocation and use of resources: finance, personnel, land and property. By comparison, committees focus-ing on the problems of *particular areas* are rare, and more rarely still are they likely to be permitted any significant policy-making role. It is true that there have been some notable decentralising initiatives in recent years (Gyford, 1991, pp. 174 ff), but the service committee still constitutes the setting in which the greater bulk of council business is conducted. There can, as a consequence, be a tension here for councillors who, as ward representatives, wish to know about and perhaps contribute to *all* policy likely to affect their particular community, yet find that their position and status on the council are increasingly dependent on their membership of one or two specialised service committees, on which they are constantly being exhorted to consider the authority as a whole. The two roles are not incompatible, but they may need consciously reconcil-ing.

In the context of policy-making, it is important to recognise that individual councillors can be surcharged for supporting unlawful local expenditure. As noted in Chapter 2, the surcharge was strongly recom-mended for abolition by the July 1997 report of the Nolan Committee on Standards in Public Life. At present, though, councillors can still be made bankrupt, as well as being disqualified from holding locally elected office. In recent years, as Joan's career demonstrates, a number of Labour councillors in Lambeth and also in Liverpool have suffered this fate. They were very much the exceptions, but they serve as a continuing reminder of the quite different form and scale of sanction faced by councillors on the one hand and ministers and civil servants on the other.

☐ *Manager*

The management role in local government can be seen as the converse of the policy-making role. Policy-making, we noted, should primarily and ultimately be the responsibility of elected members, though with the supportive advice and guidance of officers. The operational management of the authority should, by the same token, be primarily the responsi-bility of officers – but not exclusively so. As John Stewart (1990, p. 27) argues:

Although officers carry out the work of operational management, the council remains responsible for that work. The council must be satisfied with the economy, efficiency and effectiveness of operational management. Councillors determine the framework within which management operates and must be concerned with its results.

Stewart, it should be emphasised, is not advocating that members should become immersed in day-to-day management issues. Very far from it. There is a clear distinction between, on the one hand, doing something oneself and, on the other, taking overall responsibility and making the occasional intervention. The latter is the proper and necessary role for councillors.

☐ *Monitor and progress chaser*

The policy process is best visualised as a continuous cycle – from initiation, through formulation, enactment, implementation, with the cycle completed by evaluation, the outcome of which may lead in turn to a further policy initiative or adaptation (see Figure 12.1). The cycle does not stop with legislation or enactment, and nor does the councillor's policy responsibility. To quote Stewart again (1990, p. 27):

> Councillors are concerned not merely with policy, but with how policy is carried out, for in implementation policy succeeds or fails. Policy and implementation can never be completely separated. Policy is made and re-made in implementation.

As with operational management, the suggestion is not that the monitoring of policy implementation and impact and the evaluation of the effectiveness of service delivery are jobs for councillors themselves to be involved with in great detail. No, their role is again one of responsibility and control. It is *their* policy, and it is up to them to ensure it is being implemented in the way they intended – like Maureen and her housing committee's policy of tenants' choice. They are the elected

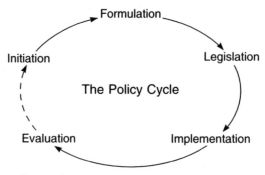

Figure 12.1 *The policy cycle*

politicians, the ones we shall want to hold to account for policy failure – whether that failure be one of conception or implementation.

■ The workload

There can be no doubt that the job of councillor in the UK is multi-faceted and potentially extremely demanding. So how much time does it all take?

There is no simple answer. Like an MP, a councillor could 'get away with' doing an absolute minimum: attending the occasional council and committee meeting and avoiding, as far as possible, all contact with constituents. All the available evidence suggests there are few such councillors nowadays, and that the far more frequent behavioural pattern adopted is a maximalist and proactive one. That was certainly the impression formed by the authors of a study of councillors and their partners which they entitled *Married to the Council?* (Barron *et al.*, 1987; also Barron *et al.*, 1991). Their findings, from an albeit limited sample of about 60 councillors from just three English county councils, were that these members were spending an average of between about 20 and 35 hours *per week* on their council duties. These figures are significantly higher than the still very substantial time commitments recorded in other recent and rather larger studies of councillor workloads.

The survey commissioned by the Widdicombe Committee in 1985 found that the average time spent by members of all types of authority on their council work was estimated at 74 hours per 'typical' month, or some 18½ hours per week. This was much more than the average of 52 hours per month recorded by the Maud Committee researchers in the mid-1960s, though slightly *lower* than had been found by the Robinson Committee in 1976.

Warnings were given at the time about the dangers of 'over-interpreting' this apparent 1976–85 trend, not least because there were simply so many reasons why councillors' workloads might be expected to have increased, not decreased, over that time (Widdicombe, 1986b, p. 63). These warnings might be said to have been borne out by Alice Bloch's 1991 survey of ex-councillors, in which the average time spent was reported as 82 hours per month, or over 20 hours per week (Bloch, 1992), and Nirmala Rao's 1992 non-random sample survey in which the average was 97 hours per month (Rao, 1994, p. 151).

Time spent on council and committee meetings had apparently risen slightly in these latest surveys – to the point where up to two-thirds of members' time is in some way meeting-related: attending them, preparing for them by reading papers or meeting council officers, and travelling to and from them. But so too had the now roughly one-fifth of their time spent on the representational aspects of their role: dealing with electors' problems and pressure groups. Taken as a whole, the relative consistency of these sets of figures – 1976, 1985 and 1991/92 – strikes one more forcefully than the minor variations between them. The problem of 'overload' is clearly evident.

■ Financial compensation

The jobs of councillor and MP may be similar in their open-endedness. In their financial rewards they are emphatically different. MPs have index-linked salaries of £43,000, office allowances of around £30,000, plus substantial travel concessions and motoring allowances. The average MP received up to £250,000 in allowances during the course of the 1992–7 Parliament.

By way of comparison, that sum would nearly have covered the *total* allowances paid out in a year to all 100 or so members of one of the largest county councils in the country. The councillors, moreover, do *not* receive salaries, index-linked or otherwise. Yet ironically, of the two groups, the councillors have by far the greater and more immediate personal power – in the sense of contributing directly to decisions to spend budgets and allocate contracts of hundreds of millions of pounds. MPs can merely question, scrutinise, approve or disapprove the spending decisions of government ministers.

Councillors today are no longer literally unpaid, as they were until 1948. But they are unsalaried – all of them, although, since the deregulation of the system in 1995, the Leaders of some of the country's largest councils have for the first time been able to earn at least the equivalent of an average graduate starting salary, and other leading members well over half that sum (see Exhibit 12.3). These councillors, however, are very much the exception. Most of the 23,000, as shown in the *Local Government Chronicle* survey summarised in Exhibit 12.3, still receive annual allowances more comparable to the maximum undergraduate student grant. Nor in many authorities, especially the smaller and more rural ones, are they likely to be much better resourced administratively and organisationally than they are financially. The findings of a 1987 survey of councillors' support services would still be recognised by a great many:

> Most councillors bear both the *workload* and the *majority of costs* of dealing with enquiries, correspondence and other work. (Association of Councillors, 1987, p. 53, emphasis in original).

■ So why do they do it?

We have established, then, that there cannot be many councillors who would claim that a desire for financial reward was their prime

---

Exhibit 12.3 *Members' allowances deregulated*

1. HISTORY
   - 1972 Attendance Allowances introduced – £10 per day maximum
   - 1980 Special Responsibility Allowances payable to Leaders, Chairs, etc.
   - 1991 3 allowances available to every local authority, within limits defined by Environment Secretary:
     - (a) Basic flat-rate Annual Allowance
     - (b) Special Responsibility Allowances
     - (c) Attendance Allowance (see Wilson and Game, 1994, p. 224)

2. PRESENT SYSTEM
   - 1995 Government-imposed limits removed.
     Councils encouraged to build *job description* for each councillor by allocating *day sessions* in line with their responsibilities and payable at rate of the average non-manual wage (approx. £89 in 1997).

3. SOME HYPOTHETICAL EXAMPLES

   (a) *Backbench shire district councillor*

Basic	8 days
Membership of 3 committees	18 days
Total: 26 days @ £89	£2,314

   (b) *Committee chair on county council/unitary authority*

Basic	10 days
Membership of 3 committees	28 days
Chair of committee	60 days
Total: 98 days @ £89	£8,722

   (c) *Leader of metropolitan district council/unitary authority*

Basic	12 days
Membership of 3 committees	24 days
Chair of committee	60 days
Leader	80 days
Total: 176 days @ £89	£15.664

4. SOME ACTUAL FIGURES

   Average allowances paid to councillors and leaders in 1996/97

	Councillors (£)	Leaders (£)
All councils in England	**2,413**	**5,925**
English districts	1,627	4,242
London boroughs	2,598	7,218
English counties	3,126	8,979
Metropolitan districts	4,621	12,702

   Source: Local Government Chronicle survey, 16 May 1997.

5. SOME COMPARISONS

	Members (£)	Chairs (£)
Health Authorities	5,000	18,000
	(= 20 days p.a.)	(= 3 days per wk)
Urban Development Corporations	5,430	68,410

Notes:
(1) All allowances are subject to income tax and National Insurance contributions and can affect those social security benefits subject to earnings rules. Quoted figures exclude travel and subsistence reimbursements.
(2) Allowances in Scotland tend to be rather higher than in England and Wales, partly in recognition of Scottish councillors' relatively higher time commitments. Allowances in the new English unitary authorities are also likely to be at the high end of the scale, reflecting their new service responsibilities.

motivating force in becoming a councillor. So what are councillors' motives? What drives them to put in these large numbers of hours for rather paltry compensation and apparently little public recognition or gratitude?

Power, status, self-aggrandisement, ambition, compensation for personal insecurity, or even sexual inadequacy . . . the drives and motives attributed to politicians are legion, and mostly unflattering. They are not to be ridiculed or lightly dismissed, but this is not the place in which to speculate about councillors' essentially private motivations. Our intention is to conclude this chapter in the way we started: with our own small castlist of members, to see what we can conclude about *their* motivations.

Our first observation must be the apparent *lack* in most of their political careers so far of any deep-rooted and single-minded wish to become councillors. Maureen's original candidacy was a kind of natural progression from her increasingly active involvement in her local Labour Party and her wish to further its policies and goals. Richard had had a rather more conscious long-term plan to stand for the county council after his retirement, but then 'events' conspired to bring to process forward. For the other three, 'events' might almost be said to have been the key recruiting agent: specific local issues for Keith and Joyce, and for Joan increasingly Labour Party-related campaigns.

Far from it being carefully planned, most of our small group of members found themselves projected almost unpreparedly into council membership. They were not exactly 'reluctants', but neither can they be seen as very driven 'self-starters', actively seeking and scheming for an additional career. They were all working full-time, bringing up young children, looking after elderly relations, or all three. As a result, the almost insatiably time-demanding nature of council work has involved for them, as for most councillors, potentially costly occupational choices, and at least some sacrifice of home and family life.

If they have a 'lust for power', most of our group of members manage to keep it fairly well concealed. They do seek *influence* and *involvement*: in the planning and development of their local environment, in getting a better deal for their constituents and local community, in furthering a particular cause or, more generally, the policies of their parties: activities which may bring them more direct satisfaction and sense of achievement than their day-to-day jobs. Likewise, they value being in or close to the places where decisions are taken and the quality of people's lives are determined.

They appreciate too the company of their fellow councillors, the shared interests and experience, and the gossip-laced conversations and negotiations – including those, initially unexpected, across the political divide. As Maureen recalls:

The first meeting I went to, I didn't understand why we even sat in the same room as these Tories. But they're mostly quite helpful, and I find that most councillors are fully committed to what's good for the borough. Often you walk out of a meeting and they'll tell you privately they agree with you. These are the things nobody ever told you – that you could and do co-operate.

■ Changing responsibilities, evolving roles

The recent reorganisation of local government has significantly reduced the numbers of councillors as well as councils. Yet, compared with other Western European countries, the UK is, as we have seen, *already* disadvantaged in this respect. Jones and Stewart (1993a, p. 15) note:

> Although ministers and officials may find it more convenient for their purposes to have fewer members, citizens and consumers will suffer if the number of their representatives is reduced. After all, the point of local government is not to serve ministers and officials but local communities, and local people.

Other changes too in the working of local government have necessarily changed the role of councillors. Compulsory competitive tendering (see Chapter 19), requiring a separation of the roles of client (specifying the service required) and contractor (service provider) within the local authority, means that councillors on service committees no longer control their service directly, 'as it happens', but through the allocation and monitoring of a contract. On the contractor side, the committees over-seeing service provision by direct service organisations (DSOs) are often known as management boards, and they too require a new, more business management, role of their councillor members. Local management of schools, devolving budgetary responsibility to governing bodies, similarly reduces the direct involvement of the Education Committee in the running of schools. Enabling councils in the future will be more 'hands off' organisations than in the past, which, coupled with the diminution in their financial discretion, may be less appealing to some councillors.

Already the number of councillors 'voluntarily' standing down greatly exceeds the number defeated in elections, by a factor of more than three to one across the country as a whole and at least twice that level in London (Game and Leach, 1993). Mostly the immediate reasons are personal, family- or work-related, but there are plenty of signs of a growing frustration and disenchantment with the direction local government has taken over the past decade. If this 'non-electoral turnover' is not to increase, there is urgent need to address the role of councillors in the

---

Exhibit 12.4   *The Audit Commission on councillors' roles*

A.   Making more productive use of committee system

What's good about committees?
*   allow decisions to be publicly scrutinised
*   allow opposition councillors to put alternative proposals
*   allow representations of special interests
*   offer forum for calling officers and contractors to account for performance.

So what should committees focus on?
*   major policy issues – e.g. service priorities in the budget
*   major operational issues – e.g. letting of large contracts
*   minor, but politically contentious, issues – e.g. establishment of travellers' site
*   monitoring of performance of services and implementation of policy.

What do they mostly spend too much time on?
*   operational detail
*   lengthy reports for information only
*   rediscussion and rubber-stamping of decisions already effectively taken by majority party group.

What can suffer?
*   councillors' time and interest
*   quality of decision-taking
*   senior officers' management time – in preparing reports and attending meetings
*   financial cost to council, often hidden (up to 4½% of total spending)
*   quality of service management
*   effective performance review.

What some councils are doing – is yours?
*   reviewing numbers and sizes of committees, and frequency and length of meetings
*   setting a few key policy objectives for committees to focus on
*   removing 'information only' items from agendas

Exhibit 12.4 (*cont.*)

* using more short-term working parties on specific, often cross-departmental, issues - e.g. crime, employment, children's services
* delegating more uncontroversial operational issues to officers
* scheduling time and establishing systems for reviewing performance against clearly specified targets
* using deregulated allowance system to remove incentives for unnecessary and unnecessarily long committee meetings.

B. Developing a wider community representational role

What does the representational role involve?
* individual casework
* advice to/spokesperson for groups with special interests
* representing the ward as a whole
* representing and promoting the interests of the whole council area
* acting as council's representative on other bodies

How can councillors' wider representation of their community be assisted?
* area committees and neighbourhood groups, to air local concerns of individuals and organisations
* a senior officer nominated to advise and support councillors representing each ward or district
* 'street surgeries', making councillors accessible at popular locations, not just at timetabled advice bureaux
* 'open forums'/question times, attended by all local councillors – county, district and parish
* local consultation exercises on key issues
* committee encouragement of direct communication of views of users and community groups
* 'scrutiny commissions' – enabling an exchange of views with groups and individuals on key topics – e.g. leisure strategy, community safety, public health, transport
* proper officer briefing of councillors representing council on outside bodies.

light of their expectations, motivation and potential contribution. Councillors, with all their diversity, remain the essential democratic ingredient in our local government system. Careful thought needs to be given to their new role in the 'brave new world' of enabling unitary authorities.

We conclude this chapter, therefore, with a summary of a recent report by the Audit Commission (1997) which does just that. Looking at the two key dimensions of councillors' workloads – their committee and their representative work – the Commission argues that the former could frequently be organised more efficiently and enjoyably, thereby freeing up more time for the latter, which should also be given more recognition and support by most councils. The Commission's analysis and proposals are summarised in Exhibit 12.4, and they amount to a useful checklist of topics to raise with any councillors you may be able to talk with personally.

Guide to further reading

Councillors in Crisis by Barron and her colleagues (1991) is a good starting point for understanding, as their subtitle puts it, 'the public and private worlds of local councillors', as is the research report on which it was based (1987). For (relatively) recent data on who councillors are, see Widdicombe (1986c), Gyford *et al.* (1989), Rao (1994), and, for Scotland, Martlew (1988). The main contributors to the discussion of councillor roles are cited in the text of this chapter, to which can be added Stewart and Game (1991). Looking back, by contrast, the best historical account of the changing character of members must be Lee (1963), while for an atmospheric depiction of life on a rural county council in the early 1930s see Winifred Holtby's 'factional' portrayal of her Alderman mother (1936), almost certainly the best English local government novel available.

■ *Chapter 13* ■

The Local Government Workforce

■ Introduction

For a sector of our society supposedly in decline, almost everything about British local government is remarkably large-scale: the population size of our local authorities, their expenditure, the electorates that our councillors are expected to represent, and, as we see in this chapter, those whose job it is actually to carry out their policy decisions. To impose some structure on our discussion of a local government workforce at least five times the size of central government's civil service, we have divided this chapter into four sections. First, we identify some of the key facts and features of local government employment. Secondly, a view from below is offered as we examine what it is like to be a manual or lower-grade clerical worker for a local authority. Thirdly, we take a view from above and look at the roles of senior managers and professionals. Finally, we examine the advent and implications of more flexible employment structures.

■ Local authority employment: some quick facts and figures

Local authorities are, by any standards, major employers. They are highly labour-intensive; up to half their total expenditure goes on staff costs. The chances are that your own council either is or is very close to being the largest single employer in its area; you might try to find out. In 1996 the UK workforce numbered about 25.3 million, of whom over 2½ million worked for local authorities. In other words, about 10 per cent of all full- and part-time jobs in the UK are provided by local authorities, a total paybill of more than £33 billion. Their division into major service areas for England and Wales can be seen in Exhibit 13.1, and to these aggregate figures should be added a quarter of a million FTEs for Scotland, essentially similarly distributed. Inevitably, given the decentralised, multi-service and multi-functional nature of local government, its workforce is hugely diverse, comprising professionals such as social workers and teachers, administrative and clerical staff, skilled manual

Exhibit 13.1   Local government employment, England and Wales, 1996

Service	Full-time ('000)	Part-time ('000)	FTEs ('000)	% of Total	% Part-time	% Female	% p-t Female	% change 1991–96
Education – teachers	362	133	401	27	27	71	22	–20
– others	125	483	285	19	79	88	74	–25
Social Services	167	187	264	18	53	84	49	+4
Housing	63	14	70	5	18	62	17	+2
Recreation, parks, baths	51	41	67	4	45	46	31	–20
Construction	64	1	65	4	2	6	2	–29
Engineering	56	7	59	4	11	28	9	n/a
Finance and computing	54	8	59	4	13	58	12	n/a
Other corporate services	59	19	66	4	24	60	22	n/a
Fire service	41	2	42	3	5	13	4	=
Libraries and museums	23	23	31	2	50	77	45	–9
Planning	27	4	29	2	13	44	11	+17
Refuse collection and disposal	27	2	27	2	7	9	4	=
Environmental health	18	2	19	1	10	39	8	–11
Other services	16	22	23	2	58	56	45	n/a
TOTAL	**1,153**	**948**	**1,507**	**61**	**45**	**70**	**41**	**–16**
	2,101							

Notes: FTEs = Full-time equivalents
n/a = not available in directly comparable form

Source: Local Government Employment Digest (monthly).

and non-manual staff, and a large number of semi-skilled and unskilled manual employees as cleaners, gardeners and caretakers. It is also highly fragmented, being spread in any large authority across hundreds of different service centres and locations.

☐ Changing numbers

The major growth in local authority employment took place in the 1960s and the early part of the 1970s. From 1979 until 1991, despite the efforts of the Conservative Government to reduce the size of the public sector, numbers remained fairly static at around 3 million – the steady reduction of manual workers during this period being largely cancelled out by the increase in non-manuals. The biggest losses during the 1980s were brought about by the abolition of the GLC and the metropolitan county councils in 1986, the change in status of bus and municipal airport staff in 1986/87, and the 1989 transfer of polytechnics and higher education institutions out of LEA control.

But at least twice the total numbers involved in these 1980s changes (i.e. over 100,000 FTEs) were lost in 1993 alone, when further education institutions became the responsibility of the Further Education Funding Council. There was a further significant drop in 1995/96, with the advent of free-standing police authorities. Quite apart from these changes resulting from functional transfers, there has been a steady fall in the local government workforce during the 1990s of between 1 and 2 per cent each year, the full effect of which can be seen in the final column of Exhibit 13.1. This trend, however, has varied from service to service. Police, up to 1995, and social services, for example, actually *increased* their numbers – reflecting on the one hand the government's commitment to law and order, and on the other the increased demands for social support stemming from an ageing and more dependent population.

☐ Changing composition

Recent years have seen a disproportionate growth in the *part-time employment of women*, resulting today in a predominantly female local government workforce. In 1954 more than half of local government's employees were men working full-time; by 1996 women made up 70 per cent of the workforce, with the growth substantially attributable to the large increase in part-time women workers – 31 per cent of the workforce in 1974 and 41 per cent in 1996 (see Exhibit 13.1). The composition of local government employment has, therefore, changed markedly over the last twenty years.

About a quarter of all employees are teachers, although, with any further spread of 'opting out', this proportion will inevitably decline. Other education staff represent an additional nearly 20 per cent of the total workforce. This figure includes administrators, special advisers, cleaning staff and school meal providers – the great majority female and part-time. Social services account for 18 per cent of employment. Social workers are only part of that number; various assistants, administrators, residential carers and home helps make up the total, which again is overwhelmingly female and substantially part-time. Law and order was, until its removal from local authority control, another major heading and included both police officers and the various civilian support staff. All the other employment headings in Exhibit 13.1 cover rather smaller numbers of staff, including those services that tend to be most closely associated with local government in the public mind: housing, refuse collection and public libraries.

☐ *The gender-biased hierarchy*

At the top of the local authority employment ladder is an echelon of senior managers and salaried professionals. The Chief Executive, the most senior of all managers, may receive a salary nowadays of over £100,000 depending on, among other things, the size of the authority (see Exhibit 13.2). A LGMB survey in 1996 found that more than a quarter of chief executives were paid 10 per cent or more above the top of the national scale, which ranged from £74,000 for shire districts to £90,000 for unitary and metropolitan councils. Chief officers, senior managers and senior professionals are also well rewarded for their service. They have, though, the sometimes unenviable responsibility for running the local authority or their particular department, advising councillors, and managing threatened budgets and possible personnel cuts (see Exhibit 13.3).

At chief officer level women are still poorly represented. While women make up 70 per cent of the total local government workforce, this is not reflected at the top managerial levels. In no sense at all is Heather Rabbatts a typical chief executive. The 1996 LGMB survey showed that only 5 per cent of chief executives and 9 per cent of chief officers in English and Welsh councils were women. This compared only slightly adversely with the equivalent top three grades in the civil service, 10 per cent of whom were female, but lagged well behind the former Department of the Environment's 19 per cent and even more so the NHS, where women had roughly 30 per cent of chief executive and almost half of general manager and senior manager posts. In Scotland women actually appeared to lose ground with reorganisation, as none of the new unitary councils operating from 1996 initially had female chief executives. Three Scottish councils, East Ayrshire, Glasgow and Moray appointed women as deputy chief executives, and Falkirk Council appointed a woman assistant chief executive. Six of the new Scottish councils, however, had no women at senior management level.

Exhibit 13.2 *'Arguably the worst job in local government'*

Heather Rabbatts
Chief Executive, Lambeth LBC (1995–)

Early life and education
Born in 1955 in Jamaica, to Jamaican clothes modelling mother and English soldier father; came to England aged 3.
School in Chatham, Kent, then FE College in London.
University College, London – specialising in British party politics, 1916–24.
LSE – MSc in International Relations.

Career
Into local government by accident, then meteoric rise.
Barrister, 1982–83 – represented Greenham Common Women protesting against cruise missiles.
Local Government Information Unit, 1983–86 – first women's officer.
Hammersmith & Fulham LBC: Director of Women's Department, 1987–9; Director of Personnel, 1989–91; Deputy Chief Executive, 1991–3.
Merton LBC, Chief Executive, 1993–5.
Then to neighbouring borough and – Lambeth's own job advert – 'arguably the worst job in local government'; also highest paid – £115,000 p.a.

Present job
London's Rudolph Giuliani – New York's crusading mayor and ex-attorney, elected to stamp out City Hall waste and corruption.
'Lambeth had the reputation of being corrupt, inefficient, loony left, typical of all that can go wrong in local government. My agenda is to turn Lambeth around . . . to change both the culture and some of the people.'
Insisted on having powers to hire and fire who she wanted.
In first year:
£40 million saved; work force cut by 1,200 to 9,000; council tax cut by 5p and collection rate up from 56% to 74%; 'Bulb Blitz' repair of 6,500 broken lights on council estates; mass evictions for non-payment of rent; creation of Anti-fraud Team to lead fight against housing benefit fraud.

Personal
'My day is mad and manic, but never boring.' Always running down corridors, rushing between meetings – 'I've become famous for changing my clothes in taxis.'
Caffeine and McDonalds' choc doughnut addict.
'At weekends I go to good restaurants with my friends, drink vast amounts of champagne, and buy expensive designer clothes' – and chauffeur teenage son and friends around in her yellow Fiat.

Useful quotes
'I readily admit my maths is probably as bad as the Chancellor of the Exchequer's, but I can get an overall grasp of a budget strategy, and we have accountants to do the adding up.'
'Signalling that I wish to be know by my first name is part of my interpersonal managerial style. It's about me being seen as a human being and relating to others here without all these huge tiers of hierarchy separating us.'

Sources: *Local Government Chronicle*, 25 June 1993; *Independent*, 8 July 1996; *Sunday Times Magazine*, 3 March 1996.

Exhibit 13.3   *The reluctant privatiser*

Peter Smallridge
Director of Social Services,
Kent County Council (1991–).

Education	North Western Polytechnic – training as psychiatric social worker; LSE – Diploma in Mental Health (1970)
Early career	Shire counties, with academic sabbatical. West Sussex CC (1965–71) – mental health social worker; area officer. Croydon College (1971–5) – Senior lecturer. Norfolk CC (1975–83) – Divisional manager. Warwickshire CC (1983–91) – Director of Social Services (1984–91). Created prototype public/private sector partnership: charitable co. to raise private finance to take over half of county's old people's homes and refurbish other half.
Present job	'Unrecognisable' from what it was in 1984 – esp. savage cash limits and no longer being monopoly provider of social services. Kent's 96/7 grant shortfall led to £23.7 mill (10.7%) cut in departmental budget, the loss of up to 1,200 jobs, and to Kent possibly becoming first county to privatise its in-house domiciliary care services – at same time as preparing for transfer of services to new Medway Towns unitary authority. 'No one in their right mind would ask a manager to deal with a budget reduction of more than 10% and simultaneously restructure the county. No business would attempt it, but we have to do it.'
Personal	Father also in social work – but none of his own three children. Ex-chain smoker; now cigars only, and not in office. Will leave Kent at end of fixed-term contract in 1998, when 55 – to play more golf, do some consultancy on social care management, and perhaps write novel.
Useful quote	'The position of director of social services is unique in local government, managing substantial resources to the benefit of disadvantaged people. You can actually have an impact on the quality of life of those individuals.'

Source: *Local Government Chronicle*, 7 February 1997, p. 22.

A similar 'glass ceiling' exists in England and Wales, although the number of female chief executives has gradually been increasing in recent years, albeit from a very low base. In 1997 there were some 30 women 'heads of the paid service', as they are sometimes called, in England and Wales, compared to just 6 in 1990. The London boroughs very much lead the way, with women holding about one in three chief executive posts, but women are now at least represented among chief executives both in English counties – e.g. Cheryl Miller in East Sussex, Jill Barrow in Lincolnshire – and in Welsh unitaries – e.g. Viv Sugar in Swansea and Joyce Redfearn at Monmouthshire. It is still true, though, as Leach *et al.* noted (1994, p. 200), that the discussion of equal opportunities in local government 'has been characterised by high levels of rhetorical excess, and the results have been very limited'. Rhetoric and practice are frequently poles apart, particularly at chief officer level.

The work of chief officers is shared with middle-ranking managers and professionals who will combine an expert knowledge of a particular service or support function (e.g. finance, personnel, the law, IT) with experience and involvement in overseeing the resources and employees of the authority. The number and range of these top and middle-management posts are considerable, as can be seen from the very brief selection in Exhibit 13.4. The final element in this group of senior managers and salaried professionals are those with professional training operating at the service frontline, such as teachers, field social workers, environmental health officers, development control planners.

Beneath the top managers and salaried professionals are the 'worker bees': a vast network of employees in a variety of lower status clerical, manual and non-manual jobs. These people receive relatively modest financial rewards and indeed many can be described in official terms as low paid (see Exhibit 13.5). Local authorities have nearly 750,000 administrative, technical and clerical (ATC) 'white collar' staff – including typists, clerical assistants, clerks in schools, technicians, nursery nurses and welfare assistants. They also employ about a million full-time or part-time manual workers. These are the people who clean streets and schools, the caretakers, council gardeners, home helps and road maintenance operatives. In addition, there is a substantial number of miscellaneous workers whose jobs are neither wholly clerical or manual: cashiers in canteens, ticket sellers, pest controllers, and so on.

So far, the discussion has presented the structure of employment within local government in general terms. The scale and nature of any individual authority's employment depends, as you will by now appreciate, on its size, responsibilities and particular circumstances. To pick just one example, Leicestershire County Council, before it lost the new unitary authorities of Leicester City and Rutland, employed over 19,000 full-time and roughly 16,400 part-time staff, giving an overall total of well over 35,000. Education, with 9,000 teachers and lecturers (25 per cent

Exhibit 13.4   *Some officer posts and what they pay*

	Advertised post (February 1997)	*Approx. salary*
Medway Towns Unitary Authority	**Chief Executive** To work with newly elected Shadow Council in setting up new North Kent UA of 240,000 people, formed by merger of former district councils of Rochester-upon-Medway and Gillingham.	£90,000
Bedford BC	**Director of Environmental and Community Services** New post, following amalgamation of two departments. Responsible for implementation of policies relating to planning, housing, environmental health, engineering, economic development, arts and leisure.	£65,000
Orkney Islands Council	**Chief Executive** To provide leadership, co-ordinating service delivery to Council's 20,000 residents on 20 inhabited islands off Scottish mainland, and to maintain partnership development of Atlantic oilfields.	£60,000+
Sandwell MBC	**Director of Housing** Responsible for delivery of all public and private housing services for country's 7th largest landlord, through network of 30 local offices and 800+ staff.	£55,000
St. Helens MBC	**Director of Contract Services** To manage one of Council's four departments, responsible for delivery of range of services including highways, engineering, building, cleansing, catering, grounds maintenance, transport, recreation, security services, building design.	£52,000
Croydon LBC	**Head of Committee Services** Reporting to Head of Corporate Services, responsible for developing and servicing committee system, elections, electoral registration, official visits, and members' services.	£45,000+
Nuneaton & Bedworth BC	**Human Resources Manager** To develop best recruitment and selection strategies for Council's 1000+ employees.	£33,000
Eastbourne BC	**National Lottery Officer** To research, develop and produce bids to National Lottery Distribution Agencies in line with Council's public and voluntary sector projects.	£25,000
Newham LBC	**Employment Development Officer** Member of Council's Local Regeneration Team, responsible for developing and implementing projects to assist local people to secure jobs.	£22,000

Exhibit 13.5 *Some less well paid local government posts*

Advertised post (February 1997)	Pay
Part-time School Cleaner Responsible for cleaning of a designated work area within the school site.	£3.83 per hr
Domestic Assistant, Children's Home To maintain a clean, healthy and warm environment for young people living in a 12-bedded mixed adolescent unit. All have behavioural, social and educational problems and at times will present challenging and unco-operative behaviour.	£3.98 per hr
Part-time Gardener/Conservationist To assist manager of special walled garden environmental centre designed for children with physical and sensory deprivation and for whom access to wild places is otherwise difficult or impossible.	£4.02 per hr
School Crossing Patrol Warden Caring, reliable person to make sure that the busy roads of Birmingham are safe for our children.	£4.20 per hr + retainer fee of £5.78 per week.
Part-time Building Maintenance Supervisor Responsible for day-to-day maintenance of school buildings, liaising with contractors, emergency cleaning, and general portage duties.	£62.12 for 15-hr wk
Crematorium Organist To play organ at funeral services and during arrival and departure of mourners.	£5,107
Carpenter, Housing Department To undertake repair, maintenance, renovation and some new work in both public buildings and council owned dwellings.	£192.42 per wk + production bonus
Motor Vehicle Fitter City and Guilds certificated and fully qualified fitter required to carry out MOT preparation, servicing and maintenance on variety of vehicles at vehicle repair works.	£212.69 per week + bonus
Clerk/Typist, Youth Justice Centre To provide clerical support to busy Youth Justice Team – including reception duties, word processing and computing, dealing with members of the public, petty cash and budgets.	£62.12 for 15–hr week
Library Assistant For library serving two inner city multicultural communities. Must be flexible in nature and able to learn new skills, from reading stories to children to using new technology.	£7,714–£10,215
Markets Police Patrol Officer To work in a team responsible for security of the Bull Ring markets. Duties include traffic and pedestrian patrol, security patrols, and enforcement of market by-laws.	£10,884–£11,647

of the total) and 13,000 support staff (37 per cent), was by far the largest employer, followed by social services with nearly 6,000 (17 per cent). When still the direct responsibility of the County Council, the police service, including traffic wardens and civilian staff, numbered over 3,500 (7 per cent), and the fire and rescue service nearly 800 (2 per cent). Your own council's Annual Report and Accounts will also contain details of both its current employment and recent changes. You might try comparing the figures with these from Leicestershire, which at the time was an above average-sized county with a population of about 900,000.

To summarise this section on the employment structure of local authorities, it is clear that, even following some significant contraction in recent years, councils are still, by any standards, large-scale employers of extremely heterogeneous workforces. They are thus of great economic importance within their communities and in a position to serve as an example to other employers.

Local authorities have at the top a range of well-paid senior managers and professionals, and beneath them a vast army of lower status administrative, clerical, manual and non-manual employees. These people are essential to the process of service provision, yet the financial rewards they receive are relatively modest. Compare, for example, Exhibits 13.4 and 13.5 and the more than tenfold pay differentials between jobs being advertised simultaneously. Employment packages incorporating non-transferable rewards such as cars and private health insurance are worlds apart from the experience of manual and clerical workers.

■ A view from below: degrees of alienation

This section is concerned with the experience and perceptions of those lower status employees that form the bulk of the local authority workforce. They are rarely studied by social scientists, yet an understanding of this 'hidden world' and of its rewards, frustrations, potential and limitations is essential for a comprehensive account of how local authorities perform their tasks and duties.

There is within all organisations a great mixture of cultures and activities. A local authority viewed from the perspective of a school cleaner is a very different organisation from that viewed by the Chief Executive, the Director of Education, or even a headteacher. Indeed, it may be very difficult for senior managers and councillors to know all the different cultures or perspectives of the hundreds or even thousands of employees they oversee. In part, this may reflect the fact that some knowledge and information is deliberately hidden from managers. Painter (1992, p. 67) suggests that local authorities like other organisations have front and back 'settings':

Front regions are the public parts or settings in which relations between management and workers, or between the council and service users, take place. The sorts of relations which take place in back regions are rather different and would include the tea break, those periods when the boss is out of the office, the staff rest room, and those operations which occur out of sight of service users. It is in the back regions that workers are able to satirise the management, to drop the special politeness reserved for customers/users and to tell jokes at the council's expense.

It is these hidden, 'back setting' cultures and perspectives that we want to try to understand. If you work in a local authority, you will be aware of the chasm that can exist between the official image of the authority and the opinions and practices of its own employees. If you do not work in local government, you could perhaps obtain a flavour of what we are talking about by discussing the issue with friends or relatives who do. Or why not, the next time you meet some council workers, ask them what they think of their employer and their jobs! We lack any really systematic studies at the moment and all that can be provided in this chapter are a few fragmented impressions.

What, then, do we know about the diverse views of those working in the lower status, less glamorous jobs in local government? Some revealing findings emerged from a range of surveys conducted by Services to Community Action and Trade Unions (SCAT) in co-operation with local authorities and their trade unions. The SCAT (1985) survey of Darlington Borough Council workers from building, maintenance, parks, refuse, street cleansing, catering and cleaning services found that:

* A third of the workforce had low or moderate job satisfaction compared to 24 and 45 per cent respectively who had average and high/very high satisfaction. The main cause of job dissatisfaction was poor management.
* 77 per cent of workers wanted to have their own area of work for which they would be responsible either individually or as a small team. Most workers wanted more say over how they carried out their work. The need for more training was a common concern.
* 43 per cent of workers thought they would be victimised if they refused to do an unsafe job. Half of park workers and 37 per cent of building workers said they did not receive the proper agreed protective clothing and equipment.
* 93 per cent wanted more information on council policies. A substantial number of employees were keen to offer their ideas about how services could be improved.

A similar set of opinions emerged from other SCAT surveys in Sheffield, Lewisham and Harlow. A survey of manual and clerical workers in Sheffield City Council's parks and recreation department (SCAT, 1985) revealed a widespread wish to have more control and responsibility in their work, backed up by more training. Thirty-eight per cent of manual workers believed they might be victimised if they refused to use unsafe machinery, although a large majority (86 per cent) said they received all necessary protective clothing and gear. Lack of communication again emerges as an issue, with workers feeling that their views about how to improve services were not considered by management. Significant job dissatisfaction was expressed by 40 per cent of clerical workers and 26 per cent of manual workers. Varied explanations for this situation were offered, of which one of the most graphic was: 'the job is boring and run by idiots' (p. 7).

The surveys by SCAT produce some valuable insights into how, viewed from below, employment by a local authority may be experienced. Many manual workers and lower status clerical workers have a lack of job satisfaction, a feeling of lack of control over their work, a view that communication channels within the authority are substantially blocked and that their health and safety concerns are not always taken into account. The modest level of financial reward is also a constant source of tension. These findings are not really surprising. Groups of workers in similar positions in the public or private sector are likely to experience some degree of alienation. Indeed, the nature of work is such that some feelings of dissatisfaction and discontent are inevitable.

Understanding something of the hidden culture of local authority employment is important, given the current concern with changing the way local authorities work and operate. Much management reform requires people working for local government to become more 'consumer-orientated', competitive, or concerned with 'value for money'. Senior managers may become convinced about the virtue of cultural change but others lower down the organisation may take some persuasion. For them, the change often creates not a new dynamic but a sense of chaos.

A case study of a radical decentralisation initiative in Tower Hamlets illustrates some of these points (see Lowndes and Stoker, 1992). In 1986 Tower Hamlets launched a major change in the way it provided services, setting up seven neighbourhood units to replace the previously centralised, traditional administrative system. The reform was to a degree successful, creating a new dynamic within the management of the authority and encouraging much experiment and innovation in meeting the needs of the people of Tower Hamlets. A survey of staff revealed that, when asked to describe the management style of the new neighbourhood organisation, half chose the description: 'boldly experimental, but with a tendency not to consolidate good ideas', and a further third chose 'crisis management in an environment of chaos'. There were plenty of more positive views, but for many in the organisation the experience of change was evidently disturbing and difficult.

In some settings – for example, where the challenge involves the introduction of compulsory competitive tendering (CCT) – the impact of change can be seen as very negative by manual and clerical staff. Painter (1992, p. 65) comments:

> In Wandsworth some trade unionists I spoke to were insistent that I should not divulge to others that I had been speaking to them. In Milton Keynes manual workers' shop stewards spoke of the complete demoralisation they were experiencing at the prospect of the service in which they worked being bought out by its management with the likely unsettling effect on their security of employment.

Not all experience of CCT has led to the development of a fearful and worried response. In some instances it has liberated new thinking and provided new opportunities for participation. The main point is that it cannot be assumed that change will be positively welcomed by all in an organisation.

For those towards the bottom of the local authority employment hierarchy the world appears in many respects profoundly different from that of senior managers and councillors. A dilemma for those seeking to understand and influence the performance of local authorities is how to get to grips with the diverse cultures and perspectives within the organisation. A commitment to customer service and value for money will take hold only if a substantial number of an organisation's employees can be persuaded of its value and benefit. Promoting such cultural change is unlikely to be easy. Creating a climate of fear from the top runs the risk that employees will respond with a 'let's-just-keep-our-heads-below-the-parapet' approach: not reporting problems, difficulties and failures. If a more consensual, open style is favoured, it may still be difficult to reconcile change with a maintenance of employees' sense of security and confidence. As Painter (1992, p. 65) argues:

> Blue-collar and clerical workers have traditionally had much less control over their work process and are thus more likely to experience change as unsettling and uncontrollable.

Realistic strategies for change require an understanding of the dynamics and nature of the hidden world of the lower status workers that form the bulk of the local authority workforce.

■ A view from above: the roles of management

We turn now from those who actually provide the services of a local authority to those whose job it is to manage them and it: the senior

officers at the top of the organisation. We have identified three dimensions of the senior management role which will be examined in turn:

* supporting, advising and monitoring politicians;
* representing the authority's interests externally;
* managing staff and resources within the authority.

□ Working with the politicians

The relationship between senior officers and councillors is explored fully
in Chapter 15. Senior officers are likely to be heavily involved in the
process of developing strategies and policies for the authority. Much of
their time is taken up meeting with councillors, writing reports for
committees, and liaising with officer colleagues in other departments
to provide policy advice and guidance. In addition, two other strands of
the councillor-senior officer axis can be mentioned. First, many councils
give officers considerable *delegated powers* in, for example, the granting of
certain categories of licence or planning permissions.

A recent trend has been for senior officers to be given also a *monitoring
role* in relation to the performance of the council and councillors. Part of
the Conservative Government's legislative reaction to the 1986 Widdicombe Committee Report was to make chief executives and chief finance
officers responsible for reporting directly to the council to ensure the
maintenance of legality and financial probity. More generally, most chief
executives nowadays will see the protection of the rights of minority
party groups and members as a key part of their role.

Senior officers stand at the heart of the decision-making processes of
local authorities. Their delegated powers and monitoring responsibilities
give them some powers, but above all it is their ability to influence the
choices, thinking and approach of councillors that gives them real
decision-making influence. Their proximity to the formal holders of
decision-making authority – the councillors – gives them an opportunity
for influence not afforded to such a degree to those in the lower ranks of
the organisation.

□ External relations

Managing relations with the world outside the council is also a substantial part of the daily workload of senior officers. Links with central
government officials, local authority colleagues in other areas, debates
within professional associations all contribute to a powerful network of
influence for the modern senior officer. They constitute important
sources of information and ideas. They provide a national forum in
which senior officers can present themselves as policy entrepreneurs and

learn from the experience of others. A senior officer can gain a reputation for pioneering new developments or approaches to service delivery.

Meetings, conferences and seminars contribute to the development of a complex network of 'national local government communities' in which senior officers locate themselves (see Chapter 8). Beyond the formal relationships with local authority associations and central government officials are informal opportunities for testing out new ideas, learning about new developments and gaining a sense of 'which way the wind is blowing'. Senior officers whose careers may involve moves around several authorities find that these networks within the local government community provide a valuable source of learning and information about potential opportunities (perhaps even their next career move!). More generally they enable senior officers to make sense of the local government world and to put the work of their own department, profession and council in a broader context – especially important in an era of rapid change.

Senior officers and professionals have in recent years been expected to develop a network of local links with private and voluntary sector organisations to match their already strong non-local ties. Indeed, if local authorities are fully to develop an enabling role (see the discussion in Chapter 20), then the enhancement of local ties – for instance in the spheres of economic development and urban renewal – is vital.

Senior officials in social service departments will certainly be in regular touch with voluntary groups and agencies. Land-use planners will have to represent the authority in public meetings and debates. Senior housing officers will attend evening meetings with tenants' associations and community organisations. In contrast to the position 30 years ago, these senior officers have come to expect a relatively 'rough ride'. People are generally less willing to accept professional explanations of what is best and are more prepared to question the policies and actions of the local authority.

☐ Internal management

The third role of senior officers is the management of the staff and resources of the authority. In recent years this role too has become more challenging. The shift from an era of growth in local authority spending to a period of standstill and cuts has made the management of finances and other resources such as building and equipment more problematic. Senior officers can face difficult choices about what to fund and what to cut (see Exhibit 13.3).

Gyford *et al.* (1989, pp. 105-8) identified a number of growing pressures and problems which could challenge senior officers' capacity to manage:

* New generations of officers joining local government have become progressively better educated and more assertive. Such officers are more likely to challenge conventional wisdom and call into question non-participative management styles.
* Resource problems limit promotion opportunities and this situation creates frustration among staff, making them less willing to co-operate with senior management.
* An intensification of union activity amongst manual, clerical and also professional staff has increased their readiness to strike, work-to-rule and engage in demonstrations in response to issues of concern.
* Staff are more likely themselves to be active in local political parties or campaigning groups, which can create problems for senior managers.
* Links between councillors and lower-ranking staff can create tensions. Such links may stem from trade union or other community-based connections. In some cases councillors may seek to influence appointments in the lower reaches of the authority – getting jobs for their friends or supporters.

The kinds of problems identified above have made the staff management task of many senior officers more challenging. There have, however, been a number of counter-trends that have helped to restore their 'right to manage'. First, the increased legislative restrictions on the taking of industrial action have had an impact in both public and private sectors. Secondly, the introduction of compulsory competitive tendering has allowed many senior officers to reassert control over their staff in an effort to make them 'fit for competition'. Work practices and operational efficiency have been reviewed in the light of a spreading competitive ethos. Senior managers in some instances have found they have had the upper hand in negotiations with the unions and the workforce for the first time. Finally the introduction of new management techniques has eased some of the burden on senior staff.

The devolving of budgets, the growing use of performance targets and performance-related pay, the development of quality circles and team-working, the use of IT to collect information and monitor activity have all in different ways created new opportunities for senior managers to guide and steer the management of staff and resources within their authority. What is being developed is a different style of *indirect management* which creates a range of powerful tools for senior managers. By involving staff in their own management, control over detail may be lost in return for greater leverage with respect to the overall performance and operation of the organisation (see Stoker, 1989, for a discussion).

■ From model employer to flexible employment structures

Local authorities have for most of the post-war period been seen as 'model employers'. They have been willing to recognise trade unions, adopt proper negotiating procedures, encourage equal opportunities, pay fair wages and provide stable employment. At least in comparison with some private sector employers, local authorities offered a relatively stable and safe employment. However, a number of changes – notably financial constraints and the impact of competitive tendering – have called into question this way of operating. There is evidence that a more flexible employment structure is emerging. Peter Smallridge's authority, Kent County Council, for example, has partly broken away from national bargaining and made its own pay settlements. More generally, as Leach *et al.* (1994, p. 199) note:

> authorities have found it difficult to maintain national pay and conditions in services that are subject to competitive tender and where there is a strong private sector. There is a movement away from formal systems for the management of industrial relations towards more ad hoc approaches reflecting the organisational interests of management.

The financial squeeze on local authorities in the 1990s brought in its wake further redundancies. The spread of compulsory competitive tendering from blue-collar to white-collar services means that the majority of employees in local government face the prospect of competing for their jobs on a regular basis. For some, the loss of a tender may mean redundancy. For those that remain in post new conditions of employment are likely. In this environment it may well not be possible for local authorities to maintain the 'good employer' tradition. As a councillor from Stroud comments:

> It is all very well for a council to aspire to the highest conditions of employment; but, if the consequence is failure to win that vital contract, and with it the resultant loss of jobs for dozens of people, are councillors entitled to adopt such a principled stance?

In response to such dilemmas and the changing environment, many local authorities have sought to introduce greater flexibility into their employment patterns. In 1996, for example, a fifth of chief executives were employed on fixed-term contracts and the Local Government Management Board's evidence showed that this was an increasing trend. In local government as a whole, the number of staff on fixed-term arrangements is more than double that for the whole economy. The

Labour Force Survey for Spring 1996 found 8.5 per cent of staff in English and Welsh councils were on fixed-term contracts compared with 3.6 per cent across all sectors in the two countries. Southampton Unitary Authority, for example, hired its new team of five directors and a chief executive on five-year fixed-term contracts. Resources sub-committee chair Richard Bates observed: 'It gives us the opportunity of looking again at our structure so we can alter it again in the light of what we learnt during reorganisation . . . if you've got a permanent contract it's very difficult to dismiss senior officers' (*Local Government Chronicle*, 27 September 1996).

The search for flexibility involves a number of dimensions, only one of which is the fixed-term contract. Others include:

1. *More flexible establishment control* – Several authorities have adopted flexible staffing structures in which the Personnel Committee exercises detailed control over senior appointments and below that chief officers can employ and deploy staff as required, within limits on numbers and grades set by the authority.
2. *More flexible contracts and job descriptions* – which can make it easier to transfer staff from unit to unit and adopt new working practices. A few authorities are making appointments which permit transfers between departments at the authority's discretion. Such an approach may be particularly useful for the clerical and administrative work that exists in all departments. There is increased interest in flexible job descriptions which emphasise what the job should achieve rather than how the work is done.
3. *Performance-related pay* – Central government remains strongly in favour of performance-related pay (PRP) as a means of linking pay to output and productivity. PRP is one of a number of approaches to improving performance. Others include Performance Management (PM), Performance Appraisal (PA) and Performance Indicators (PIs). Many authorities use PM or PA without PRP. A survey of local authorities by the LGMB in 1993 found nearly a half using PM and over a quarter operating PRP schemes. (See also Chapter 18.)
4. *Flexible working conditions* – In meeting community social and leisure needs a rigid 9 to 5 Monday to Friday pattern of working is by no means always the most appropriate. Many authorities have negotiated more flexible working arrangements in establishments such as leisure centres. A few authorities are experimenting with home-based working for certain categories of staff.

■ Conclusion

This chapter has provided an overview of the local authority workforce. What emerges is a picture of a complex range and variety of people involved in the process of delivering services and developing strategic local policies. Many of the industrial relations and other workplace issues faced in local government are similar to those found in large-scale private sector organisations. In general, the traditional bureaucratic approaches to managing staff have been replaced by managers with devolved budgets and responsibility for their own staff. The position of local authority managers, however, is complicated by their base within the public sector. Issues such as wage awards, redundancies, and competitive tendering become the subject of political argument and debate. The task of management is further complicated by the involvement of councillors in the management and oversight of the authority. Given a commitment to democratic control, the involvement of councillors is inevitable. Yet for some senior managers in local government there can be no doubt that councillors just add to the trials and tribulations of the job.

The role of leading councillors and managers in creating the conditions for better public services can, however, be exaggerated. Unless the local government workforce as a whole is well-motivated and committed to public service, the everyday experience of services by the citizen will not be positive. As Fowler (1988, pp. 2–3) comments:

> People constitute the resource by which the inanimate factors of finance, land, property and equipment are converted into the delivery of services ... Consider the different outcomes which are likely from two different kinds of workforce. The first is well-trained and highly motivated, the second has low morale and inadequate skills. It takes little imagination to see that in the former case, good decisions will be made and members of the public concerned will be dealt with courteously and efficiently. In the latter instance, the public will probably be treated brusquely and unhelpfully, and decisions will be taken with the primary aim of avoiding anything that smacks of hard work.

The secret of success, it appears, is for councillors and managers to value their workforce. Valued people will be more likely to provide responsive, sensitive and efficient service delivery to the public.

Guide to further reading

Once again, you should ideally start by finding out about your own local council's present staff structure and recent employment trends, which should be set out in its Annual Report. More generally, Poole (1978) is this chapter's equivalent of Hepworth on finance in Chapter 10: the traditional authoritative introduction, but now more outdated than dated. Regrettably, it has not been fully replaced, though Fowler (1988) and Laffin (1989), specifically on industrial relations, go some way towards filling the gap. Modern management approaches and practices are presented in Leach *et al.* (1994). Pratchett and Wingfield (1996) provide an interesting discussion of the public sector ethos in local government.

■ *Chapter 14* ■

Political Parties

■ Introduction

Like it or not – and we conclude this chapter by examining both sides of the case – party politics nowadays is a central feature of local government across most of the UK. In the first part of the chapter, therefore, we look at the current political landscape of local government and briefly at how that landscape has come to look as it does. We then compare the organisation and impact of the principal political parties, inside and outside the council. We examine too the role of the national parties in relation to local government and their respective policies and programmes.

■ The survival of non-partisanship

It is important to get the balance right when dealing with party politics in local government. Understate its significance, and you risk completely misunderstanding where and how many of the most important council decisions are made: behind the scenes and in advance of the public committee and council meetings. Overstate it, and you fall into the trap of assuming that all councils are run on disciplined party lines and that all decisions are party-based. The truth is that, as with almost everything to do with local government, the variety of practice is almost infinite. Nothing is universally true of all 450 or so authorities in the country, as can be seen in outline in Exhibit 14.1.

Exhibit 14.1 summarises the range of party, and non-party, systems in Great Britain in 1996/97. In the metropolitan areas of the country, in most of the English counties and new unitaries, and in the larger shire districts there are *fully developed party systems*. Nowadays over four-fifths of all councils come into this category and, because they include nearly all county and unitary councils, they touch the lives of almost all British voters. All or a great majority of the councillors on these authorities are elected under the labels of national or nationalist political parties and, having been elected, they organise themselves into separate party groups. Independents and representatives of local or fringe parties find it hard to get elected to these councils and are in many places non-existent (see also Exhibit 14.2).

Exhibit 14.1 Party systems in local government, Great Britain, 1996/97

PARTY SYSTEM AND DEFINITION	ENGLAND					WALES	SCOTLAND	GREAT BRITAIN	
	New Unitaries	Counties	Non-Met Districts	Met Districts	London Boroughs	New Unitaries	New and Former Unitaries	Total	%
COMPLETELY/PREDOMINANTLY NON-PARTISAN (60% or more seats held by Independents)	–	–	8	–	1	3	5	14	3
WEAK PARTISAN (20–59% of seats held by Independents)	–	1	46	–	–	4	3	54	12
MULTI-PARTY/FRAGMENTED (20% or more seats held by third party/parties)	3	24	51	2	7	1	–	88	20
TWO-PARTY (80% of seats held by two parties, neither more than 55%)	2	6	32	3	3	–	1	47	10
ONE-PARTY DOMINANT (55–69% of seats held by one party) Cons	–	–	5	–	–	–	–	5	
Lab	–	2	35	7	7	3	10	65	
LD	–	–	24	–	–	–	–	26	
(SNP)							1	1	22
ONE-PARTY MONOPOLISTIC (70% or more seats held by one party) Cons	–	–	–	–	3	–	–	3	
Lab	8	1	62	24	10	11	10	126	
LD	1	1	11	–	2	–	–	15	
(SNP)	–	–	–	–	–	–	2	2	33
TOTAL	14	35	274	36	33	22	32	446	100

Source: Municipal Yearbook, 1997.

In the more rural areas of England and in Wales and Scotland the picture can be very different. Here there are many English district and Scottish and Welsh unitary councils with *weak party systems* (12 per cent as defined in Exhibit 14.1) and others that are actually or effectively *non-partisan*, almost all councillors having stood as Independents or perhaps Ratepayers' or Residents' Association representatives.

Perhaps the best examples of complete non-partisanship are the three Scottish Island authorities: Orkney, Shetland and the Western Isles. But predominantly non-partisan councils are to be found in many parts of the country that are by no means parts of any Celtic fringe: Cambridgeshire, Cumbria, Devon, Dorset, Durham, Gloucestershire, Humberside, Lincolnshire, Oxfordshire, Shropshire, Somerset, Staffordshire, Surrey.

■ Varieties of party systems

The extent of nominal partisanship is the first clue to understanding how a council is likely to operate. At least as important, however, is its *party mix*. In Exhibit 14.1 we identify four varieties of developed party systems:

1. *Multi-party or fragmented* – relatively few Independents, but council seats divided among several party groups. Most of these councils will be 'hung' or 'balanced', in the arithmetical sense of there being no one party with an overall majority. Their actual forms of administration can vary greatly – from single-party minority rule, through different types of informal co-operation, to the rare two- or even three-party formal coalition (see Chapter 15). In countries with proportional representation systems of election multi-party hung councils are the norm. Our first-past-the-post system reduces their number, but it is still far easier for third and minority party candidates to win election in the smaller wards and divisions of local councils than in our much larger parliamentary constituencies.
2. *Two-party* – relatively few third party and Independent members, council seats being split fairly evenly between the two leading parties. Depending on the actual party balance, some of these councils too will be hung. In others control will swing regularly from one party to the other.
3. *One-party dominant* – one party holds a decisive majority of seats, and will expect to run the council most of the time.
4. *One-party monopolistic* – self-explanatory; the extreme product of our electoral system, one party having unbroken, and often effectively unchallenged, control of the council.

Exhibit 14.2 Party affiliations of councillors, Great Britain, 1997/98

PARTY AFFILIATION	ENGLAND										WALES		SCOTLAND		GREAT BRITAIN			
	New Unitaries		New Counties		Non-Met Districts		Met Districts		London Boroughs		New Unitaries		New and former Unitaries		1997/98		1979	
	No.	%	No.	%	No.	%	No.	%	No.	%	No.	%	No.	%	No.	%	No.	%
Conservative	423	17	881	40	2,306	21	197	8	518	27	42	3	82	7	4,449	20	12,143	53
Labour	1,372	57	746	34	4,263	40	1,875	76	1,047	55	725	57	615	49	10,643	48	7,351	32
Liberal Democrat	550	23	495	22	2,829	26	357	14	321	17	78	6	126	10	4,756	21	1,032	4
Nationalist Parties	–	–	–	*	–	–	–	–	–	–	115	9	186	15	301	1	278	1
Ratepayers/ Residents' Ass'n	–	–	2	*	120	1	7	*	24	1	1	*	1	*	155	1	} 2,232	10
Independents and Others	80	3	79	4	1,242	12	45	2	7	*	311	24	234	19	1,998	9		
TOTAL	**2,425**		**2,203**		**10,760**		**2,481**		**1,917**		**1,272**		**1,244**		**22,302**		**23,036**	

Notes: * = less than 0.5%

'Others' include Liberals, Social Democrats, Greens, other small local parties – the Morecombe Bay Residents (Lancaster), the single Monster Raving Loony (North Devon); also vacant seats.

In Northern Ireland party affiliations of the 582 district councillors were as follows: Official Unionist Party 205; Democratic Unionist Party 97; Social Democratic and Labour Party 121; Sinn Fein 51; Alliance 45; Independent 35; others 28.

Figures for the London Boroughs exclude the 157 members of the Common Council of the City Corporation of London which claims to have no party politics.

Source: Local Government Chronicle Elections Centre, University of Plymouth, May 1997.

Exhibit 14.3 Pattern of control of local authorities, Great Britain, 1997/98

| TYPE OF CONTROL | ENGLAND | | | | | | | | | | WALES | | SCOTLAND | | GREAT BRITAIN | | | |
| | New Unitaries | | New Counties | | Non-Met Districts | | Met Districts | | London Boroughs | | New Unitaries | | New and former Unitaries | | 1997/98 | | 1979 | |
	No.	%	No.	%	No.	%	No.	%	No.	%	No.	%	No.	%	No.	%	No.	%
Conservative	2	4	9	26	8	3	–	–	4	12	–	–	–	–	23	5	256	49
Labour	29	63	8	24	85	36	32	89	17	52	14	64	20	63	205	47	113	22
Liberal Democrat	6	13	2	6	39	16	–	–	3	9	–	–	–	–	50	11	2	*
Nationalist Parties	–	–	–	–	–	–	–	–	–	–	1	5	3	9	4	1	4	1
Independent	1	2	–	–	13	6	–	–	1	3	4	18	6	19	25	6	68	13
No overall control	8	17	15	44	93	39	4	11	8	24	3	14	3	9	134	30	75	14
TOTAL	46		34		238		36		33		22		32		441		518	

Notes:
*=less than 1%
'No overall control' is a purely arithmetic definition of councils on which no single party has more than 50 per cent of all seats. It may therefore include councils on which a single party holds exactly half the seats and, through the casting vote of the mayor or chair of the Council, may be in a position of effective control.
In Northern Ireland 2 councils were controlled by the Official Unionists and 2 by the Social Democratic and Labour Party. The remaining 22 were under no overall control, as defined above.

Source: *Local Government Chronicle* Elections Centre, University of Plymouth, May 1997.

■ Labour's present local dominance

It can be seen from Exhibit 14.1 that in 1996/97 the vast bulk of these predominantly one-party councils were in Labour hands. To an extent this is almost invariably the case, particularly in the party's modern-day strongholds in Wales, Scotland, and much of metropolitan England. But it has a more recent and probably less permanent element also: the by-product of the Conservatives' unprecedented dominance of the national parliamentary stage.

A party in power nationally usually expects to lose a certain number of seats in local elections to protest votes, and by 1986 Labour, for the first time since the 1972–3 local government reorganisation, controlled more councils than the Conservatives. The trend continued, until by the early 1990s Conservative local representation had been eroded to the point where the party had fewer councillors and ran fewer councils than at any time in modern memory. The party made a small recovery in the May 1992 district elections, compounding Labour's General Election demoralisation, but then in the four-year cycle of local elections from 1993 to 1996 it suffered by far its worst set of results on record. Across the country as a whole, therefore, Labour is for the foreseeable future the overwhelmingly dominant party, locally as well as nationally, in terms of both councillors' party affiliations (Exhibit 14.2) and councils controlled (Exhibit 14.3). The Liberal Democrats in 1997 were in an unambiguous second place, ahead of the Conservatives, who during their long period of national government lost 242 (nearly 95 per cent) of the councils they controlled in 1979 and nearly two-thirds of their 12,000 councillors.

It is several years now since the declining number of Independent councillors was passed by the rising numbers of Liberal Democrats or their Liberal and Social Democrat predecessors. Yet it should be noted that in 1997 they too held sway on more councils than were controlled on their own by the Conservatives.

■ The history of local party politics

Nearly 20 years ago, as James Callaghan's Labour Government was nearing its end, the local government landscape looked vastly different from that we have just described. The Conservatives, in opposition nationally since 1974, were overwhelmingly in the ascendant locally, with a total of one in every two councillors and control of more than half of the country's councils. Labour, by comparison, held just 15 per cent of councils and, with under a quarter of all councillors, they hardly out-numbered Independents. The 1980s and 1990s thus saw two parallel trends operating in tandem: the swing from Conservative to Labour dominance, and the continuing decline in the number of Independents. It is this second trend that we shall now examine.

The present-day hold of party politicians on so much of the country's local government is a comparatively recent phenomenon. At the same time, the role of parties in many towns and cities dates back at least as far as the Municipal Corporations Act 1835 (see Chapter 4). We should therefore view the emergence of a more politicised local government as 'a steady long-term trend, beginning in the nineteenth century, spreading in this century first through the major cities and then, if less evenly, to the shires' (Young, 1986a, p. 81). The trend has been well described in recent years, by Young himself and also by Gyford, who usefully identifies five stages to the story, which we summarise in Exhibit 14.4.

Our chief concern in this chapter is naturally with Gyford's final Reappraisal stage, incorporating as it does both a quantitative extension of the scale of party politics in local government and also some fundamental qualitative changes in its character. Much of the quantitative change occurred suddenly and immediately upon reorganisation in the early 1970s. Up to that time about half the councils in England and Wales and two-thirds of those in Scotland could be defined as 'non-partisan', in that over half their elected members resisted all conventional party labelling. There was, as ever, an urban–rural divide: between two-thirds and three-quarters of urban councils being run on party lines compared with one-third of county councils and just 10 per cent of rural district councils.

Reorganisation inevitably involved the merging of many previously non-partisan authorities with others having stronger partisan traditions. The latter invariably prevailed, and following the 1973/74 elections the proportions of predominantly partisan authorities rose immediately to nearly 80 per cent in England and Wales and to over a half in Scotland. Almost all English county councils were now party-dominated and three-quarters of all English and Welsh district councils.

In the succeeding few years this trend continued, with the Conservative Party in particular insisting that all party sympathisers stand as official party candidates and not, as often happened previously, as Independents. As we saw in our earlier Exhibits, Independent councils and councillors still survive in significant numbers, but they are being inexorably squeezed, election after election. They were squeezed even more in Scotland and Wales by the mid-1990s' reorganisation of local government. In both countries there are now far fewer Independents on the new unitary authorities than there were previously.

■ Party politicisation in practice

Counting is easy. But there is a lot more to understanding the party politicisation of local government than simply adding up the numbers of party-dominated councils. If we describe a council as party politicised,

---

Exhibit 14.4   *The party politicisation of local government*

1. **Diversity** (1835–late 1860s) – many of the new municipal councils dominated and split by party politics, but no uniform national pattern. 'Tories, Whigs, Conservatives, Liberals, Radicals, Chartists, Improvers and Economisers offered varying prescriptions in different towns' (Gyford *et al.*, 1989, p. 7). Main divisive issues: role of religion in educational provision; levels of municipal spending; drink/teetotalism.

2. **Crystallisation** (1860s-1900s) – administrative rationalisation of local government accompanied by a channelling of party politics, where it existed, into a predominantly Conservative–Liberal contest. Key catalyst: Joseph Chamberlain's Birmingham Liberal Association (1860s), as both a successful electoral organisation and a radical pioneer of municipal collectivism – local government's pro-active involvement in gas and water supply, slum clearance, public health, parks and gardens.

3. **Realignment** (1900s-1940s) – Labour's displacement of the Liberals as the principal radical force in local government, offering 'a distinctive municipal programme calling for better wages and conditions for council workers, the provision of work for the unemployed, public baths and laundries, and adequate housing for working class families' (Gyford *et al.*, 1989, pp. 11–12). Anti-socialist response orchestrated by the Conservative Party through local groups labelled variously Moderates, Progressives, Municipal Alliance and Ratepayers.

4. **Nationalisation** (1940s-1970s) – of previously local government-run public utilities and hospitals and of local party politics. Increasing involvement of the national party organisations in local government; local elections fought increasingly on national issues and personalities; but most county and rural district councils still organised on non-party lines.

5. **Reappraisal** (1970s onwards) – rapid growth and change in character of local party politics following local government reorganisation. Quantitative change – increasing numbers of party-dominated councils and declining numbers of Independents – accompanied by qualitative change, through the formalisation of local party organisation and the intensification of policy debate.

Source: Gyford *et al.* (1989, ch. 1).

we should expect to find certain features of organisation and modes of operation. They are not new; they developed gradually, notably under the direction of Labour's influential London leader, Herbert Morrison, in the 1920s and 1930s. Morrison's model party system, described by one of his biographers, George Jones, comprises at least seven elements (Jones, 1975):

1. *The selection of candidates* by local committees of party members.
2. *The formulation of a distinctive policy programme* by a local party group, usually comprising a mix of councillors and local party representatives.
3. *The production of a party election manifesto* to which all party candidates are expected to adhere, both during the election campaign and once elected.
4. *The attempted implementation of the manifesto* in the event of the party winning a majority of seats on the council.
5. *The organisation of councillors into party groups* for the purposes of allocating committee places and other positions of leadership and responsibility, developing and co-ordinating party policy, determining strategy and tactics, and ensuring group discipline.
6. *The election of a group leadership*, comprising an individual leader and usually a committee of group executive officers, by members of the party group.
7. *The convening of pre-council and pre-committee party group meetings* to enable party group members to agree on policy and plan their debating and voting tactics.

This party political dimension rarely gets included in diagrammatic representations of the organisation and working of councils. For it inevitably complicates an otherwise fairly straightforward picture of officers and departments servicing committees of councillors who make policy decisions that are then publicly approved in full council. In Figure 14.1 we acknowledge that complication, but, in the interests of realism, we try to show not only where party politics fits into the policy making process, but how in many councils it actually drives it.

Accordingly, the party groups, often omitted altogether, feature here almost at the centre. For these party groups and their respective sizes are the direct outcome of the local elections and will determine who is to run the council and how. The elected leader of the majority or largest group will generally become Leader of the Council. The majority group's manifesto becomes the council's agenda, to be translated into practical policy proposals by the relevant departments. Councillors of the majority group will chair all committees and sub-committees, and liaise closely with departmental chief officers in preparing their committee agendas. The majority group will dominate the membership of all the committees

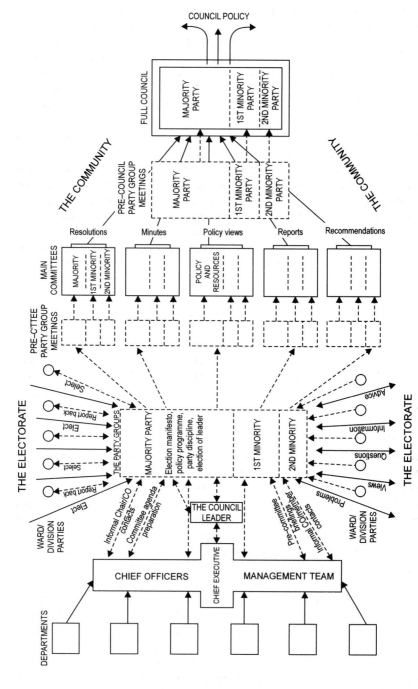

Figure 14.1 *Council policy making: where the parties fit in*

and sub-committees that will debate, amend and approve proposed policies before they go to full council for final ratification. Each public committee meeting will usually be preceded by private pre-committee meetings of the different party groups at which they determine their tactics: which issues they will focus on, who will speak to them, how they will vote. In short, for a proper understanding of how most councils work, you need to visualise the 'unofficial' organisation of the political parties completely superimposed on the 'offical' structure of committees, departments and full council.

A hung council, in which there is no overall majority party, will inevitably operate differently in practice, but not in principle. There may have to be negotiated compromises on manifesto proposals. Committees may be chaired by members of more than one party, and of course no votes – either in committee or full council – can be won simply through the exercise of tight party discipline. Officers may find themselves dealing with and briefing spokespersons from two or three different parties. But the essential process and relationships will be the same as depicted in Figure 14.1.

■ Party differences – organisation and leadership

Any political party would recognise most of the organisational principles in Morrison's model and our diagrammatic representation of them. True, practice may sometimes deviate from principle. A dearth of willing and capable volunteers may 'informalise' candidate selection procedures, as we saw illustrated in the experience of some of our councillors in Chapter 12. Party manifestos will vary enormously in length and specificity, ranging from almost book-length productions to some that look as if they were lifted from the proverbial back of an envelope (Gyford *et al.*, 1989, pp. 167–72). Party discipline varies too, some groups treating potential or actual voting dissent with considerably greater tolerance than others (Gyford *et al.*, 1989, pp. 172–75). There are also some *systematic differences* of formality and emphasis across the political parties, as exemplified in Exhibit 14.5.

The fundamental difference between the Labour and Conservative Parties derives directly from their contrasting origins and objectives. Labour is a programmatic, constitution-based, ostensibly democratic party whose local operations are governed by a set of Model Standing Orders for Labour Groups. Some local parties will adhere much more rigidly than others to these Standing Orders, but there is a greater uniformity of practice than among local Conservative parties, and a significantly more influential role for outside party members in the selection of candidates and the determination of policy. There is a similar potential for internal party conflict to that at the national level between

Exhibit 14.5 *Differences in local party organisation and operation*

		LABOUR	*CONSERVATIVE*
1.	DIRECTION FROM NATIONAL PARTY	*Model Standing Orders* and regular *NEC Action/Advice Notes* on policy and practice that local party groups are expected to follow.	*Model Constitution* for Conservative groups – completely non-binding; a guide to 'good practice'.
2.	BASIC PARTY UNIT FOR LOCAL GOVERNMENT PURPOSES	Borough/District/County Labour Party, composed of delegates elected from constituency and ward parties and affiliated trade union branches.	Borough/District/County Conservative Association, less formally and less uniformly structured than in the Labour Party. Possibly also a constituency Local Government Advisory Committee.
3.	KEY OPERATIONAL UNIT OF LOCAL PARTY	*Party Executive Committee*, annually elected and a potentially conflictual combination of councillors and often more radical non-councillor members.	Small group of Association officers, annually elected, plus permanent party agent, if one exists.
4.	CANDIDATE SELECTION	By ward parties, but only from a *panel of approved candidates*, drawn up by the local party executive committee from ward party or union branch nominees. Process overseen by regional party. Candidates expected to have party/union experience.	More varied than in Labour Party. By ward branches, possibly but not necessarily from a panel of candidates. No long-standing party experience, or even membership, necessary.
5.	PARTY GROUP ON COUNCIL	Likely to be more formally run than Conservative groups: tighter internal discipline and more frequent meetings.	Usually less tightly organised than in Labour Party, and may be more accepting of strong leadership.

6. RELATIONS BETWEEN LOCAL PARTY AND COUNCIL GROUP	'Group members are part of the local party and not separate from it.' Party representatives have right of non-voting attendance at party group meetings; group nominees should report back to local party; regular joint meetings.	Informal. Party representatives – e.g. party agent or constituency chairman – may attend group meetings, usually as observers.
7. COUNCIL POLICY	Formally the responsibility of the *local party*; in practice usually debated/negotiated with party group, who determine implementation strategy.	Determined by council group and possibly discussed with constituency's Local Government Advisory Committee.
8. ELECTION MANIFESTO	Formally the responsibility of the local party, in consultation with the council group; sometimes drafted through a network of working groups of councillor and non-councillor members.	Usually drawn up by senior councillors, with group leader taking a leading role. Generally shorter and narrower in scope than Labour manifestos.
9. ELECTION OF GROUP LEADERS	Annually, usually by council group members only; very occasionally by electoral college', including outside party delegates.	By council members only. Role of leader formally more powerful than in Labour Party.
10. SELECTION OF COUNCIL COMMITTEE CHAIRS	Almost always elected by party group members.	Usually elected by party group members, but Leader or 'inner circle' of senior party members may play more significant role in nominating and even selecting.

the Parliamentary Labour Party and the Conference-elected National Executive Committee, with party activists concerned to prevent councillors becoming 'sucked into' the council and being deflected by professional officer advice from manifesto priorities.

The Conservatives, traditionally the party of the *status quo*, have evolved over a much longer period of time than Labour and are generally much less rulebound in both their national and local organisation. There is a model constitution for Conservative groups, produced by Conservative Central Office, but it is not binding and is regarded more as a guide to good practice. Liberal Democrats too tend instinctively to favour structural flexibility and to resist externally imposed discipline, although in recent years the influential Association of Liberal Democrat Councillors has endeavoured to preach the virtues of group organisation and coherence. More recently still, even Independents have had an incentive to form themselves into at least loosely-knit groupings, in order to claim their entitled proportion of places on committees, as specified in the Local Government and Housing Act 1989.

A second and obviously related dimension of party difference that emerges in Exhibit 14.5 is that of the parties' attitudes towards leadership, which again are distinctive locally as they are nationally. Leach and Stewart have identified three broad types of leadership style that can be ranged, as in Figure 14.2, along an individualistic–collective continuum (Leach and Stewart, 1990, p. 6).

At one end of the continuum there is *leadership from the front*, where the leader is looked to by the party group to take the initiative in proposing major policy developments which the group will then generally agree and adopt. The style of the *group spokesperson* is essentially the reverse: the party group is the chief source of policy decisions, the leader's main

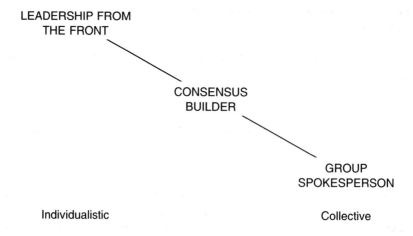

Figure 14.2 *Three basic political leadership styles*

role being to act as the group's public mouthpiece, first in the council chamber and then in dealings with the media. Somewhere in the middle of the continuum can be identified the role of *consensus builder*. Here the leader actively seeks to build consensus in the party group, arguing for what he or she feels is the most desirable or attainable policy, but positively committed too to accepting and publicly advocating the eventual majority group view.

The three principal parties differ in their receptiveness to these contrasting leadership styles. Local Conservative groups, though rarely as deferential as in the past, are still the most predisposed towards leadership from the front. Leaders are expected to lead – that is what you elect them to do.

An outstanding example was Dame Shirley Porter, Conservative Leader of Westminster City Council, 1983–91. She left some very prominent and personal legacies of her leadership: hundreds of business-sponsored white and green designer litter bins; the modern, strategically sited 'Porterloos'; and, most serious and controversial of all, accusations of wilful misconduct for having attempted to boost the Conservative vote in marginal wards through the selective sale of council houses – the 'homes for votes' scandal, as it has become known. It is not the propriety of Dame Shirley's leadership that concerns us here, though, so much as its unquestionably individualistic style:

> I am synonymous with Westminster City Council. In my years as Leader I've tried to change the culture at the Council, but . . . it's like taking the British Empire and turning it into Great Britain plc. You're changing a cosy establishment of both members and officers. We've had our battles . . .
>
> I remember asking, 'Why don't we run this Council like a business?' One of my own side, a certain uptight gentleman with a moustache, spluttered, 'This is the Council!' That was the beginning of my wanting to change the way things were run.

Her leadership was summed up by a badge she liked to wear, saying 'YCDBSOYA':

> I'll give you the polite version. It means 'You Can't Do Business Sitting On Your Armchair'. My father, Sir Jack Cohen, who built the Tesco supermarket chain, gave one to Callaghan and one to Heath, but I haven't had the temerity to give one to Mrs Thatcher yet. (Abdela, 1989, pp. 186–93)

The then Prime Minister used to figure regularly in Shirley Porter's interviews, and there were some striking similarities between the two women's pro-active leadership styles: the impatience with the traditions and conventions of public administration, the readiness to see their own colleagues as part of the problem as much as part of the solution.

In the other two parties such a highly personalised view of leadership would be much more difficult to sustain, certainly nowadays. Individualistic, let alone autocratic, leadership has become unfashionable, and politically risky. There are still plenty of strong and highly influential Labour leaders around but, out of a combination of constitutional necessity and the politician's instinct for personal survival, they will generally take considerable care to carry their party groups with them, and publicly to talk the language of consensus, teamwork, and – to use a favourite expression of Birmingham's longstanding Labour Leader, Sir Richard Knowles – 'comradeship'.

David Bookbinder, Leader of Derbyshire County Council, 1981–92, was a contemporary and in some ways a Labour version of Shirley Porter: an equally high media profile and just as concerned to challenge the 'cosy' culture of local government. But, even in a personal interview, Bookbinder's choice of first person pronoun was usually plural:

> For years and years it has always been the view that local government is a partnership between the councillors and those professionals employed to deliver services . . . Nonsense! The officers have one role and the members have another. The members are elected and the job of any government is to govern . . .

> We have a term – being officered. The officer will get hold of the Chair at a pre-committee meeting, explain to the Chair what they want to do, give them a report, and the Chair will instruct the committee members to deliver what is on the paper. But a member's role is not to say yes or no to the recommendation at the end of the report. We want to say what goes into the sausage machine. We are supposed to be the creators, elected on a political philosophy. We have changed people's quality of life: 80% of children get school meals when it used to be 50%; twice as many old folk are getting home helps; meals on wheels are the same price as when we took control in 1981; we have more nurseries. (Willis, 1990)

■ Party differences – policies and principles

David Bookbinder's declamation takes us neatly from organisation to policy. Our main political parties do organise themselves and operate differently from each other, but even more obvious are their policy differences.

As we have emphasised throughout this book, local government, its structure, functions and financing, have come in recent years to occupy a prime place on the UK national political agenda. Accordingly, no national party's manifesto is now complete without a substantial section outlining the further changes that it will impose upon local government, should it be elected to office. The party manifestos for the 1992 General Election were typical – set out in detail in Exhibit 14.6 of the first edition of this book – each party had its own proposals for the future financing of local government, for the provision of some of its principal services, and even for its basic structure and organisation. As a result, the scale, scope and shape of our local government system were all significantly different at the end of the 1992–7 Parliament from what they would have been under either a Labour Government or some form of joint Labour–Liberal Democrat Administration.

The three parties' 1997 manifestos, summarised in Exhibit 14.6, differ less fundamentally than in 1992 on structure and finance – these issues having been the subject of Conservative legislation following that 1992 election. But in other areas they each have their quite distinctive policy initiatives and emphases that make a mockery of cynics' attempts to discuss them as effectively interchangeable.

The contrasts can be just as great at local elections. Local councils are certainly more restricted and constrained in what they can do than they used to be. They cannot raise taxes as they might wish, or exceed their Government-imposed spending targets, or even spend all the proceeds from the sales of their own capital assets. But, even though the limits of their budgets are externally defined, the *content* is still largely theirs to determine, in accordance with the local and political priorities of the party or parties in control.

Local elections thus continue to be run in such a way as to suggest that the outcome makes a difference. Party manifestos and candidates' election addresses are likely to combine local issues with some of the national policies headlined in Exhibit 14.6, and the whole atmosphere and conduct of the election will be set by the party defending its record and those that may be seriously challenging it. We have tried to convey something of the flavour of these partisan contests in Exhibit 14.7.

The three elections summarised in Exhibit 14.7 were selected not for their typicality, but simply because they received a greater than average amount of media attention and because they were entirely party political clashes. All the significant candidates stood under their respective party labels, embraced publicly their parties' manifesto and campaign promises, which in turn determined the key topics of electoral debate. The parties, in short, defined and focused the campaign and probably boosted whatever interest the media and electorate might have had in it.

Exhibit 14.6 The 1997 local government manifestos

	CONSERVATIVES	LABOUR	LIBERAL DEMOCRATS
STRUCTURE	No change, except minor increase in power for parishes Maintain opposition to Scottish Parliament and Welsh Assembly	Scotland: law-making Parliament with tax-raising powers, subject to referendum Wales: assembly with secondary legislative powers London: strategic authority and mayor, both elected Regions: some devolution of power to regional chambers of councillors All councils to have annual elections	Tax-raising parliaments in Scotland and Wales Elected regional assemblies where there is public demand Strategic authority for London PR for all local elections Abolish quangos or increase their accountability
FINANCE	Retain capping Reduce business rates for small businesses More 'challenge funding' and public-private financing	Retain reserve capping power Consult with businesses on business rates Fairer distribution of grant	Long-term aim to replace council tax with local income tax Allow councils to raise more funds locally Return business rates to local control
INTERNAL MANAGEMENT	Continue CCT Legal restrictions on strikes in essential services	Abolish CCT Require councils to obtain 'best value' for services, and publish local performance plans with service targets	Power of general competence for councils Increase elected membership of police authorities

INTERNAL MANAGEMENT (*cont.*)			Increased monitoring powers for Audit Commission Encourage democratic experimentation – e.g. elected mayors
EDUCATION	Encourage more grant-maintained schools More budgetary devolution to schools More freedom for schools over employment of staff All schools permitted to select Encourage more grammar schools, where wanted Independent inspection of LEAs	Scrap nursery vouchers Guaranteed nursery places for all 4-year-olds Reduce class sizes for 5-7 year olds to 30 or less Phase out assisted places scheme More budgetary devolution to schools OFSTED and Audit Commission inspection of LEAs Parent representatives on LEAs	1p rise in income tax, to be invested in education Nursery places for all 3- and 4-year-olds Double spending on books and equipment in 1 year Reduce class sizes for 5-11 year olds to 30 in 5 years More monitoring of LEAs LEAs to devolve as many powers as possible to schools Bring GM schools and city technology colleges into LEA framework Phase out assisted places scheme
HOUSING	Councils to sell inhabitable houses empty for 1 year Encourage council tenants to transfer to new landlords	Phased release of capital receipts to fund building and repairs Duty on councils to protect the unintentionally homeless Private finance to be used, with tenants' consent, to improve housing	Phased release of capital receipts to fund building and repairs More public-private partnerships to build homes More powers for councils to deal with unfit private housing Rights for tenants to manage their estates

---

Exhibit 14.7   *Three local elections: three policy battlefields*

(1) WANDSWORTH, 1990 – MRS THATCHER'S FLAGSHIP LONDON BOROUGH
Recent history: won by the Conservatives from Labour in 1978; run since then, together with Westminster, as one of London's two radical, privatising, tax-cutting Thatcherite 'flagship' authorities.
Conservative record: council workforce halved, partly through compulsory redundancies of manual workers; long list of services subject to competitive tendering, with claimed savings of £6.5 million p.a.; 16,500 properties sold to tenants and developers; cash from sales, plus efficient tax collection, produced lowest poll tax in England and Wales; pioneering programme of specialist 'magnet' secondary schools under way, streamed by academic progress rather than age.
Labour challenge: cost-cutting and contracting-out of services has left the poor, elderly and vulnerable with inadequate and highly charged social services; council rents are among the highest in London; low poll tax achieved only by Conservative Government 'massaging' its grant allocation to Wandsworth and by running down financial reserves.
Liberal Democrats: effectively absent from this two-party battle.
1990 result: Conservatives gained 17 seats from Labour, greatly strengthening their council majority.

(2) RICHMOND UPON THAMES, 1990 – LIBERAL DEMOCRAT SHOWCASE
Recent history: traditional Conservative suburban stronghold, won in early 1980s by Alliance predecessors of Liberal Democrats, who by 1990 held 46 of the 52 council seats.
Liberal Democrat record: consultation with and involvement of local residents, previously ignored by Conservative administrations, to provide responsive, quality services; poll tax lower than in surrounding Conservative-controlled Surrey districts; 'Green' Charter.
Conservative challenge: more efficient management could produce significantly lower poll tax; threatened loss of borough's world-famous ice rink for housing development without guarantee of replacement; wasteful and unpopular public sculpture in concourse of Council's new civic offices.
Labour: no seats to defend, or likely to win.
1990 result: Liberal Democrats gained 2 seats, strengthening their hold on the council still further.

(3) EDINBURGH, 1992 – LABOUR'S SCOTTISH CAPITAL
Recent history: won by Labour from Conservatives in 1984, for first time this century; run initially by 'hard left', who abolished civic robes, flew red flag and African National Congress banner above the City Chambers, and confronted the Government over spending limits; run since 1986 internal party coup by respectable 'soft left' Labour group.
Labour's record: building a modern European city, venue of December 1992 Euro-summit, with emphasis on public investment and service provision; five new sports centres and swimming pools, with more planned, which the Conservatives would allegedly turn into private leisure clubs; new libraries opened; use of council house sales receipts (unfrozen in Scotland) to build 400 new houses plus 500 sheltered homes; 'green' plan to protect city's environment.
Conservative challenge: council must change from being 'municipal socialist' service provider to 'enabler', contracting out services cutting spending, and using sales receipts to cut poll tax.
Liberal Democrat hope: to hold the balance of power in a hung council – 'we would discuss anything with anybody'; emphasis on local issues; more home improvements, fewer 'prestige projects'.
Scottish Nationalists: also hope for balance of power; campaigning for national constitutional change: a multi-option referendum on devolution.
1992 result: Labour lost 2 seats and overall control of the council.

■ The pros and cons of party politics

It is at election time that we see most clearly both the positive and negative features of the extensive role played by party politics in our modern-day local government. We have already alluded to some of the claimed positive features, which would include:

* *More candidates, fewer uncontested seats* in local elections.
* *More active campaigning*, more information for electors, more debating of the issues.
* *Clarification of the issues*, as the parties are challenged by their opponents to defend and justify their arguments and assertions.
* *More citizen awareness and interest* in local government generally and the local council and its services in particular, resulting probably in a higher electoral turnout.
* *Stimulation of change and initiative*, as parties with their underlying principles and collective resources develop policies to put before the electorate.
* *More opportunities for public involvement in community life.*
* *Enhanced accountability*, as the parties collectively and their candidates individually make public commitments and promises which, if elected, they must seek to implement, and for which they can subsequently and electorally be called to account.
* *Governmental coherence* – the existence, following a decisive election result, of a single-party administration, clearly identifiable by the electorate and council officers alike, able to carry out the policies on which it was elected.
* *Enhanced local democracy* – the existence of electorally endorsed party policies and programmes reducing the potential policy influence of unelected and unaccountable officers.

The logic underpinning most of these claims seems indisputable. Yet it remains the case that many of us are unpersuaded by them. When asked, as in the 1985 Widdicombe Committee survey, a majority of us (52 per cent) say we would prefer local councils to be run on non-partisan lines, with only a third of us (34 per cent) feeling that a party system is better (Widdicombe, 1986d, p. 88). We need to examine, therefore, the other side of the coin: the alleged costs and disbenefits of party politics in local government, which would include:

* *More party candidates, fewer Independents* – as the major parties, with their institutional resources, make it increasingly difficult for minority party candidates and Independents to get elected.
* *More narrow debating of the issues* – with rounded discussion displaced by the strident adversarial clash of party rhetoric.

* *Less electoral enlightenment* – as uncommitted voters become disenchanted by the polarisation of debate and by politicians' apparent convictions that their party alone possesses all the answers.
* *Electoral boredom* – with electors staying at home, invoking 'a plague on all their houses'; others not bothering to vote because the outcome seems a foregone conclusion.
* *Less public involvement* – with the many citizens not wishing to join a political party being excluded from areas of local community life.
* *Nationalisation of local elections* – as supposedly local campaigns focus much of their attention on national issues and personalities.
* *Reduced representativeness of councils* – as the winning party takes all positions of responsibility and seeks to implement its policies to the exclusion of all others.
* *Excessive party politicisation of issues* – with the parties feeling obliged to adopt usually adversarial positions on subjects that might more satisfactorily be approached consensually.
* *Reduced local democracy* – as councillors are 'disciplined' into voting with their party, regardless of their personal convictions or judgement.
* *Exclusion of professional advice* – as all effective decisions are made by party groups, usually without the benefit of professionally trained and experienced officers in attendance.

■ Conclusion

Set out in this way, the arguments may seem evenly balanced. Certainly, you must form your own conclusions, preferably with reference to your personal experience and impressions. Realists that we are, we would be inclined to point first to the historical trends we identified earlier in the chapter. The comprehensive party politicisation of most of our local government is not only here to stay, but has recently received a hefty boost, with reorganisation and the spread of geographically larger, unitary authorities.

Finally, we would refer back to the argument we put forward in Chapter 12: that politics, properly understood, is at the very heart of what local government is necessarily about. It is about the management and resolution of the inevitable conflict of local views concerning the provision and distribution of public goods and services. That being so, there is something to be said for these conflicting views being marshalled and articulated openly by consciously accountable party politicians, rather than by self-styled 'non-political representatives', whose motives and policy objectives may be left publicly unspecified.

Guide to further reading

John Gyford has probably contributed most to our understanding of local party politics in recent years, starting with his introductory text (1984) and contributions to the sections on party politics in the Widdicombe Committee research (Widdicombe, 1986b) and in Gyford *et al.* (1989). The nearest equivalent to the Widdicombe Committee in the 1990s has been the independent Commission for Local Democracy. Among the Commission's key concerns were the extent and impact of the party domination of much of local government, which were addressed in one of its commissioned research papers (Game and Leach, 1995 and 1996). From an earlier period but also retaining their interest are Bulpitt (1967) and Grant (1978). Some of the best studies of individual local authorities of varying party political complexions include Hampton (1970) in Sheffield, Dearlove (1973) in Kensington and Chelsea, Newton (1976) in Birmingham, and Green (1981) in Newcastle upon Tyne. Goss (1988) takes a longer historical perspective of the London Borough of Southwark – one of the 'municipal left' councils studied by Lansley, Goss and Wolmar (1991).

■ Chapter 15 ■

Who Makes Policy?

■ Introduction – the internal politics of policy-making

The last three chapters have looked at three of the key elements in a local council's policy making process: elected councillors, the professional officers who advise them, and the political parties and party groups of which most of them are members. We turn now to the end-product of the process, as presented for example in Figure 14.1 – the actual formulation and determination of policy. We know from several of the chapters in Part 1 that much of the framework, and especially the financial framework, of local government policy nowadays is laid down by central government. But we have also seen how local authorities can still determine their own spending priorities, respond to specific local circumstances, and launch their own policy initiatives. Our concern in this chapter is therefore mainly with the *internal*, rather than external, influences on policy-making, with the internal politics of the town or county hall.

While formally policy is invariably made in full council and in various committees and sub-committees, other elements – notably political party groups and networks, relationships within and between departments, 'deals' between parties when councils are hung or balanced, as well as alliances between leading officers and councillors – all help to shape particular policies at specific points in time. It is these informal relationships – the levers and channels of informal influence – that this chapter is about.

■ Analytical models

There are three main models which have been widely used to describe the distribution of power and influence inside local authorities. Each is considered briefly before the chapter goes on to emphasise the need to broaden out the discussion beyond the narrow confines of these three models.

□ *The formal model*

This model takes as its frame of reference the 'legal–institutional' approach which dominated the study of local government until the early

1970s. Its proponents tended to see power relationships in purely formal terms and to focus on the formal structures of decision-making – the council, its committees and departments. The model could hardly be simpler: councillors make policy, while officers advise them and carry it out. No overlaps or qualifications are countenanced.

Advocates of this formal model argue that, if you understand the formal, legal position, you understand reality. Critics retort that reality, and certainly political reality, is considerably more complex, as already suggested in our discussion of councillor roles in Chapter 12. A model which sees councillors making policy through the council and its committee system, while officers merely advise and implement, tells us more about what perhaps *should* happen than about what *actually* happens. Thus Greenwood *et al.* (1980, p. 4) maintain that the formal approach fails to recognise the complexity and organisational variety within local authorities. They argued that it

> neglects variations between the decision structures of local authorities, variations that may well have important consequences for the involvement of councillors and members, for the pattern of decision-making, and, ultimately, the balance of service provision.

Furthermore, the approach is essentially static in orientation. It pays little attention to the way local authorities 'change and develop, even within an unchanging institutional environment' (Greenwood *et al.*, 1980, p. 4). Dearlove too is critical (1979, p. 55): 'the orthodox view of the relationship between councillors and officials is at best simplistic and at worst wrong'.

Yet one must beware of dismissing any model too readily. The Thatcher years saw real assertiveness by councillors of both the New Urban Left and the Radical Right. They set out to run authorities themselves in the way that the formal model delineates. Remember the quote in Chapter 14 from David Bookbinder that could easily have been echoed by Dame Shirley Porter: 'the officers have one role and members have another. The members are elected and the job of any government is to govern.' For a time at least, therefore, this model, often dismissed as naive, had its forthright advocates.

☐ *The technocratic model*

A rival to the formal model has been the technocratic model, which views *officers* as the dominant force in local politics. Their power resides, it is asserted, in their control of specialised technical and professional knowledge unpossessed by and possibly incomprehensible to part-time, amateur, generalist councillors.

This model too, however, is something of a stereotype and should not be accepted uncritically. Highly paid, professionally trained officers, heading large departments, with all the staff and other resources of these departments at their disposal, can appear formidable to the inexperienced newly elected councillor entering the council offices for maybe the first time. But the relationship is by no means all one-sided.

Plenty of leading and long-serving councillors, including those likely to be chairing the key committees, will have the experience, knowledge and political skill to assert themselves effectively in any negotiation with officers. Moreover, even the neophyte councillor comes with that vital source of democratic legitimacy that no officer, however senior, can ever have: the authority of having been *elected*, on what is now an endorsed political platform, to represent all the citizens of their locality.

In Exhibit 15.1 we construct a kind of balance sheet of the respective resources of officers and councillors – a little like that in Exhibit 1.6 in which we compared the resources of central and local government. We argued then that local government has access to more resources than is sometimes suggested, and so it is with councillors in their relations with officers.

Exhibit 15.1   *The resources of officers and councillors*

OFFICERS	COUNCILLORS
* Professional knowledge, training, qualifications	* Political skills, experience; possibly training, expertise, qualifications in own field of work
* Professional networks, journals, conferences	* Party political networks, journals, conferences
* Full-time, well-paid employee of council	* Member of employing council, spending an average of 20 hours per week on council work
* Resources of whole department	* Resources of whole council
* Knowledge and working experience of other councils	* In-depth (possibly lifetime) knowledge of own council, ward, its residents and service users
* Commitment to professional values and standards	* Commitment to personal and political values, to locality and community
* UNELECTED 'servant of the council' – appointed to advise councillors and implement their policy	* ELECTED on political manifesto to make policy and represent hundreds/thousands of residents and service users

It will be apparent from Exhibit 15.1 that it has been the politicisation, and particularly the intensified *party* politicisation of local government during the past two or three decades, that has done more than probably anything else to shift the balance of power between officers and elected councillors. We come back again to the rise of ideologically committed and politically skilful councillors of both the new left and the new right, which inevitably served to check any independent policy aspirations of officers. In the 1990s, for example, ruling Conservative Party groups in Westminster LB, Wandsworth LB, Wansdyke DC in Avon and Rochford DC in Essex were particularly assertive in the introduction of competit-ive tendering and the enabling/purchasing philosophy – just as a decade earlier the 'municipal left' had introduced their public transport and council housing subsidies, and their job creation and anti-discrimination policies.

Notwithstanding such examples, the professional and technical knowl-edge possessed by officers remains a tremendous resource, equipping them to act as powerful policy-makers *in the absence* of any positive policy lead from members. As professionals, they are always there to fill any policy vacuum. It is up to councillors to set their own clear policy agendas and thus to ensure that there is no vacuum.

□ The joint élite model

Deficiencies in the formal and technocratic models have encouraged the development of another perspective – the joint élite model – which argues that policy-making is dominated by a small group of senior councillors *and* officers, with backbench councillors and junior officers at most only marginally involved. This joint élite model is widely proclaimed. Blowers (1980, pp. 9–10) observes:

> The power to make policy and take decisions is concentrated among a few leading officials and politicians. The interaction of these decision-makers, and the transmission of ideas and hopes and fears among them, reveals how power is exercised and to what purpose.

This interpretation is supported in a number of studies. Saunders' research in Croydon (1980, pp. 216–30) revealed a picture of town hall politics where chief officers and political leaders work as 'close allies' maintaining a powerful control over policy-making. Green (1981, p. 102) found that in Newcastle the principal participants in defining problems and suggesting solutions were the chairman and the chief officer who had a symbiotic, mutually supporting relationship. Cockburn in her study of Lambeth saw the backbencher 'excluded by the high-level partnership between the leadership and senior officers' and as a con-sequence 'taking little part in the policy planning process'. Council decision-making was, Cockburn maintained, dominated by 'a tightly-knit hierarchy under the control of a board of directors (the chief officers) in close partnership with a top-level caucus of majority party members' (Cockburn, 1977, p. 169).

The joint élite model thus has plenty of supporters. It distinguishes, in a way that seems reflective of reality, between senior councillors and officers and their more junior colleagues. But it too has its critics, who question the virtual monopoly of influence apparently attributed to this élite. Young and Mills (1983) argue, for example, that the very exercise of routinised power by those at the top of a hierarchy makes them less likely *sources of policy change* than actors lower down. These junior actors learn from direct operational experience and often have the creative energy that is necessary for the development of new initiatives. Important though the leading councillors and officers in any authority obviously are, a thorough understanding of the policy process requires a recognition that they will rarely constitute a united cohesive group. In the real world relationships are both more complex and also frequently characterised by tension and conflict.

■ Broadening the debate: additional influences

There is far more, therefore, to an understanding of the distribution of policy influence in a local authority than simply an analysis of the activities of the most senior personnel. As Stoker and Wilson (1986) show, other factors need to be incorporated into any genuinely realistic model. The joint élite model requires supplementing if the dynamism of internal power relationships is to emerge. Figure 15.1 provides a diagrammatic representation of the model which is outlined in the remainder of this chapter. The elements illustrated in Figure 15.1 can be categorised, in a clockwise order, as follows:

* *Intra-party influences* – relations *within* especially ruling party groups, and between groups and the wider party;
* *Inter-departmental influences* – relations between and across departments and professions;
* *Intra-departmental influences* – relations within departments;
* *Inter-party influences* – relations *between* party groups, especially in hung authorities, where they have to take account of one another.

□ The ruling party group and party networks

The ruling party group as a whole, not just its leading councillors, can have a significant influence on policy-making. Very few party groups are homogeneous; often there are factions that make it difficult to achieve

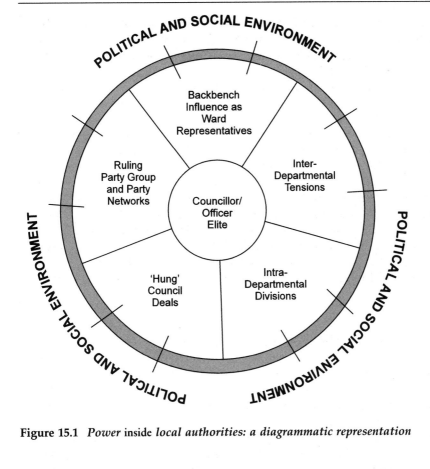

Figure 15.1 *Power* inside *local authorities: a diagrammatic representation*

and maintain unity. Policy initiatives can emerge from the backbench members of a group; additionally, backbenchers can veto leadership proposals with which they disagree. Stoker (1991, p. 98) shows that, while over many issues and for most of the time a group may

> simply endorse decisions taken elsewhere, at the very least senior councillors and officers must be careful not to offend the core political values and commitments of backbenchers. The role of party groups in local policy-making is, with the increased intensity of party ideology and organisation, a potentially crucial area for decision-making.

Given the factionalism within groups, a leadership can rarely take for granted the automatic support of all party group members. The party group can flex its muscles to remove the group leader. In November 1995, for example, two majority group leaders – Stewart Foster in Leicester and Valerie Wise in Preston – were overthrown on the same day, following votes of no confidence by their respective Labour groups. More routinely, groups will reject or refer back policy proposals presented by committee chairs. As the Widdicombe report noted (1986b, p. 90):

> The days seem to be fast disappearing when a leader could hope to deliver the group's vote without first consulting it in any way. Leadership styles still cover a wide spectrum from the ultra-democratic to the downright authoritarian. The trend however seems clearly in the direction of more open and consultative leadership under which discussions in group become a crucial, perhaps the crucial, element in final decisions.

The *local party network* also requires consideration. Links with the wider party organisation can be a valuable resource for individual group members, especially in the Labour Party where such networks have a greater policy significance, with local election manifestos, for example, being drawn up in consultation with non-councillor party members (see Exhibit 14.5). It was thus the district parties in Walsall and Rochdale, rather than the party groups on council, who were the real originators of the decentralisation policies in those boroughs. Local councillors and council leaders must respect the role of the wider movement; disregard can easily lead to conflict.

☐ *Backbench councillors*

Backbench councillors, in their capacity as ward representatives, can play their part in shaping policy. In promoting or defending local ward interests, councillors can sometimes enter the policy arena in a very influential way. In Leicester in 1983 two Asian Labour councillors initiated a campaign which overthrew the majority Labour group's housing policy by blocking a demolition plan in their ward (see Stoker and Brindley, 1985). Local ward interests can easily cut across party interests, and in authorities with relatively weak party systems (see Exhibit 14.1) these local interests are likely to be compensatingly stronger. In such circumstances councillors can, by developing alliances and lobbying, contribute regularly and effectively to the shaping of council policy.

To suggest, as some role classification schemes do, that councillors are predominantly interested in *either* ward representation or policy development is both demeaning and misleading. They can be and frequently are involved in both. On particular issues at specific points in time they can exert considerable influence, although it has to be said that much new legislation (e.g. CCT) requires 'a hands-off approach from councillors in relation to the detailed management of services, and a broad change in emphasis from the organisational role to the representational role' (Leach *et al.*, 1994, p. 183).

☐ *Inter-departmental tensions*

Different departments represent different interests and therefore have different, and potentially conflicting, sets of priorities. At times of zero growth or, increasingly, cuts in services and staffing, such differences surface and can lead to arguments across departments in the fight for scarce resources, and conceivably for departmental survival.

There are also instinctive *professional rivalries* – between, for example, the technical departments involved in land development. 'Planners, architects, housing managers, valuation officers and engineers all claim an involvement and there is a long history of rivalry between these professions' (Stoker, 1991, p. 102). Dominance of specific departments and professions will inevitably change over time; unacceptable policies will be delayed and favoured policies will be accelerated. Increased professionalisation within the local government service has meant that inter-departmental tensions are never far from the surface. They will spill over into the policy sphere with some regularity.

According to Pratchett and Wingfield (1996), the dual impact of market competition (especially through CCT) and of the internal reforms associated with the advent of the 'New Public Management' has led to some erosion of the public service ethos in local government. The divisions of functions between client and contractor that are engendered by market competition have led to increasingly antagonistic and adversarial relations between different parts of the same organisation, encouraging more reticent and secretive behaviour within local authorities. Employee loyalty is frequently perceived nowadays to be to a specific 'cost centre' rather than to the broader authority.

☐ *Intra-departmental divisions*

Intra-departmental divisions are a further factor in the policy-making equation. Individual departments are frequently no more homogeneous than are party groups. The size and diversity of many departments mean that, in effect, the span of control a chief officer can exercise must be limited, thereby providing junior officers, often with greater technical expertise by virtue of their more recent training, with scope for influence.

Most departments in larger local authorities consist of hundreds, even thousands, of employees in a range of relatively separate hierarchies and organisational divisions. Indeed, given the recent trend towards departmental mergers in many authorities, there is increasing scope for competing priorities and internal friction *within* a single department. The Planning and Transportation department of Leicestershire County Council, for example, had in 1996 the following eight major areas of responsibility: public transport services; traffic; road safety; highways;

street lighting; environment; planning; waste regulation. Kirklees Metropolitan District has five strategic directorates overseeing the whole of the authority's activities. In such contexts senior managers play the role of directors of larger groups of more disparate, if related, services than would have been the responsibility of their predecessors.

Divisions within departments can also arise with the introduction of decentralised management and service delivery. Area-based housing officers, for instance, may develop a dual loyalty, not only to the local authority but also to their specific operational area and its residents. Conflict is by no means uncommon between area offices and central departments or between a number of decentralised area offices. Additionally, junior officers working in decentralised offices within a local authority can develop close ties with local ward councillors – another source of potential influence for junior officers. Failure to incorporate *junior* officials in any model of decision-making inside the town hall is to ignore a group which can be extremely influential.

☐ *'Hung' or 'balanced' councils*

The increasing prevalence of hung or balanced councils – those on which no single party has an overall majority of councillors – raises further questions about the adequacy of the joint élite model, which assumes the existence of a small group of leading majority party councillors. In 1979, one in seven councils was hung; in 1997/98 the figure was nearly one in three (see Exhibit 14.3). On twice as many councils, therefore, party groups now *have* to take account of each other's policies and actions; otherwise any proposal they put forward can in principle be defeated at any time. First, though, they need to determine amongst themselves how council business is actually going to be conducted. There are several possible forms of hung council administration, of which the three most prevalent are:

(a) *Minority administration* – where one party, usually the largest, is prepared and permitted by the other parties to take all committee chairs and vice-chairs and, in this sense at least, to 'govern' as if it were in overall majority. About a third of recent hung authorities have adopted this model, examples among county and regional councils including Bedfordshire, Cumbria, Hertfordshire and Warwickshire (Labour), Devon, West Sussex and Wiltshire (Liberal Democrats), and Tayside (SNP).

(b) *Power-sharing* – where two or more parties agree to share committee chairs, but without, usually, any more far-reaching agreement on a shared policy programme; in other words, a deal or arrangement, rather than a formal coalition. About half of all hung authorities have been run in recent years by such power-sharing agreements, most frequently involving Labour and the Liberal Democrats.

(c) *No administration/rotating chairs* – where there are no permanently held chairs, the positions being rotated for procedural purposes amongst two or more parties, but without their having any policy significance. Among English counties, Avon, Leicestershire, North Yorkshire and Oxfordshire have recently operated such systems.

All these forms of hung council administration – especially the latter two – involve extensive inter-party contact and negotiation of the sort that is rarely seen in majority controlled councils. Officers too – particularly the chief executive and chief officers – have to assume different roles, working with and briefing spokespersons from possibly several parties rather than just one. They may, indeed, perform a brokerage role, actually bringing the different parties together in order to negotiate some policy or procedural agreement. Backbench members can also find their position enhanced, as, in both committee and full council, every single vote becomes precious. Bargaining thus becomes the order of the day, because there is no élite of members from a single party who can be sure, unaided, of delivering a policy programme.

■ Conclusion – constantly shifting alliances

The three conceptual models presented in the first part of this chapter – the formal, the technocratic, and the joint élite models – provide insights into local policy-making but have demonstrable deficiencies. Even the joint élite model is overly simplistic. While 1970s changes in management structures towards a more corporate approach certainly strengthened the positions of leading councillors and senior officers, it is misleading to see policy-making as a process restricted to this joint élite. While their centrality is not questioned, their exclusive dominance certainly is. Local authorities are *political* institutions – in both the narrowly partisan and broader senses of the word. They incorporate a whole range of additional actors and influences that may impinge on policy-making, depending on an authority's traditions, culture, leadership, political balance, and so on. The policy process in the real world is a complex and changeable one. It can be regarded as a series of shifting alliances, forming and re-forming over time and from issue to issue (Greenwood and Wilson, 1989). These networks and alliances vary enormously, but they are by no means solely the preserve of leading councillors and officers.

Guide to further reading

The Widdicombe Committee Report and accompanying research volumes (1986) are still relevant reading in this area, as is Gyford *et al.* (1989), which summarises much of it. One of the best books for providing insights into departmental politics is Young and Mills (1983). Stoker and Wilson (1986) offer both a critique of traditional analytical models and a discussion of alternative perspectives. For recent accounts of political parties in local government and the operation of hung councils, see Game and Leach (1996) and Leach and Pratchett (1996).

■ *Chapter 16* ■

Local Pressure Groups: The Exercise of Influence

■ Introduction

Most studies of local communities point to an extensive local pressure group universe. Newton, in an exhaustive study of Birmingham City Council in the 1960s, entitled his chapters on local pressure groups 'The Politics of the Four Thousand', reflecting the fact that he had identified no fewer than 4,264 local voluntary organisations in the city – at a time when, to take a rough and ready indicator, there were in the country as a whole less than a third of today's total of registered charities. More recently, Bishop and Hoggett (1986) found extensive group networks even in small district councils. Our interest in this chapter, though, is not so much in the numbers of groups – a sizeable majority of whom, as in Newton's study, will not be politically active on any regular basis – as in the influence of a minority of them on the making of local policy and the delivery of local services.

■ An all-embracing definition

It is easy to get side-tracked into discussions of alternative definitions of pressure groups – or indeed of whether, since many of them in practice have little effective pressure they can bring to bear on government, it might not be more strictly accurate to label them all 'interest groups'. We confess to being a little careless about such matters and therefore propose adopting Moran's exceedingly straightforward definition (1989, p. 121):

> any group which tries to influence public policy without seeking the responsibility of government.

An all-embracing definition of this nature acknowledges that the apparently least political of groups can be drawn into the political process, if only intermittently. Thus a local gardening association resisting a proposal to build a road over its land becomes temporarily a pressure group.

At local level many groups are precisely such single purpose groups which rise and fall with specific issues – e.g. local planning matters.

The latter part of the definition is important too. For it enables us to include those groups who may put up candidates for local elections, alongside candidates from other larger and mostly nationally-based parties that most definitely *are* seeking the responsibility of government. Single-issue parties and candidates are using the electoral process in this instance as a means of publicising their cause, not because they themselves want to govern the locality. Leicestershire CC elections have seen several of these single-issue candidates, including three in 1989 seeking a 'Voice for Rutland', prior to the then district being granted unitary status, and one in 1993 leading a 'Campaign Against the Road'. In each instance these candidates were seeking an additional publicity platform for their cause.

They neither wanted the responsibility of government, nor attempted to field remotely enough candidates to enable them to take it on, even if successful. By the same token, councils can themselves on occasion become pressure groups in larger political arenas, in making representations to Parliament, central government, or the EU. Some councils indeed nowadays employ professional parliamentary lobbyists to make their case as effectively as possible – those companies that have been in the news for their employment and payment of MPs. *Westminister Advisers*, to pick just one example, has worked for Lincolnshire, Humberside and Bedfordshire CCs, helping them to campaign against nuclear waste dumping; also for Hart DC in its fight against the Foxley Wood settlement.

■ Some classifications

The inevitable consequence of adopting a deliberately catch-all definition is that it produces a vast population of groups which then require some form of classification. In the literature on nationally organised pressure groups the most common distinction drawn is between, on the one hand, sectional or interest groups and, on the other, promotional, cause or attitudinal groups. You will find this idea – the significance to a group of there being a *congruity* between its aims and mode of operation and the political and policy objectives of the controlling party group(s) on a council – is one to which we return regularly throughout this chapter.

Sectional groups exist to defend and advance the interests of their own members involved in usually some economic activity – e.g. trade unions, business and employers' organisations, professional associations. *Promotional* groups exist to promote or campaign for some cause or principle – e.g. the environment, civil liberties, animal rights, the welfare of children, single parents, pensioners or the handicapped.

Exhibit 16.1   *A classification of local groups*

1. **Producer or economic groups** – incorporating businesses, trade unions and professional associations. *Partnerships* with such groups have become increasingly important in recent years, aided by various central government initiatives e.g. City Challenge, the Single Regeneration Budget.

2. **Community groups** – which draw on distinct social bases for their support, e.g. amenity groups, tenants' associations, women's groups, and groups representing ethnic minorities. They vary in their policy influence and *financial and administrative support* depending on the congruence of their aims and activities with those of the local authority. Grants are the major vehicle of support for such groups.

3. **Cause groups** – concerned with promoting a particular set of ideas and beliefs rather than their immediate material interests. Typically *not* the type of organisation which receives much official support from a local authority. Again, grants are the main form of relationship, and one would expect a consistency between the local authority's political agenda and that of any groups chosen for support.

4. **Voluntary sector groups** – organisations established to meet a perceived need in the community on a non-commercial, non-statutory basis. These groups have expanded a good deal in recent years, *especially* since the introduction of the purchaser/provider split in social services. Increasingly the form of relationship is becoming *contractual*.

Source: Stoker (1991).

At local level Stoker (1991, pp. 315–17) has produced an elaborated version of this classification summarised in Exhibit 16.1, which emphasises the importance of *local council attitudes* in determining the nature of the relationship with different types of groups.

Another classification scheme – perhaps more useful if you want to try to find out which groups in your area are being at least partially grant-funded by your own council tax payments – is the one most readily recognised by most local authorities: by *service* or *department*. We have illustrated this approach to classification in Exhibit 16.2, which shows some of the local groups supported by Birmingham City Council under four of its committee budgets.

All the groups in Exhibit 16.2 receive some kind of support from the City Council. From their point of view the financial support is almost inevitably the most important element, often determining whether they can simply stay in existence for another year. Grants may vary from a few hundred pounds to, in the case of a large council like Birmingham, several tens of thousands. With the more substantial grants in particular, the Council will naturally wish to protect its own and its taxpayers'

Exhibit 16.2   *Some groups supported by four Birmingham City Council committees*

Economic Development Committee
Birmingham Co-operative
  Development Agency
Black Business in Birmingham
Disability Resource Centre
Midlands Industrial Association
Motor Industry Local Authority
  Network
Trade Union Resource Centre
West Midlands Low Pay Unit

Housing Committee
Birmingham Women's Aid
Focus Housing Association
Homeless Alcohol Recovery
  Project
Housing Plus One Mother and
  Baby Project
Private Rented Sector Forum
Salvation Army
South Aston Housing
  Co-operative

Education Committee
Birmingham Social Sports
  Federation
The Chinese and Vietnamese
  Cultural School
Duke of Edinburgh Award
  Scheme
Bengali Women's Association
Big Brum Theatre in Education
  Company
Muslim Parents' Association

Leisure Services Committee
Birmingham Association of
  Youth Clubs
Birmingham Readers and Writers
  Festival
Birmingham Repertory Theatre
Cycling Advisory Group
Friends of the Library
Muhammed Ali Centre
Scout Association
Tree Lovers' League

---

interests and ensure that the money is spent on what it was allocated for and that a properly audited set of accounts is available. In such cases it is likely to nominate one or more councillors to sit on the management board of the organisation, and in all instances it will designate a contact officer in the relevant department to perform a mixture of an advisory and monitoring role.

Obviously, a group receiving, let alone depending upon, funding from its local council is hardly in a position to start imposing or threatening pressure on that council, and it is here that the very term 'pressure group' can appear misleading. In the local government world especially, many groups are, as Moran notes (1989, p. 122), not so much conflictual as natural *collaborators and agents* of government in policy-making and policy implementation. Many groups, particularly in the social services field, work in *partnership* with local authorities in service provision – a tendency naturally encouraged by the growing importance of the enabling role for local councils. Only if a group finds itself excluded by its council, and apparently without realistic hope of future inclusion, will it feel it necessary or advantageous to resort to pressure as opposed to attempted persuasion.

Exhibit 16.3   SHARP: Shelter Housing Aid and Research Project

Aims	To secure a decent home for every household in Leicestershire and Northamptonshire at a price they can afford.
How?	Free, confidential, impartial information and advice on housing rights and opportunities • help and practical assistance to those unable fully to exercise their housing rights • encouragement and support for initiatives to house those currently homeless or badly housed • education and training, to develop knowledge and expertise of individuals and housing agencies.
Staff	10 full-time, 4 part-time staff.
Funding	Income of £150,000 (1995): half from Leicester City Council, a quarter from Shelter HQ, remainder from donations.
Caseload	About 1,000 p.a., plus hundreds of enquiries
Current concern	Leicester City Council's introduction of 'Grand Aid Contracts', setting grant recipients numerical performance targets for the services it funds. 'Can those targets be met, while still enhancing the range and quality of our work?'

This brings us to a further classification, perhaps the simplest of all. Dearlove (1973, p. 168) argued that local pressure groups can be divided into two basic types: *helpful* or *unhelpful*. Helpful groups are those whose interests reinforce those of the ruling party group and council. Unhelpful groups, by contrast, 'either do not make claims on the council, or else make claims that conflict with the councillors' own views as to the proper course of council activity'. Is the local pressure group universe quite as easily divisible as that? In Exhibits 16.3 and 16.4 we summarise the operations of two local groups currently active in Leicestershire. How would you classify them: helpful, unhelpful, or a possibly mixture of both?

■ Who benefits? The pluralist/élitist debate

We have so far mentioned almost three dozen groups by name in this chapter. Some – like the Salvation Army and Scout Association – are obviously very longstanding. Most, however, are of much more recent origin, and local single-issue groups in particular are springing up all the time. Given this growth and, as already noted, the increasing involvement of groups in the delivery of local services, it is important to ask

---

Exhibit 16.4   *ENVIRON*

Aims	To provide advice on environmental management to businesses and local authorities in Leicestershire. As co-ordinators of Leicester–Environment City, to challenge the local community to care for the environment and create a better, greener future.
How?	Much of ENVIRON's work is based on partnership with: Leicester City Council – development of city centre shop-front to make people more environmentally aware; large-scale public consultation exercise to create a 'Blueprint for Leicester'; County Council – environmental education in every school; work with community on numerous nature conservation projects; Leicestershire TEC and Business Link – launched advisory Business Line.
Management	Board of Directors (unpaid) from local government, local businesses, universities.
Staff	40-strong multi-disciplinary team of landscape architects, teachers, ecologists, business managers, etc.
Funding	£60,000 from central government's Urban Programme, to fund 20 community projects; £10,000 from Leicester City Council; other grants from Leicestershire County Council, Leicestershire TEC and European Commission. Quarter of income self-generated.
Other projects	'Grass Roots' – supports residents of two Leicester neighbourhoods in improving their environment by collecting residents' views; petitioning City Council on traffic speed reduction measures, improved street lighting and dog fouling prevention. Research – 33 local and 22 national media articles published in 1994/95.

---

questions about which particular sections of society benefit from pressure groups. Is democracy enhanced by their activity, or do local groups simply reinforce the existing distribution of power in the community?

Pluralists would naturally see them as an enhancement of democracy. As Dearlove puts it (1979, p. 46):

> the interest group world is one of reasonably perfect competition, where the rules of the game ensure fair play and equal access for all to the favourable decisions of those in government.

Dearlove, however, concluded that in practice the world – and certainly the slice of it in Kensington and Chelsea that he studied – was not like this. He found that only a relatively small selection of groups was actually drawn into the local council's policy deliberations – in an élitist process that reinforced the dominance of producer interests, rather than opened up decision-making to a broader range of groups.

Dearlove's study (1973, ch.8) showed that the council's response to groups revolved around councillor assessment of group demands and communication styles. As we saw earlier, groups were seen as either helpful or unhelpful, their demands as being either acceptable or unacceptable. Their methods of communication with the council were seen as either proper or improper. Groups that were seen by the ruling Conservative councillors as most helpful were those whose demands most mirrored those of the majority group. Thus, the Kensington Housing Trust was most widely regarded as very *helpful*, since it contributed towards solving local housing problems, thereby lessening the need of the local authority to build more council houses; indeed the Council made money out of the enterprise since it charged interest on money it loaned to the Trust. Such a pressure group reinforced the policy priorities and ideological orientations of the ruling group – hence its favourable treatment.

By contrast, the *unhelpful* groups (e.g. Kensington and Chelsea Council Tenants' Association or the Kensington and Chelsea Inter-Racial Council) canvassed demands which only a minority of councillors supported and which ran counter to the policy priorities of the ruling Conservative administration. Such unacceptable demands had necessarily to be channelled through what the ruling group perceived as improper routes, e.g. petitions and demonstrations. 'Unhelpful' groups were thus faced with a dilemma: either continue to pursue demands which run counter to the majority group's dispositions and remain relatively powerless, or moderate their demands with a view to gaining access, acceptability and policy influence. This interpretation would see radical left groups being marginalised in Conservative-controlled authorities, and radical right groups being left equally impotent in Labour-controlled authorities.

Newton's study of Birmingham (1976) came to similar élitist conclusions. He found that 'established' groups enjoyed 'easy access to decision-makers' and were able to 'press for the maintenance of the status quo' in a 'relatively quick and unnoticed way'. On the other hand, the 'poorly established' groups frequently found it difficult to contact decision-makers and so had to resort to 'pressure group campaigns', which only served to underline how powerless they were in the local political system. 'Propositions from pluralist theory', Newton suggested (1976, p. 62), fare 'poorly against the empirical evidence'.

Writing more recently, though, Stoker (1991, p. 128) argues that such élitist interpretations of local pressure group influence now lack credibility, principally because times and attitudes have changed fundamentally. From the mid-1970s onwards, he maintains, 'many local authorities have opened out, providing access not only to producer groups but to a wider range of groups including community, cause and voluntary organisations'. Linked with this greater council receptivity, he identifies an increased assertiveness, a spread of resources, and a greater willingness to become involved in service delivery on the part of many groups. What are we to make of these conflicting views? Is the élitist model now redundant? Or do councils vary as much in their approach to and relations with local groups as they do in so many other respects?

The notion that radical groups have either to modify their policies or else remain relatively powerless certainly needs some qualification. Several Labour authorities, for example, have encouraged groups which challenge the status quo; indeed, many have provided them with generous grants. Best known was probably the GLC, where the Labour administration in the early 1980s increased grants to voluntary bodies to a massive £82 million by the time of its abolition in 1985–6. While many of the groups receiving grant aid were well established, a significant number were closer to being 'anti-establishment'. Such organisations included:

* Black Female Prisoners Scheme
* London Gay Teenage Group Research and Counselling
* Pakistan Welfare Society
* WEFT, Women's Resource Project
* Irish in Britain Representation Group
* Commission of Philippino Migrant Workers.

These and similar groups were often drawn into the delivery of services, thereby contributing to the radical policies supported by the Greater London Council. But the increased involvement of not-for-profit organisations in local service provision is not confined to Labour or urban councils. The precise mix of groups involved in service delivery or consulted on policy by a particular council will obviously depend on that council's political make-up, as well as on local needs and the assertiveness and effectiveness of groups themselves. Councils will differ one from another in their own amenability to groups, and they will also change over time.

■ Service delivery through grants and contracts

As already emphasised, the significance of local pressure groups has grown partly because of the way in which many groups now collaborate with local authorities in the provision of services. Local authorities are increasingly prepared to provide grants to, or establish *service level agreements* with, local groups in exchange for help with the provision of community services. Such services are thereby frequently provided more cheaply and arguably more efficiently through these specialised networks. As indicated in Exhibit 16.2, any large city or county council nowadays will be providing financial support for literally hundreds of local groups. Much of this finance is used in providing services for specific sectors of the local community. The council thereby acts as a facilitator or enabler for the provision, by voluntary groups, of a wide range of community services.

As always, though, it is important to recognise that different councils, even of the same type, will have different policy agendas and different approaches to service delivery. Looking at district councils within Leicestershire, for example, while Leicester City Council in 1994/95 allocated over £8 million (14 per cent of its revenue budget) on grants to voluntary bodies, Oadby and Wigston DC's allocation was a mere £34,500 (0.8 per cent). Among West Midlands metropolitan districts, Birmingham awarded £22m (2.4 per cent of its budget) while Dudley allocated £2.5m (1.2 per cent). There are wide variations in practice, with county councils and big cities almost inevitably spending proportionately more than smaller district authorities; and also Scottish authorities tending to spend proportionately more and Welsh authorities less than their English counterparts.

A survey by the National Council for Voluntary Organisations (NCVO) showed that local authorities projected that they would provide voluntary organisations with around £687m in revenue grants and fees for the 1994/95 financial year. This figure represents some 12.5 per cent of total voluntary sector income. Compulsory competitive tendering requirements and community care funding incentives have exerted pressure on local authorities to contract with either private or voluntary organisations. This has had a significant impact on the pattern of support offered by local authorities to voluntary organisations. There is more emphasis nowadays on negotiated service level agreements rather than 'no strings attached' grants. This enables local group agendas to be increasingly shaped by local authorities, which was one of SHARP's concerns in Exhibit 16.3. ENVIRON too (see Exhibit 16.4) faced a comparable dilemma in seeking to pressurise the city council on traffic speed, street lighting and dog fouling.

Local authorities are approaching relationships with local groups in a more contractual manner. This does not always sit happily with small groups or with the traditional local pressure group roles of advocacy, research and campaigning. As one district council chief executive told the authors (1995): 'Many authorities see grants increasingly as means by which the public sector can control voluntary sector activity, sometimes through service level agreements.' Budgets, including those which go to local voluntary bodies and pressure groups, are bound to reflect the policy objectives of local authorities. Does this mean that only 'conformist' groups are likely to be considered for funding? Birmingham City Council notes on one of its grant forms: 'The purpose of giving financial assistance in the form of grants is to achieve an outcome desirable in the city.' Are groups with different policies and outlooks to the local authority effectively marginalized by such a policy? Tighter controls over grants and, more particularly, the advent of service level agreements are both potentially constraining influences on local group activity.

■ Local policy networks

In local communities informal networks develop, linking commercial and industrial enterprises with the local council. Indeed, an apparent dearth of pressure group activity in a particular sector may be 'precisely because that interest is built into the very heart of the council itself' (Dearlove, 1979, p. 49). In a mining area the interests of the NUM are likely to permeate the local authority, just as in rural Norfolk agricultural interests will be prominently represented. Pressure group activity by these sectors may appear low key *because* their interests are being defended at every level of the local political system. As 'insiders' already, they have no need to 'go public'. Producer groups too – Chambers of Trade and Commerce – may well have particularly close relationships with their respective local authorities (see King, 1983, 1985; Grant, 1983), although not all studies have found such good relations (see Stoker, 1991, p. 122). Indeed, the obligation imposed by the 1984 Rates Act upon local councils to consult with non-domestic ratepayers led to acrimony rather than harmony in several localities.

In recent years local authorities have paid increasing attention to what has become known as their 'public service orientation' – recognising more proactively than they once did that they exist to provide services for the public. This has involved many councils using questionnaires and other devices to identify the needs and views of their residents about existing services and how they might be improved. This 'opening out' of debate about service delivery has to some extent gone hand in hand with the 'opening out' of the local pressure group world and the growing involvement of community and voluntary organisations in service delivery that we have described.

■ Conclusion – a more complex world

The world of local pressure groups and their interactive relations with local authorities were probably always more varied and complex than apparently simple classification schemes implied. Certainly that is the case today. Many councils, as we have seen, now create and maintain sizeable networks of voluntary and community groups that are likely to develop sufficient dynamism of their own to survive considerable political change on the part of their sponsoring councils.

For, in today's more fragmented world of local governance, local authorities are no longer the automatic hub of the local political system. Groups are increasingly – partly from necessity, partly from choice – finding sponsorship and support from other elected and non-elected agencies, as we saw, for instance, with ENVIRON (Exhibit 16.4) and its multi-source international, national and local funding.

At the same time, though, there have been several key legislative changes that have increased the dependence of local authorities on the voluntary sector to implement its programmes and deliver its services. Community care is one obvious illustration. Likewise, some of the measures incorporated in recent environmental legislation require councils to look to the voluntary sector for help and technical assistance. As with so much else we have dealt with in this book, the changing form of local government and particularly its enabling orientation are having their effect way beyond the formerly dominant local councils themselves.

Guide to further reading

First, see if you can obtain from your own council details of their grant funding and formal links with outside groups and organisations. You will probably need to go, as we have, to individual committee reports and accounts and to the council's yearbook. For pictures of other authorities, see Jones (1969) on Wolverhampton; Hampton (1970) on Sheffield; Newton (1976) on 'the politics of the four thousand' in Birmingham; and Dearlove (1973) on Kensington and Chelsea. Gyford (1984) and Stoker (1991) discuss as well as classify local interest group activity, while Stoker and Wilson's journal article (1991) seeks to shed light on 'the lost world of local groups'. A useful addition to the literature is Baggott (1995).

■ *PART 3* ■

AN AGENDA OF CHANGE

■ *Chapter 17* ■

Reorganisation and Beyond

■ Introduction – the reorganisation roundabout

In Chapters 4 and 5 we outlined the current structure of local government in the UK and how it had come – and was continuing to come – into existence. We described the almost continuous process of structural reform, starting with London in the 1960s and embracing the rest of the country in the early 1970s, that produced, for a brief period, an almost nationwide and thus fairly easily comprehensible two-tier system of principal sub-central government. Except in Northern Ireland and the Scottish island authorities, we had counties or regions divided into districts or boroughs with most local functions and service responsibilities allocated to one or other tier. We also indicated, though, how short-lived this system was to prove. For, by the mid-1980s, we had seen the abolition of the Greater London Council and the English metropolitan county councils and the reorganisation roundabout was revolving once again. Each main party thus went into the 1992 General Election with its own restructuring agenda and of course, with the Conservatives' victory, it is their manifesto proposals that have since been implemented.

It is that process of implementation, of translating manifesto headlines into a detailed operational structure, that we describe in the first part of this chapter. We look respectively at the work of the Secretaries of State for Scotland and Wales and of the Local Government Commission for England (LGCE) that have shaped the new structure. In each country the process has resulted in a reduction of both elected local authorities and councillors, and we discuss therefore the concept of 'democratic deficit'. This is followed by an evaluation of what is increasingly called 'local governance'. The chapter concludes by exploring the usefulness of structural reform and asking whether or not structural reform can ever be 'neutral' in its effects.

■ An 'enabling' context

There is a long tradition in British local government of institutional change, the focus of which is invariably territory or structure. There is an almost obsessive search for *structural* solutions to the perceived problems of local government, and it has regularly in the past taken precedence over more pressing matters relating to role, constitutional position and accountability. Despite the fact that structural change ought logically to *follow* decisions on role and purpose, it has tended to dominate the reform agenda, ahead of, say, a consideration of the increasing number of other non-elected agencies providing local services. We like to term it the *'cartographic approach'* to local government reform: the idea that solutions are to be found by either politicians or civil servants drawing lines on maps, and thereby changing the localities in which people live and with which they identify.

The most recent examples of this cartographic approach have been the work of the Local Government Commission for England and the structural reorganisations, implemented from April 1996, in Scotland and Wales. In this instance, though, even if not as clearly articulated as it might have been, the Major Government did have at least some underlying rationale for its reform agenda. This is set out most clearly in the 1991 White Paper *Competing for Quality*:

> The Government's model for local government in the 1990s and into the 21st century is that of the enabling authority. The task of local authorities lies in identifying requirements, setting priorities, determining standards of service and finding the best way to meet these standards of service and ensuring they are met. This implies a move away from the traditional model of local authorities providing virtually all services directly and a greater separation of the functions of service delivery from strategic responsibilities.

From the Conservative Government's standpoint, therefore, restructuring was about enabling. It was about local authorities directly providing less services themselves. The problem with the concept of enabling, however, is that it is almost infinitely elastic, with many different meanings (see also Chapter 20). At one extreme is the minimalist position taken by the late Nicholas Ridley (then Secretary of State for the Environment), in which the key role of the enabling authority should be simply to find a range of *other* – preferably private sector – organisations to provide services and carry out its responsibilities. A very different and more expansive model is one based on the idea of *enabling communities* meeting their needs and resolving their problems in the most effective way – which might or might not involve the local authority directly providing services itself. The 1991 White Paper, with its reference to 'the best way' of doing things, read as if it favoured this more expansive interpretation, but without much more detailed definition it is hard to be sure. It is questionable therefore whether such a contestable concept is a suitable base on which to attempt to build a substantially new predominantly single-tier structure of local government.

Moreover, structural change was not a necessary prerequisite for the realisation of the government's enabling vision; it is perfectly attainable within a two-tier structure. Indeed, as Travers *et al.* note (1993, p. 19), the DoE's own view that 'the development of the enabling authority has altered the presumption that there is an ideal size of authority for the most efficient delivery of service' makes structural change less important than in previous eras of direct service provision when there was much talk of there being some optimum size. The Major Government's presumed vision of enabling, with an emphasis on contracting out services wherever possible, can be made to work irrespective of structure. Yet structural reform, aimed at the creation of a smaller, single-tier system of unitary authorities throughout Britain, remained a government priority.

■ The reform process

Chapter 5 summarised the outcomes of the work of the Local Government Commission for England. In Scotland and Wales there were no Commissions; the respective Secretaries of State proposed and more or less imposed unitary solutions – 22 unitary authorities in Wales and 32 in Scotland. The LGCE, however, undertook a massive public consultation exercise in England; the government's initial goal was one which saw unitary authorities as the almost nationwide norm, but what ultimately emerged was very different.

The Conservative government made it clear in its original *Policy Guidance* that it expected 'to see a substantial increase in the number of unitary authorities as a result of the Commission's reviews'. Indeed, initially it looked as though it would succeed in its aim, since the LGCE's *first set* of recommendations was for the creation of 99 new unitary authorities covering more than two-thirds of the population of English shire counties, and based primarily on single or merged existing district councils. Figure 17.1 reflects the counties' anxiety that they would be the overwhelming losers in what they feared would be a far from neutral structural reorganisation.

The final outcome of the deliberations of the LGCE and the ministers to whom it reported was, however, very different. The initial network of 99 new unitary authorities ended up as a total of just 46, as listed in Exhibit 5.1. As Game (1997) shows, one of the major factors accounting for this retreat from an almost wholesale unitary solution was the massive public consultation exercise. The Commission leafleted people in their millions with details of its unitary proposals for their particular area. Polling organisations sampled and questioned them systematically. They were encouraged to attend meetings, write letters, sign petitions and complete newspaper questionnaires. While many of them liked the *idea* of unitary local government, far more, when asked, were opposed to

Figure 17.1 *Cartoon: County Councils under threat*

Source: Local Government Information Unit, *LGIU Briefing*, No. 52, September 1991.

the Commission's detailed plans and their likely upheaval and cost, and they made it clear that they would prefer the status quo.

In county after county, therefore, the Commissioners were confronted with evidence of substantial slippage between people's majority support for the *principle* of unitary authorities and their subsequent lack of enthusiasm for *specific* unitary solutions. To quote the LGCE's own report on the 1992–5 Structural Review (p. 63): 'when presented with specific local structures, there was often a decided shift in opinion. In many county areas most people preferred no change to any of the unitary structures put forward by the Commission.' In virtually every county in which it was actually presented as one of the LGCE's options, the status quo proved the most popular, as it did in several counties where it had to be spontaneously nominated as an 'other option'.

The result is either '*hybridity*', to use the technical expression, or a bit of a mess – the latter obviously being the view presented in Figure 17.2 showing Sir John Banham, the Commission's first Chairman, hammering a final piece of the reorganisation puzzle into place. To be fair, the picture is not quite as chaotic as the cartoon suggests. To the four counties for which the Commission's initial recommendation had been 'no change' a further 10 were eventually added. In rather more cases, county-wide unitary proposals were overturned in favour of less radical hybrid solutions. These involved one or two usually large towns or cities

Figure 17.2 *Cartoon: A confusing solution*

Source: *Local Government Chronicle*, 16 September 1994.

regaining the unitary status that they had had as county boroughs until 1974, while elsewhere in their counties the two-tier system continues as before. One county, Hereford and Worcester, was divided, back into its pre-1974 parts, with Herefordshire becoming unitary and Worcestershire remaining two-tier. In the end, therefore, only five of the 39 English counties were abolished, and one of them, the Isle of Wight, has been reincarnated in unitary form – all of which represents a very different outcome from that envisaged and feared in our first cartoon.

In Exhibit 17.1 we both summarise this reorganisation process in a more systematic fashion and also enable you to see what happened in your own area. By comparing any post-review outcome with the initial preferences of the relevant county and districts, you can form at least an impression of the 'winners' and 'losers'. You can certainly see the extent to which the Commission's early recommendations were subsequently amended, and also how most counties' worst fears were unrealised. As for the districts, most of them, responding to what they took to be the government's intentions, tried to argue to the Commission in the first instance that they both should be and were sufficiently equipped and experienced to become unitary authorities in their own right. Many have inevitably been disappointed, though for most of them a continuation of the status quo represents a perfectly acceptable second choice – if only they could have been spared the cost, time, energy, expectation and disruption that putting together an initial unitary bid had entailed.

In that sense, the Major Government, in setting up a process which was allowed to 'drift' in the way it did, has a serious case to answer. On the other hand, the more centralised, even autocratic, process followed in

Exhibit 17.1 *What happened and might have happened to your county in the Local Government Review?*

COUNTY	PRE-REVIEW (COUNTY AND DISTRICTS)	POST-REVIEW County	POST-REVIEW Districts	START OF NEW STRUCTURE (APRIL)	INITIAL PREFERENCES County	INITIAL PREFERENCES Districts (average)	INITIAL PREFERENCES LG Commission
Avon	1 + 6	abolished	4 UA	1996	S.q.	5 UA	4 UA ✓
Bedfordshire	1 + 4	hybrid	1 UA + 3	1997	1 UA	3 UA	2 UA
Berkshire	1 + 6	abolished	6 UA	1998	4 UA	5/6 UA ✓	4 UA
Buckinghamshire	1 + 5	hybrid	1 UA + 4	1997	S.q.	4 UA	3 UA
Cambridgeshire	1 + 6	hybrid	1 UA + 5	1998	2 UA	4/5 UA	3 UA
Cheshire	1 + 8	hybrid	2 UA + 6	1998	S.q.	7 UA/S.q.	5 UA
Cleveland	1 + 4	abolished	4 UA	1996	2 UA	4 UA ✓	4 UA ✓
Cornwall	1 + 6	unchanged		–	1 UA/S.q. ✓	2 UA + S.q.	S.q. ✓
Cumbria	1 + 6	unchanged		–	S.q. ✓	5 UA	2 UA
Derbyshire	1 + 9	hybrid	1 UA + 8	1997	1 UA + S.q. ✓	4 UA/S.q.	1 UA + S.q. ✓
Devon	1 + 10	hybrid	2 UA + 8	1998	1 UA + S.q.	5/7 UA	1 UA + S.q.
Dorset	1 + 8	hybrid	2 UA + 6	1997	3 UA	4/5 UA	3 UA
Durham	1 + 8	hybrid	1 UA + 7	1997	1 UA + S.q. ✓	4 UA/S.q.	1 UA + S.q. ✓
East Sussex	1 + 7	hybrid	1 UA + 5	1997	1 UA + S/q. ✓	5 UA + S.q.	3.3 UA
Essex	1 + 14	hybrid	1 UA + 12	1998	S.q.	7–10 UA + S.q.	2 UA + S.q. ✓
Gloucestershire	1 + 6	unchanged		–	S.q. ✓	3 UA + S.q.	S.q. ✓
Hampshire	1 + 13	hybrid	2 UA + 11	1997	S.q.	7–12 UA	2 UA + S.q. ✓
Hereford and Worcester	1 + 9	divided – reduced to Worcs CC	1 UA: (1 CC) + 6	1998	1 UA + S.q. ✓	5/6 UA	3 UA
Hertfordshire	1 + 10	unchanged		–	S.q. ✓	6/9 UA	S.q. ✓
Humberside	1 + 9	abolished	4 UA	1996	S.q.	5/7 UA	4.1 UA ✓
Isle of Wight	1 + 2	abolished	1 UA	1995	S.q./1 UA ✓	S.q./1 UA ✓	1 UA ✓

County								
Kent	1 + 14	hybrid	1 UA + 12	1998	S.q.	7–9 UA + S.q.	2 UA + S.q.
Lancashire	1 + 14	hybrid	2 UA + 12	1998	S.q.	10/11 UA + S.q.	8 UA
Leicestershire	1 + 9	hybrid	2 UA + 7	1997	S.q.	7 UA + S.q.	2 UA + S.q.✓
Lincolnshire	1 + 7	unchanged		–	S.q.✓	3 UA + S.q.	S.q.✓
Norfolk	1 + 7	unchanged		–	S.q.✓	5 UA	4.5 UA
Northamptonshire	1 + 7	unchanged		–	S.q.✓	3–5 UA	3 UA
Northumberland	1 + 6	unchanged		–	S.q.✓	1 UA + S.q.	S.q.✓
North Yorkshire	1 + 8	hybrid	1 UA + 7	1996	S.q.	6/7 UA	2.9 UA
Nottinghamshire	1 + 8	hybrid	1 UA + 7	1998	S.q.	8 UA	1 UA + S.q.
Oxfordshire	1 + 5	unchanged		–	1 UA	4 UA	3 UA✓
Shropshire	1 + 6	hybrid	1 UA + 5	1998	S.q.	2 UA + S.q.	2 UA
Somerset	1 + 5	unchanged		–	S.q.	3 UA	3 UA
Staffordshire	1 + 9	hybrid	1 UA + 8	1997	1 UA + S.q.✓	8 UA	1 UA + S.q.✓
Suffolk	1 + 7	unchanged		–	S.q.✓	4/5 UA	3.5 UA
Surrey	1 + 11	unchanged		–	S.q.✓	5–8 UA + S.q.	5 UA
Warwickshire	1 + 5	unchanged		–	S.q.✓	3 UA	2 UA
West Sussex	1 + 7	unchanged		–	S.q.✓	3–5 UA	0.7 UA + S.q.
Wiltshire	1 + 5	hybrid	1 UA + 4	1997	1 UA + S.q.✓	3 UA	3 UA
39 + 296		**abolished 5 / divided 1 / hybrid 19 / unchanged 14**				**New unitaries 46 / Shire Districts 238**	

Notes S.q. = status quo, i.e. no change
✓ = initial preferences achieved or very nearly achieved

For details of the new unitary authorities see Exhibit 5.1

Source: Local Government Chronicle Special Supplements, June 1994, October 1994.

Scotland and Wales can be seen as more unsatisfactory still. The respective Secretaries of State were convinced of the case for unitary authorities throughout and hence did not establish Commissions. As Leach (1995, p. 54) observes, this is an interesting example of the inconsistencies which can develop between approaches to the same problem in the three countries. 'If a uniform unitary solution is right for Scotland and Wales, why not for England? If a Commission is needed in England, why not in Wales and Scotland?' In both Wales and Scotland consultation papers were published setting out alternative patterns of unitary authorities. While there was discussion with interested parties there was widespread discontent, especially from the respective local authority associations, about the arbitrariness of both the process and the ultimate proposals (see Wilson, 1996a).

■ Democratic deficit?

Fewer elected local authorities and fewer councillors were the end-product of structural reform in the mid-1990s. In non-metropolitan England there were 335 authorities before the review process began; by 1998 there will be 318, the 46 new unitaries replacing five former counties and 58 districts (see Exhibit 2.2), producing a net loss of 17 authorities. In both Wales and Scotland, however, the consequences of reform have been much more drastic, as Exhibit 17.2 indicates. Wales now has less than one-eighth of the councils it had a quarter of a century ago, while Scotland, in terms of average population per elected council, stands as about the most locally under-represented nation in Western Europe (also Exhibit 12.2).

The unitary reorganisation of the 1990s, which halved the numbers of Scottish and Welsh councils, inevitably reduced the numbers of councillors in these areas, as it has done in the 'unitarised' parts of non-metropolitan England. The reduction is nothing like as severe as it would have been under the LGCE's initial proposals, but it is still sufficient, we feel, to justify our use of the term 'democratic deficit' – more usually applied to the alleged deficiencies of the European Parliament. Exhibit 17.3 shows how the affected areas of Great Britain have lost between them almost a third of their former councillors, with Wales being particularly adversely affected.

This 'democratic deficit' associated with the reduction in the numbers of local authorities and elected councillors is part of a broader debate about the changing nature of public accountability at local level. Central to this debate is the concept of local *governance*, to which we drew attention in Chapter 6: a recognition that elected local government is only

Exhibit 17.2   *The growing scale of British local government*

	Before 1974/75	*1974/5 to 1996/8*	*New structure*	*Increase in scale since 1974/5*
England				
No. of councils	1,246	c.410	387	
Av. population per council	37,000	113,000	121,000	3.3 ×
Scotland				
No. of councils	430	65	32	
Av. population per council	12,000	78,000	153,000	12.8 ×
Wales				
No. of councils	181	45	22	
Av. population per council	15,000	62,000	128,000	8.5 ×
Great Britain				
No. of councils	1,857	520	441	
Av. population per council	29,000	106,000	128,000	4.4 ×

Exhibit 17.3   *Unitary councillors: the missing third*

	NUMBER OF COUNCILLORS			
	New unitary authorities	*In previous two-tier system*	*The democratic deficit*	
			No.	*%*
Non-Metropolitan England	2391	3476	1085	31
Scotland	1245	1695	450	27
Wales	1273	1977	704	36
Total	**4909**	**7148**	**2239**	**31**

one of a number of bodies providing services locally. The Local Government Review, however, ignored the numerous non-elected elements and instead focused exclusively upon the elected element. In doing so it failed to recognise what we described in Chapter 7 as 'the full complexity of sub-central government' and the rise of partnerships between elected and non-elected bodies. An opportunity was missed to study comprehensively and debate the issues involved in the modern-day governance of our localities (Wilson, 1996b).

■ Reorganisation and local governance

The *fragmentation* implicit in the term 'local governance' – the shift away from a system in which local authorities were the overwhelmingly dominant actors in their localities to one where decision-making authority and service provision are divided among a number of agencies – has major implications. Elected councillors are today *directly* responsible for providing fewer and fewer services. Local authorities no longer make appointments to District Health Authorities or to Family Health Service Authorities. Health Service Trusts have been appointed to run hospitals and community health services. Training and Enterprise Councils in England and Wales (Local Enterprise Companies in Scotland) exercise substantial training and development functions at local level, many of which were once the responsibility of local authorities. Grant-maintained schools, sixth-form colleges and colleges of further education have been removed from local authority control and are governed by appointed boards which are funded nationally. Housing associations are increasingly taking over the social housing functions previously exercised by elected local authorities. New police authorities, on which five out of seventeen members are appointed in addition to three magistrates, were set up in April 1995. Urban Development Corporations, City Challenge initiatives and Housing Action Trusts also have major responsibilities for redevelopment in selected localities.

Add all these together, as we did in Chapter 6, and you find nearly 5,000 bodies, not directly elected, that are likely to be involved nowadays in the governance of our local communities, and spending well over half the total money spent by elected local government. Fairly obviously, such developments beg the question: with the erosion of local authorities' and local councillors' role in direct service provision, is it not reasonable for there to be fewer of them? Are more councillors necessarily the answer if, once in office, they have relatively little influence on policy initiation and implementation? True, their representational role remains, but is this in itself, in an era of 'customer charters', sufficient reason to clamour for more of them?

Traditionalists have no doubts, arguing that local government is enhanced as local democracy by the closeness of councillors to their constituents. A greater number of members, they maintain, makes local government more responsive to the local community and its needs. We ourselves admitted at the start of Chapter 3 a predisposition in favour of the decentralisation of power and a preference for that decentralised power to be in the hands of electorally accountable local representatives. Indeed, we devoted a whole chapter to the justification of elected local government. We recognise, though, that such a view has its critics, who would argue that it is idealistic and even romanticised. It is, they would argue, some distance removed from today's reality of large, bureaucratised, party-dominated councils, elected on embarrassingly low turn-outs, and apparently unloved by many of the citizens they purport to serve.

It is difficult to dispute some of these points, and we would not want to. We have no wish to be guilty of what might be labelled the *Animal Farm* defence of local democracy: in which the pigs' 'four legs good, two legs bad' becomes 'elected good, appointed bad'. We certainly would not claim, therefore, that either the concept of quangos is inherently bad or that, as usually single-functional bodies able to set clear performance targets, they are not capable of delivering efficient and high quality services.

We fully recognise that there is nothing magical about accountability through the ballot box, and that in our present-day system of local government it has demonstrable inadequacies:

* many people simply do not vote in local elections;
* many of those who do vote are influenced at least as much by national as by local considerations;
* they are required to cast their, at most, annual vote for or against whole party programmes, rather than on specific policies or issues;
* they are likely to have had considerable difficulty, even if they were inclined to try, finding out enough about the detailed performance of their council to be able to make an informed judgement even about its general efficiency, let alone its efficiency in specific policy areas;
* council policies are frequently decided not so much by election outcomes as in party group meetings behind closed doors;
* many voters, because of our electoral system, will have little real choice between parties or candidates;
* much of what councils do nowadays, and particularly how much they are able to spend, is determined more by central government than by councils themselves.

It is easy in the extreme, therefore, to find weaknesses in our present system of elected local government and electoral accountability. At the same time, it should be pointed out that:

* elected councillors are, by definition, removable;
* their identities are known or knowable and they can be easily contacted and complained to;
* their council and committee meetings are publicised and open to the public, as are most of their papers;
* they do have to produce annual reports and audited accounts of their activities.

So, if councillors are to be displaced, or their numbers significantly further reduced, it is reasonable to ask of the appointed bodies that take over their former responsibilities what alternative mechanisms of scrutiny and accountability will take the place of the ballot box. A supposedly comprehensive review of local government might have been expected to raise and discuss some of these issues. As we have already indicated, though, the mid-1990s restructuring process did not; in fact, it was prohibited by its terms of reference from doing so. It was another cartographic exercise that increased the scale of our local government system and reduced its democratic element, while leaving more lasting questions about its future role and accountability unaddressed.

■ Is structural reform 'neutral'?

It is important to recognise that governmental arrangements are not neutral – they can affect the access of different interests and groups to decision-making authority. According to Dearlove (1979, p. 14), a political perspective on reorganisation 'has to recognise that new boundaries, new structures, and new processes *all* have implications for the access of different interests to local government, and therefore for the likely direction of public policy'. One difficulty, however, is that much of the literature treats local government reform as a neutral process benefiting all sections of society. The reform obsession has been with efficiency – notably issues about size and resources – and with the so-called 'calibre' of local councillors.

Dearlove provides a rather different interpretation of the motives lying behind the reform process. First, the concern to increase efficiency might appear to be a neutral political objective, but, he suggests (p. 78), it is a 'political objective which comes from, and embodies the interests of, those who seek first to restrict the cost of government before moving on to restrict the scope of government activity itself'. Those people who have least need for public services can call for increased efficiency as a way of reducing their own financial contribution. Efficiency thus becomes the highly political objective of pruning 'unnecessary' services:

> A little detective work among the books on the problems of local government quickly makes it abundantly clear that the desire to increase efficiency is perhaps better expressed in terms of the concern to cut public spending and the scope of government. (Dearlove, 1979, p. 78)

The same author also suggests that 'councillor calibre' can be a euphemism for social class:

The concern about declining councillor calibre embodies a bitter lament that a variety of changes have conspired to result in a situation in which there is now a less close and direct relationship between economic power, social status, and the political control of local government than was once the case in the Victorian age when local government enjoyed the leadership of businessmen and local notables.   (Dearlove, 1979 pp. 104, 105)

Business interests feel themselves threatened by some aspects of local decision-making and for them the attempt to increase calibre 'embodies a concern to recapture the social relations, style of politics, and class of leadership that existed before the franchise was extended and before the working class rose to some sort of position of local political power through the Labour Party' (p. 105). For commentators such as Dearlove, reorganisation cannot be treated as a neutral process; rather, it reflects the aspirations of certain dominant sectors in society. The abolition of the GLC and the six 'Mets' plus the abolition of ILEA in 1990 thus reflected a national government's concern to trim the wings of those local units committed to different political objectives and policies from itself – just as did the creation of that same GLC two decades earlier, through the incorporation of Conservative outer suburbs into the metropolis to end the longstanding Labour control of the London County Council.

The Dearlove perspective is useful because it sees any such structural change in political terms. By elevating the political dimension it introduces a crucially important variable. Nevertheless, it can be challenged. First, the accusation that the intention behind local government reorganisation has been to reduce working class influence makes one big assumption: namely, that local government is or has in the past been vulnerable to such influence. Second, it is possible to identify counter-tendencies to the growing central government and business control over local government: notably the spread of party politics and the rise of radical pressure groups operating in 'urban left' authorities. The 'values' involved in local government reorganisation are many and varied.

Leach (1993, p. 35) argues that it is tempting to bring forward conspiracy theories, which imply 'hidden agendas' in the context of the recent Local Government Review. Could it be, he wonders, that the reorganisation process was a 'smokescreen', designed to distract local authorities from more fundamental changes taking place in sub-central government?

Distract it certainly did. As can be surmised from Exhibit 17.3, enormous resources were expended by counties and districts alike, especially in the early stages of the LGCE review, putting together cases claiming that they were the more suitable candidates for unitary status. It was unmistakeably wasteful and at least temporarily injurious to county–district relations. As to whether it was government conspiracy as opposed to cock-up, we remain to be convinced.

■ Conclusion – the inevitable limitations of structural reform

Structural reorganisation has been centre-stage in England, Scotland and Wales since the early 1990s. In April 1996 new unitary authorities began operating in Scotland and Wales, but in England the process has been rather more drawn out. Here the first new unitary was the Isle of Wight, established in 1995, while the final batch, as indicated in Exhibit 5.1, are scheduled for a 1998 start. The Major Government's original vision of leaner, less costly unitary authorities throughout Britain has not materialised. Stout opposition from the Association of County Councils; a judicial review which forced the government to back down from its emphasis on unitary solutions in England and issue new more open-ended guidelines; opposition from elements within the Conservative Party, especially Conservative MPs in areas threatened with merger into larger unitaries – all contributed to the 'policy drift' which characterised the LGCE Review. Damage limitation ultimately became the government's major objective. As Midwinter (1992, p. 53) reminds us: 'A reform strategy developed without sound policy analysis will, as history shows, fail.'

It is possible to argue that structural change should be jettisoned from any local government reform agenda altogether. Certainly the limits of structural change need to be recognised. Changes in policy formulation and implementation are not dependent on new structures being created. Indeed, with the advent of enabling, they are becoming increasingly independent of structure. Structures obviously have an effect on institutional capacity, but new authorities do not need to be created before there can be dramatic shifts in the balance of power between central departments and local councils.

It is unlikely that there could ever be a universally agreed solution to the politically-charged issue of local government restructuring. It is an inherently political process, and divisions are bound to exist both between and within political parties. What is certain, however, is that democratically elected local government is in the throes of being re-placed by an increasingly complex and fragmented pattern of local governance in which the local council is simply one of several agencies involved in shaping policies and delivering services. In many policy areas, such as community care, education and housing, local authorities now share strategic decision-making and service provision with other institutions. New territorial structures are unlikely to stem the flow of this tide; indeed, some would see *structural* debate as an irrelevant distraction. Identifying inter-organisational alliances, shaping a strategic vision and devising appropriate mechanisms for effective local accountability and empowerment are much more pressing tasks.

Guide to further reading

Leach (1996) provides a useful explanatory framework for the work of the Local Government Review. Boyne *et al.* (1995) have produced an interesting critique of the reorganisations in Scotland and Wales. Cochrane (1993a) is a stimulating essay on local government which incorporates an early analysis of reorganisation. The advent of local governance is discussed in Pratchett and Wilson (1996). A special edition of *Public Administration* (Spring 1997) contains a number of excellent articles on local government reorganisation. It is not easy to keep pace with the speed of change; the best way of keeping up to date is to glance regularly at either the *Local Government Chronicle* or *Municipal Journal*.

■ *Chapter 18* ■

Developments in Internal Management

■ Introduction – the neglected review area

The 1990s opened with the arrival of a new Prime Minister, John Major, and a new Secretary of State for the Environment, Michael Heseltine, whose initial challenge to Mrs Thatcher's leadership had been responsible for the change of Premiers. Mr Heseltine immediately launched a wide-ranging review of the local government system, focusing in particular on finance, structure and internal management. We have now dealt with the first two of these – in Chapters 10 and 17 respectively – and we thus arrive at the third and least heralded, the internal management arrangements of the local authority, which we introduced in the second part of Chapter 5.

Of the three-part 'Heseltine Review', finance was bound to take precedence, given the role that the bitterly unpopular poll tax had played in Mrs Thatcher's downfall and the political importance of the Government's being able to pronounce it dead before the impending General Election. It was equally politically inevitable – if by no means logical – that structural reorganisation should come next, because of the sheer impact it would have on any authority potentially affected by it. At the end of Chapter 17 we questioned the idea of the reorganisation saga being some kind of diversionary government conspiracy, but emphasised that it certainly constituted a massive distraction – from, among other things, the intended third element of the Heseltine Review, internal management.

As we shall see, the Conservative Government's principal policy paper on the subject received comparatively and disappointingly little attention at the time it appeared. With reorganisation largely completed, though, interest in internal management is reviving – partly because of the Labour Party's 1997 Election manifesto commitment to 'encourage democratic innovations in local government, including pilots of the idea of elected mayors with executive powers in cities'.

Obviously, even on a pilot basis, directly elected mayors would represent a dramatic innovation in our local government system. We therefore give it some detailed, and to some extent cautionary, consideration at the end of the chapter. There is, though, a very great deal more to internal management reform than 'flashy' institutional transplants like elected mayors. So the bulk of this chapter discusses some of the less headline-grabbing developments that took place in the 1980s and 1990s, leaving the biggest and most far-reaching change of all – the introduction and consequences of CCT – a chapter in its own right.

Here we identify and outline a series of six interconnected trends that have impinged upon the management of local authorities during the past few years. As ever in local government, you would not expect all councils to have embraced all of these developments to the same degree. But if you talk to officers and councillors in your own authority, you can be pretty sure of hearing at least some of the ideas and some of the terminology mentioned before very long. How can we be sure? Partly through our own regular visits to councils around the country, and partly through the experience of someone who, as noted in the opening paragraphs of Chapter 1, in the past ten years has visited over 300 of them, Professor John Stewart. He has recorded a fascinating 'Observer's View' of *Local Government Today*, from which the following checklist of trends is adapted.

■ Six managerial trends

□ *A recognition of organisational culture*

Every organisation has its own culture: some collection of understandings and assumptions about the nature of the organisation, its values, goals, norms, expectations and ways of working that are shared by its members. They may not be publicly discussed very often, because they tend to be learned and to operate subconsciously. That is their nature and their strength. But they are there all right, and nowadays more and more authorities are making them *explicit*, rather than implicit. The chances are, therefore, that your own council will have adopted some *mission* or *core value statement*, designed to spell out both to its employees and the public the kind of organisation it thinks it is, or is trying to be.

□ *The customer service revolution*

Without doubt one of the most fundamental developments in the public service in the past two decades has been what Skelcher has termed 'the service revolution' (1992): the publicised commitment to put customers first, or, rather, to label them customers and then tell them they are being put first. Twenty years ago local authorities had residents, tenants, clients and claimants *to* whom, rather than *for* whom, they provided services in the way and to the standards they felt most appropriate. Then, prompted to an extent by the private sector, came what was variously termed the *public service orientation* (PSO) or *customer care*: the gradual realisation by councils that these previously passive recipients of their services should be treated more as customers, with at least a voice, if not totally free choice, and entitled to be consulted and even actively involved in decision making.

The practical manifestations of a council's customer focus can be seen in a host of ways: user surveys and residents' questionnaires, advertised complaints procedures, service days, customer care training, neighbourhood forums, user groups, public question times at council and committee meetings, and perhaps most notably *customer charters* and *service guarantees*. Charterism and specifically the Citizen's Charter have come quite understandably to be associated personally with John Major, whose 1991 White Paper sought to empower the citizen as an individual service consumer, if not more ambitiously as a participant in the process of local self-government. It is worth emphasising, though, that the Prime Minister's initiative was predated both by the Labour Party's *Quality Street* policy review following the 1987 General Election, which included service guarantees with redress mechanisms and financial compensation, and also by a number of mainly Labour councils developing their own charters and customer contracts. Of these latter, York City Council's was the most interesting:

> not merely as an example of local government innovations anticipating a major central government initiative, but because of the way it attempts to weave together the concerns of citizens, customers and community. The commitment to citizenship – to people's *civic rights* as citizens of York – is explicitly stated in terms of rights to know; rights to be heard and to influence; rights to be treated honestly, fairly and courteously; rights to participate and be represented. These general civic rights are subsequently translated into practical entitlements, through, for example, the establishment of:
> – area committees where you can have your say about decisions affecting your neighbourhood;
> – special arrangements to involve some of the people who are not often listened to: people with disabilities and other special needs.
> (Prior, 1995, pp. 91–2 – our emphasis)

☐ Quality systems and quality assurance

'Customer first' initiatives, like mission statements, can easily backfire on the authority by appearing as little more than pious rhetoric unless there is a genuine institutional commitment and capacity to translate them into service quality. This recognition has prompted many authorities to develop quality control (QC), quality assurance (QA), and total quality management (TQM) systems, as means of improving their service quality. The three processes are clearly differentiated and discussed by Skelcher (1992, c.8).

Quality control – 'is an inspection and checking process which occurs *after* the service has been or is ready to be provided' (our emphasis). Its purpose therefore is to measure performance against pre-set standards and thereby identify any failure rate in the service provision. An example would be a post-repair tenant satisfaction survey. Knowledge of tenants' dissatisfaction will hopefully help improve the service next time.

Quality Assurance – is the attempt to stop the substandard service being provided in the first place. It involves designing delivery systems and procedures so that a certain standard of service can be guaranteed every time. Originally developed in the manufacturing sector, where product standards can be precisely measured and specified, QA does not translate easily into the local government world of personal service delivery. Nevertheless, the British Standards Institute has developed a recognised benchmark (BS 5750), against which local and NHS authorities can assess their QA systems and a number have been accredited. Developing an accreditable QA system can be a protracted and resource intensive exercise, necessitating as it does the detailed codification of policies, procedures, performance standards and monitoring systems. On the other hand, confronted, say, with a case of alleged child abuse in a council residential home, it is not hard to see it as a worthwhile investment.

Total Quality Management – can be seen as making service quality the driving force of the whole organisational culture of the authority. As Oakland puts it (1989, p. 14): 'it is essentially a way of organising and involving the whole organisation; every department, every activity, every single person at every level' in the commitment to quality. Its demands are immense, as Skelcher shows by instancing the chain of employees needed in any complex organisation to delivery even a fairly straightforward service (1992, p. 103):

> For a home help to deliver her service to the highest quality, she needs others in the organisation to operate effectively:
>
> * her supervisor – to give support and advice;
> * the training section – to convey skills and knowledge;
> * the finance department – to pay her wages and expenses promptly;
> * the research section – to provide information on new services and voluntary organisations;
> * managers and members – to secure the resources, policy and organisational framework necessary to provide a quality service.

In principle, one defective link in the chain is enough to jeopardise your TQM, which is one reason why Stewart suggests that it 'is often an aspiration imperfectly realised or perhaps understood' (1996, p. 19). As he adds, however, 'the search for quality remains important'.

☐ *Strategic management*

Self-evidently, any authority even aspiring to TQM requires a *strategic approach,* ensuring that the multiplicity of activities and policies of the authority are consistent and are all contributing to the corporate objectives and values. Increasingly, though, authorities of all types, not just those setting out down the QA/TQM route, have come to see the need systematically to take stock of their activities in a constantly changing environment, and either set new directions or at least state some vision of where the authority will be in so many years' time and what it will be doing.

That, in essence, is what strategic management and planning are about: providing information and developing decision-making processes that enable elected members and officers alike to set priorities, direct their energies to key issues, and thereby develop a means of coping assertively with change. It can be contrasted to, and is a means of getting away from, the limitations of operational or reactive management, as indicated in Exhibit 18.1. It involves standing back from the everyday pressures of operational management and taking a broader, corporate, longer-term view of the authority and its function.

Exhibit 18.1   *Strategic vs. operational management*

Strategic management can:	. . . where operational management:
* Be long-term	* Is short-term
* Expose choices	* Reinforces continuities
* Be guided by political priorities	* Emphasises professional concerns
* Encourage the organisation to pause for thought before deliberation	* Produces a ceaseless treadmill of activities and routinised meetings
* Take account of the changing environment	* Is grounded in the organisation
* Be concerned with the impact of its activities	* Is concerned with getting activities done
* Look outwards to the network of community organisations	* Is limited by organisational boundaries
* See interrelationships between tasks	* Is centred on specific tasks

Source: Adapted from M. Clarke and J. Stewart, *Strategies for Success* (LGMB, 1991), p. 15.

Strategic management necessarily therefore involves some breaking down of traditional departmental and committee boundaries, and in that respect it links back to the ideas of the corporate approach of the early 1970s that we encountered towards the end of Chapter 5. Certainly, strategic management is likely to involve some of the corporate structures that were advocated at that time by the Maud, Bains and Paterson Committees – chief executives, policy and resources committees, chief officers' management teams – reinforced by some more recent institutional innovations, such as corporate member panels and officer/member working parties on key issues. The big difference is that there is a much more solid policy substance to strategic management than was often the case in the early 1970s, when we described the structural innovations as 'corporate icing' on a traditional cake. For strategic management to be effective, there must exist a well-designed and robust *policy process* through which objectives are determined, key issues identified and explored, choices emerge, targets are set, and decisions taken, implemented and monitored.

As an additional way of fostering strategic thinking and breaking down traditional departmental and professional boundaries, many authorities have appointed *strategic directors*, who may oversee a number of combined departments, but who are freed from the day-to-day responsibility of departmental management. The intended outcome is a streamlined strategic management team, comprising the chief executive and strategic directors, who are better able to focus on major policy issues and secure co-ordination between services (see Griffiths, 1992).

☐ *Devolved, cost centre management*

An almost necessary concomitant of strategic management is a devolution of actual management responsibility. Once the authority's overall objectives and policies have been established, they need, if they are going to stand a realistic chance of being achieved, to be translated into clearly defined targets or key tasks for individual managers. Somebody, in short, has to be able to be held to account; but, to make that accountability meaningful, that person has to be given the necessary discretion to deploy financial and other resources in such a way as to attain the specified targets. The principle behind such devolved management is that it releases initiative among middle and junior managers who would previously have been constrained within a steep management hierarchy, and thereby leads to greater efficiency and, in the case of a local authority, a better quality service to the public.

The managerial logic is the same as that behind the Next Steps Initiative within the civil service, which has involved setting up separate units or executive agencies to perform the executive functions of government which were previously the responsibility of Whitehall departments. Next Steps Agencies – ranging in scale from the massive Benefits Agency to the Vehicle Inspectorate, Royal Mint, and Public Record Office – remain part of the civil service, but, under the terms of individual framework documents, they have responsibility for their own financial, pay and personnel decisions. Similarly, cost centre managers, whether within a university or local authority, remain part of the corporate body, but have the authority to use the resources they have been allocated to achieve the key tasks and standards of performance with which they have been entrusted.

☐ *Performance management*

The establishment of cost centres is likely to lead in turn to performance management (PM): the specification, measurement, and evaluation of the performance both of individuals and of the organisation. Tasks are devolved to cost centres and expressed in measurable terms, enabling the performance of the cost centre and the cost centre manager to be regularly reviewed, appraised, and then rewarded or penalised accordingly. Generally, when it is the organisation that is being evaluated, the term used is performance review (PR); when an individual, performance appraisal (PA). But what, for a service-providing local authority, is 'performance'?

For the Audit Commission, it meant the '3 Es', which, in the early 1980s, were Economy, Efficiency and Effectiveness.

Economy – relates to *inputs*, and is concerned with minimising the cost of resources involved in producing any given standard of service.

Efficiency – is concerned with the *relationship between inputs and outputs*. It is not, as is often wrongly supposed, a measure of cost, but of the relationship of output quantity and quality to the cost of inputs. It is about getting more or better for less: either minimising inputs in relation to outputs, or maximising outputs in relation to inputs, or both.

Effectiveness – is also about a *relationship, between intended and actual outputs*, or, to put it slightly differently, between outputs and outcomes.

It will be immediately apparent that any attempted measurement of these '3 Es' is likely to be much more difficult for a political, sometimes monopolistic, multi-service delivering local authority than for a single-product, profit-maximising manufacturing company. At the very least, account has to be taken of the council's political values and objectives, which are likely to be considerably more complex than the maximisation of profit; also of the problems involved in even defining, let alone measuring, outcomes of, say, the educational experience or some of the social services. Partly in recognition of this public service complexity, additional, equally problematic Es have been added over the years, such as:

* Equity
* Excellence
* Enterprise
* Entrepreneurship
* Expertise
* Electability

(Jackson and Palmer, 1992, pp. 19–20; Rouse, 1993, p. 61).

More relevant for us here, however, are the various kinds of measures that can be used to assess performance, and in Exhibit 18.2 we list some of the commonest types of Performance Indicators (PIs) and relate them to the corresponding E.

As noted in Chapter 7, all councils are now required to produce for the Audit Commission and also to publish themselves dozens of such performance indicators. They do so, of course, albeit in some cases grudgingly. For the initial instinct of almost everyone involved in service delivery – and certainly high trained professionals – is to claim that the really significant aspects of their work are simply not amenable to measurement, or to 'time and motion' study as they are likely disparagingly to put it. The same will be argued on behalf of the whole local authority: so-called performance measures are really only measures of the socio-economic deprivation of the area, or of the government's refusal to grant it adequate funding.

Exhibit 18.2 *Performance Indicators and the 3 Es*

Type of Indicator	*Corresponding 'E'*	*Example*
Cost indicators	Economy	Annual cost per aged person in residential accommodation
Productivity indicators	Efficiency	No. of library books issued per staff member per hour
Time targets	Efficiency and Effectiveness	Response time for dealing with grant application
Quality of service indicators	Effectiveness	% of users/clients satisfied with the service
Demand for service indicators	Effectiveness	Numbers using a service
Availability of services	Effectiveness and Equity	Access to library service in different areas
Outcome of policy indicators	Effectiveness	Reduction of unemployment through operation of training scheme

Source: Jackson and Palmer (1989, pp. 5–6); Fenwick (1995, p. 116).

These points are not to be dismissed lightly – any more than they can be in relation to the measurement of the academic performance of schools and children. PIs are certainly not going to go away with the arrival of a Labour Government. To quote its 1997 Manifesto:

> Every council will be required to publish a local performance plan with targets for service improvement, and be expected to achieve them. The Audit Commission will be given additional powers to monitor performance and promote efficiency. On its advice, government will where necessary send in a management team with full powers to remedy failure.

The solution, for any currently dissatisfied local authority, is the one advised by the Audit Commission itself: if you feel the Commission's statutory PIs are faulty or misleading, go ahead and supplement them with your own, more sensitive, ones. For the individual employee subject to appraisal, that option is not so readily available, which is one reason why, as noted in Chapter 13, only about half the authorities operating systems of performance management have gone as far as introducing performance-related pay schemes.

■ Addressing the councillor's role

All these managerial developments we have described have implications for councillors as well as for the officers that are probably most directly affected by them. Yet some councillors have undoubtedly felt marginalised in all the conceptual discussions of mission statements, quality management, strategic planning, performance measurement, and so on, which have seemed far removed from their day-to-day party political and constituency experience. They were hardly reassured by the contribution of the Audit Commission, who produced in 1990 a well-intentioned but insensitively argued publication, *We Can't Go On Meeting Like This*.

The paper, subtitled 'The Changing Role of Local Authority Members', examined the existing role of councillors and pointed a way ahead in the light of new imperatives. Its main emphasis was upon the role of councillors in the management of an authority and it all sounded very positive. Strategy setting, policy planning, performance review and cultural change – all those developments, in fact, that we have been discussing – should, the paper argued, be the priorities for councillors, *not* detailed administration and financial control.

The aim of the Audit Commission paper was (p. 3) 'to suggest ways in which members could encourage better management and obtain better results'. There were clear implications that many authorities would need to change the ways in which their business was organised and also devise means for developing relevant 'strategic' skills in elected councillors. It maintained that the specialisation of members in one or two service areas and a general tendency to become excessively involved in day-to-day operational detail had sometimes hindered the development of effective strategic management. Councillors were, in other words, responsible for many of the characteristics on the right-hand side of Exhibit 18.1.

The challenge for each authority, the paper argued (p. 10), was to resolve the tension inherent in the three key roles of members – Political, Representative and Organisational – and bring them together in a new and coherent manner. It advocated that all councils should have in place:

* a broad policy statement of the future direction and role for the authority;
* a Performance Review and Reporting System;
* a scheme of delegation to officers which keeps members out of day-to-day operational matters as far as possible, while retaining appropriate lines of accountability.

Central to this analysis is the role of members in determining political aims: 'Without any clear statement of direction the authority will become becalmed, or even ship-wrecked, and little different from local administration.' It was not, then, that the Audit Commission was advocating officer-led councils; quite the reverse. It wanted to see councillors spending more time and being more centrally involved in identifying and defining their political priorities, setting the authority's objectives, debating key issues and monitoring performance. Unfortunately, though, in heavily emphasising this organisational or managerial role of councillors, it at least gave the impression of neglecting their work as representatives and politicians; also of failing to acknowledge the essential inseparability of policy making and implementation that we sought to argue in Chapters 12 and 15. The result is that what should have been an influential contribution to the consideration of the role of the councillor in the local authority of the future was rather sidelined.

It was an opportunity missed, because there were plenty of proposals that might have been made for changing and enriching the way in which councillors work, and which would probably have met with a rather more positive reception. If proof be needed, we have it in the form of the Commission's more recent tilt at the subject in its 1997 paper, *Representing the People*, the arguments and proposals from which we summarised in Exhibit 12.4. The difference in the two publications is, to use John Stewart's phrase, that the first was attempting to go 'against the grain' of the way in which councillors instinctively think and work, while the second goes much more 'with the grain' and addresses itself precisely to issues that do concern councillors – namely, the frustrations and deficiencies of the traditional committee system and how to enhance their representational role.

If *We Can't Go On Meeting Like This* had expressed its concerns in the more sensitive and practical way that *Representing the People* does, it would probably have had a much more positive impact. Indeed, it could have found plenty of examples of its own suggestions already being translated into institutional form. As in any other area of local government activity, for every traditional authority or reform-resistant group of councillors, there are innovators.

The Audit Commission is supportive of the idea of area committees to boost councillors' community representative role; the Tower Hamlets' Liberal Democrats were way ahead of them. The Commission wanted some constructive thinking about alternative forms of committee systems, for ways of getting councillors to focus on major policy issues, to monitor the council's performance, to address key strategic issues; it is already taking place, possibly in your own council. In Exhibit 18.3 we list a small selection of interesting, and in some instances quite startlingly radical, institutional reforms that deserve perhaps a little more recognition than some of them have received.

■ The Internal Management Review

One possible reason why such developments have not received greater attention is that they fall short of the radical agenda that Michael Heseltine had in mind when he set up his Internal Management Review in the early 1990s. He wanted to challenge the whole basis of local government decision-making that had developed over at least the past hundred years and that the Widdicombe Committee five years previously had also found acceptable. The Heseltine Review was to raise fundamental questions that Widdicombe had left dormant: about the 'British model' in which policy is made openly and corporately by the elected council, working through committees with delegated powers but no independent authority, and on the advice of officers serving the council as a whole, not just the majority party and its leadership.

Consequently, when in July 1991 the then Environment Secretary produced his Consultation Paper on *The Internal Management of Local Authorities in England*, it put forward a range of alternative models, most of which involved replacing the committee system – which Mr Heseltine was known personally to regard as cumbersome, overly time-consuming, unbusinesslike and inefficient – with some form of either separate appointed or elected executive, thus splitting the executive and representational roles of the council. A broad distinction was drawn between officer executives and political executives, the latter in turn being divisible into the individual or collective and the directly or indirectly elected. The resulting models can be presented diagrammatically, as in Figure 18.1.

Exhibit 18.3   *Committees: some different ways of doing things*

Tower Hamlets' neighbourhood committees

In one of the most radical political management reforms, the Liberal Democrats from 1986 abolished the council's traditional borough-wide committee system and all its main professionalised departments and devolved power to 7 *multi-purpose neighbourhood committees*, some of which were Labour-controlled, and 7 neighbourhood town halls, each headed by its own chief executive. Other forms of participatory democracy followed, including residential consultative bodies and elected tenants' forums.

Kingston upon Thames' neighbourhood committees

Another Liberal Democrat decentralisation, but considerably less radical than that in Tower Hamlets. Again, 7 *neighbourhood committees*, to consider and monitor the operation of council services within the neighbourhood (though not the undevolved education and social services). All committees, including those not controlled by the Lib Dems, have their own current and capital budgets and meet in public, with public question times.

Milton Keynes' two-tier committee structure

The new unitary authority has become one of a number of councils to stratify its committee structure between *strategic committees*, dealing with major policy, and service committees, dealing with detailed issues and the monitoring of services.

Mendip's town task forces

This district council, based on 5 distinctive Somerset towns, has established a network of *town task forces*, consisting of local county councillors, district and town councillors, representatives of community organisations, local commerce and industry. The task forces produce agreed Action Plans, have led to the appointment of Town Centre Managers, and generally improve district-town council relations.

Haringey's public scrutiny meetings

The London borough has introduced a *public scrutiny procedure*, centred around a panel of councillors who subject to scrutiny particular service areas - e.g. housing benefits, prevention of rubbish dumping, services for those with physical disabilities. The public scrutiny meetings enable service users, members of the public, representatives of voluntary organisations and sometimes outside experts to question senior officers responsible for the service, and then draw up a scrutiny action plan.

Cumbria's select committees

Operating similarly to parliamentary select committees, groups of mainly backbench members take evidence, written and in oral hearings, on particular issues – e.g. youth services, care in the community - and then produce a report which is debated in full council.

Fife's Citizenship Commission

This new Scottish unitary authority has introduced several managerial innovations, including a Citizenship Commission - a full committee whose aim is the promotion and development of representative and participatory democracy in Fife.

		INDIVIDUAL	**COLLECTIVE**
POLITICAL	Appointed/ indirectly elected	(Nominated/indirectly elected mayor)	Cabinet system
	Directly Elected	Elected mayor	Elected executive
OFFICER		City/Council manager	(Collective officer executive)

Figure 18.1 *Models of separate executives*

Note: An elected mayor – however elected – is but one of several possible alternatives to the existing committee system. Bracketed entries were not specifically considered in the Heseltine Review.

Interestingly, the Consultation Paper did not nominate for further consideration all the logical possibilities. In particular it bypassed the French model of the nominated or indirectly elected mayor, thereby appearing to presume that any individual political executive should be elected directly and separately from the council – as indeed did the Commission for Local Democracy in one of its key recommendations (1995). This reflected Mr Heseltine's publicised enthusiasm for elected mayors, but did little to enhance understanding of the range of alternative forms of mayoral executive which exist elsewhere and which might be at least as transplantable to this country.

For various reasons the Consultation Paper was not enthusiastically acclaimed by local government. Councillors were predictably unimpressed by the democratic implications of the emphasis on streamlining the decision-making process and the likely reduction in the numbers of elected members. There was also a disconcerting lack of detail about how some of the optional models, that authorities were recommended to pilot, would actually operate. The government's next move, therefore, was to set up a joint working party of DoE nominees and representatives of the local authority associations, which produced in July 1993 a report entitled *Community Leadership and Representation: Unlocking the Potential.*

The potential to be unlocked was that of councillors, and indeed the whole report was written much more from their perspective than had been the Consultation Paper.

The Working Party's considered view was that:

1. There is a need to *strengthen the role of all elected members* in:
   - formulating council strategies,
   - leading and representing their communities,
   - acting as consumer champions, and
   - holding to account those responsible for providing those services.
2. There is a need to *develop the framework for effective leadership within local authorities*, which involves:
   - giving clear political direction,
   - identifying the needs and priorities of local communities, and overseeing the provision of high quality services to them.
3. To these ends, it is important that councils seek to 'unlock the potential of councillors' by:
   - acknowledging the reality and importance of party political groups;
   - reducing councillors' focus on detailed administration by enabling them to concentrate on strategic issues;
   - ensuring that they are adequately trained and supported;
   - ensuring that the system of allowances is adequate, and
   - looking for ways of decentralising procedures to involve local people.
4. In particular, *councils should review their internal management arrangements* to assess whether they are the most appropriate ones to achieve the above objectives.
5. They should *recognise the diversity of models of internal management that are possible within existing legislation* and that are *already in operation* somewhere in Great Britain.
6. Finally, councils should at least *consider the merits of more radical and experimental forms of internal management* that would require changes to existing legislation, but that the government might be prepared to see piloted in a small number of volunteer authorities. Four specific examples were identified by the joint working party:
   (a) *The Single Party Executive Committee*
   The council would delegate to a single party policy committee certain powers of strategy and policy formulation, the council itself retaining control over, for example, the annual budget and planning decisions.
   (b) *The Lead Member System*
   The council would delegate powers to named lead members rather than to a collective political executive. The lead member – e.g. the chair of the Social Services Committee – would be free to take decisions in a way that would currently be illegal, but would be accountable to the full council.
   (c) *The Cabinet System*
   The principle of delegation is extended to a single party policy committee whose membership has *both* individual and collective executive powers. Decisions taken by this executive would be

decisions of the council, and individual members would have delegated areas of responsibility. The full council would retain certain powers – e.g. setting the budget – and the right to overturn at least some decisions taken by the executive or lead members.

(d) *The Political Executive as a Separate Legal Entity*
In this scenario there would be a separate – perhaps separately elected – political executive with its own legal powers, which would take control of the decision-making process on behalf of the council. The full council would become very largely a scrutinising and reviewing body.

The differences in approach between the Consultation Paper and the Working Party's Report are manifest. The latter's emphasis on the *existing diversity* of internal management models is particularly significant, resulting as it almost inevitably does in the downgrading of the separate executive options which had been so dominant in the Consultation Paper. It should also be noted that by the time the Working Party Report was complete, not only had Mr Heseltine moved on from the Environment Department, but so too had his successor, Michael Howard. The Report was therefore received by John Gummer, who was not known to be as fascinated by internal management reform as the review's begetter.

It was certainly the case that the one option that did *not* receive much attention from the joint working party was the one that had most attracted Michael Heseltine personally, as well as some of the media: *directly elected mayors*. There are obvious potential difficulties, notably the possibility of conflict between a mayor of one party and a council controlled by another. At the same time, elected mayors could provide a powerful political voice for local government and, as noted at the start of this chapter, they reappeared in Labour's 1997 General Election Manifesto and in the Queen's Speech (see Exhibit 20.2). They thus both justify and require some more detailed examination.

Stoker and Wolman (1991), drawing on USA experience, argue that such mayors in the UK could provide a focal point and driving force for a more dynamic and influential local government. The system produces a high profile figure whom the public can identify and hold to account – but in such contexts scandals over the letting of contracts and use of public funds are not uncommon. Essentially, however, any directly elected political executive, individual or collective, would lead to a far more élitist local government system, with relatively few councillors having any really decisive policy-making significance. The 'representative' nature of local government could thereby suffer; fewer decision-takers with less detailed local knowledge could result in more streamlined but less sensitive community government. Local government might thus raise its public profile, but in doing so become less representative of grass-roots needs, unless the scrutiny role of the full council were to be considerably strengthened.

The independent Commission for Local Democracy (CLD) advocated directly elected mayors in its 1995 report; indeed this was its first recommendation: 'Local authorities should consist of a directly elected Council and a directly elected Leader/Mayor. Both Council and Leader/ Mayor should be voted in for a term of three years but the elected Leader may only serve two full terms in office' (Appendix 1). The CLD believed that a directly elected mayor was an important means of enhancing democracy in local government by providing a focus of power which would be 'highly visible and thus highly accountable' (1995, para 4.15), but at the same time the Commission recommended a number of direct and indirect means of limiting the power of such executives, thus reducing the extent to which direct accountability could be achieved (see Pratchett and Wilson, 1996, ch. 12).

Jones and Stewart (*Local Government Chronicle*, 7 July 1995, p. 8) were unimpressed, arguing that the report's section on directly elected mayors was simplistic:

> It is as if the Commission regards it as a piece of magic which will automatically increase turn-out and build a vibrant local democracy. But the magic does not seem to work in the U.S. In 1991 in Phoenix – an authority with a city manager and a directly elected mayor – only 17% of the electorate voted, and that is of the electorate who bothered to register as voters.

The debate goes on, as it should. The Labour Government's wish is that there should be experimentation: in itself a welcome recognition of local government's inherent learning capacity and of the fact that different management arrangements are appropriate for different authorities. For there to be successful experimentation, there must be enthusiasm and, although few backbench councillors are likely to be enthusiastic about changes which threaten to diminish their role, it is possible that, along with the proposed Greater London Authority, there may be leaderships of at least a few medium-sized towns who will nominate themselves as pilot authorities.

■ Conclusion

We have considered in this chapter a considerable range of internal management innovations which have been debated and in some instances implemented during the past ten years or so. We have tried to emphasise, as elsewhere in the book, that the tremendous diversity of local authorities means that it is neither necessary nor desirable to have a 'standardised package' which can be taken 'off the shelf' and applied uncritically to every authority in the UK. Internal management patterns need to relate to the particular circumstances and culture of each individual authority. Authorities need to be selective in introducing change, rather than simply following the latest fashion for its own sake. New patterns need to recognise that recent legislation has brought about a broad shift of emphasis in the role of councillors from the organisational to the representational. They need to recognise the advent of 'governance' at the local level and the consequent fragmentation of activity that has frequently ensued.

Guide to further reading

A good starting point is likely to be your own local authority's *Annual Report*, but the best source of detail about internal management change in local authorities is the Local Government Management Board (LGMB). The Board commissions and publishes regular research reports aimed at making local authorities more managerially effective, several of which have contributed to this chapter. We have drawn particular attention to the writings of Professor John Stewart, many of which have been published by LGMB itself or in a usefully practical series of books produced jointly with Longman on *Managing Local Government*. Skelcher (1992), which summarises a large amount of material on 'consumer-oriented' aspects of contemporary internal management, is also in this series. The papers we have referred to by the Audit Commission and the DoE are obviously important for the more specialist reader, but the best general overview of management in local government is probably Leach *et al.* (1994).

■ *Chapter 19* ■

The Impact of Compulsory Competitive Tendering

■ Introduction

Of all the changes introduced by the 1979–97 Conservative Governments, perhaps the most fundamental and far-reaching were those associated with compulsory competitive tendering (CCT). Successive legislative enactments forced local authorities to put specified services out to competitive tender on terms and time-scales established by the centre. In many cases, as we shall see, the tenders were won not by private companies but by in-house bids from a council's own workforce. But the very acts of putting together a tender document and drawing up and monitoring contracts produce profound changes in the internal management and operation of an authority – sufficiently profound in our view for CCT to justify a chapter in its own right.

This chapter, therefore, examines the ideological context within which CCT originated and outlines the accompanying legislative framework. It then assesses its internal management and financial implications, and concludes with a brief outline of the Blair Government's alternative to CCT, known as 'Best Value'.

■ Context – one element of the contract culture

The introduction of CCT into local government needs to be seen as one dimension of the 'New Right' privatisation or contracting-out strategy of successive Conservative Governments. Essentially, the process requires a comparison of the costs of in-house provision with those of any interested private contractors and the award of the contract to the most competitive bidder. It must be emphasised that it is the *competitive tendering* – the cost comparison – that is compulsory, *not* the contracting-out of the service, which may or may not result, depending on the competing bids. Three pieces of legislation have driven the process:

1. *The Local Government, Planning and Land Act 1980*, which introduced CCT for building construction and maintenance and highways construction and maintenance;

2.   *The Local Government Act 1988,* which extended CCT to building cleaning; grounds maintenance; vehicle maintenance; school meals, welfare and other catering (e.g. staff canteens); refuse collection; street cleaning; plus sports and leisure management (added in December 1989);

3.   *The Local Government Act 1992,* which extended it beyond these technical services into housing management and a large number of mainly 'white collar' activities at the very heart of the local authority.

The New Right has consistently argued that the contracting-out of services formerly provided monopolistically by central and local government or by agencies like the NHS will lead to both improved service provision and reduced costs. The advent and spread of CCT have meant that local authorities were entering what, for many of them, was a brave new world of *sharing* the provision of services with a range of other bodies, e.g. private industrial/commercial concerns and voluntary organisations. The role of the local authority as sole, or even major, service deliverer for its community was being challenged by governments concerned to champion *competition* at local level.

This *ideological* context of CCT is important. The 'think-tanks' of the New Right – notably the Adam Smith Institute, the Institute of Economic Affairs, and the Centre for Policy Studies – pressed hard for legislation on competitive tendering. Such organisations emphasised individualism and lamented the 'dependency culture' imbued by the Welfare State. To some extent they were pushing at an open door, particularly when Nicholas Ridley was Secretary of State at the DoE (see Ridley, 1988). CCT became a key element of the broad Conservative aim of 'rolling back the frontiers of the state'. A lesser role for the state would mean more involvement by the private sector.

For New Right theorists such as Forsyth (1982, p. 988) both local taxpayers and businesses are winners in the contracting-out game. Local taxpayers are winners because of 'the one great fact about privatised services: they are cheaper'. Businesses are perceived to be winners because the contracting-out of services offers them the chance of extra business. The contractor 'finds opportunity for enterprise development and profit in the new activity'. Those opposed to CCT, on the other hand, argue that it potentially reduces the role of not only local authorities but also trade unions. According to Ascher (1987, p. 47): 'Competitive tendering and contracting-out fit into the Conservative Government's comprehensive and sustained attack upon trade union power. In particular, they offer scope for reducing the "stranglehold" that the Party attributes to public sector unions.' A similar theme is developed by Cochrane, who argues that the imposition of CCT on local authorities increased central control over local service provision (1993b, pp. 223–4):

One might expect the extension of quasi-markets to reduce potential areas of conflict between central and local government, and to undermine existing hierarchical assumptions, as competition develops between agencies, and new ways of allocating resources become the norm. In practice, however, the new arrangements have often been experienced at the local level as increased restrictions and tighter control. . . . Market mechanisms have in practice largely been used as part of the battle to impose central authority.

■ The development of competition – the key legislation

The Conservative Government's attempt to introduce market disciplines into the operation of local authorities through competition for services had two major components:

(a) the requirement to subject some services to competitive tender;
(b) the imposition of *internal trading markets*.

Walsh noted (1995, p. 28) that, while the tendency is to focus upon the requirement to put work out to tender,

the requirement to operate an internal market has had at least as great an impact, because it has created an ethos of commercialism within the local authority. It is increasingly possible to see the local authority as a set of contracts and quasi-contracts, involving a network of internal and external trading organisations.

In what ways has this new commercialism manifested itself inside local government? The *Local Government, Planning and Land Act 1980* effectively introduced market discipline into the operation of local government. Under this Act local authorities were obliged to put out to tender their building construction and major highways and building maintenance work.

If, after competition, local authorities determined that they should themselves undertake such work, because they could provide it more cheaply than a private contractor, that part of the local authority which carried it out became known as the Direct Labour Organisation (DLO), in effect the Works Department. Such DLOs were obliged to maintain trading accounts which had to make a surplus sufficient to enable them to make a rate of return on capital of at least 5 per cent.

The initial impact of the 1980 Act was limited by the exclusion of any building maintenance work valued at less than £10,000 and highways work costing less than £100,000. Local authorities were also able to draw up contracts in such a way and on such a scale as to be unattractive to potential private sector bidders. These 'loopholes', however, were progressively closed by government regulation and certainly the tendering conditions in the 1988 Act were considerably tighter.

Before the 1988 Act, though, came the Transport Act 1985, which also extended the requirement to compete by requiring bus undertakings and some local authority airports to operate commercially. Here was one piece of local government legislation that had an almost immediate impact on the consciousness of at least the public transport-using public, as reduced subsidies led to higher fares and there were plenty of early examples of bizarre scheduling by competing companies on popular routes.

The next major piece of CCT legislation was the Local Government Act 1988, but it is important to emphasise that, before the *compulsory* element became widespread, a number of authorities had *voluntarily* put services out to tender. A *Municipal Year Book* survey in 1989 found that 223 authorities had made some voluntary use of competition in deciding how local services were to be delivered. Most of the resulting contracts, however, were fairly small and the government's view was that compulsion was required – hence the *Local Government Act 1988*. This Act extended the statutory requirement for competition to the range of technical services listed at the beginning of this chapter: refuse collection, cleaning, catering, and so on. A detailed timetable for the phasing in of contract awards was determined by the Department of the Environment. There were few exemptions this time, although there was a '*de minimis*' rule excluding contracts below a specified value.

The Local Government Act 1988 threw down one of the biggest challenges that local authorities have ever had to face. It forced councils to put a number of key services out to tender, and to do so within a defined 30–month period. Contracts were to be awarded on a strictly commercial basis, with little or no room for any political, social or non-commercial considerations. Local authorities had to keep separate accounts for work done by their own in-house Direct Service Organisations (DSOs) and were also required to submit annual reports to the Secretary of State.

The 1988 legislation required local authorities not to 'act in a manner having the effect or intended or likely to have the effect of restricting, distorting or preventing competition' (Local Government Act, 1988, S.7 (7)). This clause is the most powerful in the legislation since it means that local authorities must examine everything they do to ensure that it is not anti-competitive. The Secretary of State has power to act against local authorities which are perceived, by the private sector or consumers, to be acting anti-competitively. An authority can be required to explain its procedures, and the minister, if not satisfied with the explanation, can require re-tendering with or without an in-house bid. But despite frequent complaints from the last Conservative government about authorities bending the rules laid down by the legislation, relatively few were forced to re-tender. The DoE's annual report for 1993, for example, records 157 cases of allegedly anti-competitive behaviour in relation to more than £6 billion worth of work. This led to the issuing of 20 notices and 12 directions under the provisions of the 1988 Act – or roughly the same numbers as for the contracts that local authorities find it necessary to terminate each year for reasons of performance failure or financial collapse of the contractor.

The last of the Conservative government's three main CCT statutes was the *Local Government Act 1992*, which extended competition to a range of professional central support services: law, personnel and finance; construction-related services, such as architecture and surveying; information technology; and housing management. These 'white collar' services self-evidently differ one from another, as well as being collectively more complex and less easily opened up to external competition than the earlier technical services. The government acknowledged almost from the outset, therefore, that a much longer phasing-in timetable would be required and that initially only a proportion of work in any particular service would be involved. The intervention of local government reorganisation delayed the process still further and, with a Labour Government committed to the eventual abolition of CCT, Exhibit 19.1 may prove to be of mainly historic interest. It does, however, convey an impression of what was envisaged under the 1992 Act and of the areas in which – whether compulsorily or voluntarily – local authorities are most likely to see further extensions of competitive tendering.

It should be mentioned here that, as with the poll tax, the CCT elements of the Local Government Act 1988 were not applied to Northern Ireland. A consultative paper published by the DoE/NI Office in November 1988 discussed the possibility of introducing CCT along the same lines as in the rest of the UK, and final details emerged in the Local Government (Miscellaneous Provisions) (Northern Ireland) Order 1992 which came into operation in May 1992. CCT has been introduced gradually, with the first round, including refuse collection, completed in April 1994. Street cleansing followed in April 1995, and grounds maintenance by April 1996. A further timetable was established for other services. Contracts in the initial round all went to in-house tenders from councils' direct labour organisations (see Connolly, 1994). The likelihood is, however, that the private sector will begin to win some of the later contracts. In this event a further reduction in the role of NI local authorities as direct providers of services seems inevitable.

■ Winners and losers?

What proportion of contracts has the private sector won? Early evidence suggested that local authority 'in-house' tenders were overwhelmingly

Exhibit 19.1 The CCT implementation timetable for professional services, 1996

	Proposed implementation date	% to be put out to competition	'De minimis' level	Most suitable for 'externalisation'	Less suitable for 'externalisation'	Prospects?
Legal Services	1996–99	45%	£300,000	Litigation, advocacy, contracts and conveyancing	Advice on propriety to members and officers	Some voluntary contracting-out already; private firms reluctant to compete for new contracts, and risk spoiling existing relationships
Personnel Services	1996–99	30%	£400,000	Training, health and safety, occupational health	Equal opportunities, industrial relations, human resource management	Training already widely contracted out; 30% target easily met by most councils
Housing Management	1996–98	95%	£500,000	Suitability depends more on internal politics of council than for other CCT services. Councils known to be 'protective' will deter competition		Many councils 'de minimis'; potential competition from private sector and housing associations, but larger contracts likely to stay in-house
Finance Services	1997–99	35%	£300,000	Salaries and wages, benefits administration, pensions, council tax and business rates collection	Budgeting, housing management, internal auditing	Much voluntary contracting-out already; 35% target easily met by 'most suitable' services
Information Technology Services	1998–2000	70%	£300,000	Not much that is not suitable; but councils advised to maintain in-house capability to control purchase and delivery of service		Much voluntary contracting-out already and increasing even before postponed start dates

successful. The frequently predicted 'take over' by the private sector failed to materialise. A *Municipal Journal* survey at the end of the first year of operating CCT showed that 76 per cent of all contracts went to the authorities' own workforces. In Scotland a survey put the percentage nearer 85 per cent.

The current picture is summarised in Exhibit 19.2, which shows the significant differences both between services and between numbers of contracts and their value. We see that only in building cleaning and construction have more than half the contracts been won by outside bidders, while at the other end of the scale DSOs have been most successful at retaining in-house leisure and housing management. In every service it will be seen that DSOs have tended to win a disproportionate share of the larger contracts, so that while 40 per cent of the total number of contracts nowadays are being won by private companies, they amount to only 25 per cent of the total contract value. For every service too it should be emphasised that in Scotland a significantly higher proportion of contracts, both in number and by value, have stayed in-house.

The private sector has not, therefore, rushed into this new 'market' and totally transformed service provision overnight as some hoped and many feared. In many cases still there are no private sector bids and 'in-house' DSOs win out by default. The overall picture is, indeed, very much what you should by now have come to expect – extremely varied from one council to another, depending upon their size, type and, perhaps above all in this instance, their political inclinations.

Thus there are authorities such as Westminster, Wandsworth, Bromley and Rochford that have been keen to put as much as possible out to tender, going well beyond the requirements and in advance of the time-scales of legislation. Rather more Labour authorities have been equally keen for their DSOs to win as many contracts as possible. Estimates by the Local Government Management Board in 1996 were that there were over 120 authorities in which DSOs had so far experienced a 100 per cent success rate, while there were some 26 mainly non-metropolitan districts with no DSO contracts at all. As ever with local government, aggregate data can give you little detailed idea of what is happening in your own local area.

■ The impact upon management

It might be imagined that, with the great majority of larger contracts still staying in-house and with DSOs in around a quarter of all authorities being successful with every bid, CCT has left much of local government relatively unchanged. Let us immediately dispel any such thought, which could hardly be further from the truth. Whether retaining or

Exhibit 19.2 The scale and results of CCT, 1996

	Average annual value of individual contracts (£'000)	% contracted out		Nos of private contractors		Largest company (no of contracts and market share)
		Contracts (%)	Value (%)	Active	Winning contracts	
Building Cleaning	242	58	28	458	158	Taylorplan (38; 2.6%)
Refuse Collection	1,422	39	35	97	31	SITA (21; 5.0%)
Vehicle Maintenance	559	23	19	163	40	Serco (3; 2.1%)
Catering (Education and Welfare)	1,897	25	19	68	19	BET (16; 10.2%)
Grounds Maintenance	240	44	26	607	231	Brophy (67; 5.2%)
Sports and Leisure Management	470	15	7	147	33	Relaxion (10; 1.2%)
Housing Management	1,057	11	7	68	12	Hyde H.A. (3; 1.6%)
Legal Services	281	37	16	88	14	Stoneham Langton Passmore (1; 6.8%)
Construction and Property	1,153	56	49	141	34	Babtie (2; 11%)
Information Technology	1,403	n/a	n/a	46	18	CFM (16; 31.2%)
Financial Services	914	n/a	n/a	62	35	Capita (8; 24%)
Weighted average		40	25			

Source: Municipal Year Book, 1997, vol. 1, pp. 121 ff.

'losing' contracts, all authorities have had to adapt quite fundamentally their patterns of management and organisation in response to CCT.

The major change is the need to separate the roles of client and contractor within the authority. *Clients* are those responsible for the specification and monitoring of services; *contractors* are those responsible for the direct production and delivery of the service. The separation of these roles can be made within a single department or by creating separate contractor departments. As noted above, some people were fearful that the 1988 Act would herald the beginning of the end of the local authority as a *direct* provider of services. But the threat presented a challenge to many local authorities to win the contracts in-house – which could be secured only by streamlining management structures. One of the by-products of the 1988 Act, therefore, has been a *strengthening* of local authority management as a means to an end, namely winning contracts in-house.

■ Financial effects

As Walsh (1989, p. 42) pointed out early on in the debate, 'much of the evidence that is presented either to prove or disprove the value of competitive tendering is tendentious, produced by those concerned either to promote or oppose competition'. A healthy scepticism is needed when examining financial data; methodologies require close scrutiny. The Audit Commission's study (1987) of housing maintenance found that costs 'tend to be higher when work is not subject to competition' (Audit Commission, 1987, p. 2). After a study of refuse collection the Commission found that privatised services had lower than average costs, but that some services provided in-house did equally well (Audit Commission, 1984). Other studies of refuse collection have found cost savings when competition has been introduced, but this does not mean that these results can be automatically applied to the many other diverse services subjected to CCT. Indeed, it would seem to be the introduction of competition, rather than the awarding of contracts to private firms, which is the critical factor in producing lower costs. The major savings come from a reduction in the number of staff employed to do the work, often by 20 to 30 per cent. Pay and conditions have been cut, but this has been a secondary source of saving. As Walsh (1995, p. 38) later observed, methods of work have changed too, 'and new equipment has been introduced, for example, larger refuse wagons. Any full social costing would have to take account of the unacknowledged costs of unemployment, and increased benefits following pay reductions.'

Whilst authoritative data about the financial implications of CCT are somewhat elusive, Walsh (1991) showed the following:

* on average the annual cost of a service in the 40 councils examined was 5.7 per cent lower after competition;
* the largest savings have come in building cleaning;
* employee costs have been reduced as a proportion of total costs;
* the average cost of preparing for competition was 10.7 per cent of annual contract value or 2.5 per cent of the total cost.

While there were a number of teething troubles in the early stages of CCT, there were relatively few outright failures. The LGMB in 1996 had records of only 190 contracts being terminated, or well under 2 per cent of the total. The major areas of difficulty have been grounds maintenance (69 terminations), building cleaning (40), and sports and leisure management (32). As exemplified in Exhibit 19.3, there will always be a debate about service quality under CCT, with the DoE under a Conservative Government arguing that standards had improved and the trade unions and other critics claiming the reverse. To close this section on a more objective if less dramatic view, therefore, we turn again to Walsh, who drew three conclusions about the impact of contracting and competition on the quality of service (1995, p. 42):

(a) Service failure is most likely at the beginning of contracts, largely because of problems of transition;
(b) Both the public and private sectors are equally competent in most cases;
(c) Standards of service have become more uniform as a result of competition.

■ Conclusion – performance plans to replace compulsion

The introduction of CCT has had a major impact on both the culture and management of local authorities. It necessitated numerous organisational changes along with the need for closer monitoring and inspection of work in the interests of providing quality services. One possible implication, however, of the division between client and contractor is fragmentation *within* an authority and the loss of corporate identity as a series of separately accountable units operate within a single council.

Politically, of course, as we have shown, CCT remains highly contentious. Opponents argue that Conservative governments compelled local authorities to put specific services out to tender by means of standard rules applied throughout the country without regard for local needs or conditions. They emphasise that such legislation gives the government yet more power and weakens the freedom of locally elected people to decide what services they want and how they should be run.

Exhibit 19.3 *CCT – competing perspectives*

The last Conservative Government's view

Research undertaken for the Department indicates that CCT for blue collar services produced annual cost savings of around 7% in the first round of tendering and over 9% in the second round, while maintaining or improving service standards; and has led to tighter specifications, more attention to the needs of customers, and improved monitoring of performance and management.   (DoE Annual Report, 1997, p. 133)

The disenchanted customer's view

Croydon's closed pools

Croydon LBC had to close down its swimming pools and sports facilities following the financial collapse of private contractor, Contemporary Leisure, and staff concern about the health and safety of users.
The Council took on most of the company's staff, some of whom had not been paid for weeks, but had to wait for special authority from the Environment Secretary to reopen its sports facilities, because the 1988 Act forbids councils taking over a function that has been taken over by a private firm.

Stockport's toadless holes

School children in Stockport complained of being asked to choose between having either gravy or vegetables, and being served undersized sausages and 'toadless' hole by BET Catering under its £3 million per annum school meals contract. Councillors issued default notices and fined the company for failing to meet quality controls laid down by the contract.

West Wiltshire's fast-growing grass

West Wiltshire DC sacked private contractor, CSG (Bath), for failing to keep council verges tidy. Taking a proverbial leaf out of British Rail's book of imaginative excuses for inconvenienced punters, the company claimed it had been unable to keep up with 'the unusually fast-growing grass'.

Bristol's uncollected rubbish

Bristol City Council threatened the French-owned contractor, SITA, with financial penalties after it had failed to collect more than 156,000 of the city's rubbish bins on the agreed day over a 20–week period of monitoring under its refuse collection contract.

Source: *The Daily Telegraph*, 24 April 1995.

Critics perceive it as unfair that, whilst the private sector could compete for council services, council departments were not allowed to compete for private contracts.

Under the 1988 Act councils have no say on the terms and conditions of employment operated by contractors. They are not able to take into account a competing firm's practices when it comes to trade union rights, employment protection, sickness benefit, pensions, training and apprenticeships or many aspects of equal opportunities. Issues of *quality*, critics argued, are always secondary to issues of cost. Nevertheless, even most opponents of CCT recognise, albeit reluctantly, that elements of the 'contract culture' are with us to stay; it is the compulsion and the bias against public service provision that need to go.

Exhibit 19.4   *The 12 Principles of Best Value*

1 Councils will owe a duty of best value to local people, both as taxpayers and service customers. Performance plans should support local accountability

2 Best value is about effectiveness and quality, not just economy and efficiency. Target-setting should underpin the new regime

3 The best value duty should apply to a wider range of services than CCT

4 There is no presumption that services must be privatised or delivered directly. What matters is what works

5 Competition will continue as an important management tool but will not in itself demonstrate best value

6 Central government will continue to set the basic framework for service provision

7 Local targets should have regard to national targets and performance indicators to support competition between councils

8 National and local targets should be built on performance information

9 Auditors should confirm the integrity and comparability of performance information

10 Auditors will report publicly on whether best value has been achieved and contribute to plans for remedial action

11 There should be provision for DoE intervention, on Audit Commission advice, to tackle failing councils

12 The form of intervention, including requirements to expose services to competition and accept external management support, should be appropriate to the nature of the failure.

Source: Local Government Chronicle, 6 June 1997.

Under the Labour Government elected in May 1997 they *will* go – by April 1999, legislative timetable permitting. The Party's manifesto was unambiguous on that part of its programme at least: 'Councils should not be forced to put their services out to tender. . .'. It was the next part, however, that is potentially the most interesting and innovative: '. . . but [they] will be required to obtain *best value*' (our emphasis).

In both Scotland and Wales the moratorium on CCT (introduced because of structural reorganisation) was immediately extended for a further year (to July 1998 in Scotland and October 1998 in Wales) to allow for the rapid introduction of a 'best value' system of service delivery. The Blair Government announced that in England CCT would be relaxed for a smaller number of pilot councils on condition that they adhered to a 'best value' regime. The basis of this pilot scheme was to be the '12 Principles of Best Value' set out by the Local Government Minister (see Exhibit 19.4). While competition was set to continue to be an 'important management tool', it would be insufficient on its own to demonstrate best value.

It is the unenviable task of civil servants in the Department of the Environment, Transport and the Regions' competition and quality division to transform this rhetoric into practical regulations.

Guide to further reading

The advent of CCT has had a major impact on both the culture and management of local authorities. Best further reading on *culture* is Painter (1992); the most useful sources on *management*, and certainly on Labour's evolving performance plans, are probably the *Local Government Chronicle* and the *Municipal Journal*, largely because this is such a fast moving scene. Ministerial statements come thick and fast; without regular reading of the professional local government press your knowledge will inevitably soon become dated. An excellent source of detailed information about the *extent* of CCT is the LGMB's CCT information service database, updated at regular intervals and summarised in the annual *Municipal Year Book*, available in most local libraries. Midwinter (1995) sketches the Scottish dimension very clearly, while Connolly (1994) does the same for Northern Ireland. As you will have gathered, much of the most useful evaluative work on CCT was carried out by an INLOGOV colleague of ours, Professor Kieron Walsh. Kieron died suddenly in 1995 and is, academically and personally, still sorely missed. Some of his later writing, however, is still of direct relevance – notably his chapters in Stewart and Stoker (1995) and Leach, Davis *et al.* (1996).

■ *Chapter 20* ■

The Shape of Things to Come

■ Introduction – New Labour, new change

Throughout this book one theme has received emphasis in chapter after chapter: change. UK local authorities have in the past two decades had to manage and adapt themselves to a scale of change and upheaval that has approached the revolutionary. So, more recently, has this book – which is why this second edition differs so substantially from the first. At least the book, though, has retained its 20-chapter format. For much of British local government even its external structure has changed in the past five years.

Indeed, that is how we started Chapter 2: with reference to the Conservative Government's structural review and our annually changing number of councils. In Chapter 5 we described the nearly completed 'hybrid' structure in England that resulted from that review, and the fully unitary systems already in operation in Scotland and Wales; then in Chapter 6 the changing nature of some of the major services and of local government's service responsibilities – from provider to commissioner or enabler. Chapters 7 and 8 dealt with some of the new institutions involved in the world of sub-central governance, including the recently unified Local Government Association, and Chapters 9 and 10 with local finance – now relatively stabilised, but only after the violent disruption of the poll tax era.

In short, in every one of those principal chapters in Part 1 – outlining what we called 'The Basics' – we find that today's world of local government is sufficiently different from that of the early 1990s to necessitate significant rewriting, rather than merely amendment. That was before we even reached Part 3, which was actually supposed to be about change. Then, just as we completed the book, we were confronted with potentially the greatest change of all: the election of a new Labour Government, and one, moreover, with its own agenda of ideas for the further reform of sub-central government.

That national Labour administration, and particularly the expanded Department of the Environment, Transport and the Regions presided over by the Deputy Prime Minister, John Prescott, will inevitably play a leading role in determining 'the shape of things to come' for local government. It is only appropriate, therefore, that we conclude this final chapter by summarising the early legislative initiatives of the new government and its longer-term proposals.

Not even the most radical government, however, could overthrow immediately all the changes and developments of the recent past. As we indicated at the end of the previous chapter, for example, the 'contract culture' ushered in by CCT will outlast its eventual abolition. Performance management, described in Chapter 18, will be reinforced through the proposed annual performance plans. Above all, the progressive movement of local authorities from being largely self-sufficient service providers to enablers is set to continue – not least because it is consistent with Labour's manifesto view of their role (p. 34):

> We reject the dogmatic view that services must be privatised to be of high quality, but equally we see no reason why a service should be delivered directly [by local councils] if other more efficient means are available.

The first main part of this chapter, therefore, examines more closely than we have previously the concept of 'enabling': a concept with such elasticity of definition and interpretation that governments of both major parties are able to see it as central to their future visions of local government. We then present three alternative models of enabling that might be adopted by three hypothetical authorities – Ridleyburg, Contractopolis and Communitown – and compare them with each other and with the more traditional but equally hypothetical Tradsville.

Each of the four models represents a form of response to what the Local Government Management Board (1993b) has suggested are the three major strategic choices facing local authorities as they approach the millennium:

* the extent to which they wish to exercise a *wider role of local governance,* as opposed to concentrating on their narrower responsibilities for service delivery;
* the degree to which they wish to incorporate *market mechanisms –* competition and 'market-testing' – into their operations beyond the requirements of legislation;
* their *interpretation of 'community'* and the relative importance they put on responding to the needs of wider communities, over and above their service to individual consumers and household units.

We are not suggesting that any particular pattern of responses is better than any other. The strategic choices are linked and it is perfectly possible for an authority to seek a balance between the different emphases. We do feel, however, with the LGMB, that these choices are better addressed explicitly by authorities, and that the conscious adoption of any model is likely to be preferable to a continuing directionless drift, with no strategic vision to serve as a guide to political action and to internal organisation.

■ The elastic concept of enabling

At one time, in the 1987–9 period, when Margaret Thatcher was Prime Minister and Nicholas Ridley was Secretary of State for the Environment, it appeared as if a coherent and minimalist vision of local government was beginning to emerge, epitomised by the Adam Smith Institute's *Wiser Counsels* (1989a) and Ridley's own pamphlet for the Centre for Policy Studies, *The Local Right* (1988). This vision proposed a *residual* or safety net role for local government. Local authorities were envisaged as 'enablers' in the limited sense of elected agencies which made arrangements for the provision of a small number of services which the market could not provide. Such authorities would be encouraged or, increasingly, required not to provide even this residual range of services directly, but rather to specify the form of service needed and contract out its actual provision to the private sector, the voluntary sector, housing associations – to anyone, it appeared, in preference to the local authority itself. Even the regulatory role was minimised, for the private sector was not seen as requiring more than a minimal degree of regulation.

This minimalist vision lost much of its force with the disappearance from the centre-stage of British politics of its main enthusiasts and advocates. Nevertheless, the essence of the Major Government's view of the enabling authority was still very much concerned with finding new ways of delivering services through agencies other than the council itself.

By contrast, the concept of enabling developed by Clarke and Stewart involves a very different and much more *expansive* interpretation. For them (1988, p. 1):

> the role of an enabling council is to use all the means at its disposal to meet the needs of those who live within the area.

The starting point here is the identification of community needs. The enabling authority in this sense uses a wide range of powers and resources, including the powers of civic leadership, influence and campaigning, to meet those needs. Pro-active negotiation with the private sector to stimulate economic activity, empowerment of local communities, imaginative use of regulatory powers, and the positive use of links with other public sector organisations are all means to this end. This much more active conception of enabling is shared nowadays, at least in their public rhetoric, by a majority of individual local authorities (see Ennals and O'Brien, 1990), and has obvious similarities to Labour's manifesto references to 'partnership working' (p. 34):

> We will place on councils a new duty to promote the economic, social and environmental well-being of their area. They should work in partnership with local people, local business and local voluntary organisations. They will have the powers necessary to develop these partnerships.

■ Four models of strategic choice

We have, then, two almost polarised depictions or 'ideal types' of enabling authority, and obviously there are plenty of additional, less extreme possibilities (see Leach and Stewart, 1992b). We present just three here, in the form of pen portraits or cameos, following an equivalent characterisation of a fourth and more familiar model, that of the traditional hierarchical authority.

□ *Tradsville – the traditional, service-delivering authority*

Tradsville is an archetypal authority of the 1945–80 period, striving towards self-sufficiency but never really being granted the financial and policy autonomy to achieve it. It has always seen its principal role as being a direct provider of public services, in which its elected members believe just as passionately as Conservative ministers proclaimed that private provision is inherently superior. Its profession-based departments and mainly single-service committees are geared to its service-providing role, with client–contractor splits blurred, rather than accentuated, and relatively little inter-departmental working. Its response to the Conservative Government's grant cutbacks of the early 1980s was to raise domestic rates in order to maintain the levels of service which it believed local residents wanted, and, throughout the era of ministerial capping of local rates, taxes and expenditures, Tradsville's leading councillors have complained bitterly and publicly about the outrage of Whitehall usurping *their* rights to set their own budgets and tax rates according to the needs of *their* local people.

CCT has been doubly resented, for its compulsion and for its inbuilt bias against public services, and every effort has been made – including some that have come to the attention of the DoE as allegedly 'anti-competitive' – to ensure that as many contracts as possible are won by in-house bids. Considerable expectations have been invested in a new

Labour Government abolishing CCT, removing capping, and releasing more resources to authorities like Tradsville. Councillors, though, are less enthusiastic about all the current talk, including that in Labour's own manifesto, of community governance, public/private partnership, 'enabling' councils working through other organisations, or 'arm's-length units' within the authority. Local councils, in their view, were set up to provide local services to local people; that is what they are professionally equipped to do, and what should continue to be their core business.

☐ *Ridleyburg – the residual enabling authority*

Ridleyburg, as will be appreciated from the above discussion of enabling, is Tradsville's ideological mirror-image. Its councillors are the very opposite of empire-builders. They have come into local government, which several hope may serve as a stepping-stone to a national political career, to play their part in implementing locally as complete a version as possible of the Thatcherite project of minimising councils' direct service-providing responsibilities. Rather, they believe, councils should be providers of last resort, employing only skeletal workforces, and responsible only for a limited set of services which cannot be provided directly through the private market or through some other more appropriate mechanism – e.g. quango, development corporation, local office of central government.

Even in the case of those residual services for which a local authority like Ridleyburg would retain responsibility, it is preferable for that responsibility to be one of contract-monitoring, rather than direct service provision. The authority should specify the level of service required, contract out the service to a private company, or exceptionally a local authority in-house contracting agency, and then monitor the contractor's performance. There is some provision for regulation of private sector activity, but even this role is best minimised, because the market can be trusted as the most efficient and effective mechanism for providing goods and service of all kinds, with only a limited need for external intervention. Organisationally, both committee and departmental structures have been slimmed down.

The key accountability relationship, Ridleyburg councillors will claim, is not the traditional but ineffectual electoral one between local residents and themselves, but between the individual local taxpayer and the local authority: as close an approximation as possible to a supermarket transaction between customer and market organisation. Considerations of any wider community role are seen as largely irrelevant: the council's function is simply to enable the delivery of a limited range of public goods and services which the market cannot or does not wish to provide.

□ *Contractopolis – the commercial enabling authority*

Like Ridleyburg, Contractopolis believes in the virtues and efficiencies of market forces, but sees them as having a rather different role to play in local government. Contractopolis councillors have no intention of privatising themselves and their council out of existence. They see the local authority as having a much stronger and more active role in determining the economic future of its area than would their Ridleyburg counterparts. Indeed, the council has the potential to be the key planning and co-ordinating agency for local economic development, providing a series of mechanisms and incentives through which the local economy can flourish.

The planning role of the authority in particular is given much more emphasis, embodying a view that a longer-term planned approach to land-use, infrastructure and transportation links is necessary for the effective operation of the local economy. The relationship between the local authority and local economic concerns is seen as a two-way process. Social responsibility by the local employer is emphasised and planning agreements between developer and local authority expected and actively negotiated. As the 1997 Conservative Manifesto put it (p. 30):

> We believe local government should take a lead in the planning and development of their local communities . . . [and] work in partnership with central government, with private enterprise, and other organisations in their community. The impact of local government is multiplied when they work in this way.

There is clearly a much more pro-active role envisaged for Contractopolis than for Ridleyburg, and similarly, although both authorities firmly believe in contracting out consumption services wherever possible, their approach to the negotiation of these contracts is rather different. Contractopolis is keen on the idea of planning gain deals (see Exhibit 7.7), and so endeavours to draw up contracts that maximise benefits to the local authority, rather than necessarily picking the lowest cost option. There is also more recognition of the need to regulate the activities of the private sector, and a readier acknowledgement that contracting-out has had its service failures as well as its financial successes.

Frustrated by what they saw as the excessively time-consuming and bureaucratic departmental and committee structure, the council leadership – several of whom have some business experience – recently introduced an internal management restructuring. As a result, management boards of councillors have replaced a number of the committees, and much more responsibility is now devolved to the managers of a number of service-providing units, who operate on the basis of business plans and are evaluated on their achievement of performance targets.

☐ *Communitown – the orchestrating enabling authority*

Communitown has a considerably more sceptical view of the benefits of market mechanisms than either Ridleyburg or Contractopolis, alongside a very much more expansive conception of the role of the local authority. Communitown councillors were just as opposed as, say, their colleagues in Tradsville, to the financial and other legislative constraints imposed upon them by central government. But, in seeking to come to terms with them, they have come to recognise that Communitown and authorities like it have many more resources and levers of influence at their disposal than they had previously realised, when almost all their attention tended to be focused on direct service provision. As well as being the biggest employer and biggest purchaser in the area, Communitown Council also owns all sorts of land and property; it has powers of compulsory purchase, of regulation, inspection and licensing; it has access to central government and European funding; it gives out grants and makes appointments to a huge range of local organisations; it is, far more than any other local organisation, at the very hub of community life and can speak with an authority that no other organisation can remotely approach.

Exhibit 20.1   *Key features of the four strategic models of local authorities*

	Primary role	*Main functions*	*Scope for discretion*
TRADSVILLE	Direct provider of a wide range of services	Service provision Co-ordination External advocacy	Moderate
RIDLEYBURG	Provider of last resort Filler of market gaps	Contract specification and monitoring Limited regulation	Low
CONTRACTOPOLIS	Key agency for local economic development Advocacy	Contract specification and monitoring Bargaining	High (policy content) Low (mode of service delivery)
COMMUNITOWN	Comprehensive identification of community needs, and responsibility (not necessarily direct) for meeting them	Mixed mode of service provision Strategic Advocacy Redistribution	High

The council may have lost much of its direct control over its schools, lost its former further and higher educational involvement, sold off many of its council houses, and been forced to compete to retain other of its services. But it still has a unique capacity, if it chooses, to take on a role of community leadership and governance – attempting to identify and respond to the needs of the many different local communities within its area. After all, as one councillor put it, 'if we don't give it a go, there's no one else who can'.

To assist the development of this community leadership role, Communitown has strengthened its strategic capacity by grouping a number of different services together into directorates – housing and social services; education, leisure, recreation and community development; planning, economic development, traffic and highways – each headed by a director whose main responsibility is strategic development. The small management team of directors has a strong external orientation, and is constantly on the look-out for ways to work with and through other agencies – not just contractually – for the benefit of the authority and the community. The council leader, in a rare burst of eloquence, was once heard to describe Communitown's enabling role as similar to that of the well-known conductor of the local symphony orchestra: interpreting the score and bringing in different contributors to create as full a musical experience as possible. He then rather over-extended the metaphor by trying to equate individual instruments with particular statutory and voluntary sector bodies, and claiming that the acoustics of the whole orchestral hall would be better and the seats cheaper, were it not for central government, but you could see what he meant.

■ Fitness for purpose

These four models, summarised in Exhibit 20.1 and presented here in a much more curtailed form than in the first edition of the book, derived originally from a report produced by the Local Government Management Board entitled *Fitness for Purpose*. The message in that title is an important one. Its intention is to emphasise that, while the areas of discretion open to local authorities have unquestionably decreased in recent years, there remains significant scope for strategic choice about the *kind of authority* they wish to be. It is important that authorities themselves recognise and address this choice because, while there is no single model of 'good' local authority management and organisation, there is 'fitness for purpose'.

Unless an authority makes a clear choice about its role and purpose, it can hardly hope to develop appropriate or fitting organisational arrangements, structures, processes, personnel skills, and so on.

The contrast is clear, as one of the authors of the LGMB report, Steve Leach, illustrates in a more recent publication (Leach, Davis *et al.*, 1996, p. 160):

> Such choice opportunities have not been recognised in all authorities. Some continue to cope with external crises and demands on an incremental basis . . . However, other authorities have made and acted on such choices. There are unmistakable contrasts between the political priorities and organisational cultures of Tower Hamlets, where the devolution of power to neighbourhoods was taken so far that the role of the authority itself became almost residual, and Birmingham, where in recent years the city council has attempted to transform Birmingham into an 'international city'. There is a similarly striking contrast between Rutland, which has developed the involvement of the private sector (and other alternative sources of service provision) well beyond what is required by law, and many South Wales authorities which, whilst acting within the law, have attempted to minimise the impact of CCT on their operations and organisational structures and maximise the chances of winning contracts internally.

■ Labour's strategic choice – community governance?

One of the reasons why the LGMB argued that it was necessary for local authorities to make such strategic choices was that no one else was going to do so for them – central government included. For all the constraint and control, direction and intervention imposed by Conservative governments, the Board's view in 1993 was that:

> there is no inexorable logic in the range of measures introduced by central government which requires a set of specific organisational design features . . . the absence of a coherent vision leaves scope for local authorities to make choices. (LGMB, 1993b, p. 9)

As we have indicated, there was indeed no 'coherent vision' guiding the comprehensive review of the structure, finance and management of local government that was set in motion by Michael Heseltine in 1990. Financial reform was dealt with immediately, for party political reasons, before structure was even addressed. When it was addressed, the outcome was the 'hybridity' compromise, which may have been, in England, responsive to local public opinion, but was certainly not driven by any coherent vision. Internal management, as we saw in Chapter 18, came in the middle, and presented a selection of interesting options and recommendations, but again no single model. Which raises the obvious question: does the Labour Government have any clearer a conception of the role and purpose of local government that can offer strategic guidance to individual local authorities? To which our answer, already hinted at in our reference to the Party's manifesto and key policy documents, is at least a tentative 'yes'. As far as can be discerned from these publications, the Government would seem to favour our Communitown model of community governance.

■ 'Good local government' – the early legislation

The local government section of Labour's 1997 General Election manifesto, *New Labour – Because Britain Deserves Better*, was characteristic of the whole 40–page, 19,000–word document: rather heavier on broad rhetorical pledges than on specific new policy commitments. Under the heading 'Good local government' there were plenty of what, in management training jargon, might be termed 'warm fuzzies' – positively worded statements designed to make, in this instance, Labour councils and councillors feel good, valued and optimistic about the future. They certainly sound closer to a vision of community governance than to any of our other strategic models:

> Local decision-making should be less constrained by central government, and also more accountable to local people ... [councils] should work in partnership with local people, local business and local voluntary organisations. They will have the powers to develop these partnerships.

> 'Labour councils have been at the forefront of environmental initiatives under Local Agenda 21, the international framework for local action arising from the 1992 Earth Summit. A Labour government will encourage all local authorities to adopt plans to protect and enchance their local environment.

> 'A Labour government will join with local government in a concerted attack against the multiple causes of social and economic decline – unemployment, bad housing, crime, poor health and a degraded environment.'

There was no attempt, though, amidst all the encouragement and promise of concerted action, to confront the detailed and difficult questions – How? When? Where is the funding coming from? – and clearly nothing specific enough to be translated into first-term legislation. Indeed, it will be noted from Exhibit 20.2 that there was no Local Government Bill *per se* in the Labour Government's first Queen's Speech, intended to cover the first 18 months of the 1997 Parliament.

Instead, there was promised legislation about certain local government services and particularly about the structure and organisation of sub-central government. Most prominently of all, there was Scottish and Welsh devolution, closely followed by another Bill involving a preliminary referendum: this one for an elected Greater London Authority headed by a separately elected mayor. This latter announcement

---

Exhibit 20.2   *The Labour Government's Queen's Speech, May 1997*

Proposed legislation affecting local and regional government

Scotland and Wales

Referendum (Scotland and Wales) Bill
To enable the holding of referendums in September 1997 on the establishment from May 1999 of a 126–member Scottish legislative and tax-raising Parliament and a 60–member Welsh Assembly/Senedd without such powers, both to be elected by proportional representation. Would bring a measure of home rule to Scotland and Wales for the first time since the Acts of Union in 1707 and 1535.

London

Greater London Authority (Referendum) Bill
To pave the way for a referendum in May 1998 on the establishment from May 2000 of a strategic authority for London – the only Western capital city without an elected city government – headed by a separately elected mayor.

The English Regions

Regional Development Agencies Bill
To establish from April 1999 Agencies in the regions (outside London) to work with the existing Government Offices for the Regions (see Chapter 7) in promoting inward investment, helping small businesses, and co-ordinating regional economic development. The Agencies would be based on the Scottish and Welsh Development Agencies set up in the 1970s and would constitute the first step towards directly elected regional government.

Education

(1)   Education (Reduction in Class Sizes) Bill
An immediate Bill to stop independent schools offering new 'assisted places' to children from poor families – the resulting savings from phasing out these subsidies to be used to reduce class sizes in infant schools.
(2)   Education Bill
A wide-ranging Bill, based on an early White Paper, to include:
* steps to raise school standards by setting 'improvement targets'
* expansion of nursery provision
* work experience for 14–16 year olds
* reform of curriculum for 16–19 year olds
* abolition of grant maintained status for opted out schools
* three new categories of foundation, community and aided schools with varying degrees of autonomy
* new policy on school admissions, selection and grammar schools
* new role for LEAs, requiring the appointment of parent representatives and the formation of public/private sector partnerships to tackle £3 billion backlog of school repairs
* new arrangements for long-term student loans
* reforms to the teaching profession.

Housing

Local Government Finance (Supplementary Credit Approvals) Bill
To allow local authorities to reinvest up to £5 billion of their accumulated receipts from council house sales in building new homes and renovating old ones. The money will be distributed through supplementary credit approvals (see Chapter 9) and could produce up to 70,000 new and 140,000 refurbished homes.

immediately sparked off more speculation about possible mayoral con-
tenders – including Richard Branson; London Transport Minister Glenda
Jackson; her Conservative predecessor Steven Norris; and Sports Minister Tony Banks – than about the actual powers he or she or the strategic
authority itself might have. The popular enthusiasm, though, is both
understandable and, for local government as a whole, a welcome
novelty, for a London mayoral election would indeed be a quite
unprecedented event. As one observer put it (Kettle, 1997):

> Even Tony Blair, presidential in style as he may be, will not be able to claim
> such personal authority from the voters as the Mayor of London.

> If the post is to mean anything at all, the Mayor of London will become the
> most important person in British local government. The mayor of London will
> have a larger electorate than any putative prime minister of Scotland, Wales or
> Northern Ireland. He or she will speak for more voters than the leaders of
> Denmark, Ireland, Luxembourg or Finland. For that reason too, London's
> mayor will become the most prominent extra-parliamentary politician in the
> land. It will be a post on a par with the Cabinet and, as devolution elsewhere
> takes shape, it could be more important than most ministries.

The English regions are not, at least for the foreseeable future, to
receive a similar injection of electoral democracy. Instead, they will have
new quangos in the form of Regional Development Agencies. These are
intended to be a first step towards the implementation of one of Labour's
explicitly longer-term commitments, although on the face of it they
appear an odd form of response to the Party's criticism of its predecessors:

> The Conservatives have created a tier of regional government in England
> through quangos and government regional offices. Meanwhile local authorities
> have come together to create a more co-ordinated regional voice. Labour will
> build on these developments through the establishment of *regional chambers* to
> co-ordinate transport, planning, economic development, bids for European
> funding and land use planning.

> In time we will introduce legislation to allow the people, region by region, to
> decide in a referendum, whether they want directly elected regional
> government. (our emphasis)

Other early legislation affecting local government included two Education Bills and the Local Government Finance (Supplementary Credit
Approvals) Bill, all anticipated in the manifesto (see Exhibits 14.7 and
20.2). Some of Labour's supporters in local government had been hoping
that the capital receipts measure would be but one of several in a more
extensive local government bill, which might also pick up other manifesto promises:

* the abolition of CCT;
* the new duty on councils to 'promote the economic, social and environmental well-being of their area';
* the abolition of 'crude and universal capping';
* annual election of a proportion of councillors in each locality;
* the encouragement of 'democratic innovations', including elected mayors with executive powers in cities outside London.

These commitments, however, were destined to have to wait for later legislative enactment, together with one or two others of which there was rather more suspicion. For, in addition to its well-publicised intention to retain *reserve* capping powers, 'to control excessive council tax rises', the manifesto also emphasised that:

> The Audit Commission will be given additional powers to monitor performance and promote efficiency. On its advice, government will where necessary send in a management team with full powers to remedy failure.

Taken together with the Blair Government's commitment to accept for its first two years the last Conservative Government's public spending allocations, these centralist powers – and particularly the management hit squads – make local government nervous. Is local decision-making really to be 'less constrained by central government', as promised, or merely less constrained only so long as it acts in tolerable accordance with central government's wishes? It is perhaps an aptly rhetorical question on which to conclude.

Guide to further reading

The first section of this final chapter is our fairly freely adapted interpretation of the 1993 LGMB report, *Fitness for Purpose*. Its analysis originated in a study led by Steve Leach and Murray Stewart and supported by the Rowntree Foundation (Leach and Stewart, 1992b). The same authors and other colleagues have since produced a useful collection of essays (Leach, Davis *et al.*, 1996), pleasingly, if unusually, 'dedicated to Britain's local councillors who, week in, week out, freely give of their time and efforts in the service of their communities'. An even more readable, and outspokenly critical, overview of recent trends is Simon Jenkins's *Accountable to None* (1995), now available in a Penguin edition. The second part of the chapter is based on the 1997 Labour Party manifesto – a document read probably more extensively since the Election than before, and by which the Government will of course be judged. Its local government section is a distillation of an earlier policy document, *Renewing Democracy, Rebuilding Communities* (1995). Our final recommendation you will by now be able to guess: there simply is no substitute for a regular scanning of both the quality press and, whenever possible, the news sections at least of the weekly practitioner journals.

Bibliography

Abdela, L. (1989) *Women With X Appeal: Women Politicians in Britain Today* (London: Optima).

Adam Smith Institute (1989a) *Wiser Counsels* (England and Wales) (London: Adam Smith Institute).

Adam Smith Institute (1989b) *Shedding a Tier* (Scotland) (London: Adam Smith Institute).

Alexander, A. (1982a) *The Politics of Local Government in the United Kingdom* (Harlow: Longman).

Alexander, A. (1982b) *Local Government in Britain since Reorganisation* (London: Allen & Unwin).

Allen, H. J. B. (1990) *Cultivating the Grass Roots: Why Local Government Matters* (The Hague: International Union of Local Authorities).

Ascher, K. (1987) *The Politics of Privatisation* (London: Macmillan).

Association of Councillors (1987) *Support Services for Councillors* (by P. Arnold and I. Cole) (Croydon: Charles Knight Publishing).

Atkinson, R. and Moon G. (1994) *Urban Policy in Britain: The City, the State and the Market* (London: Macmillan)

Audit Commission (1984) *Securing Further Improvements in Refuse Collection* (London: HMSO).

Audit Commission (1987) *Competitiveness and Contracting Out of Local Authorities' Services*, Occasional Paper, 3 (London: HMSO).

Audit Commission (1988) *The Competitive Council* (London: HMSO).

Audit Commission (1990) *We Can't Go On Meeting Like This* (London: HMSO).

Audit Commission (1991a) *A Response to the Government's Consultation Paper – 'A New Tax for Local Government'* (London: HMSO).

Audit Commission (1991b) *A Rough Guide to Europe: Local Authorities and the EC* (London: HMSO).

Audit Commission (1997) *Representing the People* (Abingdon: Audit Commission)

Baggott, R. (1995) *Pressure Groups Today* (Manchester: Manchester University Press).

Bailey, N. (1995) *Partnership Agencies in British Urban Policy* (London: UCL Press)

Bailey, S. and Paddison, R. (eds) (1988) *The Reform of Local Government Finance in Britain* (London: Routledge).

Bains, M. (Chairman) (1972) *The New Local Authorities: Management and Structure* (London: HMSO).

Barron, J., Crawley, G. and Wood, T. (1987) *Married to the Council? The Private Costs of Public Service* (Bristol: Bristol Polytechnic).

Barron, J., Crawley, G. and Wood, T. (1991) *Councillors in Crisis* (London: Macmillan).

Ben-Tovim, G. *et al.* (1986) *The Local Politics of Race* (London: Macmillan).

Beresford, P. (1987) *Good Council Guide: Wandsworth 1978–1987* (London: Centre for Policy Studies).

Bishop, J. and Hoggett, P. (1986) *Organizing Around Enthusiasms: Mutual Aid in Leisure* (London: Comedia).

Blais, A. and Carty, R. J. (1990) 'Does Proportional Representation Foster Election Turnout?', *European Journal of Political Research*, 18, pp. 167–81.

Bloch, A. (1992) *The Turnover of Local Councillors* (York: Joseph Rowntree Foundation).

Blowers, A. (1977) 'Checks and Balances – The Politics of Minority Government', *Public Administration*, Autumn, pp. 305–16.

Blowers, A. (1980) *The Limits of Power* (Oxford: Pergamon).

Bogdanor, V. (1988) *Against the Overmighty State: A Future for Local Government in Britain* (London: Federal Trust for Education and Research).

Bongers, P. (1992) *Local Government in the Single European Market* (Harlow: Longman).

Boyle, Sir L. (1986) 'In Recommendation of Widdicombe', *Local Government Studies*, 12:6, pp. 33–9.

Boyne, G. *et al.* (1995) *Local Government Reform: A Review of the Process in Scotland and Wales* (LGC/Joseph Rowntree Foundation).

Brooke, R. (1989) *Managing the Enabling Authority* (Harlow: Longman).

Budge, I., Brand, J., Margolis, M. and Smith, A. L. M. (1972) *Political Stratification and Democracy* (London: Macmillan).

Bulpitt, J. (1967) *Party Politics in English Local Government* (Harlow: Longman).

Bulpitt, J. (1983) *Territory and Power in the United Kingdom* (Manchester: Manchester University Press).

Bulpitt, J. (1986) 'The Discipline of the New Democracy: Mrs Thatcher's Domestic Statecraft', *Political Studies*, 34, pp. 19–39.

Bulpitt, J. (1989) 'Walking Back to Happiness?', in C. Crouch and D. Marquand (eds), *The New Centralism* (Oxford: Blackwell) pp. 56–73.

Bulpitt, J. (1993) Review in *Public Administration*, Winter, pp. 621–3.

Burns, D. (1992) *Poll Tax Rebellion* (London: AK Press and Attack International).

Burns, D., Hambleton, R. and Hoggett, P. (1994) *The Politics of Decentralisation: Revitalising Local Democracy* (London: Macmillan).

Butcher, H., Law, I., Leach, R. and Mullard, M., (1990) *Local Government and Thatcherism* (London: Routledge).

Butler, D., Adonis, A. and Travers, T. (1994) *Failure in British Government: The Politics of the Poll Tax* (Oxford: Oxford University Press).

Byrne, T. (1994) *Local Government in Britain*, 6th edn (Harmondsworth: Penguin).

Campbell, M. (1990) (ed) *Local Economic Policy* (London: Cassell).

Carmichael, P. (1992) 'Is Scotland Different? Local Government Policy under Mrs Thatcher', *Local Government Policy Making*, 18:5, May, pp. 25–32.

Cawson, A. (1977) 'Environmental Planning and the Politics of Corporatism', *Working Papers in Urban and Regional Studies, No. 7* (University of Sussex).

Chandler, J. A. (1988) *Public Policy-Making for Local Government* (London: Croom Helm).

Chandler, J. A. (1991) *Local Government Today* (Manchester: Manchester University Press).

Chandler, J. A. (ed.) (1993) *Local Government in Liberal Democracies* (London: Routledge).

Clarke, M. and Stewart, J. (1988) *The Enabling Council* (Luton: LGTB).

Clarke, M. and Stewart, J. (1990) *General Management in Local Government: Getting the Balance Right* (Harlow: Longman).

Clarke, M. and Stewart, J. (1991) *The Choices for Local Government for the 1990s and Beyond* (Harlow: Longman).

Cloke, P. (ed.) (1992) *Policy and Change in Thatcherite Britain* (Oxford: Pergamon Press).

Cochrane, A. (1993a) *Whatever Happened to Local Government?* (Buckingham: Open University Press).

Cochrane, A. (1993b) 'Local Government', in R. Maidment and G. Thompson (eds), *Managing the United Kingdom* (London: Sage).

Cockburn, C. (1977) *The Local State* (London: Pluto).

Colenutt, B. and Tansley, S. (1989) Draft Interim Monitoring Report on UDCs (Manchester: CLES).

Commission for Local Democracy (1995) *Taking Charge: The Rebirth of Local Democracy* (London: Municipal Journal Books).

Connolly, M. (1986) 'Central–Local Government Relations in Northern Ireland', *Local Government Studies*, September/October 1986.

Connolly, M. (1990) *Politics and Policy Making in Northern Ireland* (Hemel Hempstead: Philip Allan).

Connolly, M. (1992) 'Learning from Northern Ireland: An Acceptable Model for Regional and Local Government', *Public Policy and Administration*, 7:1, pp. 31–46.

Connolly, M. (1994) *Lessons from Local Government in Northern Ireland* (Luton: LGMB).

Connolly, M. (1996) 'Lessons from Local Government in Northern Ireland', *Local Government Studies*, 22:2, pp. 77–91.

Connolly, M. and McAlister, D. (1990) 'Public Expenditure and Management in Northern Ireland', in P. Jackson and F. Terry (eds), *Public Domain Yearbook 1990* (London PFF/KPMM).

Conservative Party (1997) *You Can Only Be Sure With the Conservatives: The Conservative Manifesto* (London: Conservative Central Office).

Cook, P. (1992) 'Corseted and Never Cosseted', *Local Government Chronicle*, 20 March, pp. 16–17.

Corina, L. (1974) 'Elected Representatives in a Party System: A Typology', *Policy and Politics*, 3:1, pp. 69–87.

Cousins, P. (1976) 'Voluntary Organisations and Local Government in Three South London Boroughs', *Public Administration*, 54:1, pp. 63–83.

Cox, D.C. (1989) *Shropshire C.C.: A Centenary History* (Shropshire CC).

Craig, F.W.S. (1989) *British Electoral Facts, 1832–1987* (Aldershot: Parliamentary Research Services).

Crequer, N. (1991) 'Agents of Change Waiting in the Wings', *The Independent*, 3 June.

Crossman, R. (1977) *The Diaries of a Cabinet Minister, Vol. 3: Secretary of State for Social Services* (London: Hamish Hamilton and Jonathan Cape).

Davies, H.J. (1988) 'Local Government Under Siege', *Public Administration*, 6:1, pp. 91–101.

Davis, H. (1996) 'Quangos and Local Government: A Changing World', *Local Government Studies*, 22:2, pp. 1–7. Special Issue on Quangos.

Deakin, N., and Edwards, J. (1993) *The Enterprise Culture and the City* (London: Routledge).

Dearlove, J. (1973) *The Politics of Policy in Local Government* (Cambridge: Cambridge University Press).

Dearlove, J. (1979) *The Reorganisation of British Local Government* (Cambridge: Cambridge University Press).

Democratic Audit (1994) *Ego Trip: Extra-Governmental Organisations in the United Kingdom and their Accountability* (London: The Charter 88 Trust).

Department of the Environment (1981) *Alternatives to Domestic Rates*, Cmnd 8449 (London: HMSO).

Department of the Environment (1983a) *Rates*, Cmnd 9008 (London: HMSO).

Department of the Environment (1983b) *Streamlining the Cities*, Cmnd 9063 (London: HMSO).

Department of the Environment (1986) *Paying for Local Government*, Cmnd 9714 (London: HMSO).

Department of the Environment (1991a) *The Structure of Local Government in England* (London, April).

Department of the Environment (1991b) *The Internal Management of Local Authorities in England* (London: HMSO).

Department of the Environment (1993) *Community Leadership and Representation: Unlocking the Potential*, Report of the Working Party on the Internal Management of Local Authorities in England (London: HMSO).

Department of the Environment (1996) *Local Government Financial Statistics, England* No. 6 (London: HMSO).

Doig, A. (1984) *Corruption and Misconduct in Contemporary British Politics* (Harmondsworth: Penguin).

Doogan, K. (1995) *Market Forces and Local Public Service Jobs*, Economic Policy Institute Economic Report, December.

Dunleavy, P. (1980) *Urban Political Analysis* (London: Macmillan).

Dunleavy, P. (1984) 'The Limits to Local Government' in M. Boddy and C. Fudge (eds), *Local Socialism?* (London: Macmillan), pp. 49–81.

Dunleavy, P. (1986) 'Explaining the Privatization Boom: Public Choice versus Radical Approaches', *Public Administration*, 64:1, pp. 13–34.

Dunleavy, P. and Rhodes, R. A. W. (1983) 'Beyond Whitehall' in H. Drucker *et al.* (eds), *Developments in British Politics*, chapter 5 (London: Macmillan).

Dunleavy, P. and Rhodes, R. A. W. (1985) 'Government Beyond Whitehall', in H. Drucker *et al.* (eds), *Developments in British Politics 2* (London: Macmillan).

Dynes, M. and Walker, D. (1996) *The Times Guide to the New British State* (London: Times Books).

Elcock, H. (1989) 'The Changing Management of Local Government', in I. Taylor and G. Popham (eds), *An Introduction to Public Sector Management* (London: Unwin Hyman).

Elcock, H. (1991) *Local Government* (London: Methuen).

Elcock, H. (1994) *Local Government: Policy and Management in Local Authorities*, 3rd edn (London: Routledge).

Elcock, H. and Jordan, G. (eds) (1987) *Learning from Local Authority Budgeting* (Aldershot: Avebury).

Elcock, H., Jordan, G. and Midwinter, A. (1989) *Budgeting in Local Government: Managing the Margins* (Harlow: Longman).

Ellwood, S., Nutley, S., Tricker, M. and Waterston, P. (1992) *Parish and Town Councils in England: A Survey* (London: HMSO).

Ennals, K. and O'Brien, J. (1990) *The Enabling Role of Local Authorities* (London: Public Finance Foundation).

Fenwick, J. (1995) *Managing Local Government* (London: Chapman & Hall).

Flynn, N. (1985) 'Direct Labour Organisation', in S. Ranson, G. Jones and K. Walsh (eds), *Between Centre and Locality* (London: Allen & Unwin).

Flynn, N., Leach, S. and Vielba, C. (1985) *Abolition or Reform? The GLC and the Metropolitan County Councils* (London: Allen & Unwin).

Forsyth, M. (1982) 'Winners in the Contracting Game', *Local Government Chronicle*, 10 September.

Foster, C.D., Jackman, R. and Perlman, M. (1980) *Local Government Finance in a Unitary State* (London: Allen & Unwin).

Fowler, A. (1988) *Human Resource Management in Local Government* (Harlow: Longman).

Game, C. (1981) 'Local Elections', *Local Government Studies*, 7:2, pp. 63–8.

Game, C. (1991a) 'How Local are Local Elections?', *Social Studies Review*, 6:5, pp. 202–7.

Game, C. (1991b) 'County Chronicles: A Collective Appreciation', *Local Government Policy Making*, 18: 2.

Game, C. (1997) 'Unprecedented in Local Government Terms – The Local Government Commission's Public Consultation Programme', *Public Administration*, 75:1, pp. 67–96.

Game, C. and Leach, S. (1993) *Councillor Recruitment and Turnover: An Approaching Precipice?* (Luton: LGMB).

Game, C. and Leach, S. (1995) *The Role of Political Parties in Local Democracy, CLD Report No 11* (London: Commission for Local Democracy/Municipal Journal Books).

Game, C. and Leach, S. (1996) 'Political Parties and Local Democracy', in L. Pratchett and D. Wilson (eds), *Local Democracy and Local Government* (London: Macmillan), pp. 127–49.

Gasson, C. (1992) 'Freedom at a Cost', *Local Government Chronicle*, 4 December, p. 12.

Gibson, J. (1990) *The Politics and Economics of the Poll Tax: Mrs Thatcher's Downfall* (West Midlands: EMAS Ltd).

Godfrey, J. *et al.* (1988) *A Very Special County: West Sussex CC – The First 100 Years* (West Sussex CC).

Goldsmith, M. (1986a) *Essays on the Future of Local Government* (Wakefield: West Yorkshire Metropolitan County Council).

Goldsmith, M. (1986b) 'Managing the Periphery in a Period of Fiscal Stress', in M. Goldsmith (ed.), *New Research in Central–Local Relations* (Aldershot: Gower).

Goldsmith, M. (ed) (1986c) *New Research in Central–Local Relations* (Aldershot: Gower).

Goldsmith, M. and Newton, K. (1986a) 'Central–Local Government Relations: A Bibliographical Summary', *Public Administration*, 64:1, pp. 102–8.

Goldsmith, M. and Newton, K. (1986b) 'Local Government Abroad', in *Widdicombe Committee of Inquiry into the Conduct of Local Authority Business, Research Vol IV: Aspects of Local Democracy*, Cmnd 9801 (London: HMSO) pp. 132–58.

Goss, S. (1988) *Local Labour and Local Government* (Edinburgh: Edinburgh University Press).

Grant, M. (1986) 'The Role of the Courts in Central–Local Relations', in M. Goldsmith (ed.) *New Research in Central–Local Relations* (Aldershot: Gower) pp. 191–206.

Grant, W. (1978) *Independent Local Politics in England and Wales* (London: Saxon House).

Grant, W. (1983) *Chambers of Commerce in the U.K. System of Business Interest Representation*, Working Paper 32 (University of Warwick: Department of Politics).

Gray, A. and Jenkins, W.I. (1989) 'Public Administration and Government 1988–89', *Parliamentary Affairs*, 42:4, pp. 445–62.

Gray, C. (1994) *Government Beyond the Centre* (London: Macmillan).

Green, D. (1981) *Power and Party in an English City* (London: Allen & Unwin).

Greenwood, J.R. and Wilson, D.J. (1989) *Public Administration in Britain Today* (London: Unwin Hyman).

Greenwood, R. *et al.* (1980) *Patterns of Management in Local Government* (Oxford: Martin Robertson).

Griffith, J.A.G. (1966) *Central Departments and Local Authorities* (London: Allen & Unwin).

Griffiths, D. (1992) 'Strategic and Service Management – The Kirklees Experiment', *Local Government Studies*, 18:3, pp. 240–8.

Gyford, J. (1984) *Local Politics in Britain*, 2nd edn (London: Croom Helm).

Gyford, J. (1988) 'A Councillor's Case-Work', *Local Government Studies*, 14:3, pp. 9–12.

Gyford, J. (1991) *Citizens, Consumers and Councils* (London: Macmillan).

Gyford, J. and James, M. (1983) *National Parties and Local Politics* (London: Allen & Unwin).

Gyford, J., Leach, S. and Game, C. (1989) *The Changing Politics of Local Government* (London: Unwin Hyman).

Hall, W. and Weir, S. (1996a) *The Untouchables: Power and Accountability in the Quango State*, Democratic Audit Paper No. 8 (University of Essex: The Scarman Trust and Human Rights Centre).

Hall, W. and Weir, S. (1996b) 'Rise of the Quangocracy', *Local Government Chronicle*, 30 August, p.12.

Hampton, W. (1970) *Democracy and Community* (London: Oxford University Press).

Hampton, W. (1991) *Local Government and Urban Politics*, 2nd edn (Harlow: Longman).

Hebbert, M. and Travers, T. (eds) (1988) *The London Government Handbook* (London: Cassell).

Heclo, H. (1969) 'The Councillor's Job', *Public Administration*, 47:2, pp. 185–202.

Hedley, R. (1991) 'First Principles – The Reorganisation of New Zealand Local Government', *Local Government Chronicle*, 11 January, p. 18.

Hennessy, P. (1990) Whitehall (revised ed.) (London: Fontana Press).

Hepworth, N. (1984) *The Finance of Local Government*, 7th edn (London: Allen & Unwin).

Herbert, Sir Edwin, Chairman (1960) *Royal Commission on Local Government in Greater London 1957–1960, Report*, Cmnd 1164 (London: HMSO).

Hill, D. (1974) *Democratic Theory and Local Government* (London: Allen & Unwin).

Hirst, P. (1995) 'Quangos and Democratic Government', *Parliamentary Affairs*, 48:2, pp. 341–59.

HMSO (1971) *The Reform of Local Government in Wales: A Consultative Document* (London: HMSO).

Hogwood, B. (1995) *The Integrated Regional Offices and the Single Regeneration Budget, CLD Research Report 13* (London: Commission for Local Democracy/ Municipal Journal Books).

Hollis, G. Ham, G. and Ambler, M (1992) *The Future Role and Structure of Local Government* (Harlow: Longman).

Hollis, G., *et al.* (1990) *Alternatives to the Community Charge* (York: Joseph Rowntree Trust/Coopers & Lybrand Deloitte).

Hollis, P. (1987) *Ladies Elect: Women in English Local Government, 1865–1914* (Oxford: Oxford University Press).

Holtby, W. (1936) *South Riding* (London: Collins).

Houlihan, B. (1988) *Housing Policy and Central–Local Government Relations* (Aldershot: Avebury).

House of Lords (1996) *Select Committee on Relations Between Central and Local Government, Vols I–III* (London: HMSO).

Imrie, R. and Thomas, H. (eds) (1993) *British Urban Policy and Urban Development Corporations* (London: Paul Chapman).

INLOGOV (Institute of Local Government Studies) (1990) *Competition for Local Government Services* (DoE report).

Isaac-Henry, K. (1980) 'The English Local Authority Associations', *Public Administration Bulletin*, 33, August, pp. 21–41.

Isaac-Henry, K. (1984) 'Taking Stock of the Local Authority Associations', *Public Administration*, 62:2, pp. 129–46.

Jackson, P. M. and Palmer, B. (1992) *Developing Performance Monitoring in Public Sector Organisations* (Leicester: University of Leicester Management Centre).

Jefferies, R. (1982) *Tackling the Town Hall* (London: Routledge & Kegan Paul).

Jenkins, S. (1995) *Accountable to None: The Tory Nationalisation of Britain* (London: Hamish Hamilton).

Jennings, R. E. (1982) 'The Changing Representational Roles of Local Councillors in England', *Local Government Studies*, 8:4, pp. 67–86.

John, P. (1989) *Introduction of the Community Charge in Scotland* (London: Policy Studies Institute for the Joseph Rowntree Memorial Trust).

John, P. (1994) 'Central–Local Government Relations in the 1980s and 1990s; Towards a Policy Learning Approach', *Local Government Studies*, 20: 3, pp. 412–36.

Jones, G. (1969) *Borough Politics* (London: Macmillan).

Jones, G. (1973) 'The Functions and Organisation of Councillors', *Public Administration*, 51, pp. 135–46.

Jones, G. (1975) 'Varieties of Local Politics', *Local Government Studies*, 1:2, April, pp. 17–32.

Jones, G. and Stewart, J. (1985) *The Case for Local Government* (London: Allen & Unwin).

Jones, G. and Stewart, J. (1992) 'Selected not Elected', *Local Government Chronicle*, 13 November, p. 15.

Jones, G. and Stewart, J. (1993a) 'When the Numbers Don't Add Up to Democracy', *Local Government Chronicle*, 8 January, p. 15.

Jones, G. and Stewart, J. (1993b) 'Different Domains', *Local Government Chronicle*, 8 April, p. 15.

Jones, G. and Travers, T. (1996) 'Central Government Perceptions of Local Government', in L. Pratchett and D. Wilson, *Local Democracy and Local Government* (London: Macmillan).

Jordan, A. G. and Richardson, J. J. (1987) *Government and Pressure Groups in Britain* (Oxford: Clarendon Press).

Keith-Lucas, B. and Richards, P. (1978) *A History of Local Government in the Twentieth Century* (London: Allen & Unwin).

Kellas, J. (1989) *The Scottish Political System*, 4th edn (Cambridge: Cambridge University Press).

Kent CC/Price Waterhouse (1992) *Facing the Challenge: Making Strategic Management Work* (Kent C. C.).

Kettle, M. (1997), 'Chains of Power', *The Guardian*, 17 May, p.25.

King, R. (1983) 'The Political Practice of Local Capitalist Associations', in R. King (ed.), *Capital and Politics* (London: Routledge & Kegan Paul).

King, R. (1985) 'Corporatism and the Local Economy', in W. Grant (ed.), *The Political Economy of Corporatism* (London: Macmillan).

Kingdom, J. (1991) *Local Government and Politics in Britain* (Hemel Hempstead: Philip Allan).

Kitchen, H. (1996) 'A Power of General Competence for Local Government', in L. Pratchett and D. Wilson, *Local Democracy and Local Government* (London: Macmillan).

Knox, C. (1989) 'Local Government in Northern Ireland', *Public Money and Management*, 9:2, pp. 59–63.

Knox, C. (1991) *Compulsory Competitive Tendering in Northern Ireland Local Government*, Ulster Papers in Policy and Management, no. 10 (University of Ulster).

Labour Party (1995) *Renewing Democracy, Rebuilding Communities* (London: Labour Party publications)

Labour Party (1997) *New Labour – Because Britain Deserves Better* (London: Labour Party publications)

LACSAB (1991) CCT Information Service Survey Report, no. 2 (London: LGTB/LACSAB).

Laffin, M. (1986) *Professionalism and Policy: The Role of the Professions in the Central–Local Relationship* (Aldershot: Gower).

Laffin, M. (1989) *Managing Under Pressure* (London: Macmillan).

Laffin, M. and Young, K. (1990) *Professionalism in Local Government* (Harlow: Longman).

Lambert, C. and Bramley, G. (1991) 'Local Government', in F. Terry and H. Roberts (eds), *Public Domain Yearbook 1991* (London: Public Finance Foundation) pp. 53–66.

Lang, I. (1992) 'Bringing the Union Alive', Address to the Monday Club, Brighton.

Lansley, S., Goss, S. and Wolmar, C. (1991) *Councils in Conflict: The Rise and Fall of the Municipal Left* (London: Macmillan).

Lawson, N. (1992) *The View From No. 11* (London: Bantam Press).

Layfield Committee (1976) *Report of the Committee of Enquiry into Local Government Finance*, Cmnd 6543 (London: HMSO).

Leach, S. (1989) 'Strengthening Local Democracy? The Government's Response to Widdicombe', in J. Stewart and G. Stoker (eds), *The Future of Local Government* (London: Macmillan) pp. 101–22.

Leach, S. (1993) 'Local Government Reorganisation in England', *Local Government Policy Making*, 19:4, pp. 30–5.

Leach, S. (1995) 'The Strange Case of the Local Government Review', in J. Stewart and G. Stoker (eds), *Local Government in the 1990s* (London: Macmillan) pp. 49–68.

Leach, S. (1996) 'The Indirectly Elected World of Local Government', *Local Government Studies*, 22:2, pp. 64–76.

Leach, S. and Game, C. (1989) *Co-operation and Conflict: Politics in the Hung Counties*, Common Voice Research Study no. 1 (London: Common Voice).

Leach, S. and Game, C. (1992) 'Local Government: The Decline of the One-Party State', in G. Smyth (ed.), *Refreshing the Parts: Electoral Reform and British Politics* (London: Lawrence & Wishart).

Leach, S. and Pratchett, L. (1996) *The Management of Balanced Authorities* (Luton: LGMB).

Leach, S. and Stewart, J. (1990) *Political Leadership in Local Government* (Luton: LGMB).

Leach, S. and Stewart, J. (1992a) *The Politics of Hung Authorities* (London: Macmillan).

Leach, S. and Stewart, M. (1992b) *Local Government: Its Role and Function* (York: Joseph Rowntree Foundation).

Leach, S. *et al.* (1987) *The Impact of Abolition on Metropolitan Government* (Birmingham: INLOGOV).

Leach, S. *et al.* (1992) *After Abolition: The Operation of the Post-1986 Metropolitan Government System in England* (Birmingham: INLOGOV).

Leach, S. *et al.* (1994) *The Changing Organisation and Management of Local Government* (London: Macmillan).

Leach, S., Davis, H. *et al.* (1996) *Enabling or Disabling Local Government: Choices for the Future* (Buckingham: Open University Press).

Lee, J. (1963) *Social Leaders and Public Persons* (London: Oxford University Press).

Lindblom, C. (1980) *The Policy-Making Process* (Englewood Cliffs: Prentice-Hall).

Livingstone, K. (1987) *If Voting Changed Anything, They'd Abolish It* (London: Collins).

Lloyd, P. (1985) *Service Administration by Local Authorities* (London: ICSA).

Local Government Chronicle (1993) 'Poll Tax is Not Quite Sucked Up the Nozzle of History', 2 April, p. 11.

Local Government Information Unit (1991) *Powers to Act: The Case for Local Government* (London: LGIU).

Local Government Information Unit (1993) *Guide to Local Government Finance* (London: LGIU).

Local Government Information Unit (1995) *The Quango File* (London: LGIU).

Local Government Management Board (1992) *Getting On With It: Managing Local Authorities* (Luton: LGMB).

Local Government Management Board (1993a) *Challenge and Change* (Luton: LGMB).

Local Government Management Board (1993b) *Fitness for Purpose: Shaping New Patterns of Organisation and Management* (Luton: LGMB).

Local Government Management Board (1995) *Renewing Local Government in the English Shires: A Report on the 1992–95 Structural Review* (London: HMSO).

Local Government Management Board (1996) *Guide to Europe* (Luton: LGMB).

Loughlin, M. (1996a) *Legality and Locality. The Role of Law in Central–Local Relations* (Oxford: Clarendon Press).

Loughlin, M. (1996b) 'Understanding Central–Local Government Relations', *Public Policy and Administration*, 11:2, pp. 48–65.

Loughlin, M. Gelfand, M.D. and Young, K. (eds) (1985) *Half a Century of Municipal Decline, 1935–1985* (London: Allen & Unwin).

Loveday, B. (1996) 'Police Reform: Problems of Accountability and the Police and Magistrates' Courts Act 1994' in S. Leach, H. Davis *et al.*, pp. 131–43.

Lowndes, V. (1996) 'Locality and Community: Choices for Local Government', in S. Leach, H. Davis, *et al.* (eds), *Enabling or Disabling Local Government* (Buckingham: Open University Press), pp. 71–85.

Lowndes, V. and Stoker, G. (1992) 'An Evaluation of Neighbourhood Decentralisation Part 2: Staff and Councillor Perspectives', *Policy and Politics*, 20:2, pp. 143–52.

Lynn, J. and Jay, A. (1983) *Yes, Minister: The Diaries of a Cabinet Minister, Vol. 3 – The Challenge* (London: BBC).

Macrory, P. (Chairman) (1970) *Review Body on Local Government in Northern Ireland, Report*, Cmnd 540 (NI) (HMSO: Belfast).

Madgwick, P. J. and James, M. (1980) 'The Network of Consultative Government in Wales', in G. Jones (ed.), *New Approaches to the Study of Central-Local Government Relations* (Aldershot: Gower) pp. 101–15.

Martlew, C. (1988) *Local Democracy in Practice* (Aldershot: Avebury).

Mason, D. (1985) *Revising the Rating System* (London: Adam Smith Institute).

Mather, G. (1989) 'Thatcherism and Local Government: An Evaluation', in J. Stewart and G. Stoker (eds), *The Future of Local Government* (London: Macmillan) pp. 212–36.

Maud, Sir John (Chairman) (1967) *Committee on the Management of Local Government, vol. 1: Report* (London: HMSO).

Midwinter, A. (1989) 'The New Conservatism and Public Expenditure in Scotland', *Political Quarterly*, 60:3, pp. 357–65.

Midwinter, A. (1992) 'The Review of Local Government in Scotland – A Critical Perspective', *Local Government Studies*, 18:2, pp. 44–54.

Midwinter, A. (1995) *Local Government in Scotland: Reform or Decline?* (London: Macmillan).

Midwinter, A., Keating, M. and Mitchell, J. (1991) *Politics and Public Policy in Scotland* (London: Macmillan).

Miller, W. (1988) *Irrelevant Elections? The Quality of Local Democracy in Britain* (Oxford: Clarendon Press).

Milton Keynes Liberal Democrats (1995) *Quangos in Milton Keynes* (Milton Keynes).

Montgomery (1984) *Report of the Committee of Inquiry into the Functions of the Island Councils of Scotland*, Cmnd 9216 (Edinburgh: HMSO).

Moran, M. (1989) *Politics and Society in Britain* (London: Macmillan).

Murray, N. (1989) 'A Service Business', *Local Government Chronicle*, 18 August.

Newton, K. (1976) *Second City Politics* (Oxford: Oxford University Press).

Newton, K. (1979) 'The Local Political Elite in England and Wales', in J. Lagroye and V. Wright (eds), *Local Government in Britain and France* (London: Allen & Unwin) pp. 105–13.

Newton, K. and Karran, T. (1985) *The Politics of Local Expenditure* (London: Macmillan).

Nolan, Lord (Chairman) (1997) *Committee on Standards in Public Life: Report on Local Government* (London: HMSO).

Norton, A. (1986) *Local Government in Other Western Democracies* (Birmingham: INLOGOV).

Norton, P. (ed.) (1991) *New Directions in British Politics?* (Aldershot: Edward Elgar).

Oakland, J. (1989) *Total Quality Management* (London: Butterworth Heinemann).

Paddison, R. and Bailey, S. (eds) (1988) *Local Government Reform: International Perspectives* (London: Routledge).

Page, E. and Goldsmith, M. (eds) (1987) *Central–Local Relations: Comparative Analysis of West European Unitary States* (New York: Sage).

Painter, J. (1992) 'The Culture of Competition', *Public Policy and Administration*, 7:1, pp. 58–68.

Parry, G., Moyser, G. and Day, N. (1992) *Political Participation and Democracy in Britain* (Cambridge: Cambridge University Press).

Paterson, I. V. (Chairman) (1973) *The New Scottish Local Authorities: Organisation and Management Structures* (Edinburgh: Scottish Development Department).

Pearce, C. (1980) *The Machinery of Change in Local Government 1888–1974* (London: Allen & Unwin).

Peters, T. and Waterman, R. (1982) *In Search of Excellence* (New York: Harper & Row).

Poole, K. P. and Keith-Lucas, B. (1994) *Parish Government 1894–1994* (London: National Association of Local Councils).

Poole, R. (1978) *The Local Government Service in England and Wales* (London: Allen & Unwin).

Pratchett, L. and Wilson, D. (eds) (1996) *Local Democracy and Local Government* (London: Macmillan).

Pratchett, L. and Wingfield, M. (1996) 'The Demise of the Public Sector Ethos', in L. Pratchett and D. Wilson (eds), *Local Democracy and Local Government* (London: Macmillan).

Prior, D. (1995) 'Citizen's Charters', in J. Stewart and G. Stoker (eds), *Local Government in the 1990s* (London: Macmillan), pp. 86–103.

Pross, P. (1986) *Group Politics and Public Policy* (Oxford: Oxford University Press).

Pyecroft, S. (1995) 'The Organisation of Local Authorities' European Activities', *Public Policy and Administration*, 10:4, pp. 20–33.

Rallings, C. and Thrasher, M. (1991) 'Local Elections: The Changing Scene', *Social Studies Review*, 5:4, pp. 163–6.

Rallings, C. and Thrasher, M. (1992a) 'Democracy Needs a Health Audit', *Local Government Chronicle*, 13 March, pp. 20–1.

Rallings, C. and Thrasher, M. (1992b) 'The Impact of Local Government Electoral Systems: Some Thoughts for the Local Government Commission', *Local Government Studies*, 18:2, pp. 1–8.

Rallings, C. and Thrasher, M. (1997) *Local Elections in Britain* (London: Routledge).

Ranson, S. (1992) 'Education', in F. Terry and P. Jackson (eds), *Public Domain Yearbook 1992* (London: Public Finance Foundation).

Ranson, S. (1995) 'From Reform to Restructuring of Education', in J. Stewart and G. Stoker (eds), *Local Government in the 1990s* (London: Macmillan) pp. 107–25

Ranson, S. and Thomas, H. (1989) 'Education Reform: Consumer Democracy or Social Democracy?', in J. Stewart and G. Stoker (eds), *The Future of Local Government* (London: Macmillan) pp. 55–77.

Ranson, S., Jones, G. and Walsh, K. (eds) (1985) *Between Centre and Locality* (London: Allen & Unwin).

Rao, N. (1993) *Managing Change: Councillors and the New Local Government* (York: Joseph Rowntree Foundation).

Rao, N. (1994) *The Making and Unmaking of Local Self-Government* (Aldershot: Dartmouth).

Rawlinson, D. and Tanner, B. (1990) *Financial Management in the 1990s* (Harlow: Longman).

Redcliffe-Maud, Lord (Chairman) (1969) *Royal Commission on Local Government in England 1966–1969, vol. I Report,* Cmnd 4040 (London: HMSO).

Redlich, J. and Hirst, F. W. (1958) *The History of Local Government in England,* rev. edn (London: Macmillan).

Regan, D. E. (1977) *Local Government and Education* (London: Allen & Unwin).

Rhodes, G. (1970) *The Government of London: The Struggle for Reform* (London: Weidenfeld & Nicolson).

Rhodes, R. A. W. (1979) 'Research into Central–Local Relations in Britain: A Framework for Analysis', unpublished paper, Department of Government, University of Essex.

Rhodes, R. A. W. (1981) *Control and Power in Central–Local Government Relations* (Farnborough: Gower).

Rhodes, R. A. W. (1986a) *The National World of Local Government* (London: Allen & Unwin).

Rhodes, R. A. W. (1986b) *Power Dependence, Policy Communities and Intergovernmental Networks,* Essex Papers in Politics and Government, no. 30 (University of Essex).

Rhodes, R. A. W. (1988) *Beyond Westminster and Whitehall* (London: Allen & Unwin).

Rhodes, R. A. W. (1991) 'Now Nobody Understands the System: The Changing Face of Local Government', in P. Norton (ed.), *New Directions in British Politics?* (Aldershot: Edward Elgar) pp. 83–112.

Rhodes, R. A. W. (1992) 'Local Government Finance', in D. Marsh and R. A. W. Rhodes (eds), *Implementing Thatcherite Policies* (Milton Keynes: Open University Press).

Rhodes, R. A. W. and Marsh, D. (1992) 'Policy Networks in British Politics: A Critique of Existing Approaches', in D. Marsh and R. A. W. Rhodes, *Policy Networks in British Government* (Oxford: Clarendon Press) pp. 1–26.

Richards, P. (1988) 'The Recent History of Local Fiscal Reform', in S. Bailey and R. Paddison (eds), *The Reform of Local Government Finance in Britain* (London: Routledge).

Richardson, J. J. and Jordan, A. G. (1979) *Governing Under Pressure* (Oxford: Martin Robertson).

Ridge, M. and Smith, S. (1990) *Local Government Finance: The 1990 Reforms*, IFS Commentary no. 22 (London: Institute for Fiscal Studies).

Ridley, N. (1988) *The Local Right* (London: Centre for Policy Studies).

Robinson, D. (Chairman) (1977) *Remuneration of Councillors: Vol I: Report; Vol II: The Surveys of Councillors and Local Authorities*, Cmnd 7010 (London: HMSO).

Robson, W. (1954) *The Development of Local Government*, 3rd edn (London: Allen & Unwin).

Rose, R. (1983) *Understanding the United Kingdom* (Harlow: Longman).

Rouse, J. (1993) 'Resource and Performance Management in Public Sector Organisations', in K. Isaac-Henry, C. Painter and C. Barnes (eds), *Management in the Public Sector: Challenge and Change* (London: Chapman & Hall), pp. 59–76.

Saggar, S. (1991) *Race and Public Policy* (Aldershot: Avebury).

Saunders, P. (1980) *Urban Politics: A Sociological Interpretation* (Harmondsworth: Penguin).

Saunders, P. (1981) 'The Crisis of Central–Local Relations in Britain', unpublished paper presented to the Issues in Contemporary Planning Seminar, University of Melbourne.

Savage, S. P. and Robins, L. (eds) (1990) *Public Policy under Thatcher* (London: Macmillan).

SCAT (1985) *Working Report on Job Satisfaction Survey of Manual and Clerical Workers in Parks and Recreation Departments* (London: Services to Community Action and Trade Unions).

Sharpe, L. J. (ed.) (1967) *Voting in Cities: The 1964 Borough Elections* (London: Macmillan).

Sharpe, L. J. (1970) 'Theories and Values of Local Government', *Political Studies*, 18:2, pp. 153–74.

Skelcher, C. (1980) 'From Programme Budgeting to Policy Analysis: Corporate Approaches in Local Government' *Public Administration*, 58:2, pp. 155–187.

Skelcher, C. (1992) *Managing for Service Quality* (Harlow: Longman).

Smith, B. C. (1985) *Decentralization: The Territorial Dimension of the State* (London: Allen & Unwin).

Sophal, R. and Muir, C. (1996) 'Survey of Councillors' in *Facing the Challenge: A Report of the First National All-Party Convention of Black, Asian and Ethnic Minority Councillors* (London: LGIU)

Spencer, K. M. (1989) 'Local Government and the Housing Reforms', in J. Stewart and G. Stoker (eds), *The Future of Local Government* (London: Macmillan) pp. 78–100.

Spencer, K. M. (1995) 'The Reform of Social Housing' in J. Stewart and G. Stoker, *Local Government in the 1990s* (London: Macmillan) pp. 145–65.

Stanyer, J. (1976) *Understanding Local Government* (London: Fontana).

Stewart, J. (1988) *Understanding The Management of Local Government* (Harlow: Longman).

Stewart, J. (1989) 'The Changing Organisation and Management of Local Authorities', in J. Stewart and G. Stoker (eds), *The Future of Local Government* (London: Macmillan) pp. 171–84.

Stewart, J. (1990) 'The Role of Councillors in the Management of the Authority', *Local Government Studies*, 16:4, pp. 25–36.

Stewart, J. (1991) 'The councillor as elected representative' in J. Stewart and C. Game, *Local Democracy – Representation and Elections* (Luton: LGMB).

Stewart, J. (1993) *Supporting the Councillors in Local Government: Some Ways Forward* (Luton: LGMB).

Stewart, J. (1995) 'The Internal Management of Local Authorities' in J. Stewart and G. Stoker (eds), *Local Government in the 1990s* (London: Macmillan) pp. 69–85.

Stewart, J. (1996) *Local Government Today: An Observer's View* (Luton: LGMB).

Stewart, J. and Game, C. (1991) *Local Democracy – Representation and Elections* (Luton: LGMB).

Stewart, J. and Stoker, G. (eds) (1989) *The Future of Local Government* (London: Macmillan).

Stewart, J. and Stoker, G. (eds) (1995) *Local Government in the 1990s* (London: Macmillan).

Stewart, J., Greer, A. and Hoggart, P. (1995) *The Quango State: An Alternative Approach, CLD Research Report No. 10* (London: Commission for Local Democracy/Municipal Journal Books).

Stodart (1981) *Report of the Committee of Inquiry into Local Government in Scotland*, Cmnd 8115 (Edinburgh: HMSO).

Stoker, G. (1988) *The Politics of Local Government* (London: Macmillan).

Stoker, G. (1989) *New Management Trends* (Luton: LGTB).

Stoker, G. (1990) 'Government Beyond Whitehall', in P. Dunleavy *et al.* (eds), *Developments in British Politics 3* (London: Macmillan).

Stoker, G. (1991) *The Politics of Local Government*, 2nd edn (London: Macmillan).

Stoker, G. (1992a) 'Local Government', in F. Terry and P. Jackson (eds), *Public Domain Yearbook 1992* (London: Public Finance Foundation) pp. 67–77.

Stoker, G. (1992b) 'The Structure and Size of Local Government: Some Thoughts from the UK', Paper presented to the Council of Europe, Krakow, April.

Stoker, G. (1993) 'Europe and Local Government: Cultural and Structural Differences and Similarities', paper presented to ICM *Strategies for Europe* Conference, January.

Stoker, G. (1995a) 'Intergovernmental Relations', *Public Administration*, 73, pp. 101–22.

Stoker, G. (1995b) 'Introduction', in D. Marsh and G. Stoker (eds), *Theory and Method in Political Science* (London: Macmillan).

Stoker, G. (1996) 'Understanding Central–Local Relations: A Reply to Martin Loughlin', *Public Policy and Administration*, 11:3, pp. 84–5.

Stoker, G. and Brindley, T. (1985) 'Asian Politics and Housing Renewal', *Policy and Politics*, 13:3, pp. 281–303.

Stoker, G. and Wilson, D.J. (1986) 'Intra-Organizational Politics in Local Authorities', *Public Administration*, 64:3, pp. 285–302.

Stoker, G. and Wilson, D.J. (1991) 'The Lost World of British Local Pressure Groups', *Public Policy and Administration*, 6:2, pp. 20–34.

Stoker, G. and Wolman, H. (1991) *A Different Way of Doing Business – the Example of the US Mayor* (Luton: LGMB).

Stoker, G. and Wolman, H. (1992) 'Drawing Lessons From US Experience: An Elected Mayor for British Local Government', *Public Administration*, 70:2, pp. 241–67.

Travers, T. (1986) *The Politics of Local Government Finance* (London: Allen & Unwin).

Travers, T. (1992) 'So You Think There's Been a Revolution?', *Local Government Chronicle*, 27 March, pp. 16–17.

Travers, T. *et al.* (1993) *The Impact of Population Size on Local Authority Costs and Effectiveness* (York: Joseph Rowntree Foundation).

Truman, D. B. (1951) *The Governmental Process* (New York: Knopf).

Vize, R. (1994) 'Northern Ireland: The Acceptable Face of Quangos', *Local Government Chronicle*, November 25, pp. 16–17.

Walker, D. (1983) *Municipal Empire* (London: Temple Smith).

Walsh, K. (1989) 'Competition and Service in Local Government', in J. Stewart and G. Stoker (eds), *The Future of Local Government* (London: Macmillan) pp. 30–54.

Walsh, K. (1991) *Competitive Tendering for Local Authority Services* (London: HMSO).

Walsh, K. (1995) 'Competition and Public Service Delivery', in J. Stewart and G. Stoker (eds), *Local Government in the 1990s* (London: Macmillan) pp. 28–48

Warburton, M. (1996) 'The Changing Role of Local Authorities in Housing', in S. Leach, H. Davis *et al.* (1996) *Enabling or Disabling Local Government* (Buckingham: Open University Press), pp. 114–30.

Weir, S. (1995) 'Quangos: Questions of Democratic Accountability', *Parliamentary Affairs*, 48:2, pp. 306–22.

Weir, S. and Hall, W. (eds) (1994) *Ego Trip: Extra-governmental Organisations in the United Kingdom and their Accountability*, Democratic Audit Paper No. 2 (University of Essex: Human Rights Centre).

Welsh Office (1971) *The Reform of Local Government in Wales: A Consultative Document* (London: HMSO).

Welsh Office (1993) *Local Government in Wales: A Charter for the Future* (London: HMSO).

Wendt, R. (1992) 'A View From the Local Authority Associations', paper presented to PAC, University of York, September.

Wheatley, Lord (Chairman) (1969) *Royal Commission on Local Government in Scotland*, Report, Cmnd 4150 (Edinburgh: HMSO).

Widdicombe, D. (Chairman) (1986a) *The Conduct of Local Authority Business: Report of the Committee of Inquiry into the Conduct of Local Authority Business*, Cmnd 9797 (London: HMSO).

Widdicombe, D. (Chairman) (1986b) *Research Volume I – The Political Organisation of Local Authorities* (by S. Leach, C. Game, J. Gyford and A. Midwinter), Cmnd 9798 (London: HMSO).

Widdicombe, D. (Chairman) (1986c) *Research Volume II – The Local Government Councillor*, Cmnd 9799 (London: HMSO).

Widdicombe, D. (Chairman) (1986d) *Research Volume III – The Local Government Elector*, Cmnd 9800 (London: HMSO).

Widdicombe, D. (Chairman) (1986e) *Research Volume IV – Aspects of Local Democracy*, Cmnd 9801 (London: HMSO).

Willis, J. (1990) 'David Bookbinder: Behind the Mythology', *Local Government Chronicle*, 12 January, pp. 24–5.

Wilson, D. (1995) 'Quangos in the Skeletal State' *Parliamentary Affairs*, 48:2, pp. 181–91.

Wilson, D. (1996a) 'Structural Solutions for Local Government: An Exercise in Chasing Shadows?' *Parliamentary Affairs*, 49:3, pp. 441–54.

Wilson, D. (1996b) 'The Local Government Commission: Examining the Consultative Process', *Public Administration*, 74:2, pp. 199–220.

Wilson, D. and Game, C. (1994) *Local Government in the United Kingdom* (London: Macmillan).

Wistow, G. *et al.* (1992) 'From Providing to Enabling: Local Authorities and the Mixed Economy of Social Care', *Public Administration*, 70:1, pp. 24–45.

Wood, B. (1976) *The Process of Local Government Reform, 1966–74* (London: Allen & Unwin).

Young, K. (1986a) 'Party Politics in Local Government: An Historical Perspective', in Widdicombe (1986e) (London: HMSO).

Young, K. (1986b) 'The Justification for Local Government', in M. Goldsmith (ed.), *Essays on the Future of Local Government* (Wakefield: West Yorkshire Metropolitan County Council), pp. 8–20.

Young, K. (ed.) (1989) *New Directions for County Government* (London: ACC).

Young, K. (1990) 'Approaches to Policy Development in the Field of Equal Opportunities', in W. Ball and J. Solomos (eds), *Race and Local Politics* (London: Macmillan), pp. 22–42.

Young, K. and Mills, L. (1983) *Managing the Post-Industrial City* (London: Heinemann).

Index